By the same author

The Hallé Tradition
The Works of Ralph Vaughan Williams
Portrait of Elgar
Portrait of Manchester
History of the Royal Manchester College of Music

Recording at EMI in 1965

Michael Kennedy

Barbirolli

Conductor Laureate

The authorised biography

With a full discography compiled by Malcolm Walker

MacGibbon & Kee   London

Granada Publishing Limited
First published in Great Britain 1971 by MacGibbon & Kee Ltd
3 Upper James Street London WIR 4BP

Second impression 1972

ISBN 0 261 63336 8
Printed in Great Britain
by Richard Clay (The Chaucer Press), Ltd.,
Bungay, Suffolk

FH

In grateful memory,
with love

Contents

❧ *Illustrations*

Frontispiece Recording at EMI in 1965

❦ Preface

John Barbirolli hoped to write an autobiography but he never gave himself enough time and left only a few hundred words of rough notes about his childhood. From about 1960 it was understood between us that I would be his biographer and he kindly gave effect to this in his Will. We knew each other for nearly thirty years and though we spoke only once very briefly about the biography as such, over the years he told me many things about himself and his fascinating career. He was also, thank goodness, a hoarder, so that when he died all his letters, papers, programmes, press cuttings, recordings, tape recordings and photographs were carefully filed and ready. 'It's all there in order, waiting for you when I'm gone,' he said; and I confess I was slightly sceptical. But I had no need to be. So this is what is rather chillingly known as an 'authorised' biography. It is certainly authenticated; and I hope it is also a personal portrait. If it is, that is largely because Sir John was such a prolific and natural letter-writer. Indeed I would call him a great letter-writer; and because they were the spontaneous product of the hour, written for pleasure with no thought of later publication, his letters recall his turn of speech, his tone of voice, with vivid clarity.

Therefore my first debt of acknowledgment is due to Sir John himself. The next is due to Lady Barbirolli, who has co-operated fully and frankly, answered innumerable questions, read the book at all its stages, corrected many points of factual detail and helped me in every conceivable way. I am also deeply indebted to Miss Audrey Napier Smith for placing her large correspondence with Sir John at my disposal and for much invaluable advice; to Mrs Ralph Vaughan Williams, Mr D. C. Parker, Mr Brian Douglas and Mr Martin Milner for lending letters and other material; to Miss Brenda Bracewell for much time, talk and trouble and for some letters; and, for various assistance, to Miss Tina Gibilaro, Miss Norah Winstanley, Miss Zenovia Goonan, Mr Clive Smart, the Hallé Concerts Society, Dame Eva Turner, Mr Bernard Herrmann, Mr Arthur Judson, Mr Bruno Zirato, Dr Wolfgang Stresemann, members of the Berlin Philharmonic and Hallé Orchestras, Mr T. E. Bean, Mr Roger Casini, Mrs Parry Jones, Mrs Percy Heming, Miss Helen Henschel, Dr N. Campbell Brown, Dr D. L. Jones and last but not least my typist Mrs A. Wragg. I am also greatly indebted to Mr Malcolm Walker for providing his superb and comprehensive discography.

Finally I should like to thank the hundreds of people who answered my letter in the press and sent me reminiscences, letters and appreciations of Sir John. To them all, I express heartfelt gratitude and the hope that they may think my book tries to be worthy of its subject.

M.K.
Sale, Cheshire,
1971

PART ONE

*The
Young
Maestro
1899-1943*

I
Cockney Johnny

There were musicians among the Venetian Barbirollis from the beginning of the nineteenth century. Tommaso Barbirolli of Bologna had two sons, Lorenzo, born in Bologna in 1798, and Luigi, born in Rovigo in 1802. The former became choirmaster – *maestro di capella* – at Ferrara and composed an opera, *I Trojani in Laurento*, which was produced at the Teatro Apollo, Ferrara, in 1837. His brother Luigi was a violinist and pianist in addition to being a professor of literature at Rovigo. It is the second of Luigi's two sons, Antonio, born in Rovigo in 1838, who has the first connections with the subject of this biography, his grandson. Antonio was a gifted violinist who spent an important part of his career in the orchestra at Padua, where from 1874 until 1883 he was in the first violins, becoming leader in 1879. His son Lorenzo, born in Padua in August 1864, joined him in the first violin section in 1881 at the age of seventeen.

Antonio was a close friend of the great opera conductor Franco Faccio, a noted interpreter of Verdi but also responsible for the first Italian performance of Wagner's *Die Meistersinger*, and it was no doubt because Faccio knew of the talents of the Barbirollis, father and son, that both became members of the orchestra of La Scala, Milan, and thus took part in all the rehearsals and the first performance (5 February 1887) of Verdi's *Otello*. Another member of the orchestra that evening was a nineteen-year-old cellist, Arturo Toscanini. Antonio and Lorenzo belonged to the group of experienced players who went as 'stiffening' to local opera orchestras when *Otello* had its first performances in other Italian towns. Lorenzo passed on to his son John many reminiscences of these occasions. 'It was a rare privilege,' John wrote in 1969,[*]

> for me to hear these, not from some old man searching back in the recesses of his memory, but from a man still in the prime of his life who remembered everything with great clarity... During rehearsals Verdi had no hesitation in correcting Faccio in regard to any tempo which was not to his liking. Normally rather silent, Verdi would at such moments produce a tremendously loud clicking of his thumb and second finger which resounded throughout the empty theatre and put everyone on their proper course again... Of [Tamagno's] voice, temperament and power [as Otello] much has been written, but such voices are difficult to manipulate and my father, to the end of his days, used to shudder at the recollection of Tamagno's inability to sing the A flat at the end of the first act at anywhere near its proper pitch... In a letter to Faccio at the time when he was preparing the first performance of *Otello*, Verdi expresses, somewhat ironically, the hope that the conductor will be able to persuade the tenor to sing 'something approximating to what I have written!'

Despite the distinction of such occasions as the *Otello* première, life was not easy in Italy for the professional musician and Lorenzo decided to leave and to make his living elsewhere. First he went to Paris and played in a 'Hungarian band' in the Café Anglais, Rue de la Paix. His younger cousin, Alfredo Barbirolli (1872–1921), a pianist and composer, was living there and together they went one evening to a restaurant in the Faubourg-St-Honoré. The niece of the restaurateur was staying in Paris and was helping her aunt to serve the dishes on this particular evening. When she saw Lorenzo she asked to be allowed to take his order to the table. Her name was Louise Marie Ribeyrol. She was born on 3 October 1870, at Arcachon, on the south-west coast of France, near the Pyrenees.

Louise and Lorenzo were soon in love: he spoke good French and she began to learn Venetian. The Hungarian band was booked to play at the Savoy Hotel in London from 1

[*] *Memories of Otello*, EMI booklet with recording.

May 1892, and Lorenzo went with it, but he promised to send for Louise as soon as possible so that they could be married. According to her own version of events as she amusingly told it in later life, she waited impatiently but no word came. It did not come because all the orchestra had been sacked when the leader's affair with the manager's wife was discovered. She would have gone to England earlier had she not put all her savings on a horse at Longchamp in an attempt to raise enough for the fare. Nothing if not determined, she eventually set off for England to find that Lorenzo had found no new work and was having a hard time. She helped to save money by working as a dressmaker in New Bond Street and eventually they were married at the Italian church in Clerkenwell and found lodgings in Wardour Street.

Lorenzo found work in the orchestra at the Alhambra, Leicester Square, and they were joined by his father and mother, Antonio and Rosina, and Lorenzo's sister Elisa. In 1895 their first child, Rosa, was born. Shortly afterwards Louise found six rooms on two floors above a baker's shop in Southampton Row. ('It was not a baker's shop,' she said many years later, 'it was a high-class confectioner's. It said so above the door.') There on 2 December 1899 a son was born, named Giovanni Battista after his great-uncle who had been a professor of pianoforte and singing. He was known to the family by the customary Italian diminutive Tita, which was varied by English friends to Tito. Tita was thus born a true Cockney, well within the sound of Bow bells.

The Barbirollis adored their adopted country and especially London. Other Italian families lived near them, and the area of Bloomsbury in which they dwelt had a colourful cosmopolitan air. When Tita was still a baby the family moved to lodgings at 37 Drury Lane. Music was the principal topic of conversation: Antonio and Lorenzo now shared the first desk of violins in the orchestra at the old Empire Theatre, Leicester Square, which was conducted by Leopold Wenzel. They had played when the orchestra performed by royal command at Windsor Castle on 23 November 1897, as accompaniment to 'cinematograph pictures'.

The London of his childhood remained vividly in John Barbirolli's memory all his life. He was taken walks or to the theatres by his father and grandfather, and shopping (which bored him) by his mother. Being precociously observant and receptive he absorbed the atmosphere of the city ineradicably. 'It is hard for those who did not know it,' he said when he was over sixty,* 'to realise the magic, beauty and overwhelming personality of pre-1914 London. Even its sordid side went towards creating this vivid and vital tapestry of a vanished age. London wasn't vulgar as it is today.' To the end of his days John loved exploring his 'favourite bits' of London, especially if he could show them to a sympathetic friend. Dean's Yard, Little Cloister, the alleys off Fleet Street, Lincoln's Inn Fields and Gough Square, the last with Dr Johnson's House as the *pièce de résistance* of the tour – he would show it to you with knowledgeable enthusiasm and with a proprietorial air, as if he had built it all himself.

His earliest recollection was of a fit of temper when he was four: he threw a ring into the middle of the road walking down Long Acre with the family, 'then a street of magic for me,' he wrote in 1954 – 'nearly all the shops were carriage makers, harness makers and saddlers, ending up at Aldridge's salerooms for horses. I can still smell that neighbourhood.' He was taken to ballet rehearsals at the Empire in its heyday and met Adeline Genée.

I must have been very small and light for I remember her saying what a dancer I would make. (God forbid.) I was fascinated even then by the conductor, Wenzel, who wore white gloves and conducted sitting down. I would lock myself in a room with some sort of stick and white gloves taken from Mémé [the family's name for Louise Barbirolli], Auntie or Granny and sing and conduct away for hours, but would never do it for anybody as a stunt.

Barbirolli had vivid recollections of his grandfather ('Nonno') although he was only six when Antonio died. 'He was tall, with a great sense of humour, and he was extremely kind, but he had a frightful temper. Everyone adored him and was terrified of him.' He was also striking in appearance and

* In the following pages the quoted passages in Sir John Barbirolli's own words are taken either from some fragmentary notes for an autobiography which were found among his papers or from a tape recording of a speech he made at a private dinner in the Town Hall, Manchester, in December 1961, on the occasion of the fiftieth anniversary of his first public appearance.

would say to his daughter-in-law when they were out in Soho: 'Drop a few paces behind me and you'll see all the girls winking at me.'

It was Antonio who put his grandson on the right musical path. Obviously, in a family of violinists, playing a stringed instrument was taken for granted and both Rosie and Tita began their musical education with the violin, although both graduated to other instruments, Rosie the pianoforte and Tita the cello. Their natural aptitude was remarkable, in fact Tita once said of himself that 'if such a medical monstrosity were possible, I was a pre-natal prodigy.' But while he practised the violin, five-year-old Tita, who was a fidget, walked from room to room. 'This used to drive my grandfather mad and one day he went to Edward Withers's in Wardour Street, bought a quarter-size cello and brought it home in a hansom cab. "Now," he said to me, "play that and you'll *have* to sit down".' Unfortunately Antonio did not live to see the result of this tactical success, for he died suddenly in July 1907, at the age of sixty-nine. Two days before, the family had found themselves thirteen at dinner. Throughout his life John was very superstitious in little ways: he would never sit thirteen, and if wine was spilt while he was dining he would dip his finger in it and go round everyone at table marking the sign of the Cross on their foreheads. Yet, apart from thirteen at table, thirteen was his lucky number. He won his scholarship on the thirteenth of the month and he intentionally gave his first public recital on 13 June, his grandfather's name-day.

Life at 37 Drury Lane was happy. For Rosie and Tita it was a thrill to go with their father to buy hors d'œuvres for the family lunch. 'My Dad had a damned good lunch beforehand anyway,' Barbirolli recalled,

tasting all that was on offer under the pretext of seeing that it was fit to eat. He had a mania for dressing me up like himself, in bowler hat, coat and stick. My mother hated this, so the bowler was bought in secret and only brought out outside the door. One day we were out like this and were outside the London Hippodrome when a crowd collected and followed us. It suddenly dawned on us that a famous giant and dwarf circus act was appearing at the theatre and the crowd were convinced that they had come upon them in person.

Sundays were quiet and special days when the family went to
the big Mass in the French Church of Notre Dame in Leicester Square.

When sermon-time came my father would listen to the first
few sentences in French, then whisper to us 'We've heard
this one' and take Rosie and me to the superb pastrycook's,
Bertaux, and he'd time it exactly so we'd all be back for the
rest of the service after the sermon.

Near No. 37 was the 'Old Mo' – the Old Mogul music-hall,
now the Winter Garden Theatre – but where now stands an
imposing set of Masonic buildings was a network of

rather unsalubrious little streets including a beloved little
shop where they sold newspapers, tobacco and cheap sweets
(a 'farving's' worth of suckers was a fact) and toys. I remember I used to buy masks with funny or hideous faces
($\frac{1}{2}$d or 1d) and whips, for my other ambition besides conducting was to be a hansom driver. I used to rig up a chair
on top of a table (very precarious) and pretend to drive a
cab. There was an Italian greengrocer opposite. My Saturday night treat was an ice cream and to stand by the
window with Granny watching the drunks. Those were the
days when 'bobbies' were 'bobbies', all very large with their
thumbs in their belts. The same old girls were removed
regularly. I remember the almost Hogarthian scene of their
publicly relieving themselves on the pavement.

The house seemed always to be full of musicians. The
Barbirollis had an English maid, who taught herself Italian in
the Venetian dialect, and they also took in lodgers to help out
with the money, 'though how well we lived.' One of the
lodgers before Tita was born was the Italian bass Arturo
Pessina, the first man to sing Falstaff in Verdi's opera in London, in 1894. He was paid £80 a performance, 'a fabulous sum
in those days,' and Lorenzo went with him to the bank to pay
in his own modest sum and to watch eighty gold sovereigns
being 'shovelled over the counter' by the celebrity.

Tita was about six when the family moved again

to a nice old Georgian house in Granville Street, No. 17
[now demolished] at the corner leading to Brunswick

Square, then so lovely and quiet. Here I first heard of an apartment called the 'drawing room', which I took very literally and immediately went to a desk there and proceeded to draw (or what passed for that art). The neighbourhood still had much character and what seemed to me a certain dignity. There were many interesting people we used to see, to whom Father raised his hat and occasionally spoke. Lionel Monckton* was one, who lived in what seemed a very grand house with its own grounds where now there are shops, at the corner of Russell Square and Southampton Row. About this time I used to be taken to Lincoln's Inn Gardens by my grandpa in the mornings where a band played in the little bandstand. Chairs were $\frac{1}{2}$d and on the way there Nonno used to call at a very good pork butcher, Shortland, and buy a huge ham sandwich, of which I was always offered a bite but I deeply regretted the amount of mustard in it for I felt it spoilt the taste. (Later in life I used to lunch there when at Covent Garden, sumptuously and cheaply.) My conducting mania was certainly furthered at Lincoln's Inn and when the performance was over I used to go and stand where the conductor had stood and hope that perhaps one day I might achieve such eminence. (The last night I played in the orchestra at Covent Garden I did the same thing and returned seven years later on the 'box'.)

Tita and Rosie first went to school at the kindergarten of the French church in Leicester Square.

We went in the green horse-bus which plied between King's Cross and Victoria. To give an idea of the leisure and grace of those times: the bus would stop in front of our house, my father and grandfather would emerge, offer a cigar or cigarette to the conductor and driver, my sister and I would be deposited in the bus and off we went to school. I was taught by two very beautiful nuns, Sister Paquin and Sister Monique. One I believe was Irish and I loved just to look at her. I must have been very susceptible even at that age, for not long after, in 1907, I fell in love with Lily Elsie when taken to see *The Merry Widow* in its original production at Daly's. Father and Mother both loved the

* 1862–1924, composer of *The Arcadians, A Country Girl,* etc.

theatre and I was taken if the play was thought suitable. Never shall I forget the thrill of queueing up for the Daly's gallery in a long alleyway, and the rush for the best seats. At the theatres of those days I had thrills I have never recaptured in my days of comparative affluence. All the buskers, acrobats, singers entertaining the queues – we had a two-hour variety show before we got into the theatre. How I pity those who have begun their theatre-going in booked seats, though I suppose such unfortunates must exist.

His first contact with the Royal Opera House, Covent Garden, was in 1905 when Lorenzo and Louise went to the first London performance of Puccini's *Madam Butterfly* and little Tita took sandwiches and sustenance to them in the queue for the gallery.

Another aesthetic remembrance and a very nostalgic one (which always had the queer effect of unsettling me a little, I felt so happy and then a rapid thought would come that it might not last) was the smell of lilac in Russell Square in the Springtime. This I also always associate with Mémé, for Father would be busy in the evenings and Mémé usually took us (Rosie and me, for Peter was not born till 1911) for a walk after supper. Of course the Square was reserved for the residents, and we walked round it, but the scent and colour were no different from inside or out, and one never felt any envy or class-consciousness. Although the divisions then were more marked, everyone seemed to be content to be what they were and thought no more about it.

In the foregoing can plainly be found some of the influences which moulded Barbirolli's taste and character and made him such a compelling interpreter of Elgar's *Cockaigne* overture and symphonies and of Vaughan Williams's *A London Symphony*, in which the slow movement recaptures the solitude of an Edwardian Bloomsbury Square. As he would often say, the closing pages of Elgar's Second Symphony never failed, even at a morning rehearsal, to bring tears to his eyes, caused not only by the intrinsic beauty of the music but because, for Barbirolli, they represented his nostalgia for the era that ended in 1914 and for the way of living that perished with the First World War. That music was associated in his mind with Sir Edward Grey's words, 'The lamps are going out all over Europe; we shall not see them lit again in our lifetime.' Nor did Barbirolli lose his affection for the light music of this epoch, which was his father's bread-and-butter, not only Lehár and Edward German but Haydn Wood and Monckton. But music was not all. As he has described, the magic of the theatre was almost equally potent. The career of Sir Henry Irving was of lifelong fascination to him, and when Laurence Irving's great biography was published in the 1950s John soaked himself in it, savouring the details and thinking it not a word too long. He also liked the smell of size, of which the backstage of the theatre is redolent.

Childhood memories for Barbirolli meant not only the Lincoln's Inn bandstand but the tale of how his father's violin was smashed in the excitement on Mafeking night at the Lyric Club, of wonderful Christmases, with Lorenzo returning home in a hansom cab laden with gifts for the family from the Queen's Hotel, Leicester Square, where he conducted the orchestra, the building by Oscar Hammerstein of the London Opera House in Kingsway, bank holidays on Hampstead Heath, visits to Paris exploring the old streets and buildings and listening to Père Gay's sermons on Sunday mornings at Notre Dame, and summer holidays at Brighton, a town he always loved, remembering the elegance of the piers and the church parades. Yet, he noted in his fragmentary memoirs, at holiday times he was 'always inclined to be a little sad,' so early did his chronic fits of depression manifest themselves. He wrote years later to his friend Canon Joseph Thompson: 'The word "rest" has been anathema to me since childhood!' On those Brighton holidays he begged to be allowed to take his cello. Music absorbed him all the time, even then. At the age of eight he was practising scales for two hours a day. One day Tita went with other boys to fish in a lake near Brighton at Barcombe Mills, but soon he had vanished and was found studying the score of a symphony. 'Why didn't you stay and fish?' he was asked, and he replied: 'It seemed such a waste of time. If you want some fish we can buy it on the way home.'

John's father dominates these childhood memories, 'a wise and gentle counsellor,' he wrote in 1969, 'who exercised his benevolent influence until his end.' After his end too: in 1952, after conducting a compelling performance of *Aïda*,

Barbirolli said to my wife: 'That was one for my dear old Dad.' He believed that he unconsciously derived all his instinctive sense of feeling and tempi of Italian opera from his father and grandfather. Lorenzo's life in England, in the thirty-seven years he spent there, was passed mostly within the famous Victorian–Edwardian social playground of Leicester Square, in the Alhambra, the Empire and the Queen's Hotel. From 1904 he was musical director of two little orchestras at the Queen's, one in the restaurant and one in the grill room. They played selections from *San Toy* or *Carmen* or *My Lady Molly*, the dances from *Nell Gwynne* by Edward German, the *Valse Lente* 'Seduction', and music by Lehár, Leslie Stuart, Lionel Monckton and Tosti – and, 'by request,' in February 1912 *Alexander's Ragtime Band*. A long way, it must sometimes have seemed, from *Otello* under Faccio at La Scala but, as Lorenzo would tell Tita, 'an A is an A and a quaver is a quaver wherever it is played.'

Sometimes, at the after-dinner concerts, promising singers appeared, the tenor Walter Hyde for example. It was Hyde who asked Lorenzo to give a first London engagement, at a fee of a guinea, to the great Irish tenor John McCormack, and it was the accompanist at the Queen's, Charles Marshall, who wrote for McCormack the song 'I hear you calling me.' Then there would be 'morning' concerts ('to commence at THREE o'clock precisely') at the Steinway Hall at one of which Signor Barbirolli's Quintet played selections from Cilèa's *Adriana Lecouvreur*, and Charles Santley and Manuel Garcia sang.

Lorenzo's hopes were centred on his son Tita, in whom he perceived an exceptional musical talent and responsiveness. From the child's earliest days Lorenzo took him to concerts and recitals – together they heard Santley and Ben Davies sing, they heard a pianoforte recital by Saint-Saëns, Beethoven violin sonata recitals by Eugen Ysaÿe and Raoul Pugno, recitals by Kreisler, Kubelik and Pachmann, orchestral concerts conducted by Henry Wood and Thomas Beecham. Lorenzo even awakened his son's lifelong interest in the world of politics during the famous general election of 1906. 'My father, I discovered, was a Liberal so a Liberal I became too and took a most passionate interest in the results.' Later in life he always voted Conservative, and made sure he had his postal vote if he was abroad at election times.

Father and son were like brothers and friends. Tita was

treated as an adult, even from the age of four being allowed to drink wine. He admired his father's musicianship not merely from filial devotion but with professional judgment. 'I never forgot the beautiful phrasing of my father in playing the various arias in the operatic selections at the Queen's.' Lorenzo was greatly liked by his fellow-musicians, who called him 'Barbi' and went to him for advice and help. His pianist at the Queen's for many years summed him up in a letter written to Tita in February 1931, nearly two years after Lorenzo's death:

> It signified to me the passing of one of the few real gentlemen of the profession, a great heart, a lovable nature and one of the best friends I had, who...bore with my failings and inexperience as no other man would... Well can I remember how enthusiastically he would express his determination that you should be 'at the top of the tree'. Nothing gave him greater pleasure than that topic.

Tita left his attractive nuns at kindergarten to enter the preparatory class of St Clement Dane's Holborn Estate Grammar School, then in Houghton Street, Strand. (Its tuck shop was on the site of what is now the London School of Economics, and Barbirolli thought the site was put to better use in his schooldays.) A pupil in the girls' school remembered years later the morning when a little boy, hand in hand with two little girls, went through the school hall. He wore long trousers, tee shirt and looked very Italian, his eyes sparkling. It soon became clear that ordinary school lessons held little interest for him – and he was thrown out of the choir because his voice was 'unmusical.' Only the cello really mattered, only music was to be taken really seriously, and when he played at school speech days, dark, intensely concentrating, even the non-musical were impressed, including perhaps Lord Roberts who was the guest on one occasion and to whom Tita was introduced: 'He was about as big as I was.'

In 1910 he won a scholarship to Trinity College of Music to begin his academic musical education. His cello teacher, then in his seventies, was Edmund Woolhouse, a pupil of the leading British cellist of the first half of the nineteenth century, Richard Lindley (1777–1855), who had known Beethoven and often played with Dragonetti, the double-bass virtuoso. Tita had a great affection for Woolhouse and went to the performances of Bach's *St John Passion* in St Anne's Church, Soho, to hear his teacher play the viola da gamba obbligato in the aria 'It is finished.' In his spare time Tita buried his head in the scores of Beethoven symphonies and quartets and Haydn quartets. By the time he was eleven or twelve he was going to hear operas armed with the full score. Probably the first mention of his name in print was in the *School Music Review* of 1 May 1911, which included a photograph of him, unmistakably J.B., clad in sailor-suit (he even had a whistle in his pocket), his right hand holding his bow and clearly showing that long slender thumb later to be familiar to concert-hall audiences the world over. An accompanying paragraph recorded the 'remarkably good performance' of a movement from Mendelssohn's D minor Pianoforte Trio which Richard Ball Johnson (pianoforte), Samuel Kutcher (violin) and Tita had given at De Keysers Hotel on 18 April at a dinner given to examiners and local representatives of the college.

John remembered 1911 especially, because it was the year his beloved horse-buses ceased running and the year of the Coronation of King George V, with the 'beauty and grace of the street decorations and illuminations.' But it was to have a personal significance also, because at the Trinity College's orchestral concert in the Queen's Hall on 16 December conducted by Wilhelm Sachse, one of the violin teachers, he made his first public appearance as the soloist in a performance of one movement, the Cantilena, from the Cello Concerto in A minor, Op. 14, by Georg Goltermann (1824–98), the German cellist and conductor. The concerto is of immense difficulty, rather like the Vieuxtemps violin concertos, and it is hardly surprising that even this intrepid twelve-year-old was not expected to tackle the whole of it. The critic of the *Musical News* amused the Barbirolli family by complaining that although the execution was good, the tone was not large – which, considering that there was an orchestra of about ninety and he was using a half-size cello, was 'faintly excusable,' as John said years later.

Tita missed most of the spring term of 1912 because of a severe attack of German measles, and spent some of the time arranging for strings the *allegretto* movement of a cello sonata by Benedetto Marcello. (Thirteen years later he conducted it with his string orchestra.)

On 11 July 1912 the Trinity College orchestra gave another concert in the Queen's Hall, conducted by Herr Sachse. Tita had a complete concerto this time, the A Minor, Op. 33, by Saint-Saëns, and the performance was heard by the thirty-five-year-old viola player, Lionel Tertis, who said at a dinner fifty years later that it was 'most amazing – quite wonderful technically and musically. He was a prodigious prodigy; why, he could play my head off when he was twelve and a half.' The critic of the *Musical News* mentioned Tita's pure tone but again complained that it was 'not strong.'

Tita's exceptional gifts were noticed by Edgardo Levy, who suggested to Lorenzo that the best teacher for such a gifted boy was Herbert Gregor Walenn, at that date forty-two years old. Walenn was trained at the Royal Academy of Music and later in Frankfurt with Hugo Becker. For five years at the turn of the century he was cellist in the Kruse Quartet and was appointed professor at the Royal Academy of Music in 1901. He gave private lessons at No. 10 (later re-numbered 34) Nottingham Place, and it was there, in the summer of 1912, that Tita was taken by his father. Master and pupil became at once devoted to each other. 'From that day,' Barbirolli wrote after Walenn's death in 1953, 'until two days before his death we remained in constant and close touch. During my fleeting visits to London it was nearly always my first port of call...not because I thought I was fulfilling a duty but because I always felt refreshed and much the better for breathing for a few peaceful moments the air of his serene and kindly wisdom...'

Although Tita was offered another scholarship by Trinity College, Lorenzo did not accept its terms, to the regret of the principal who wrote that 'your boy...has been a general favourite.' Lorenzo was determined that Tita should stay with Walenn and so the boy competed for and won the Ada Lewis Scholarship at the RAM, which he entered in September 1912. The critics' notices of RAM concerts over the next few years regularly referred to 'that clever young cellist Tita Barbirolli.' At one of Gwynne Kimpton's 'concerts for young people' in the Duke's Hall of the Academy on 8 November 1913, he played the Marcello Sonata in C already mentioned. On 14 July 1914, with the Principal of the Academy, Sir Alexander Mackenzie, conducting, he played Max Bruch's *Kol Nidrei* 'with astonishing ease and feeling,' according to *The Strad*, which went on to say: 'This very musical boy is developing rapidly.' He was Boughton Packer Bath Scholar and Bronze Medallist in 1913, Charles Rube prizewinner, Bonamy Dobrée prizewinner and Silver Medallist in 1914, and Piatti prizewinner and certificate of merit in 1915. He played a good deal of chamber music at the Academy, in trios with Winifred Small (violin) and Egerton Tidmarsh (pianoforte) and later in a string quartet with Wolfe Wolfinsohn (later leader of the Stradivarius Quartet) as first violin, Joseph Shadwick (later leader of the Sadler's Wells Orchestra) as second violin, and Frank Howard (to be leader of the violas when Beecham formed the London Philharmonic in 1932). His regular partner in cello sonatas was the pianist Ethel Bartlett.

In those days the Ravel String Quartet was not allowed to be played at official Academy concerts, only at recitals organised by the students' club. The four young players rehearsed in the men's lavatory. Debussy, too, was barely admitted to these academic precincts. Tita was captivated by some of the contemporary music of his youth. One 'infatuation' which was to last all his life began at a Sunday afternoon concert at the Queen's Hall when he was twelve. After the overture, Delius's *Dance Rhapsody No. 1* was played. Tita had never heard of the work or its composer. But, he said many years later, 'I thought it the most beautiful music I'd ever heard – it just knocked me out. At the final violin solo I was in a daze and even today that music still stirs me.' Thenceforward he was a passionate Delian, and the last recording he was to make, a few days before he died, was of music by Delius. Curiously he hardly ever conducted the *Dance Rhapsody*.

Barbirolli's second study instrument at the Academy was the pianoforte, taught him by Bernard Symons, a pupil of Tobias Matthay. Mr Symons remembered after Barbirolli's death that his pupil was 'not much good.' Meeting him years afterwards he asked him how his piano-playing was faring. Barbirolli replied: 'My dear chap, absolutely ghastly, but it wasn't your fault. Nobody could possibly teach me to play the piano.'

This musical education proceeded against the background of the happy and close-knit family life of the Barbirollis. In 1913 they moved again to rooms above a chemist's shop at 46 Marchmont Street, near Russell Square. In 1916 a local musician, Marblacy Jones, went to see Tita at this address where he noticed a copy of Cyril Scott's *Pierrot amoureux*. 'I picked it up to look at it more closely. He asked me if I was interested and would I care to play it with him. We did so and his comment was that no one at the Academy could play it. He then showed me a copy of Cyril Scott's *Russian Dance* for piano which his piano professor had torn into four pieces saying this was not music. Tita collected the pieces from the wastepaper basket and put them together.' By this time Tita had had his first professional orchestral engagement in the pit at the Duke of York's Theatre (in about 1915) – for which he had bought a pair of long trousers which, he said, 'hurt under the armpits.' A girl who lived opposite the Barbirollis in Marchmont Street would watch Tita leaving home carrying his cello. He would 'take a few steps, pause, look back and wave to his mama who was always sitting by the window.' Sometimes he left carrying not a cello but boxing gloves, for he was very keen on boxing as a means of keeping fit and took part in flyweight bouts at the YMCA. He was light on his feet and fearless. It was in a boxing match that his nose received a blow which put it out of shape and caused him a lifetime of sinus trouble.

Barbirolli left the Academy at the end of the summer term, 1916. So gifted a cellist was able to obtain a fair amount of free-lance work. He became the youngest player in Henry Wood's Queen's Hall Orchestra, he played in the Carl Rosa Opera orchestra and for Beecham's opera at the Aldwych and Shaftesbury Theatres, including a performance of *The Magic Flute* in which the Queen of the Night was sung by Dorothy Moulton, who later became the wife of Sir Robert Mayer and a good friend of Barbirolli. He played also for pantomime at the old Surrey music-hall, when the smell of oranges pervaded the front stalls, and in a small theatre orchestra. 'There was not much to do,' he wrote twenty years later; 'incidental music to plays had fallen into disuse; all we did was to play the people to and from the bar in the intervals. In the long waits between the act-intervals I studied scores.' For playing at the Promenade Concerts in 1916 and 1917, Tita received 65s. a week, for six concerts and three rehearsals, and when the air-raids reduced the audiences they also reduced his wages to 37s. 6d. But if someone were to say that this amount 'did not go very far' in those days, he would have vehemently disagreed. On 13 June 1917, he gave his first solo recital in the Aeolian Hall, New Bond Street, playing – from memory, which was unusual then – Boëllmann's A Minor Sonata and Debussy's Sonata with Ethel Bartlett, the Piatti arrangement of Locatelli's solo Sonata, the Prelude, Sarabande and Bourrées

I and II from J. S. Bach's Suite in C Major and (accompanied by Harold Craxton) Scott's *Pierrot amoureux*, Cui's *Orientale* and Davidoff's *Am Springbrunnen*. The notices were outstandingly good, his maturity and breadth of style being generally remarked upon. 'Indeed so far as his natural ability and his technique are concerned he has nothing to fear from even the most gifted of his contemporaries,' the critic of the *Daily Telegraph* wrote. The date of 13 June had been specially chosen because it had been Grandpa Antonio's name-day.

The autumn and winter of 1917 were an anxious time for Londoners because of the Taube and Zeppelin raids. In May 1916 Tita's sister Rosa had married Alfonso 'Fofo' Gibilaro, a Sicilian pianist, and they now had a daughter, Maria Concetta (Tina), born in March 1917. Louise Barbirolli took Peter, now six, and the baby Tina to Bournemouth at this time while Tita stayed in London where he was playing in the Beecham season of opera at Drury Lane. He wrote to Louise:

My dear Mama. – I think the best thing to do will be to stay just the three weeks as you originally intended and then come back. It will be no use coming back before the three weeks otherwise all the money we have spent will be of no use, as the doctor says you must be away at least 3 weeks to do the baby's cough any good... Our recital is fixed for the 22nd or 29th November in the afternoon. I have not been wearing my nice blue suit since you went away. I am having it cleaned and pressed and put away and will not take it out till the day of the recital as it would be very silly to have a new suit made just for that afternoon. The audiences at the opera considering the raids last week were surprisingly good... Will stop now as I must practise a little.

The recital to which Tita referred was given in the Aeolian Hall on 29 November when, with Ethel Bartlett, he played sonatas by Brahms (the E Minor, Op. 38), Debussy, Grieg and the *Rhapsody* by Eugène Goossens. Their playing of the Debussy attracted the most favour: 'an interpretation of extraordinary perceptiveness and conviction,' said the *Morning Post* critic.

This was to be Barbirolli's last London concert for some time. Three days later he was eighteen, and on 12 December he went to enlist in the Army. But he was not immediately called up, so there was Christmas at home. The family were delighted by their new member, Rosie's pianist husband Alfonso Gibilaro.* He had left Palermo for England in pursuit of better opportunities. He began in a pier orchestra at Weston-super-Mare but soon went to London where he played at the Ritz and then became pianist for De Groot's famous orchestra at the Piccadilly Hotel. After their marriage he and Rosie stayed in Marchmont Street, and 'Fofo' or 'Fof,' as he was called by the family, learned the Venetian dialect. From the first Tita loved him, and since Rosie too was a pianist and sometimes played with her father at the Queen's – as did Tita on occasions – the musical *camaraderie* was consolidated. It was this close-knit circle that Tita left when he joined the Army.

52537 Private G. B. Barbirolli joined up on 2 February 1918, going first to Hounslow Barracks from Whitehall. He was to spend most of the next fourteen months in Kent and wrote home to his parents several times a week.

...Today has passed a little quicker as from 7 to 8.30 I had to help clean the hut out. You would laugh if you saw me putting the beds straight and cleaning the grate. Still that's better than having to scrub tables and benches. After breakfast I had to go and help in the kitchen. I had to peel the parsnips for dinner and take them to the cook... At 1.30 had to go on parade. I was given nothing to do so am enjoying myself writing to you, dear Mama, and Ethel [Bartlett]... For breakfast we had ham, very nice, and quite a decent dinner, boiled mutton and vegetables. I was lucky and had a good lot of meat... The Army does teach you to appreciate home, but after all I didn't expect to come to Buckingham Palace. We had a lecture this morning about saluting etc. as it was raining and the Sergeant didn't want to make us march about in the rain...

* He was also a composer of good light music. One of Gigli's finest records is of Gibilaro's 'Sicilian Waggoner's Song', originally written as an oboe solo for Evelyn Rothwell.

Tita was eventually posted to the 1st (Reserve) Garrison Battalion of the Suffolk Regiment at Gravesend. The colonel, C. F. Grantham, was, according to John, 'a very bad violinist' but enthusiastic (he had known the cellist Piatti well) and had encouraged the formation of a voluntary orchestra. Tita wrote to Mémé: 'Tonight if I have time hope to see the conductor of the orchestra here and perhaps I might get in…'

The colonel was delighted to have such a fine cellist to strengthen the orchestra. All the rehearsing and concerts were in the men's free time. The oboist was described by Barbirolli years later as 'an old Indian Army regular, a drunken old Irishman and enchanting person.' He could not cope with the name Barbirolli, so he called Tita 'Bob O'Reilly.' The sort of programme the orchestra played can be gauged from one given at the Port Victoria aerodrome on 12 March 1918: *Poet and Peasant* overture, 'Roses of Picardy,' *Invitation to the Waltz*, selections from *Chu Chin Chow*, Rachmaninov's C Sharp Minor Prelude, *Henry VIII Dances*, the *Indian Love Lyrics* and cello solos by Musician Barbirolli. Tita was able to get sheet music from Lorenzo and a composition from his brother-in-law Gibilaro.

In April 1918 he wrote:

Monday 7.30 p.m.

My dear Mama… Last night I played at the concert and had a great success. It is funny what music does. The sergeants etc. are very nice to me and talk about music. This morning my sergeant was giving us a lecture on drill order and finished up talking to me about Beecham, opera etc…

The battalion moved to the Isle of Grain, and it was there, in May 1918, that Tita first conducted when the regular conductor, an officer, was on leave.

Grain, Saturday

Father, I have conducted two rehearsals of the orchestra here with great success. Last night for the first time I did the *Petite Suite* of Coleridge-Taylor, *Marche Triomphale* from Cleopatra, Mancinelli, and *The Maid of the Mountains*. I was surprised myself at some of the effects I got

B

without much trouble. Some of the chaps came to congratulate me and said they had never enjoyed a rehearsal so much and what a pleasure it was to play with me...

A few days later:

If I hadn't been on guard today I should have gone to see the doctor. My back and stomach are not quite right... Yesterday we had a medical inspection by our doctor and, although I'm not sure, I fancy I was passed B1, unfit for overseas... The first thing the doctor said on looking at my medical history sheet from Whitehall was 'This man is deaf.' Then he examined my heart and dismissed me. Last week I conducted a splendid rehearsal. We did *Rosamunde* overture, *Ballet Egyptien* and Coleridge-Taylor suite. I was really surprised at *Rosamunde*. The band seem to play smoother under my direction. Funny how difficult it is to make people play piano. I got some fine pianissimos. I hope you don't think it swank writing this, but I thought you would like to know.

Sometimes on a Sunday evening he played his cello at the church service. After one such occasion he wrote to Lorenzo: 'Will you please if you can spare it send me that trio arrangement of the Schubert *Serenade* to play in the church here. It is a lovely little place and the effect of the *Träumerei* just as it was getting dusk was wonderful. I did enjoy it so.' He also played often at informal chamber music recitals – known as PSEs (Pleasant Sunday Evenings) at the home of the organist of Gravesend parish church.

May, 1918

Yesterday being Whit Monday we had a half holiday. The boys arranged a rehearsal and I conducted and also lost my temper a little but it was all for their good and they all thanked me after and told me how they enjoyed it... Tomorrow start firing my course.

This last sentence referred to rifle-firing which took place at Sheerness.

Finished firing my course yesterday and have passed out as 1st class shot. Apart from the honour, that means after six months 3d a day extra pay. Have not been able to write much lately as I have been so tired in the evenings after coming back from the ranges. We had a march every day of $5\frac{1}{2}$ miles with full marching order... I had to fire with what was left of my glasses, only one glass is broken. Still, you have to shut one eye when you fire so it was all right. I couldn't have done anything without.

In the summer of 1918 Tita had a spell in hospital. Some weeks earlier he had written home: 'The medical board came this morning and passed me B1. My medical history sheet read: "Irregular action of the heart, slight deafness left ear, bad discharge two years ago." I wanted to tell him about my back and stomach but didn't get a chance.' His ear trouble, combined with chronic catarrh, caused the army doctor to send him to a specialist and he went to Dr James Donelan, surgeon to the throat and ear department of the Italian Hospital in London. His report, dated 16 August 1918, read:

I treated him at the Italian Hospital in 1914 for right chronic suppurative otitis media with a large perforation. This healed under treatment... He has a slight deflection of the nasal septum to the right side which has become much more marked since I last saw him and this should be resected. The deafness is due to the chronic middle ear disease on the right side and primarily to the neglect of his adenoids and tonsils until he was 15 years old... He suffers at times from Eustachian obstruction and catarrh, due to obstruction within the nose.

For the rest of his life Barbirolli was never to be free from sinus trouble.

On 6 November 1918 Tita went to Crowborough on an anti-gas warfare course. He eventually became an instructor and was promoted to acting Lance-Corporal. His notes made during this course have been kept. They are as thorough as one of his rehearsal schedules. He had good reason to remember Armistice Day: as part of the course each participant had to inhale gas in a little wooden shed. Never one to do things by halves, he exceeded the limit when it was his turn on 11 November and had to be resuscitated. Nevertheless he came top of Southern Command in his exams – he understood nothing, he said in later years, but he had memorised the gas manual.

On 30 March 1919, acting Lance Corporal Barbirolli, medical category BIII, went on twenty-eight days' demobilisation leave, being transferred to Army Reserve as from 27 April 1919. His conducting career had begun during this episode in his life and the experience had convinced him that this was where his future lay. As far as the physical actions were concerned, he told me many years later, 'I conducted on that first night as I do today.'

sometimes he...

3
Except in
the Street

Tita left the Army to begin his career in earnest and to pick up the threads where he had left them in 1917. On one thing he was determined: that he would be independent and lose no chance of gaining experience. He knew he could always earn a living with his cello, but in the forefront of his mind was the determination to abandon it for the conductor's 'box' at the first opportunity. But opportunities were not many in the world of English music in 1919–20. Before the war music in Britain had been dominated by foreign conductors like Richter and Nikisch. Only Cowen, Beecham and Wood of native conductors had made any great reputation. There were few orchestras, most of them on an *ad hoc* basis, and in London the system of deputies still prevailed by which a player could send a substitute to a concert while he accepted some more lucrative private engagement elsewhere. It was an iniquitous system, epitomised by the classic story of the conductor who at rehearsal complimented a player on his beautiful playing of a solo passage only to be told: 'Thank you, but I'm afraid I won't be here for the concert.' Barbirolli remembered the standards of those days as appalling, with a few shining exceptions among individuals. 'If you'd heard the violas when I was young,' he said, 'you'd take a bismuth tablet.' Among the shining exceptions were names he uttered with respect to the end of his life: the violist Lionel Tertis; his first principal cellist, Warwick Evans; and Alfred Brain the horn-player. Among his colleagues, though in the viola section, was Eric Coates, who has written in his autobiography, *Suite in Four Movements*, a vivid account of the Queen's Hall Orchestra from 1910 to 1919.

Tita in 1919 could rely on engagements at Royal Philharmonic Society concerts and with opera orchestras. He played in Beecham's orchestra at Covent Garden, including the performances of *Parsifal* in which Percy Heming, who was to become a close colleague and friend, sang a magnificent Amfortas. But he worked whenever he could; and in that first year after demobilisation he played in dance-halls, in hotels (with his sister Rosa and a violinist, Edward Stanley de Groot, later known as Stanelli, the comedian), in a circus orchestra, and in cinemas, where he was part of an orchestra which had to 'fit the picture,' that is to say to switch suddenly from one piece of music to another as the action on the screen changed. Sometimes he would find as many as eighty pieces of music on the stand before him; he regarded this experience as invaluable to his musicianship. 'For a start, it taught me to play rhythmically,' he said. 'One minute it would be a waltz, then a bit of *William Tell*, then something quite else.' He was able to boast that he had played everywhere except in the street. This work also taught him about the ways of the world and he learned all the dodges musicians can employ when they want to ease off or waste time at rehearsal. One of these ruses was to be tried on him in 1936 at one of his first rehearsals with the New York Philharmonic. He told the player concerned: 'Look here, old chap, I know that one and I could teach you a few you don't know.' He had no more trouble.

Two events particularly marked 1919 for Barbirolli. His cello teacher, Herbert Walenn, founded the London Violoncello School, of which Pablo Casals later became patron. Barbirolli was connected with it from the first, as teacher, performer and conductor, and there he made two good friends, Joan ('Dot') Mulholland and Douglas Cameron. Secondly, on 26 October he began his connection with Elgar's music as one of the cellists in the London Symphony Orchestra for the first performance of the Cello Concerto. At the rehearsal Elgar, who was to conduct his own work, was deprived of an hour of his already limited rehearsal time by Albert Coates who was conducting the rest of the programme and 'stole' the hour for Skryabin's *Poème de l'Extase*. When the concerto was at last reached it was clear that no really adequate performance would be achieved. Barbirolli was inwardly incensed and wanted, had he dared, to stand up and say: 'Go home, sir, refuse to conduct it until you can have a proper rehearsal'; and it is now known that Elgar seriously considered withdrawing and would have done so had it not been that he did not wish to damage the career of the soloist, Felix Salmond. The memory of this incident enraged Barbirolli to the end of his life.

In the summer of 1919 he was a member of the orchestra for Diaghilev's second post-war season of the Russian Ballet, staged at 'that beautiful theatre the Alhambra, always the best house in the capital in which to show ballet,' to quote Sir Osbert Sitwell. During this season Massine, Karsavina and Lopokova entranced audiences in *La Boutique Fantasque*, *Tricorne (The Three-Cornered Hat)* and *Parade*, and Ernest Ansermet conducted. Barbirolli's particular memory of this season, apart from the pleasure of playing in Stravinsky's *Fire-Bird* and *Petrushka*, was of Diaghilev's insistence that Manuel de Falla should conduct his own ballet, *Tricorne*. Despite the composer's protestations that he was not competent to do it, Diaghilev almost dragged him to the pit at rehearsal. After a few bars they reached some cross-rhythms. Falla stopped beating, so the orchestra stopped. 'No, no,' he cried, 'you go on.' He was totally unable to conduct the rhythms he had devised.

Barbirolli continued to play at Covent Garden and took part in the first London performances of Puccini's *Trittico*. He later recalled how Puccini liked to buy English club ties in Bond Street and appeared at rehearsal in an Old Etonian tie one day, MCC the next, and so on!

Barbirolli's first solo recital after the war was on 17 January 1920, at the Theatre Royal, Dublin. In March he was soloist in Tchaikovsky's *Variations on a Rococo Theme* with the Bournemouth Symphony Orchestra (as it was in fact called, being the Municipal Orchestra augmented to fifty players) conducted by Dan Godfrey, ever willing to give young executants and composers their chance. Engagements of this kind filled much of his time in 1920. On 25 March he was in the Royal Philharmonic's orchestra for the first public performance, conducted by the composer, of Holst's *The Hymn of Jesus*. He noticed how the short-sighted little man, whom all the orchestra loved, had his dress trousers braced too tight, revealing a pair of red socks. He went, as a deputy, with the

LSO to the first post-war Three Choirs Festival in September at Worcester and again played under Elgar's baton, this time in *The Dream of Gerontius*, with Gervase Elwes as Gerontius. 'It was extraordinary,' he wrote in 1965, 'how he could make you feel exactly what he wanted if you were in sympathy with him.'

But it was in April of 1920 that he had his most pleasing success when he was in the orchestra at the Theatre Royal, Drury Lane, for the return to London of Anna Pavlova for a season of ballet. Her *pièce de résistance* was, of course, *Le Cygne*, to Saint-Saëns's music, and in the *Daily Telegraph* of 13 April the critic complained: 'Why, by the way, are we never told, officially at least, the names of the orchestral players on these occasions?... There is a remarkable cellist for "The Swan" dance, for example...' The cellist, with harp accompaniment, was Barbirolli and on the first night Pavlova was so delighted by his playing that she split her bouquet of tiger lilies and threw half down to him in the pit. Later she asked to meet him to thank him, and he was astonished by the steely grip of her handshake – 'nearly broke all my fingers,' he said. Bertram C. Jones, a member of the London Symphony Orchestra, heard this performance. 'The exquisite playing foretold the great artist he was to become; even memories of the great Casals have not dulled that first memory of Barbirolli's playing.' John played this solo because the leader of the section was ill and the sub-principal funked it, so he was brought from the back desks to play it. 'Of course,' he said, 'I was soon sent back to the back desks. They didn't like rivalry from a young 'un.'

His experience with the Elgar Cello Concerto had spurred him to learn the work, and on 27 January 1921 he was the soloist in a performance with the Bournemouth orchestra conducted by Dan Godfrey. This was not, as Barbirolli remembered it and as a Bournemouth critic claimed at the time, the first performance outside London. Felix Salmond had played it with the Hallé in Manchester on 20 March 1920, and there were almost certainly several other 1920 performances. Nevertheless Barbirolli was perhaps the third cellist to take it up (the second being Beatrice Harrison) and a critic's account of his performance said that it was 'in evident sympathy with the composer's intentions, and the interpretation suggested some singularly refined conceptions on the part of the soloist and orchestra.'

For the next three years he continued his arduous and valuable apprenticeship in symphony, opera and cinema orchestras. In his spare time he studied scores to prepare himself for the day when he would achieve his ambition and step up to the conductor's rostrum, for his experiences with the garrison orchestra had confirmed him in his conviction that he was born to conduct. The only relaxations he allowed himself were visits to Lord's to watch Middlesex, for this English-born Italian-Frenchman had a passion for cricket. In the winter of 1922 he was again among the Royal Philharmonic cellists for the opening concerts under Albert Coates, of whose abilities he formed a low opinion. Most of his orchestral experience was under Beecham or Henry Wood. Of the latter, whose qualities of application and thorough musicianship he admired, he had a fund of affectionate and amusing anecdotes. Wood, he said, had 'the most inelegant way of expressing things that were perfectly normal.' At a rehearsal of the *Tannhäuser* overture, when the much-used special sets of orchestral parts Sir Henry had devised in order to prevent constant page-turning became difficult to keep on the stands, he exclaimed: 'Me private parts! Must have 'em sewn up.' In fugal passages he exhorted the orchestra to 'pull out your subject with vigour.'

Barbirolli's only chance at this time to further his conducting ambitions came on his twenty-third birthday in 1922 when at the London School of Violoncellos' pupils' meeting in the Kingsway Hall he conducted the first performance of a work called *Dawn*, by Felix White, scored for twelve cellos. The critics were not very impressed by this work, but another arrangement for six cellos was liked, principally, one writer said, because of 'Mr Barbirolli, who was very popular. He wielded his baton with considerable vigour, and some of his movements would not have shamed Mr Douglas Fairbanks in one of his most energetic moods.' It was in this year that he anglicised his name to John Barbirolli for a recital at the Aeolian Hall on 13 June, with Harold Craxton as pianist, when he played Elgar's concerto and Delius's sonata. He also played *Ancient Lullaby* by Ethel Bartlett, who was now married to the pianist Rae Robertson (later they became well-known as a duo). This recital was attended by Frank Machray, who had been in the Army with Tita and took his fiancée to the Aeolian Hall to meet the man to whom he had written a few days earlier: 'When I sometimes think of you, Tita, one impression always stands out in my mind and that is your thoughts about women; your ideal seemed to be so far above the people one meets every day.' Tita had been in love with Ethel. They renewed their partnership at a Violoncello Club concert on 9 June 1923, and in the autumn of the same year made their first broadcast. Barbirolli still played in theatre orchestras and it was in 1923, playing something by Massenet in the interval, that he was heard by one of the actresses in the play who was also a talented musician – Yvonne Arnaud. So began a long friendship.

At this period Barbirolli met two men who were to play important roles in his life. The first was the French violinist André Mangeot. He was born in Paris in 1883* and settled in England (of which he became a naturalised citizen) in 1903 when he was for a time a member of the Queen's Hall Orchestra and played at Covent Garden under Richter. Eventually he abandoned opera and in 1920 founded the Music Society of London and a string quartet in 1921. The Music Society was symptomatic of the upsurge of interest in music which followed the armistice. Several small enterprising organisations of this kind sprang up in London. Some flourished and some died. Some were very successful, the English Singers for example. Mangeot was specially interested in the early English composers – Purcell, Orlando Gibbons, Matthew Locke – and it was not surprising that he later collaborated in this field with Philip Heseltine (Peter Warlock). He also promoted an early London performance of Schoenberg's *Pierrot Lunaire*. He was always on the watch for rising talent and the prowess of Barbirolli soon came to his notice when they met at a house in St John's Wood and Barbirolli joined in a performance of Vaughan Williams's G Minor String Quartet. Early in 1924 Barbirolli became the cellist in the Music Society Quartet, the other members being Mangeot, Boris Pecker (a Russian born in Kiev in 1902), and Cecil Bonvalot, who was later replaced as violist by Rebecca Clarke (later to be the wife of the pianist James Friskin). Mangeot wanted to introduce English music to overseas audiences and took his

* He died aged eighty-seven in London on 11 September 1970, six weeks after Barbirolli.

quartet to Paris where, on 22 March at the Salle Pleyel, they played the Vaughan Williams quartet at a concert of the Société Nationale de Musique. At a Music Society concert in November 1926 the quartet gave the first public performance of Fauré's String Quartet, Op. 121, having prepared and rehearsed it with the composer at the beautiful home at Bray of Frank Schuster, friend of Fauré and of Elgar.

Another string quartet in which Barbirolli was cellist was the Kutcher, formed and led by his boyhood friend Samuel Kutcher in 1924. They played Dvořák and Debussy on 29 March 1924 at a Wigmore Hall concert organised by the Guild of Singers and Players and later added Delius and Franck to their repertoire. Mention of the Guild introduces the second man Barbirolli met at this period who was to be influential in his career, the tenor John Goss, who had formed the Guild after the war as a co-operative effort among artists to promote unusual concerts and to help young composers and executants. Barbirolli and Ethel Bartlett gave several recitals for the Guild, and Goss was deeply impressed by the young cellist, whom he had met at Mangeot's home. Late in 1924 when Barbirolli, with his own savings, formed a chamber string orchestra of twelve players – seven violins, two violas, two cellos and a double bass – and Goss invited him to conduct it at a Guild concert, Kutcher was the leader. The first concert was given privately on Thursday 30 October at 93 Harley Street, the home of Mrs Fergie Woods. The soloists were Goss himself and Ethel Bartlett. The orchestra's first public performance was eight days later, at the first of the Guild's new season of subscription concerts held in the delightful old Court House in Marylebone Lane.

On 25 January 1925 the orchestra gave the first performance of Warlock's *Serenade* written for Delius's sixtieth birthday. Eric Blom, in the *Manchester Guardian*, remarked that Barbirolli 'seems to be endowed with all the special gifts that go to the making of a highly competent conductor' and *The Times* had a good word for his Purcell, Vivaldi and Tartini.

In August Barbirolli travelled to Germany with the Music Society Quartet, who were the foundation of a festival of English chamber music and songs at Hamburg. They played fantasies by Purcell and Gibbons, Vaughan Williams's quartet and music by Charles Wood, McEwen and Frank Bridge, among others. Coming home through Brittany, where they played for the Queen of Rumania at La Fosse St Briac, Mangeot was astonished to see Barbirolli attired in a school blazer and setting out for the golf course carrying a bag of clubs – for the first and last time in his life. A more permanent Barbirolli feature was a wide-brimmed hat. A friend of Mangeot remembers Barbirolli at this time as 'a cheerful pipe-smoking young man.' Together they went to hear Bruno Walter conduct *Götterdämmerung* at Covent Garden. 'Barbirolli, armed with a full score, chose a seat well to the left under a lamp [in the gallery]. During the entire performance he never glanced at the stage.'

With the autumn of 1925 came an important extension of the Guild chamber orchestra's activities as a result of the opening of the New Chenil Galleries, built on a site in the King's Road next to Chelsea Town Hall to replace the old galleries which had existed since 1905. The galleries had always had the character of an arts centre and, with the new premises, a society was formed to promote art exhibitions, recitals and concerts, lectures and dances. The larger hall, which had splendid acoustics, could seat about 250 people. Augustus John, who had long been associated with the Chenil, laid the foundation stone on 25 October 1924. The music committee included John Goss, Eugène Goossens, Philip Heseltine, John Ireland, E. J. Moeran and Vaughan Williams, most of whom lived in Chelsea. Goss decided to reform the Guild's chamber orchestra as the Chenil Chamber Orchestra and to entrust the conducting to Barbirolli. Four concerts were given in the first series between 16 October and 10 December. The works played were by Vivaldi, Mozart and Purcell, a Handel Concerto Grosso, Elgar's *Elegy* and Warlock's *Serenade*. Public support was discouraging, despite one considered judgment that the orchestra produced the best and most carefully rehearsed string-playing in London, and Ernest Newman's more cautious assessment that it was 'well on the way to becoming a really sensitive instrument.' 'Marie-gold' in the *Sketch* wrote that 'those of us who like our intervals interesting as well can have no complaint to make, as not only intellectual Chelsea but Bloomsbury comes all the way to hear Mr Barbirolli and his delightful orchestra. At the Bach concert the other day I noticed Mr Augustus John, Chelsea's great man, with his wife; that distinguished young painter Mr **Duncan Grant**, Virginia Woolf, the well-known writer;

Arthur Waley, the Chinese expert, and Mr Roger Fry; and lesser highbrows filled the room.'* A strange milieu for John Barbirolli, whose Bloomsbury was not that of Virginia Woolf and her circle.

The orchestra was enlarged to include some woodwind and brass and Barbirolli broadened his repertoire to include Mozart violin concertos and divertimenti, Delius's *On Hearing the First Cuckoo in Spring* and Haydn's *Farewell* symphony. He also conducted Elgar's *Introduction and Allegro for Strings,* and when eventually he recorded it was delighted by Elgar's comment: 'I'd never realised it was such a *big* work.' The Chenil concerts made his name known in what are called select circles, but it was another enterprise by John Goss that was to have a far-reaching and dramatic effect on his life, and it took the unlikely form of a concert of the music of Bernard Van Dieren in the Wigmore Hall on 14 December 1925. From that evening was to branch the extraordinary and sensational course that took John Barbirolli in ten years from the small London halls where he had never conducted an orchestra of more than a handful of players to the liner in which he sailed across the Atlantic to assume the conductorship of Arturo Toscanini's orchestra, the New York Philharmonic-Symphony.

* Many years later, on 29 September 1959, Augustus John drew Barbirolli, not very successfully although he penetrated to his insecurity. Some of the best drawings of Barbirolli are those by Harold Riley.

4
With the BNOC

Bernard Van Dieren's name seems destined only to be remembered as a footnote in the history of English music. He was born in Holland in 1884 and trained as a research scientist. When he was twenty-five he settled in London, having by then decided that music was his calling. He became a friend of the Sitwells, of Cecil Gray, the critic and composer, and of Philip Heseltine. He was an inescapable part of that interesting and serio-comic period of English musical life when a superficial observer might have concluded that 'everybody who mattered' was singing madrigals, collecting folk-songs, editing Purcell string fantasies, running down Elgar, talking about Walton's *Façade* and acclaiming Van Dieren, on very scanty evidence, as the most neglected genius of the day. A campaign to have his music performed more often was increasingly successful during the 1920s, culminating in a spate of activity in 1925 stemming from pressure from the Oxford University Press.

The Wigmore Hall concert on 14 December 1925 included a string quartet, some pianoforte pieces (played by Kathleen Long), some songs, and a scene from a comic opera *The Tailor*. This last item was conducted by Barbirolli. The critics and the public were unconvinced about Van Dieren's genius (they agreed only that the music was of extraordinary contrapuntal complexity) but most of them agreed that the young conductor had done a fine job. One man in particular was deeply impressed, Frederic Austin, artistic director of the British National Opera Company. He asked Barbirolli after the concert if he would like to conduct some of the British National Opera Company's productions. One may easily imagine how astonished and overjoyed Tita was, and he arranged to join the company in the autumn. Equally delighted to have his own talent-spotting confirmed was John Goss. When Barbirolli received the Gold Medal of the Royal Philharmonic Society in December 1950 Goss was present in the Royal Albert Hall. The next day he wrote: 'Twenty-five years ago I knew you'd make it. And yesterday gave me a deal of satisfaction, because so few of one's prophecies come so strikingly true...'

The quality of Goss's championship can be gauged from a letter he wrote on 9 February 1926 to a critic of *The Times* who had written on 23 January that 'Mr John Barbirolli conducted with great care – indeed, with too much care, for though he is not lacking in vigour the playing of this excellent orchestra never succeeds in stirring either our imagination or our feelings.' Stronger disparagement was expressed to Goss personally, who retorted with a letter which also gives by far the most detailed account of the young Barbirolli at work:

I was sorry to hear the other night that you are unable to share my enthusiasm about Barbirolli as a conductor. I still cannot help suspecting that your reasons are either temperamental or on account of some very special theory you hold as to how conducting should be done. I suspect this latter the more, because you said nothing about Barbirolli's interpretations, and on looking up your recent *Times* notices on him I see that very little is said about them there. But you did try to raise one or two objections to the way he holds his stick.

What I mean, quite rudely, is that you are not criticising him as an artist but as someone who doesn't conduct like Adrian Boult, or Henry Wood, or someone you favour or have studied with... I think I can bring one or two facts to bear upon my theory that your reaction from Barbirolli is temperamental. These facts are adduced from my experiences as a singer to orchestral accompaniment. I have three purely technical advantages over you in this matter. I have sung to Barbirolli's accompaniment, I have listened a great deal to his rehearsing, and I have seen him tackle a Van Dieren score.

With regard to the first point, I have never been so sensitively or subtly accompanied in my life, even by a single instrument. With regard to the second point, I can most emphatically assure you that Barbirolli knows exactly what he wants and is never at a loss to transfer this knowledge to his orchestra. Rehearsals are hardly ever stopped because of any misunderstanding as to what his beat implies, but only to fix the more subtle shades of phrasing and dynamics.

The third point is probably the most important. You have, no doubt, seen a Van Dieren score. I should like to show you, some day, the score of the scene from the opera we did in December, and to get your idea of how long such a score should be in the hands of a conductor before the first rehearsal, and how many rehearsals would be needed for a working performance. Without your seeing it I cannot hope, of course, to impress you as I and the composer and the orchestra itself were impressed. Barbirolli, who had seen the complete score for the first time at 3 a.m. on Sunday morning [the concert was on Monday] and spent most of the time of rehearsal on the same morning in correcting copyist's errors, managed to pull off a brilliant performance at the end of the second rehearsal on Monday morning. This was a tour de force that I don't believe any other conductor in the country would be capable of.

I mention these things because I am certain, whatever else one might say of Barbirolli, that his technique and musicianship are of the first order, and when *The Times* talks about his 'having more force than control' it is talking unmitigated rubbish... I will tell you why I think Barbirolli has in him the making of a great conductor. He has, first of all, the greatest thing in all art, a sense of 'glamour'. This, I think, no other English conductor has, except Beecham. He has the Grand Manner, which prevents his becoming desiccated and 'niminy piminy' even when he has only a dozen or so strings under his control. He would conduct a quartet as if he were before an orchestra of 120. This I think a gloriously youthful thing to do. He has infinite delicacy. He has style...

This was a remarkably perceptive assessment. When Barbirolli replied to Goss's 1950 letter he wrote: 'I was so upset to hear you were there on Wednesday and that I did not see you, for that wonderful evening for me was the culmination of the faith and encouragement you so lavishly bestowed on me 25 years ago. John, it is not and *never* will be forgotten.'

The British National Opera Company was formed in 1921 by some of those who had been associated with Beecham's operatic ventures which came to an abrupt, though temporary, halt in 1920 when his personal financial troubles ended his musical activity. Percy Pitt was its first director and it gave its first performance in February 1922 at Bradford. Most of its work was done in the provinces, with short seasons in London. Several English operas, notably Vaughan Williams's *Hugh the Drover*, were included in a repertory which also encompassed Wagner, Debussy's *Pelléas et Mélisande* and the Italian masters. The company drew almost exclusively on English singers and many famous names were made with it. Austin took over the direction in 1924 and among the conductors he engaged were Adrian Boult (for *Parsifal*), Malcolm Sargent, John Tobin, Aylmer Buesst, Clarence Raybould, Leslie Heward and Eugène Goossens, senior. The autumn season in 1926 opened in Newcastle upon Tyne and it was there, at the Hippodrome Theatre on 22 September, that Barbirolli conducted his first opera, Gounod's *Romeo and Juliet*, followed later in the week by Puccini's *Madam Butterfly* and Verdi's *Aïda*. For them all he had only three and a half hours' rehearsal, but the reason is amusing. Austin allotted a whole day to him but it was Friday, and John's superstitious Italian grandmother ruled that even if he had to make his debut without having rehearsed, it would be unlucky to begin a new venture on a Friday. 'I had to invent the most formidable untruths to convince the directors of my inability to be present at this full rehearsal,' Barbirolli was to recall.

In a gruelling six-months baptism of visits to Glasgow, Edinburgh, Leeds, Bradford, Manchester, Liverpool, Birmingham and London (Golders Green Hippodrome) – the last four more than once – he went on to conduct *Tosca*, *La Bohème*, *Hansel and Gretel*, *The Barber of Seville* and *Il Trovatore*. Time and again the press singled out the conductor as the hero of the evening. It should be remembered that provincial music criticism was of a high standard – Herbert Thompson in the *Yorkshire Post*, A. J. Sheldon in the *Birmingham Post*, Samuel Langford in the *Manchester Guardian*, were critics of great experience and professional stature, and there were others too. Nor was this favourable reaction confined to the audience's side of the footlights. The singers in the company included Miriam Licette, Edna Thornton, Gladys Parr, Constance Willis, Robert Radford, Norman Allin, Frank Mullings, Heddle Nash, Percy Heming and Parry Jones. Many of these became John's close friends for life; none of them resented this twenty-six-year-old unknown taking charge of them, because they recognised from the first his thorough professionalism, his dedication to the task in hand and his technical knowledge. At Liverpool when the company were entertained at a hotpot supper by the Sandon Studios Society, Heddle Nash was heard to say: 'Barbirolli makes us sing the *music*. Not a note escapes him. We have never been so thoroughly rehearsed before.'

His routine with the company on tour was to rehearse with the singers in the morning; during the afternoon he would study a new opera in his hotel room; in the evening if he was not conducting he would go to the theatre to take charge of any off-stage music that might be required, or to listen; and he would regularly leave instructions at his hotel for a call at four a.m. so that he could 'do some swotting' on the score before morning rehearsal. The 'old lags' in the company told him he was like an old routine opera conductor from the start. He had to study hard, always, but once the music was in his head it was 'translated to my arms automatically.' What the singers thought about him was expressed nearly thirty years later by Percy Heming in a letter to Barbirolli. Recalling the experience of 'being one with you and the orchestra,' he added: 'It is an indescribable sensation and one that one can never forget – it seemed as if I were saying the words for the first time and that they were my own words; I never had that feeling with anyone else. I have often wanted to tell you but felt that you might think it silly, but I don't feel that now.'

D. C. Parker, writing in the *Glasgow Evening Times*, called the *Aïda* (with Mullings as Radames) a triumph. 'No orchestra will go to sleep under Mr Barbirolli. Even his National Anthem had personality.' In Leeds Herbert Thompson remarked upon the 'exceptionally fine quality' of the orchestral playing in *Bohème*. 'All the effusive emotionalism of modern Italian music was brought out without the least sense of exaggeration or awkwardness, so complete was the control he exercised upon the players.' It was during this

Leeds visit, when Edna Thornton sang Amneris, Rachel Morton Aïda, Walter Widdop Radames and Percy Heming Amonasro, that an amusing incident occurred during the last scene where Aïda goes to join Radames in the death cell. In the old Theatre Royal the ladies' lavatory was near the circle, and when Radames asked: 'Aïda, where art thou?' the answer was drowned by the ferocious sound of flushing. 'We got to the end somehow,' Barbirolli said, 'but that was the real end of the performance.'

Barbirolli made his first appearance in Manchester at the Opera House on 17 November in a matinée performance of *Madam Butterfly*. Langford's enthusiastic notice of that occasion has often been quoted. But even more prophetic and perceptive was the review of *Romeo and Juliet* by A. J. Sheldon in the *Birmingham Post*:

> What is certain is that the soul of music is in him, and there is little to be ventured in declaring that last night we made a first acquaintance with a young conductor who is going to count in our music. With his sensitiveness to melody the company might do worse than turn him on to every opera in its repertory – Wagner's not excepted – to see what new light he can throw on them. Anyhow, he can make an orchestra sing.

The next hurdle was his first London appearance with the company, in *Romeo and Juliet* at Golders Green on 12 January 1927. Again the critics were impressed. Francis Toye, in the *Morning Post*, admitted that he had not expected to find justice done to Gounod's orchestration.

> Mr John Barbirolli...showed admirable theatre sense, knew the score inside out, and clearly was able to inspire his players with something of his own understanding and enthusiasm. In short, he was, in my opinion, the real success of the evening.

But the important feature of his second visit to Manchester was the new production, in a new translation, of Rossini's *The Barber of Seville*. This was a tremendous success and was the occasion of the first of the many sustained ovations Manchester audiences were to give him. The cast reads like a

Who's Who of British singers: Heddle Nash as Almaviva, Dennis Noble as Figaro, Percy Heming as Bartolo, Robert Radford as Basilio, Miriam Licette as Rosina and Gladys Parr as Marcellina. When the company returned to London the popularity of the opera was repeated, Francis Toye writing that he 'never wanted to hear a more rhythmical or sensitive interpretation.' In Birmingham in March Barbirolli conducted his first *Trovatore* (Mullings as Manrico), having astonished everybody by calling an extra three-hour rehearsal for strings alone. 'What?' the orchestra said. 'Rehearse this old rum-ti-tum we know backwards! The lad must have lost his head.' 'But after three hours,' said Barbirolli, 'devoted entirely to the first scene, they seemed to accept my own conviction. That was, that the accompaniments of Verdi, even in his early works, are packed with dramatic meaning, and only a careful study of their potentialities will suffice. It is not a case of oompah, oompah, but a suggestive background for the stage action.' The results were appreciated by the music critic of the *Glasgow Herald* who, after a 1928 performance, wrote that Barbirolli

showed clearly by his careful handling of his forces how much can be done with simple rhythmical figures and other simplicities of accompaniment. Even such a passing touch as the phrase of three simple chords for strings that appears several times in the scene of di Luna's camp was made to contribute something real and true to the dramatic situation.

It is also worth recording the effect made by a Barbirolli *Trovatore* on a distinguished journalist, later Sir Linton Andrews, writing as W.L.A. in the *Leeds Mercury* of 14 November 1928:

I must tell you of the joys I found in watching Mr John Barbirolli conduct. He seems very young at a first glance... But what a transformation when he begins to conduct. He is fiery with energy. He crouches, springs up, flutters his fingers and is of demonic energy. He has made a good name already. Perhaps in twenty years some of us will be saying proudly 'Yes, I saw Barbirolli conduct when he was quite a youngster with the B.N.O.C. at Leeds in 1928.'

I have met many of them! Audiences responded immediately to the dynamism radiating from this small figure – he was only 5 ft 4 in. in height – with his shock of black hair and his Italianate good looks.

When the company dispersed for the summer Barbirolli was responsible for an experiment in 'off-season' opera in July and August. In June 1927 he was giving a cello recital at the Violoncello School which was attended by the mother of his cellist friend, Joan Mulholland. Mrs Mulholland owned the King's, Hammersmith, and Wimbledon Theatres. 'It suddenly struck me,' Barbirolli said in a *Daily Express* interview, 'that she had her theatres empty at this period of the year. I suggested that she might consider the possibility of my producing 'The Barber'... I spoke to her on a Saturday and by Monday it was arranged. The BNOC gave me permission to present the opera, and the BNOC artists and orchestra were engaged.'* The season was a success in every way and encouraged him to have high hopes for the future of opera in Britain. Ernest Newman in the *Sunday Times* wrote: 'Time after time it was all so good that for it to be true seemed almost unbelievable.' That fine singer Robert Radford wrote to Barbirolli at the end of the run saying it had been 'a privilege to have taken part in the really splendid performances. I thought you were in great form, not only as a musician (one takes that for granted) but in handling people and generally delivering the goods... Once again, old chap, many many thanks.'

He had not, of course, deserted his Chenil concerts and other commitments – so early in his career he contrived to cram in as much work as possible whatever travelling was involved. In January 1927, at the Galleries, he conducted the first performance of Bax's *Romantic Overture* for chamber orchestra and pianoforte (played by Rae Robertson). But the audience were warned that unless there was stronger support, the orchestra's days were numbered. The Galleries went into liquidation and were sold in December 1927, but the orchestra was not disbanded, at any rate for a time, and Barbirolli continued to conduct it at Gerald Cooper's Wigmore Hall chamber concerts and for the Guild of Singers and Players. In

*An interesting oddity about this production was that the Laughing Song from Auber's *Manon Lescaut* was interpolated in the Lesson Scene of Act III and sung by Licette (Rosina).

March 1928 he conducted his first Vaughan Williams, the 1925 Violin Concerto, with Sybil Easton as soloist, at a Cooper concert.

When the BNOC's 1927–28 season opened in Newcastle Wagner's *Mastersingers* was given into Barbirolli's charge. The company were in London, at Golders Green, during December, a lucky circumstance for the next milestone in his astonishing rise to fame. Beecham was due to conduct the London Symphony Orchestra's concert on Monday 12 December, but four days before the concert he injured his leg in a fall and cancelled his engagement. Much depended on this concert, because the LSO had been put on its mettle by the eulogies which the Berlin Philharmonic's visit had called forth. The LSO, which is self-governing, tried in vain to engage an eminent substitute. Finally Bertram Jones,* the secretary, suggested that Barbirolli, who had often played in the orchestra as a deputy cellist, should be invited to take Beecham's place. Beecham's programme had been Mozart's *Linz* Symphony, Haydn's D major Cello Concerto (with Casals) and – curiously enough, for Beecham was not an Elgarian – Elgar's Second Symphony. When Jones put the proposition to Barbirolli he went home to discuss it with his father, for although he had heard Elgar conduct the symphony, he had never studied the score and had grave apprehensions about learning such a complex work in forty-eight hours. But Lorenzo told him vehemently that he must not miss such an opportunity. So he agreed to take on the programme, substituting Haydn's *London* Symphony for the Mozart.

At the rehearsal an incident occurred which Barbirolli recounted thus: 'After the first introductory bars [of the concerto] I stopped the orchestra and made a few remarks. Casals leaned forward in his chair and said "Listen to him. He knows." I was only a boy and those few words coming from such a great artist touched me deeply. It was a wonderful thing for a man of his greatness to do.' The concert was a success. 'Expectancy turned in the course of the evening to enthusiasm,' Robin Legge wrote in the *Telegraph*. Eric

---

* Mr Jones retired in 1929 and was ninety-three in 1970 when he wrote to me: 'On meeting him some five or six years ago in the artists' room at Bexhill, immediately he saw me he came and embraced me and said "I haven't seen you since 1927 when you started me on my way."'

Blom, in the *Manchester Guardian*, discussed the Elgar in detail, noting that Barbirolli had

made himself so fully conversant with this extraordinarily complex score that he had a safe margin of energy left to expend on technicalities. What was astonishing to note, in fact, was that he did not always remain content with following Elgar's meticulous indication of the tiniest variations in tempo but actually supplied some additional modifications of his own... No liberties were taken which could not be justified by the addition of that something to the printed notes without which no music can come to life. The one point to which serious exception could be taken was the sentimentalising of the second subject in the initial movement... Here Elgar's favourite direction – *nobilmente* – was certainly violated.

Elgar was told about the performance by W. H. Reed, leader of the LSO, and by Frank Schuster, who wrote: 'I must just tell you that to my thinking Barbirolli gave a remarkably good account of your No. 2, playing it as it is written and, what's more, as it is felt. No point-making and no exaggeration but very cohesive and round and rich. But it appears that in spite of a most enthusiastic reception the highbrows don't agree with me. Am I wrong?' Schuster's question was to be echoed many times over the next forty years. Elgar wrote to the young conductor on 14 December from Battenhall Manor, Worcester: 'I hear splendid accounts of your conducting of the symphony concert on Monday last; for your kind care of my work I send you very sincere thanks. I should have sent a word before the concert had I known of it, but I was quite unaware that anything of mine was being given.' The concert had its sequel in July 1929 at a dinner of the Musicians' Club at which Elgar spoke. John was there and 'could have fallen through the floor' when Elgar addressed him personally as 'a rising hope of music in England for whom I have admiration and in whose work I have confidence.'

As Barbirolli left the platform after the Elgar symphony he was astonished to see among the violins a little man, wearing a hat, who grabbed him and said: 'Don't sign any gramophone contracts. See you tomorrow at 10. I'm Gaisberg, HMV.' This was the beginning of Barbirolli's association with HMV but it was by no means his first acquaintance with the gramophone. He had made some Edison Bell records seventeen years earlier with his sister Rosa and during 1927–28 recorded for EB Electron the *Flying Dutchman* and *Hansel and Gretel* overtures, the Prelude to Act III of *Mastersingers* and the Love Duet from *Butterfly* with Stiles Allen and Dan Jones. For the National Gramophonic Society, founded by Compton Mackenzie and Christopher Stone, he made records with the Music Society String Quartet (renamed the International String Quartet) including the *Phantasy Quintet* of Vaughan Williams with Jean Pougnet as the extra player, and the first of several recordings he made during his career of Elgar's *Introduction and Allegro*, in which he conducted his Chenil Galleries chamber orchestra. But by joining HMV he moved into a bigger league and soon was recording with singers of the eminence of Frida Leider, Chaliapin, Friedrich Schorr, Gigli, Pertile, Maria Olczewska, Peter Dawson (some excerpts from Elgar's *Caractacus*), Lauritz Melchior and Renato Zanelli, and with instrumentalists like Heifetz, Suggia and Artur Rubinstein. The assistance given to his career by this early association with gramophone recording was to be increasingly apparent, and he grew very fond of that remarkable man Fred Gaisberg, who always referred to him as 'Babrioli.'

The year 1928 opened for Barbirolli with a broadcast concert of music by Delius, including the violin concerto played by Albert Sammons. A few days later he received a letter which he realised from the postmark was from Delius, yet he hardly dared to open it for hours because, as he said, 'I loved this music so much and if Delius himself didn't like what I'd done I thought I'd better give up.' He need not have worried.

Grez-sur-Loing 7.1.28

Dear Mr Barbirolli. I was very pleased with the way you conducted my music last night. I heard it fairly well … I heard Sammons's solo perfectly, but not always the orchestra, as if they were playing *too* softly. Your tempi were perfect, just as I want them and I felt you were entirely in sympathy with the music, for which I thank you most heartily.

Yrs sincerely, Frederick Delius

This was one landmark of the year. The other was his first appearance on 30 June as a guest conductor at the Royal Opera House, Covent Garden. Since 1925 the Syndicate which ran the Royal Opera House had had as its managing director Lieut-Colonel Eustace Blois, who had worked in the City for Courtaulds. Mr and Mrs Samuel Courtauld were opera-lovers and took a sub-lease of the Royal Opera House. When they withdrew in 1927 a new company, the Grand Opera Syndicate Ltd, was formed by Blois, who had been a pupil of the conductor Leopoldo Mugnone and had studied opera and its staging in Germany and Italy. As will be seen, he had strong sympathies for British artists and for the cause of English opera, and it was his idea in the summer of 1928 to try a Saturday night performance at prices considerably lower than those obtaining for the international season. *Madam Butterfly* was the opera chosen, with Barbirolli conducting and Miriam Licette in the title-role. A gossip columnist reported in the *Weekly Dispatch* (2 July) that the unusual 'spectacle was seen of lounge suits and tweed coats in the stalls of a theatre famed for the brilliance of its dress display.' Some of the grand tier boxes had been removed and a dress circle substituted, but despite these social and sartorial disadvantages – 'there was little to discuss between the acts,' the *Morning Post* complained – the house was full and the performance a reasonable success.

Barbirolli added Rimsky-Korsakov's *Golden Cockerel* to his repertoire for Manchester, Birmingham and Liverpool, with Robert Radford as King Dodon, Noël Eadie as the Queen and Gladys Parr and Parry Jones in smaller parts. In Aberdeen he conducted the latest addition to the company's productions, Verdi's *Falstaff*, on 19 October.

It was while rehearsing *Falstaff* that Barbirolli was much troubled by a corn and conducted in a slipper. One of the trumpeters was hired locally and proved to be very bad, so bad that, aggravated by the pain from his foot, Barbirolli gave him the rough edge of his tongue. Afterwards this man approached him. 'Your foot's troubling you, sir, isn't it?' 'Indeed it is,' Barbirolli replied. 'Well,' said the man, 'I'm not really a trumpeter, you know.' 'I'd rather gathered that.' No,' the man went on, 'I'm a chiropodist!'

On 24 October, the day before Barbirolli was elected a Fellow of the Royal Academy of Music, his grandmother

(Nonna) died at the age of eighty-eight. He was now the family's chief means of support, for this was the time of unemployment and depression and Lorenzo had lost his job at the Queen's Hotel which could no longer afford an orchestra. John paid the rent and sent other money home, and sometimes added this kind of heartfelt plea to his mother: 'Please send me a little mixture of salami etc. for my suppers. I am getting a little tired of roast beef.'

John wrote to Lorenzo that 'now *Falstaff* has been produced I have started work on my concert programmes.' One of these was another Van Dieren concert organised by John Goss in the Wigmore Hall on Saturday 10 November. He had conducted *Mastersingers* in Glasgow the previous evening. This kind of thing was typical not only of his gluttony for work but also of his loyalty to old friends like Goss and Mangeot.

His next important engagements were his first Royal Philharmonic Society concert on 17 January 1929, and his re-engagement by the LSO four days later. At twenty-nine he was the youngest conductor the Royal Philharmonic had ever engaged. For them he decided to conduct Debussy's *La Mer*, which (it is almost impossible nowadays to believe) had not been performed in London for ten years. He quickly realised that he would need more than the three rehearsals allotted to him and asked for an extra three hours for *La Mer* alone. He offered to pay for it himself and this offer – which came to the exact amount of his fee – was accepted 'with alacrity.' Another feature of the concert which was exceptional enough for the *Daily Express* to comment on it was that 'not a single deputy player was in the orchestra. Every single man-jack of them had attended the four rehearsals...and Mr Barbirolli had spent much time in marking the score copies.' Eric Blom, in the *Manchester Guardian*, said that Barbirolli's 'first-rateness' was coming to be a matter of course. 'His performance of *La Mer* was a magnificent piece of work. He gave this wonderful score just that sombre glow which is a subtly calculated something between reticence and ostentation.' Philip Page noticed a Barbirollism which was to become familiar to many: 'He has one little trick of turning sideways to the first violins and addressing them with great patriotic spirit and gusto.'

These successes behind him, he returned to the BNOC in February for its weeks in Brighton and Lewisham and then during March in Bradford and Birmingham. The tour was to end in Birmingham and Barbirolli was then to spend Easter in London with his family. Lorenzo was greatly excited. He had recently had some 'fainting fits' but no one had taken them seriously. But on the Sunday he suddenly collapsed with a stroke and was taken to the Italian Hospital where he died before John arrived. He was sixty-four. John was stricken with grief and never, for the rest of his life, regarded Easter as anything but a time of sadness. He cherished his father's memory. Some years later he wrote to Evelyn Rothwell: 'He was one of the most kindly and generous souls I have ever known, and I know of many acts of his which make it both a pride and a responsibility to bear his name.'

During the sad week which followed John conducted his first London *Falstaff* with the BNOC at Golders Green Hippodrome, with Roy Henderson now singing Ford. Lorenzo died with the proud knowledge that John had been engaged to open the Italian season at Covent Garden on 27 May with Mozart's *Don Giovanni*. In an article in the *Daily Express* on the morning of the performance, John described his conflicting emotions:

I am thrilled and apprehensive; hopeful and nervous; happy and unhappy; awed and confident. And all at the same time... I am conscious of the great privilege that is being entrusted to a young Englishman to conduct at the Garden at all and especially at being entrusted with the performance of a work which is notoriously one of the most difficult in the repertoire... I have literally been living with the score in front of me. I study it the whole time. The great difficulty of this work is to sustain the dramatic unity throughout... It has all my waking moments. I dream of it, and sometimes I wake at three or four in the morning and go and turn over the pages. I feel that I must keep in touch... In all the excitement and anticipation of what tonight is going to hold for me I have only one regret – my father will not be there...

The cast was truly international: an Italian Don Giovanni (Mariano Stabile), an American Donna Anna (Anne Roselle), a German Zerlina (Elisabeth Schumann), an English Elvira and Don Ottavio (Miriam Licette and Heddle Nash), and Italians in the remaining roles. Barbirolli adhered to Covent

Garden's practice at that date of omitting the final ensemble, ending the opera with the Don's descent to Hell, and his restoration of *Dalla sua pace* was favourably commented upon. Sheldon of the *Birmingham Post* referred to the 'memorable loveliness and salience' of the orchestral playing and remarked on Barbirolli's 'unerring sense of the character in the accompaniment to every aria... We had the rare delight of feeling the music always to live a no less vital life on the instruments than it did on the voices.' Four days after the first performance John wrote to his Glasgow friend D. C. Parker, of that city's *Evening Times*: 'As you can imagine the burden of worry attached to this task has been immense. It is not unalloyed pleasure to be entrusted with the performance of such a work, which one loves and reveres so much, under such conditions as exist in opera today, but fortunately all has been well...'

These events occurred against the background of the financial failure of the BNOC. Yet another chapter in the chequered history of opera in England had come to its usual close.

5
Covent
Garden

When Barbirolli described it as a 'privilege' for a young English conductor to conduct at the Royal Opera House he was not exaggerating. In the 'grand seasons' before 1914, only Percy Pitt, Thomas Beecham, Albert Coates and Frederic Cowen occupied the rostrum hallowed by Richter, Mottl, Mahler, Mancinelli, Karl Muck, André Messager, Nikisch, Bruno Walter and Richard Strauss. Foreign conductors and foreign singers were regarded almost as *de rigueur*, and only on the rare occasions when the theatre was leased to the Carl Rosa or Moody-Manners companies did less exotic names appear. The 1919 season was run by the Grand Opera Syndicate in association with Beecham who, through his father and James White, had bought the whole of the Covent Garden estate. Beecham's own opera company had had great success during the war, especially in Manchester, while the Royal Opera House was closed, but his 1919 and 1920 seasons at Covent Garden were financially disastrous. As already related, the BNOC was formed by Percy Pitt from the remnants of the Beecham company and leased the Royal Opera House for four short seasons during 1922, 1923 and 1924. English singers were employed and among the conductors new to the Opera House were Leslie Heward, Julius Harrison, Aylmer Buesst and Frank St Leger. Hamilton Harty, who had conducted *Tristan* in 1913, conducted *Figaro*, *Die Walküre* and *Aïda* in 1923 and 1924. On other occasions the Carl Rosa company occupied the theatre. But in 1924 the Syndicate decided to revert to Grand (i.e. international) Opera, barred the BNOC from the theatre and had a glamorous summer season made unforgettable by Walter's conducting of *Der Rosenkavalier* with Lotte Lehmann and Frida Leider, Richard Mayr and Elisabeth Schumann. There followed the Courtauld-financed seasons already mentioned and the formation of another syndicate under Col. Blois in association with the naturalised Hungarian financier F. A. Szarvasy.

The provinces had for years relied for opera upon a series of companies such as Denhof, Carl Rosa, Moody-Manners and the O'Mara, which battled, with varying degrees of success, against the hazards of inadequate theatres, lack of money and variable public support. That they trained some good singers in spite of everything is undeniable. Beecham's company was easily the best and he devoted large sums of money to trying to put opera on a sound footing. When he was forced from the scene it seemed that the BNOC would be the first company to achieve some kind of consistent success but the financial odds were stacked heavily against it by one major factor – opera was not exempt from entertainment tax. In 1927–28 the BNOC paid £17,000 in entertainment tax, and its demise came in 1929 because it was £5,000 in debt. So this splendid venture foundered for the lack of a comparatively trivial sum, but this was also the year of the Wall Street crash and the beginning of Britain's 'economic blizzard.'

Beecham's role in the history of opera in England at this time is well known, Barbirolli's hardly at all, yet his was also important. Beecham, like a mercurial Svengali, hypnotised the English musical scene of his day. Even after 1920 when for a time he withdrew altogether his presence brooded over it. For 12 years he did not conduct at Covent Garden. He confined his activities to the concert-hall, but opera remained his ambition. He formed in the 1920s his Imperial League of Opera which had private subscribers rather like shareholders and aimed at running opera on a non-subsidised basis. Unfortunately the subscribers were never as numerous as Beecham hoped – he expected 250,000, but only 44,000 were forthcoming. He looked askance at any project with which he was not personally associated.

Barbirolli had been deeply, perhaps naïvely, impressed by the evidence he saw on his BNOC tours of the public appetite for opera. Speaking in Glasgow early in 1929 he called for 'amalgamation of the efforts at present so scattered and uncoordinated. You must sell music by business methods, which means that your selling organisation must be as efficient as the selling organisations of the big combines.' Colonel Blois was also convinced that only by amalgamation into one concern could opera ever be made to pay in Britain, and then only in all probability with that unheard-of assistance, a subsidy from the Government. He had the courage of his convictions when the BNOC failed in 1929. Instead of letting it be dispersed, he took it under his wing, rechristened it the Covent Garden Opera Company and, encouraged by HMV, appointed Barbirolli as musical director. He had a profound admiration for the young conductor and for the kind of musician who had prepared the singers of the ensembles in *Falstaff* for six months before the performance went on stage. So the autumn provincial tour of 1929 became a reality, and in Halifax on 27 September Barbirolli conducted the first performance in English of *Turandot*. The kind of schedule he undertook can be gauged from the week at the Prince of Wales Theatre, Birmingham, from 11 to 16 November when he conducted every performance except the Saturday matinée (*Lohengrin*, under Eugene Goossens senior) and each performance was of a different opera: Monday, *Falstaff*; Tuesday, *The Barber of Seville*; Wednesday, *Tosca*; Thursday, *The Mastersingers*; Friday, *Turandot*; and Saturday, *La Bohème*. He had most of his former colleagues with him, Arthur Fear, Heddle Nash, Dennis Noble, Percy Heming, Parry Jones, Gladys Parr, Constance Willis and Marjorie Parry. The Mimi and Liù were Noël Eadie, Turandot was sung by Odette de Foras, and the Calaf was Francis Russell. Liverpool and Manchester had similar seasons. The orchestra, of course, was much too small.

From a distance of over forty years one envies those who heard these BNOC and Covent Garden performances, yet at the time they were not fully appreciated. English singers' names were not considered glamorous attractions, and there is a faintly patronising air about much of the press criticism of the company. Barbirolli himself had the highest opinion of several of the singers, notably Heming; although they were close friends, Barbirolli was too honest a judge of artistry to have allowed that to sway words he wrote after Heming's death: * '...one of the greatest, if not the greatest, English operatic artists of our time... It was my privilege to work with

* *Opera*, Vol. 7, No. 4, April 1956.

the greatest singers of the time, then at the summit of their powers. I have only to mention names such as Chaliapin, Schorr, Stabile, Gigli, Pertile, and, amongst the women, Leider, Lehmann, Schumann, to show by what standards those words were written.' Another of his special confidants, with whom he spoke Italian, was the tenor Francis Russell.

Because of this belief in his colleagues' artistry, Barbirolli fought hard for them. He did not subscribe to the view that everything foreign was bound to be better than anything English. He went to Milan early in 1930 to hear for himself. 'I came back full of hope and confidence in our operatic future,' he wrote to D. C. Parker.

I saw a week of performances at the Scala...and heard *La Vestale, Don Giovanni* (very badly done), *Bohème* and *Forza del Destino*. Considering the wonderful resources of the place it was most disappointing. A fine orchestra of 110...chorus 120 (splendidly trained) but conductors (Guarneri and 2 or 3 others) not more than efficient, and the ensemble generally was poor. The loss of Toscanini [who had left Milan for New York in 1929] is a great blow to them and the standard of singing apart from Volpi and Fronci (artists I did not hear) is 2nd rate. The women especially are awful. The settings on the other hand are superb... The audiences except for *Bohème* were *scanty* in the extreme and terribly apathetic. *Don Giovanni* got *one* curtain at the end. The cinema and jazz have made great inroads on the time and interests of the younger generation of Italians and it is only the more popular works which seem to have a public. Of what I saw of the managerial side of the business, the less said the better... All this is said in no disparaging attitude, but let us be fair to ourselves and realise what we have achieved under conditions which would be to them unthinkable.

Sir Steuart Wilson once said that if Beecham had had more faith in British singers the BNOC might not have collapsed. But of course Beecham needed to please his rich patrons, most of whom thought that the foreign article was, *de jure*, superior. English music should remember that the young Barbirolli recognised the real merit of Heddle Nash, Percy Heming, Eva Turner and others. How ironic that when Dora

1

1 *Tita on his father's knee, with his sister Rosie and a friend*
2 *In London with his Italian grandmother (note the left hand!)*
3 *Trinity College of Music trio. The violinist is Samuel Kutcher, the pianist R. B. Johnson*

2

3

4

4 *Rehearsing opera in the 1920s with Miriam Licette and Tudor Davies*
5 *J.B., about 1931*
6 *After a swim at Rottingdean, August 1938*

5

6

7

8

7 *Rehearsing the New York Philharmonic in Carnegie Hall, 1936*

8 *New York, 1940*

9 *Greeted on return to New York, 1939 by (left to right) Vincenzo Vanni (tuba player), Joseph Schuster (principal cello), Mishel Piastro (concert-master) and John Corigliano (deputy concert-master)*

9

10 *Rehearsing with Fritz Kreisler in New York, February 1943*
11 *In the kitchen, Hollywood, 1941*
12 *A menu, in J.B.'s writing, for one of his Trafalgar Day private dinners*

10

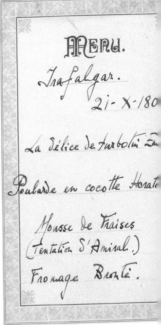

12

11

3

4

13 *On tour with the Hallé in Holland, 1949. At J.B.'s table are Norah Winstanley (left), Joyce Aldous (centre) and Mr and Mrs Thomas Cheetham*
14 *Kathleen Ferrier at Seaford, 1951 (taken by Evelyn Barbirolli)*

15 *With Augustus John after a Prom, 1953 (on the left is Amaryllis Fleming, the cellist)*
16 *Family picnic in Sussex, 1955. Left to right: Rosie, Mémé, J.B., Cecilie Barbirolli, 'Fof' Gibilaro*

17, 18 *At Ravello,*
June 1957

19 *Presenting a scientific book as a prize at St Clement Dane's School, May 1954*
20 *With Jimmy Edwards and the Hallé trombone section, Festival Club, Cheltenham, 1957*

Labbette's and Nash's recording (with Beecham) of an extract from *La Bohème* was issued in 1970, a distinguished critic should write that such a performance, if heard at the Royal Opera House today, would have the audience on its feet. Barbirolli himself described being on the receiving end of this pro-foreign bias at a Covent Garden party:

Having conducted the evening's performance I soon found myself surrounded by a crowd of society women who expressed themselves as 'too thrilled for words' by the movements of my hands, the – to me maddening but incurable – unruliness of my hair, and the performance generally. 'But how marvellously you speak English!' gushed one talkative young woman. 'Why,' I replied, 'I *am* English. I live in London.' The effect was instantaneous. Every face in that little circle fell several inches. The ingenuity of the excuses made to slip away from my vicinity should have been heard to be believed.*

An aim of Beecham's Imperial League was to establish in London both a permanent opera company and a permanent orchestra. Early in 1930 there was talk of the amalgamation of all opera interests, which Blois wanted. Beecham declared himself ready to co-operate. Barbirolli had some contacts with the Labour Government – he had been one of a small group who entertained Ramsay MacDonald to dinner at the House of Commons in March 1928, before MacDonald became Premier – and he went to see the music-loving Mrs Philip Snowden, wife of the Chancellor of the Exchequer, to enlist her aid in obtaining some sort of subsidy. She wrote from 11 Downing Street, on 24 April 1930:

Dear Mr Barbirolli. I am glad, very glad, to know all this about the Company. I am full of sympathy. The Chancellor of the Exchequer is coming up from the country to hear the singers, and if you get a chance have at him with your facts and let us see if we can pave the way to a state grant next year! Several ambassadors are coming and we will show them what English folk can do... Best regards, Ethel Snowden.

* 'Too Much in a Name,' *The Gramophone*, September 1932.

She was referring to a musical evening given at No. 11 by members of the company on 27 April, when Barbirolli played in a cello sonata, and Heddle Nash, Noël Eadie, Arthur Fear, Constance Willis and Odette de Foras sang operatic arias. It bore fruit, because later in the year the Government offered a subsidy of £25,000 a year to Covent Garden, later reduced to £17,500, through the Postmaster-General and the BBC. This was the first state subsidy of opera in English history, and Barbirolli proudly claimed the credit for obtaining it. When Beecham heard that part of the Covent Garden Syndicate's monetary contribution towards the capital of the proposed amalgamated company was this subsidy, he withdrew the Imperial League from the scheme and angrily denounced the Government, the Syndicate and the BBC. So Blois pressed on without him.

Barbirolli was one of the six conductors of the Grand Opera season at Covent Garden from 28 April to 4 July 1930, the other five being Bruno Walter, Robert Heger, Vincenzo Bellezza, Edoardo Fornarini and Giorgio Polacco. The last-named became a very close friend in New York ten years later. Barbirolli conducted *Aïda* (with Eva Turner), *Butterfly* (with Maggie Teyte singing the title role at one performance) and *Romeo and Juliet* (with Ezio Pinza in the cast). At long last *Die Fledermaus* was admitted to the Covent Garden repertoire, at the insistence of Bruno Walter, whose cast included Lehmann, Schumann, Olczewska, Habich and Gerhard Hüsch. Barbirolli's comments on this season were included in a letter to D. C. Parker, who was a devoted Wagnerian:

6 May, 1930

...The opening performance of *Meistersinger* was rather unequal. The tenor [Rudolf Laubenthal] was quite the worst exhibition ever given in C.G. I should think and it seemed to depress Lehmann whose phrasing in the Quintet was far from good. In fact with such a tenor it was quite hopeless to expect anything much in the matter of balance. Schorr magnificent, the Pogner had more quantity than quality. Fasolt would have been quite an appropriate emblem for his guild. To pick holes in a great artist, Walter seems very erratic this year. Alternately very slow and so fast as to become unsingable and unplayable (he tied Habich, superb Beckmesser as he is, in a knot once or twice through excessive speed) and I hear the 2nd perf. under Heger was far more shapely and clean. Both our young people, Nash and Gladys Parr, did splendidly. The season is a great success and *Fledermaus* will be delicious. If all goes well I will include it in the autumn tour... T.B. is as usual causing a commotion.

The autumn tour began in Glasgow in October with *Fledermaus*. As with *Falstaff*, Barbirolli had been rehearsing the company for six months. The cast included Nash (Eisenstein), Dennis Noble, Parry Jones, Nora Grühn (Adèle), Gladys Parr (Orlovsky), Marjorie Parry (Rosalinda) and Percy Heming (Frank). Walter incorporated the *Blue Danube* waltz into the ballroom scene, but Barbirolli played it as an entr'acte between Acts II and III. According to one critic he 'achieved the excessively difficult capriciousness of tempo variation that is the distinguishing mark of Viennese music.' He added *Rigoletto* to his repertoire during this tour.

If the operatic scene was in turmoil during 1930, so was the orchestral. The decision of the BBC to form its own symphony orchestra to give public concerts had been savagely criticised by existing orchestras, notably Harty's Hallé, and the vogue of the 'talkies' combined with growing economic depression had affected audiences. Yet great occasions were there to be heard. Barbirolli attended the four concerts in which Toscanini conducted the New York Philharmonic-Symphony Orchestra in London in the summer and was deeply impressed. He also met Felix Weingartner in March 1930. 'What a charming gentleman he is,' he wrote to Parker.

His performances at the Schubert concert were of wondrous beauty. Everything was there. Tone, balance, style, culture, tradition, life and above all it seemed love of the music and the instruments that were playing it. I notice the critic of the *Telegraph* called the heavenly playing of the 2nd subject 1st movt. 'Unfinished' *questionable* because of its slight change of speed. Cannot they for *once* refrain from their little quibbles when confronted with a great old artist (he is nearly seventy) who in the nature of things cannot give us much more, and just thank him for all the beauty he brings us and for the great boon he is conferring on us younger musicians by giving so generously (I call it extremely generous at his age to give so much of himself as he obviously did at this concert) of his wisdom and experience.

In that letter is epitomised the rarely bridged gap between the creative artist and the critic. Barbirolli did not take easily to criticism but he could forgive anything if he thought the writer had a real love of music.

Barbirolli's principal orchestral concert in the early part of 1930 was for the Royal Philharmonic Society on 13 March. He again chose an adventurous and difficult programme (with Casals as soloist in two works, one of them the Schumann concerto) and described it in a letter to Parker:

26.iii.30

...The William Tell Overture [played in celebration of the centenary of its first English performance at an RPS concert on 15 March 1830] brought the house down and really the vitality in that music is tremendous, and how beautiful the introduction for the 5 cellos. The Debussy piece [*Rondes de Printemps*] I love personally, and I do not think that his true worth has yet been estimated by English musicians. The Bax work [*Overture, Elegy and Rondo*] is fine stuff, especially the slow movement, which in its depth and concentration of feeling makes me think of the late Beethoven. With this work I had a rather disturbing experience. I lost the score (the only one in existence, MS) on the Sunday previous to the concert and it has never been recovered. Fortunately as is my wont I had studied it very carefully and was able to conduct the rehearsals in detail, and the performance, without it. The effort however was considerable and left me a little tired.

To Dot Mulholland he elaborated:

To conduct a work by heart is nothing but to *rehearse* a modern, complex, *new* work is a different story. Casals listened to all my rehearsals and even he did not notice it...

Casals was always one of John's musical gods, and what he thought about him he expressed nine years later in a letter from New York to Evelyn Rothwell:

> He should live on for ever in some way to inspire and teach generations still to come by the wondrousness of his art. That beauty, which few seem to realise, is *first* born of a technical accomplishment such as no cellist I have ever known possessed (including your Feuermanns, Piatigorskys etc.) and *finally* and irrefutably of a sense of beauty and integrity which surely have never been surpassed by any artist.

During this summer Barbirolli made recordings with Melchior. In November he was chosen to conduct the opening concerts of the Scottish Orchestra's Glasgow and Edinburgh seasons, early in January 1931 he first accompanied Lionel Tertis, who wrote to him that 'it was the greatest delight to me, and I shall long remember it,' and he had another Royal Philharmonic engagement on 29 January 1931 when he conducted Delius's *Brigg Fair*, Brahms's Second Symphony, two extracts from Busoni's *Doctor Faustus*, and Mahler's *Kindertotenlieder*, in which Elena Gerhardt was the soloist. She became and remained a devoted friend and admirer. This was the first Mahler that Barbirolli conducted. His view of this composer differed considerably in 1930 from what it was to become, as this extract from a letter to Parker shows:

23 April 1930

> ...I heard the rehearsal of the 2nd part of the Mahler symphony and was extremely disappointed. The material is very thin, and as regards orchestral *sound* Berlioz and Wagner have all done it far more convincingly. It seemed to be an impertinence to want all those people to make that particular music, as if *size* had become a morbid obsession with him.

The symphony concerned was, surprisingly, the Fourth, which Oskar Fried conducted.

Covent Garden was still Barbirolli's main preoccupation.

The 1931 Grand Season, from 27 April to 3 July, had only four conductors: Walter, Heger, Tullio Serafin, and Barbirolli – who had *Gianni Schicchi* and *Turandot* to himself and shared *Bohème*, *Rigoletto* and *Tosca* with Serafin. Stabile, Gigli and that fine baritone Fernando Autori were among the singers. On 16 May the historic recording was made of the Quintet from *Die Meistersinger* with Elisabeth Schumann, Gladys Parr, Lauritz Melchior, Ben Williams and Friedrich Schorr. The saga of this famous 78 was one of John's best anecdotes, told with a wealth of gesture. Take after take was ruined by wrong entries by Melchior while Elisabeth Schumann became hoarser with each new beginning. Eventually, after a day and a half, Barbirolli told Melchior to watch him implicitly. He conducted the final take with his eyes riveted on no one but Melchior and with one hand over his mouth. When he moved it away was the signal for Melchior to sing; when he didn't, Melchior was under orders to keep his mouth firmly shut. Yet the result was one of the classics of the gramophone.

Another musical event of importance was taking place that summer at the Theatre Royal, Drury Lane: the appearance of Richard Tauber in Lehár's *The Land of Smiles*. In the orchestra was a twenty-year-old oboe player from the Royal College of Music, Evelyn Rothwell. Also in the orchestra was a violist, Peter Barbirolli, John's brother. He was impressed by Evelyn's playing and mentioned her to John, who was looking for an oboist for Covent Garden. The result was a letter inviting her to an audition. Extracts from Evelyn's diary for 1931 tell the rest of the story:

13 July: Got home about 1 a.m. or thereabouts and found the most thrilling letter waiting for me... It appeared to be from someone called John Barkworth.* Most odd. Never heard of him... I wonder how he got hold of me?

15 July: Pouring wet day again. Had lunch at College and then set off for Covent Garden. Got there very early... Then *Barbirolli* came out of the office and shook hands... So that's who Barkworth was! I would not have known him by sight... He took us upstairs to the foyer... They went to fetch a music stand and so I talked to Barbirolli. He is very

* The letter still exists and the signature still looks like Barkworth!

good looking, rather plump, and looks rather foreign. He had on a mauve suit. He was remarkably nice and didn't behave like a foreigner in the least... I played a slow movement of a Handel sonata and Barbirolli accompanied me. He didn't want to hear any more. I sight-read out of *Rosenkavalier*... Then he said if he should offer me the job, would I feel like taking 6 weeks at Covent Garden and 8 weeks on tour, 2nd oboe.

In this way, Evelyn came into John's life, but eight years were to pass before they were married. Another woman was in John's life in the summer of 1931, and a formidable one too – Dame Ethel Smyth, most colourful and forthright of English women composers and a 'character' in her own right. John's efforts had been rewarded, with the help of Mrs Snowden who was on the board of the Syndicate, by a season of opera in English by the touring company at the Royal Opera House from 14 September to 24 October. Singers from Sadler's Wells, which had opened in January of this year, and the Old Vic were included in the company. They staged thirteen operas, including a revival of Ethel Smyth's *The Wreckers*, a tragic tale of adultery and smuggling on the Cornish coast. Two conductors shared the work with Barbirolli – Adrian Boult and Frederick Hay. Besides *The Wreckers*, Barbirolli conducted *Aïda, Barber of Seville, Bartered Bride* (its first Covent Garden performance since 1907), *Bohème, Fledermaus, Butterfly, Mastersingers* and *Tosca*.

Ethel Smyth was notorious for her active interest in the rehearsal of her works, sometimes carried to exasperating lengths. Once she provoked Boult, of all men, to greet her thus: 'Good morning Dame Ethel, and what are your tempi for today?' Barbirolli was not surprised, then, when he began to be pelted with letters from Coign, Woking, at the end of July. One of them contained the remark which enabled him for the rest of his life to allege, with humorous relish, that Dame Ethel had made an indelicate approach to him.

14 Aug. 1931

...(I just say things as they occur to me). I very much want to spare the Syndicate every penny of unnecessary expense, hence this letter. (a) I cannot remember what the Stage

Band is written for on p. 82. (b) I don't know what sort of 'organ' you have.

31 Aug. 1931

...If you and Mr Moor [the producer] want any rehearsals (foyer?) and Miss G. [Grühn] is too busy to rehearse, *I know her part* and all the business and shall be delighted to replace her. It will help the others and I swear to you... I will be a block of wood in your hands! No conducting – no giving of tempi! *nothing*...

In the event Odette de Foras sang in two performances and Nora Grühn in the third. Evelyn Rothwell joined the orchestra on 7 September and her first rehearsal was for *The Wreckers*. Her diary recorded: 'Ethel Smyth very much all there and *very* dictatorial. John Barbirolli is very nice, I think. Particular, though. Loses his temper quite suddenly and completely for only a few minutes.' We get other glimpses of Barbirolli at rehearsal from this diary:

8 September: Wind reh: of *Bartered Bride* at 2. Simply awful. All parts were wrong completely. We took from 2 to 6 to get through one act. J.B. very patient and nice. Said he'd have to correct parts instead of going to the Coliseum. I said I'd been to the Alhambra the night before [*Waltzes from Vienna*]. He raved about it – colours and so forth.

14 September: [opening night of the season, *Bartered Bride*]... Barbirolli conducted marvellously, though he was terribly nervy at first.

17 September: *Bohème* at 10-15 in the foyer. Very tricky. Barbirolli very patient. Everyone rather weary after last night [*Die Walküre*]. Like a damned fool I came in a bar late once and got a look from Barbirolli – it wasn't obvious either, as a matter of fact, but he hears everything.

The day after the first night of *The Wreckers*, Ethel Smyth wrote to Barbirolli: '... I don't believe anyone quite knows as well as I do what a feat you performed last night!' Later she took him and the cast 'for a treat' to lunch at Lyons's Corner

House. When she went to the cash-desk to pay the bill she astonished everyone present by hitching up her voluminous skirts, delving into the mysterious recesses thereby revealed, and producing a purse.

Evelyn Rothwell's next diary entry is of particular interest:

28 September: Went to College for a timpani lesson at 3. Wheelhouse [BBC timpanist] says the BBC orch. are all furious about Newman's attack on the opera. He says it is chiefly personal attack on Barbirolli (for Beecham, to do with a quarrel between him and J.B. apparently). It's a beastly shame.

The quarrel with Beecham was unquestionably over the subsidy. Events were playing into Beecham's hands. Throughout 1931 the country's economic situation became steadily more disastrous and a National Government was formed. The summer season of 1931 had been poorly supported and the English season was a disaster, with receipts at only a quarter capacity. People stayed away from *The Bartered Bride*, which they did not know, and from *The Wreckers*. There was also a prejudice against opera in English, in addition to the financial stringency imposed on everyone's pocket. Yet the autumn tour went forward as planned, opening in Glasgow in late October. Barbirolli now added Strauss's *Der Rosenkavalier* to his repertoire, conducting it for the first time in Glasgow on 29 October. Marjorie Parry was Oktavian, Miriam Licette the Marschallin, Nora Grühn was Sophie and Norman Allin sang Ochs.

Neville Cardus, who attended the *Rosenkavalier* performances in Manchester, recalled them nearly forty years later as one of the most understanding interpretations of the score he had ever heard. Dr A. Cranz, the music publisher, attended a 1932 Barbirolli performance of *Die Fledermaus* and said that 'for rhythm, charm and delicacy' it was the best he had heard anywhere. Before the first Halifax performance of the Richard Strauss opera in February 1932, Barbirolli gave a lecture on it to the town's music society (it was later printed in booklet form). Yet despite all this artistic success and endeavour, the touring company was doomed. The loss on the autumn tour was in the region of £8,000. The board of the syndicate were desperate, and there was revived talk of pulling down the Royal Opera House and extending the market. It was announced that there would be no international season in the summer of 1932 – immediate outcry! Beecham's hour was at hand. He let it be known that he would look favourably on renewed moves to amalgamate all opera interests, and Blois offered him the principal conductorship of the Royal Opera House for a Wagner season of four weeks in May with casts largely based on the touring company but with guest artists like Lehmann, Leider, Olczewska, Melchior, Schorr and Herbert Janssen. So, on 9 May, Beecham returned to Covent Garden after twelve years. Heger and he shared the main burden of the conducting. Barbirolli's share was, at short notice, one of the three *Meistersinger* performances, Beecham conducting the others. He had the pleasure, at any rate, of conducting Lotte Lehmann as Eva and of receiving a letter from her afterwards telling him 'Your *Meistersinger* performance was marvellous. I hope to have the chance to sing very often with you.' This was the first time he had conducted *Meistersinger* in German and he was allowed no orchestral rehearsal, only a short one with the soloists and pianoforte accompaniment. During this he corrected Lehmann on a small point. She raised an eyebrow but did what he wanted. Afterwards she said: 'It would have been all right tonight, you know.' John replied: 'Of course, I know that. But if I had not let you know I had noticed your mistake, what would you have thought of me?'

The company went on tour again in the autumn of 1932, during which Barbirolli conducted his first *Tristan and Isolde*, in Glasgow on 31 October, and again in Leeds on 21 November. Florence Austral was Isolde, Walter Widdop Tristan and Enid Cruickshank Brangäne. During this tour, however, the board of the Syndicate met and decided to amalgamate with the Imperial League, the Old Vic, Sadler's Wells and the BBC. Beecham became artistic director and at the end of the year the subsidy was finally withdrawn. In October of 1932 Beecham's new orchestra, the London Philharmonic, had been formed and became the Covent Garden Orchestra also. The effect of these changes and of Beecham's return was dramatic as far as Barbirolli was concerned, and was perhaps intensified by the death of Blois in May 1933. In the 1933 summer season of opera he conducted two *Bohèmes* and one *Aïda*. In 1931 and 1932 he conducted two Royal Philharmonic concerts; in 1932–33, when the LPO became the Society's resident orchestra, he conducted none: Beecham conducted nine of the ten concerts. Barbirolli did not conduct another RPS concert until October 1943. Something of the disappointment he felt about the demise of the touring company went into his letters to D. C. Parker describing the 1933 summer season at Covent Garden:

8 June 1933

...So far we know nothing of any future arrangements (in fact there are none). All this does not affect me as I have as much as I can cope with, but it is all very distressing for some of my colleagues. Also to think that a young ensemble like ours which was able to perform so musically and promisingly works like *Tristan, Meistersinger, Rosenkavalier, Falstaff, Schicchi,* to be put aside like that. In fact the more I hear of some of these foreign performances the prouder I am of our *musical ensemble* (*accuracy*). Much might have been built on that.

A month earlier he had discussed his fellow-conductors:

8 May 1933

...Heger, if anything, has improved. Allied to that 'artistic integrity' (which phrase so well defines him) there seems a greater freedom of expression which makes his work very outstanding at the moment. I am doubly delighted at the warmth of his receptions, not only because he thoroughly deserves it, but for three or four years when people have called him 'rather dull' I have had, what I hope I may call without undue arrogance, the sense to appreciate him at his true value, so that I can now make that unpleasant remark 'I told you so.' I was very amused at E.N.'s [Ernest Newman's] attempted whitewashing of T.B.'s *Rosenkavalier* in yesterday's [*Sunday*] *Times*. Some of the cuts were awful, and the ensemble in some instances deplorable. I was at the dress rehearsal last Saturday week when Lotte Lehmann, after a protest at his tempos, nearly walked out. I hear from one of the artists that Heger has been in the wings with a score at every performance to give them a hand. T.B. is really an enigma. Undoubtedly at times he is capable of remarkable work, but his arrogance is, I am afraid, most distasteful to me...

And was to become more so. But Beecham reigned supreme in English musical life for the next few years. With Lady Cunard, and with Geoffrey Toye as his managing director, he was now in control of Covent Garden and it was to be five years before Barbirolli conducted there again. After the resignation of Harty from the Hallé conductorship in March 1933, Beecham, though never appointed to the vacant post, had a big say in Mancunian musical affairs. With Boult firmly in the saddle at the BBC, Harty going to the LSO, and a senior generation of conductors – Sir Henry Wood, Albert Coates and Sir Landon Ronald among them – still active, there was little room in London for even the most gifted of the younger musicians. Barbirolli was turning his mind to the symphonic repertoire and by the time he had finished with the Covent Garden summer season of 1933 he had been appointed conductor of the Scottish Orchestra. How this came about will be related in the next chapter, but a further letter to Parker implies how much 'out of it' he now felt at Covent Garden.

30 June 1933

...I suppose you have seen E.N.'s onslaughts on C.G. I don't quite know how he manages to entirely divorce blame from Sir T.B. who this year was *Artistic Director* in complete control, and *went with Blois to Italy* to engage the singers. Really, musical criticism is in a funny state in London. I read the other day in one of the weeklies (Capell* it was, I think) regarding the Wagner at C.G. that 'although Heger has not the mercurial and imaginative qualities of Sir T.B. he is not a DUFFER.' One can only feel grateful for having that assurance, even though not expressed in the most elegant language! ! !

Meanwhile, there had been another important event in his life. Since 18 June 1932 he had been married to Marjorie

* Richard Capell (1885–1954), music critic of the *Daily Mail* and later of the *Daily Telegraph*.

Parry, the Oktavian and Rosalinda, among others, of his Covent Garden productions. Both were thirty-two and they were married at Bath register office with Peter Barbirolli and Marjorie's father as witnesses. Their engagement had once been broken off, but although several of John's friends in the company felt that the marriage was unlikely to be a success, he was in love. They went for a short honeymoon to Bruges and Brussels where, he told D. C. Parker, 'we found much the same tale of woe in regard to music as elsewhere.' Sadly, also, he had already begun to suspect that he had made a tragic mistake.

6
Glasgow to New York

Occupied as he was with the Covent Garden company and its fate, Barbirolli never relaxed his studies of the scores of symphonies, concertos and the other works of the concert-hall repertoire, for he had no intention of being labelled as an opera conductor, or an Italian opera 'specialist.' He had no inhibitions about catholicity of taste and none about versatility, which he once described as 'a dangerous asset in this country where, by some queer alchemy, anyone who does one particular thing persistently enough (however badly) is sooner or later labelled an "authority".'

In 1932 his orchestral repertoire was limited to the works he had conducted with his string orchestra and those in the handful of concerts with the LSO and Royal Philharmonic Society, but not much besides. He had not yet conducted a Beethoven symphony and only one by Brahms. So each concert meant months of preparatory study, because he insisted on knowing a work thoroughly before he presumed to instruct orchestral players in its performance. He listened to records, read books and went to other conductors' concerts. His opinions on contemporary composers and musicians formed and re-formed. Some of this formative time is reflected in extracts from letters to D. C. Parker:

8 June 1933

...I was able to hear one of the Koussevitzky concerts, the second; the Bax symphony I thought the best performance.

The Wagner was not too well played, and I must confess myself very disturbed by his rather ruthless disregard of all the composer's indications of speeds, and the continual substitution of 'effects' of his own. The *Meistersinger* overture surely cannot stand a dozen or so different tempos in the course of its performance, the grandeur leaves the music and it becomes hysterical emotion. This is not to deny him the glamour of his personality and perhaps his sincerity, but I do feel that his attitude of not disciplining himself at all in regard to matters of style, and in giving the impression that he must 'interpret' everything before the music can come to life, is not in the highest ideals of our art. Perhaps the simplest way to put it is that his attitude is the direct *opposite* of Toscanini. The latter radiates something very *pure* and *noble* whereas I cannot help sensing some of the showman in K.

4 April 1933

...We had an excellent concert with my Trinity College pupils on Saturday. A young girl (17) made a splendid show with the Elgar Violin Concerto. From my boyhood I have preferred this to almost any other concerto, and time does not seem to make me change that opinion.

8 May 1933

...You will be, I hope, interested that I am entirely coming round to your estimate of Elgar. Of my great admiration you have known for a long time, but as you know I was torn in my affections between him and Delius. Without in the least diminishing my love of the latter's music, I have had to confess to myself he is something of an Amateur of Genius as against a Master...

His means of studying the Brahms symphonies was typical. Since his boyhood he had known Helen Henschel, daughter of Sir George Henschel, the close friend of Brahms and a great conductor. In May 1933 he told Miss Henschel how much he would like it if Sir George, who was then eighty-three, would 'show me how to do the Brahms symphonies.' Henschel himself was delighted by this interest from a young conductor, and a week or two later they met in Miss Henschel's music room after tea, 'the Brahms scores between them while they went through them almost bar by bar, both their faces alight with enthusiasm and pleasure... There was a half-century's difference in their ages, but here were two great musicians whose lifelong dedication was the same: complete devotion to the music with no thoughts of self-glorification.' In 1956 Miss Henschel gave John Sir George's marked scores of the Brahms symphonies and reminded him of that afternoon twenty-three years earlier. He replied: 'What a precious and wonderful gift. Of course I shall use them for conducting and draw inspiration from the knowledge that I have before me the possession of a very great and noble man and artist. The afternoon you speak of is still vividly in my memory...'

His visit to the Scottish Orchestra in 1930 led to a six weeks' engagement in the 1932–33 season. This was a critical time for the orchestra. Audiences, and consequently receipts, had fallen, and there was even talk of disbanding the orchestra. But a few brave spirits, D. C. Parker among them, had faith that Scotland could do better and called for the foundation of an endowment fund to support the orchestra. At the prompting of Sir Landon Ronald, a former permanent conductor, the committee decided to offer Barbirolli half the season, in January and February 1933, obviously as a 'try-out' before making any permanent appointment. He threw himself into the task with his customary vigour and enthusiasm. His programmes were wide-ranging and bold, with a marked leaning to English music: Elgar's First Symphony (17 January), and two very recent works, Vaughan Williams's *Job* (in a disastrously shortened version) and Bax's Fourth Symphony. He also conducted Beethoven's Ninth Symphony for the first time in his career. At the end of the season it was the custom to have a plebiscite programme. This was the occasion in 1933 for speech-making and appeals for help. R. W. Greig, chairman of the orchestra's executive committee, promised the audience that in 1933–34 there would be a return to the policy of one conductor for the whole season, 'and I do not need to tell you who he is.' At which there were cheers and the singing of 'Will ye no' come back again.' As a critic had written after Barbirolli's second concert: 'It must be obvious to even the most casual listener that something definite has happened to the Scottish Orchestra. That something is Mr

John Barbirolli.' Glasgow was the first city to respond utterly
to his magnetism, and to sense the rapport between orchestra
and audience which he created. Even if people went to the
concerts at first to see his shock of black hair and his unusual
expanse of white shirt-cuff, they usually left entranced by the
atmosphere of music-making. (The shirt-cuffs, incidentally,
had a severely practical operatic origin: to enable the singers
to see his hands clearly against the background of a theatre
audience.)

Another significant guest engagement was his first appearance with the Hallé Orchestra in Manchester on 12 January
1933, when he conducted the *Suite for Strings* which he had
arranged from Purcell pieces for his Chenil Galleries orchestra, Delius's *In a Summer Garden*, Mozart's 40th Symphony
and Franck's Symphony. The Hallé's interest in him at this
stage was symptomatic of his growing reputation. Nor was this
confined to Great Britain. During 1928 he had met in London
Arthur Judson,* supreme among American impresarios,
who had been told by Hans Kindler, conductor of the Washington Symphony Orchestra, about Barbirolli's work in
opera. Now, four years later, Judson wrote from New York (7
November 1932):

Since I met you... I have been interested in watching your
career. I have been especially pleased to note your conducting in the concert field. I shall be glad if you will let me
have from time to time any material about your concert
work. Conditions in America are very difficult at the present time and it is not possible to prophesy what the situation will be another year concerning conductors. Nevertheless I think it would be highly advisable for you to keep me
fully posted...

Eighteen months later Judson put Barbirolli under contract
for any American engagements that might arise.

After the success of his Glasgow concerts, Barbirolli
accepted the permanent conductorship of the Scottish Orches-

* Judson launched his own concert agency early in his career and by
1930 was president of an 'empire' – virtually all artists visiting the
United States worked under his management. In 1915 he became manager of the Philadelphia Orchestra and in 1922 of the New York
Philharmonic.

tra. Not only was it a fine chance to explore the orchestral repertoire, it was what he enjoyed most – working with a regular team. This was what he had liked about the BNOC and his Covent Garden touring company, and this was what was eventually to bind him to the Hallé. He loved building, training, teaching and taking the audience along with him. Working with his own orchestra he could find out also his own mistakes – the only true progress, he thought; and he believed that a permanent conductor could stamp his own character, by which he meant his own ideal of music, on the orchestra. So, far away from London and glamour though it was, he was happy and proud to go to Glasgow. From 1855 the Glasgow Choral Union had provided the West of Scotland with its music, for its first years with hired orchestras and from 1873 with its own orchestra. Hans von Bülow conducted it that year. In 1898 it became the Choral and Orchestral Union with the Scottish Orchestra. One of its first regular conductors had been Henschel. For four years from 1916 to 1920 its regular conductor had been Sir Landon Ronald, who wrote to Barbirolli in the warmest terms:

19 June 1933

...I congratulate the authorities of the Scottish Orchestra on having secured you for their permanent conductor. I gave them the tip two or three years ago... Without your knowing it, I 'run' you more than any other professional I know, because I heartily believe in you and your talent. There are two posts I have recommended you for, unsuccessfully, but I still hope to live to see you in one of the premier positions in this country... P.S. Don't fail to keep in touch with me, as I am really interested in your career.

Barbirolli had a high opinion of Ronald's quality as an Elgar conductor. Elgar had dedicated *Falstaff* to him, and when John once remarked to him what a thrill this must have been, Sir Landon shook him by replying, 'Never could make head or tail of the piece, my dear boy.'

Before he took up his new post, Barbirolli went with Parker to the Bayreuth Festival. They were both ardent Wagnerians and John keenly looked forward to this pilgrimage:

2 Woburn Court
30 June 1933

...I *would* like a night in Nuremberg so that the itinerary you propose seems just the thing. I am afraid it is not possible for me to stay for *The Ring*.* The *Parsifal* at Covent Garden this year [conducted by Heger] was absolutely first-rate. I don't think there can ever have been a finer Gurnemanz than Kipnis. He sang with such dignity and understanding *and* (to me this is important) with unfailing beauty of tone. Janssen was a very moving Amfortas. What I am looking forward to most of all is the sound of the orchestra as it is constructed in Bayreuth...

In Nuremberg they visited Hans Sachs's house. Bayreuth itself was commemorating the fiftieth anniversary of Wagner's death with an exhibition of relics. Barbirolli was deeply moved to be able to examine manuscripts and to enter Wagner's study. Twenty years afterwards his eyes filled with tears and he gripped my arm in his unforgettable way as he described seeing sketches from which *Tristan* had grown. He was especially interested to discover the original number of players in the *Siegfried Idyll* and usually conducted it with this small orchestra because he thought the music's peculiar intimacy was lost with a large orchestra. His letters to Parker on their return show how much he had enjoyed the trip:

3 September 1933

...It is I who have to thank you, for I should never have gone alone, and undoubtedly I profited much from the experience... I shudder to think what it would have been like to see some of the things we did, with anybody incapable of feeling the sense of wonder and grandeur they undoubtedly call forth. I have been re-reading a little of the Newman *Wagner as Man and Artist* (not the last book) and I must say that at this time, his insistence on and assiduousness in collecting every possible piece of information as to Wagner having kissed a laundry girl or an odd chambermaid or two seems rather childish and boring to read.

* He saw *Parsifal* conducted by Richard Strauss and *Die Meistersinger* conducted by Karl Elmendorff.

Surely that side of him if it existed was but the very ordinary weakness that many men (complete fools) have in common with him. What possible relation it has to his greatness I fail to understand. The Wesendonk episode seems a beautiful one and whether it was a guilty friendship or not seems to me a mere detail... The weather here continues delightful and in the very warm periods I often say 'Zwei Helles, bitte' but all to no purpose, I fear.

While in Bayreuth, Charles Parker suggested that they should follow their Wagner pilgrimage with a visit to their other 'master', Elgar. So on 19 August they went to Worcester, first spending some time in the cathedral, and then inquiring the way to Marl Bank, Elgar's home, from a woman shop assistant. She stared at them and asked 'Does he live here?' John remembered every detail of that afternoon and of his conversation with the composer. Elgar talked to them about his music and played some of his recording of *Falstaff*, remarking of the side-drum solo: 'Well, that's a good bit anyway.' (John always let this passage have a little extra panache in memory of that remark.) He showed them his garden and apologised because the heat had 'withered up' all the flowers. He took them up to his bedroom to see the view and showed them the towers of the cathedral, saying 'That's what I see every morning when I wake up.' He also told them that the broad opening theme of the last movement of the Second Symphony was evolved from the rhythmic figure in which form it appears later in the movement. Then, as they left, he emotionally hugged John and thanked him for liking his music. Almost exactly six months later, on 23 February 1934, Elgar died. John wrote to Parker:

2 Woburn Court

My dear Friend. Our beloved Master left us today. It seems incredible that men like that should go, though of course they live on in ever increasing glory in the heritage they leave behind them. It seems but yesterday we paced his garden together, so soon after we had paced the garden of our other 'Master'. Elgar had been at various times very kind to me and that is what makes it all such a deep personal loss. The man was as noble and beautiful as his music, and I feel very humbly and deeply grateful that I was granted the privilege of having known him. To think I fulfilled his last public engagement.* I send these few words to you, my friend, in my sorrow, as I know of no one who loved his work better than you. Yours, John.

Parker and Barbirolli together attended the Memorial Service in Worcester Cathedral on 2 March and John was also at the London memorial concert on 24 March when Ronald and Boult conducted. Thirty-four years later, in 1968, I published a book about Elgar which dealt in some detail with his psychological weaknesses. John wrote to me when he had read it:

It has caused me much distress at times (for you know how much I loved and still love him). But it is fated to such men to suffer and he did not have Wagner's 'hide' to protect him... A book that has enlightened me so much in many ways, given much pain in other ways, and much pride.

Barbirolli's appointment to the Scottish Orchestra when its fortunes were at a low point was his first exercise in what he called 'musical corpse-revival.' The Committee had kept their word and made a big drive to raise funds, in which they were unexpectedly successful. Before the season began they took the unprecedented step of holding a reception in Glasgow City Chambers, on the invitation of the Lord Provost, for four hundred guests to meet their new conductor. Barbirolli urged the gathering to 'leave your wirelesses at home and go to a live concert.' As the *Glasgow Bulletin* put it, he delighted everybody present – 'his speech showed the man of brains as well as the artist and the true adroitness of the orator in getting a laugh of real amusement.' He became the talk of the town and a woman reporter who went to St Andrew's Hall to interview him at rehearsal was told by the janitor: 'He's rather like me – not much of him but what there is is good.'

The Committee had supported him in reorganising the orchestra, which began the season with twenty new members including several new principals of sections. Their faith was

---

* Barbirolli took Elgar's place at a Hallé Concert on 15 February 1934, and conducted *Froissart*, the Violin Concerto (Albert Sammons), the *Enigma Variations* and *Cockaigne*.

justified. Audiences increased and the critics approved what they heard. Barbirolli's concerts for school-children made a special impact, and many people today recall how their interest was kindled by 'the Scottish under J.B.' at these and other concerts. His enthusiasm, his expansive conducting style – his gestures in those days seeming to take in a wider radius than the length of his arms – and the improved performances he obtained from the orchestra made him popular wherever he went. He boasted that the Scottish was the only orchestra in the country which rehearsed every day of its season, and he introduced his famous sectional rehearsals: three hours strings, three hours wind, three hours everybody. The conductor nine hours, of course – 'I'm the freshest person at the end,' he said, 'because I'm completely absorbed.'

The Scottish's season was fairly short, from mid-November to mid-February, with thirteen Tuesday and fourteen Saturday concerts in Glasgow and others in Edinburgh. Barbirolli's programmes were typically varied, contained several 'first performances at these concerts,' and several works which remained in his repertoire throughout his life, including Berlioz's *Fantastic Symphony*, Strauss's *Ein Heldenleben* and Stravinsky's *Petrushka*, a work which he considered 'lifted Stravinsky into the Beethoven class.' His soloists included Adolf Busch, Artur Rubinstein and a large number of opera singers: Maria Olczewska, Florence Austral and Gerhard Hüsch. He encouraged some of the orchestral principals to be concerto soloists, and he also had the support of old friends – Ethel Bartlett and Rae Robertson, in Mozart's E Flat Concerto, and Yvonne Arnaud, who played Schumann's Piano Concerto and thanked Barbirolli for his help, charmingly adding: 'I think worlds of you as an artist, and so it reflects on me that I cannot, after all, be such a "bum" pianist.'

The Scottish was not the only provincial orchestra he conducted at this period of his career. He took on the Leeds Symphony Orchestra, which also was trying to revive a bygone prosperity and was a forerunner of the larger and ill-fated Yorkshire Symphony Orchestra formed after the Second World War. It was good enough to play Sibelius symphonies and to engage soloists like Jelly d'Aranyi, Myra Hess and Arthur de Greef. When he conducted, the hall was full for the first time for years. He conducted orchestras at Torquay, Eastbourne, Tunbridge Wells, Bournemouth and Folkestone;

opera – *Butterfly* and *The Barber of Seville* with his former BNOC colleagues – at Sadler's Wells; the Hallé in February – two concertos with Schnabel as soloist; and in August 1934 the LSO at the Welsh National Eisteddfod at Neath – 'one of the most thrilling experiences of my career,' he told Charles Parker. 'There was an audience of 14,000 which simply went wild. Such spontaneous exhibition of emotion I have never witnessed nor heard before. To end the concert I conducted, with their picked choir of 700 voices, the traditional "Land of My Fathers" and the *beautiful* sound, allied to the fervour with which it was sung, will long remain in my memory. I look forward to doing the Verdi *Requiem* and *Meistersinger* choruses with that choir one day.'

Already the thirty-four-year-old Barbirolli's appetite for work can be recognised. Even then he paid the price in his health. Always prone to over-tiredness, he also suffered at that time from severe headaches, caused partly by his sinus trouble but also undoubtedly by the severe strain he put on himself by constant studying and rehearsing. Yet he needed work like a drug to keep at bay the fits of depression which attacked him if he was idle. He dreaded the Brighton holidays with the family unless he could take work with him. Also, he was aware by now that his marriage was on the rocks. Marjorie resented his attachment to his family and found it hard to accept his devotion to his mother. They were still together, but only just.

On 9 January 1934, the soloist in a Handel oboe concerto at the Scottish Orchestra concert was the new principal oboist, Evelyn Rothwell, whom John had brought from Covent Garden after an audition at which they discovered a mutual admiration for Duke Ellington. Evelyn sent him the record of 'Sophisticated Lady' and he transcribed it as a cello solo. This still exists. (He also liked Jerome Kern's tune 'Smoke gets in your Eyes' and when, in 1956, Steve Race wrote his *Variations on a Smoky Theme* for Barbirolli and the Hallé to play at Bexhill, John was delighted because 'it enables me, with a certain decency, to conduct this lovely tune.') In a letter to her parents Evelyn described Hogmanay, 1933–34:

We had jazz on the wireless and so forth and sang *Auld Lang Syne* at 12. Barbirolli and his wife couldn't get away from their duty party till 1 a.m. or so. When they arrived it was marvellous... There were some quartets and everyone drank healths a lot and then B. said he was extremely sorry but since someone was silly enough to lend him a cello he couldn't stop playing... He played unaccompanied Bach with all the lights off! We broke up at 3.30 a.m. about. On Tuesday I had my cello lesson... Barbirolli took me to lunch at the grill of the best hotel in Glasgow. Then we got my cello in a taxi and went back to his flat [in Queen's Crescent]. I had a lesson...then we put some records on and talked about all sorts of things and he then carried my cello all the way back to the digs for me. He says he'll give me another lesson next week. Isn't it fun?

When the Scottish Orchestra's 1934–35 season began, John had left Marjorie* and thenceforward his affection for Evelyn grew. He admired her musicianship and soon found that her warm and charming personality was highly attractive to him. She came from an upper middle class background, her elderly and very Victorian father being a successful tea dealer. (John used to tell amusingly how sure he was that Mr Rothwell would not approve of him: 'I was small, a foreigner, a musician, a Roman Catholic and getting divorced!' But they grew to like each other.) All this element was a source of affectionate raillery for John, who found the very 'English,' reticent, under-stating side of Evelyn delightfully at odds with her expansive musical self. After a special holiday concert on 1 January 1935 he sent this note:

Evelyn dear. The Delius was so lovely tonight that I feel I must write you a word before going to my rest. By this time you will probably have realised what this music means to me, and to have so much of its loveliness realised for me, as it was tonight, was a very moving experience. If I want to tell you how beautifully you played in the 'Cuckoo' it is not to minimise the playing of the others. Just now, however, with all your sweetness to me, I do want you to know that the sensitiveness with which you share the music we make together, is something very precious. Bless you. John.

* When the prospectus for the season was published in the late summer of 1934 it showed her as soloist for the final concert on 9 February 1935, but another soloist took her place.

His second Scottish season was therefore a happy time for him and his programmes show not only the development of his tastes but the splendid fare set before the Glasgow and Edinburgh audiences – and the quality of soloists engaged. Carl Flesch played Beethoven's Violin Concerto, Schnabel Beethoven's Fifth Piano Concerto, Horowitz Brahms's D Minor Concerto and Liszt's A Major, Hubermann Brahms's and Tchaikovsky's violin concertos, Rubinstein Falla's *Nights in the Gardens of Spain*, Jacques Thibaud Mozart's A Major Violin Concerto (No. 5) and Chausson's *Poème*, and Nicholas Medtner Beethoven's G Major Piano Concerto. There were many English works, including Bax's *The Tale the Pine Trees Knew*, dedicated to Barbirolli whose friendship with Bax was of long standing, Elgar's *Grania and Diarmid* Funeral March, Violin Concerto, Second Symphony and *Enigma Variations*, Delius's *North Country Sketches*, *In A Summer Garden* and *Eventyr*, and Walton's Viola Concerto (soloist Eileen Grainger, a member of the orchestra). He conducted Brahms's First, Third and Fourth Symphonies, Strauss's *Don Quixote* and, among lighter pieces, the *Emperor Waltz* of Strauss. He also conducted the Marcello Oboe Concerto which Evelyn had edited. Over thirty years later, the slow movement was played at his funeral.

The season had specially commemorated Elgar, Delius and Holst, all of whom had died in 1934. Barbirolli was already beginning to regard his Elgar performances as his special mission in life. As he told Charles Parker, 'I still feel the mass of our public is still very far from a true appreciation of his greatness.' And walking in Glasgow with Evelyn one winter's night he took her to Joseph Lister's house in Woodside and there vowed to do all he could to make people both in Great Britain and overseas appreciate the true greatness of Elgar.* (Lister was one of his medical heroes – Barbirolli's interest in and knowledge of medicine was considerable – and shared a place in his pantheon with Pasteur, Henry Irving, Napoleon and, perhaps most admired of all, Horatio Nelson.) Elgar's music, and matters Elgarian, were a binding factor in

* After conducting an LSO concert in August 1934, Barbirolli was told by the leader, W. H. Reed, that Elgar wanted in the unfinished Third Symphony 'to revert to the utmost simplicity of which he was capable and talked all the time of the Mozart Symphony as his model. He was even going to have a repeat (to have the exposition twice).'

John's relationships with many people. Parker was his first *amico simpatico* in this respect and there were others. It even extended to casual acquaintances. Mr G. W. Hargreaves, with whom he had a short discussion on Elgar after a concert at Stockport, did not see him again for several years until May 1970, when that excellent Manchester record shop Avgarde put on an exhibition of Barbirolli's recordings. He noticed Mr Hargreaves there and said to him: 'I remember you.' Mr Hargreaves protested that this was surely impossible in view of the thousands of people he must have met in the meantime. 'I remember you distinctly,' John persisted. 'We talked of Elgar. You see, Elgar-lovers always fascinate me.'

He was soon to have a chance to begin to fulfil his vow about Elgar. When the Scottish and Leeds seasons ended in February 1935, he left for his first engagements as a guest conductor of foreign orchestras, something he had anticipated with mixed feelings because he had an innate dread of going to a foreign orchestra. Although he never lacked confidence, in one sense he suffered from an inferiority complex – he could never quite believe that he would be good enough for foreign orchestras. Yet, as so often in his life, once he was 'on the box' everything was all right. This fear had always been with him. In March 1930, writing to Dot Mulholland, who had gone to Brussels for cello lessons, he said: 'I have rather a horror of the continent myself, specially alone, so I admired you much for doing it.' On his first tour he took with him Thomas Cheetham, the Scottish Orchestra's Lancastrian librarian and percussion player, who was one of his most loyal friends and was later to join him in Manchester with the Hallé. Among the works Barbirolli conducted in Helsinki, Leningrad and Hilversum on this 1935 tour were Elgar's *Introduction and Allegro* and *Enigma Variations* and Delius's *In A Summer Garden*. He described the tour to Evelyn:

Torni Hotel, Helsinki
23 February. 3.15 a.m.

...I know you will be glad to hear my first concert on foreign soil has been a veritable triumph... At the end of my last rehearsal this morning the whole orchestra [the Helsinki State] stood up and cheered and played me some sort of musical honours which must be the equivalent of

out 'For he's a jolly etc.' What would please you most of all perhaps, my dear, was the speech of the leader [Arvo Hannikainen] after the concert...who said 'We have not only played with a great conductor, but with a great man with a great heart.' You know, my dear, I don't write this in conceit of myself, but with infinite gratitude that my love of music has brought these men so near to me... I marvel that they gave me so much of myself in the short time I was with them... I shall have lots to tell you when I return of this extraordinarily civilised city...

He conducted the Leningrad Radio Orchestra in a series of concerts at the end of February and beginning of March and was also thrilled to visit the Hermitage art gallery. But he was horrified by the low wages and living standards of Soviet musicians at that period. On 8 March, in the train to Riga, he wrote some of his impressions:

... After my last concert they took me in the band-room and I realised they had clubbed together and bought me a present. If you knew what they had to live on you would realise, dear, why I am almost moved to tears at the recollection of their sweet thought. The present consists of two full scores, with a dedication and signed by the whole orchestra. The man detailed to look after me (a poor fellow who has obviously seen better days and spoke excellent French) used to say to me every day 'Ils sont tous amoureux de vous'... *Also* they loved the *Enigma*, which was the loveliest thing of all... I have met two of Rimsky-Korsakov's sons (one is in the orchestra) and chatting with one of them yesterday I discovered there exists a set of variations for oboe still in MS. If I come again I will try and get them copied for you... We are going through real Christmas card country now. Fir trees, frost, sun, sleighs. This week has been much colder but very dry and have been out in my fur cap. I look 'no sae bad' in it.

In Holland he conducted another radio orchestra. He returned to England to conduct opera (*Romeo and Juliet* and *Tristan*) with the Carl Rosa company. He also worked on arranging some Pergolesi pieces as an oboe concerto for Evelyn. Other foreign tours were in the air, too:

30 March 1935
Queen's Hall

Evelyn dear... Have done some work at the concerto. The 1st mvt. is in score and completed, and last night sketched out the second in full, the oboe part and the bass... Peter on seeing the score said 'You'll have Rothy [Evelyn's father] on your track' to which remark I made hearty acquiescence... All the ailments are progressing quite well, if I could have a little rest soon all will be well... Saw [Harold] Holt about the American business and the inquiry is for concerts at the Hollywood Bowl, San Francisco and Santiago. There is no further news yet.

A few days later:

Savage Club

This morning had a word with Holt about going to the Hollywood Bowl to conduct this summer. Am to see him this afternoon. This is rather exciting, for it is the very best way of going to America first, and you don't have to be there too long!!

Nothing came of this proposal. It was a source of wry, though slightly embittered amusement to Barbirolli that although Arthur Judson wanted him for an American tour because he had heard such good reports of him from Heifetz, Horowitz, Rubinstein and others, he was now conducting fewer London concerts than he had in the late 1920s. As Ferruccio Bonavia was to write in the *New York Times* of 24 May 1936: 'John Barbirolli has made his reputation in London in spite of the factions and partisanship which are now to be found in London as well as in any other musical city... The London public is determined never to be stampeded into an admission of triumph where a young British artist is concerned. Its full confidence can only be won by a foreign reputation or else by long and steady wooing.' Irving Kolodin was also to comment on this attitude: 'There is good reason to suspect that the rapidity with which Barbirolli created a following aroused the apprehension of those who control musical jobs in England. Inevitably guest engagements became fewer.'

John's letters to Evelyn during the summer of 1935 show him in his many-sidedness. It was the year of King George V's silver jubilee and this stirred his deep-seated and very genuine patriotism. In July he conducted the Academy students in *The Mastersingers*. He went to Covent Garden and was horrified by what he heard in the theatre where, as he had confided to Robert Mayer, he would have liked to be musical director. He pondered on his music-making and what it meant to him. He gave Evelyn the Pergolesi concerto as an Easter gift, and she gave him a book on Louis Pasteur.

24 April 1935

...It is difficult to describe the feelings I have experienced in reading Pasteur these last few days. A man of that beauty of character is an inspiration and a guide to life such as can come but rarely, and it was difficult to hold back the tears when in the hydrophobia chapter I read of his own intense suffering with his little patients. Also that beautiful letter (*I* think it beautiful) to the shepherd boy when he had recovered gently telling him to take great care with his writing and his schooling and so kindly wanting to help and improve the boy. That a great man in the midst of all his labours should stop for a moment to do things like this is perhaps something that reconciles us to greatness, when we realise what forms it takes with some. To have come into contact with such a man, even only through a book, has I am sure been a blessing to me... I sometimes feel so very inadequately equipped in many ways to do all I want or should want to do for Music, but perhaps the fact that I need more plodding perseverance than some is not without its recompense. All that is acquired by dint of effort and some kind of sacrifice has value.

After a *Tristan* performance:

My sweet beloved... To plan and direct a work of that magnitude needs a great effort, and it is wonderful beyond words for me that I have found a woman who understands, and can suffer and rejoice musically with me... Life has so far dealt very fairly by me, inasmuch as, though it has had its clouds, personally and privately, it has given me great good fortune to pursue my work, and any personal setbacks I have had have all contributed towards keeping a steady balance in things, and given me the power of understanding and tolerance towards my fellows. For all this I am infinitely grateful, and moreover it is a gratitude which replenishes itself day by day and is ever present... I had ceased to hope or believe it possible that anyone could come along with an affection for me such as you have shown me.

Monday 7 May 1935

...Rose early this morning just after six and set out with Dick [his nephew] at about seven. We saw *both* processions [to and from St Paul's] very well, so the effort was well worth it. It was rather a wonderful experience... The day was ideal. A cloudless blue sky, which somehow seemed to symbolize and intensify the feelings of gratitude that we are returning (I hope really) to better days, and that our King was with us to see them... I had to do a good deal of tiptoeing and it was a pity as Rosie remarked yesterday that you could not have been there for as she said you could have lifted me in your arms and I should have had a perfect view however far back I was.

Tuesday, 1.30

I meant to finish this last night after supper and a little walk, but felt so depressed somehow, I thought it better to leave it over till the morning... I have felt so nervy these last few days and worried, not for any precise reasons, but I suppose an accumulation of everything... I am not feeling sorry for myself (I *hate* that kind of thing) but I resent not being able to concentrate well on my work. But I must be patient and realise I ask rather a lot of J.B.

1 June 1935

...Bellezza* made the Phil. sound like a 5th rate orchestra

* Vincenzo Bellezza conducted *The Barber of Seville, La Bohème, La Cenerentola* and *L'Italiana in Algeri* during the 1935 Grand Season at Covent Garden between 1 and 31 May.

...without even achieving the feat (perhaps a little excessive to ask of C.G. during the Grand Season) except now and again of being together with the singers. In such other places as it seemed from the movements of their lips that they *might* be together, the orchestra was so loud as to make any definite assertion of that remarkable fact almost an impossibility. The singing with the exception of Pinza and De Luca [who sang together only in the final performance of *The Barber of Seville* on 31 May] (a great old artist this, age about 65) was deplorable, and yet I find [Francis] Toye writing of this performance, of a work on which he is supposed to be an authority, that it was 'not only first-rate, but perhaps the best-ever and a model' etc. etc. This with bars of ensemble missed, and in one case being nearly a bar out with the orchestra. Borgioli was singing instead of Nash, and never was the sycophantic snobbery of Covent Garden better exposed when someone at the interval (not having noticed the change of cast) and picking on what they thought the only Britisher there, said to me 'Don't think much of Nash.' I agreed the tenor was awful, and then enlightened them as to who it was. It is good I do not often go to C.G. for it is difficult even to laugh at this desecration and prostitution of all ideals of sincerity, simplicity and humility in face of great music. I shall never forget when I remarked to Toscanini on his last visit here how well he looked, and his reply: 'My boy, five years *without* opera.' If it nearly broke a man of his power and prestige, it is almost impossible to expect that ever will those most gifted by nature vocally to assist an idealist such as he was be of sufficient mental calibre to understand and *serve*. This may sound irrelevant to Toye, but it is not, for if he really knows, he should do his duty and not pander further to the already over-pampered and inordinate vanity of so-called 'stars'. Evelyn my dear it is a shame to let all this off on you, but I was offended and distressed by what I saw and heard... Am going to Toscanini tomorrow and will write you about it... I hear he is delighted with the [BBC Symphony] orchestra and all goes happily which, as this is the first time he has ventured to conduct an English orchestra, 'does give me very great pleasure'...[John enjoyed reading and quoting Pepys.]

Tuesday

The Toscanini concert was grand. I was at rehearsal too and was much moved by his attitude to music, which is one of the greatest sincerity, humility and ideal of service. It is extraordinary how a man of such individual power can yet create the illusion that there is nothing coming between you and the music. A lovely tone quality he gets, and such endless lines of phrase, and all with such impeccable taste and dignity. The orchestra played well for him, strings especially, but the intonation was frankly *bad*. I really cannot understand it... It was a happy day for me to hear him again, for I know now that the path I am pursuing is the right one. It may be the difficult one, but that is of no account.

June 1935 [undated]

...Had rather a wonderful day yesterday. The two hours spent with Toscanini* were lovely. He talked much of Father and their times together, also I was able to ask him many things about the licence permissible in Verdi operas, and very relieved to find I was perfectly right in the stand I had taken in this matter. On telling him of some of the things I had heard at C.G. under so-called distinguished Italian conductors he proceeded to describe them as men who are not only ignorant, but traitors to music... So my fulminations in my last letter were rather to the point. But the most revealing thing of all was the man's great *simplicity* and burning sincerity in his love of music. He has rather a lovely face, and when he heard how Elgar died (his sufferings from cancer) the hurt look on that face was, to me, really moving. He was so sweet to me, and to hear him call me 'Caro Maestro' tickled me to death. I got him on to the subject of Glyndebourne to tell him about you, and apparently he had never heard of a female oboe player for he called it a 'cosa buffa' (comic thing)... The orchestra played better last night... The Brahms and Wagner were unforgettable. Such nobility of music-making becomes a great inspiration and I feel very secure about my methods of work. A great man should do this to his young contem-

* John invariably mis-spelt it 'Toscannini'.

poraries, not inspire them with hopelessness but with determination to go on and on and endeavour to develop to the full such poor talents as we may possess... News from Scotland is all rather worrying. The moment I leave, all seem to get cold feet and want to chuck everything – extension [of length of season], visit to London etc. It is really too bad. I have no one there to fight for me. Everything the last two years has been on my shoulders, and my only fear is I can't keep on doing this. It is not fair to ask it of me.

Later that summer he went up to Glasgow to see the committee about these 'shilly-shallyings.'

August 1935

I won't bother you with the whole tale now, but suffice to say I managed to put everything straight. Still, the negotiations were difficult and delicate and as I have told you before I manage to feel well enough now, but soon seem to wear out when put to any strain. All these things have their amusing side however, and one of the committee has offered me a directorship in their firm should I ever think of giving up music, and Barnes [secretary and manager of the Scottish Orchestra] agrees my powers of persuasion would make me the ideal League of Nations Minister. Seriously tho', I suppose any public person with ideals will always have to fight and overcome the petty and ignorant minds he must perforce be surrounded by...

On 26 May 1935 Delius's body was brought to Limpsfield churchyard in Surrey from its temporary resting-place in France. Barbirolli was one of the many musicians who attended the service.

Monday 27 May

...Found I had just time to shave before Ethel and Rae were due to call for me to go to the Delius funeral... It was a lovely afternoon and I did enjoy seeing a little country and the lovely smells that came from the may and I suppose other things which, although I am so ignorant, I can appreciate to the full... The spot they chose for Delius to rest in is so lovely, dear, that I couldn't help feeling a sense of happiness that he who had given so much loveliness of this same kind to us through his music was to be left amongst it for ever. The service was very simple, just a few prayers and a small section of the Philharmonic which played the *Summer Night on the River, Cuckoo in Spring, Serenade* from *Hassan* and *Elégie* for cello and orchestra. T.B. conducted, except for the *Elégie* which Beard did. The stone of the church was not the best sonority for that music, but T.B. has lovely feeling for it, and that part of it, and his very eloquent and dignified oration at the graveside, I like to think sum up all that is best in T.B. His love and championship of Delius I am sure is absolutely sincere... I forgot to tell you I spent Sat. rehearsing and recording with Lily Pons... The session was quite amusing, more or less with that type of songstress a case of 'chasing the Kadenz' and correspondingly not without its anxieties, but despite the fact that her average of notes in tune is about 60 p.c. we managed to make four sides. There is something wrong to me, however, in a musical world where PUBLICITY can put a 3rd rate singer like this into the position she holds...

This attitude, and his impatience with the Scottish Orchestra committee, were typical of Barbirolli. It was not that he took himself too seriously – he had enough humour, and to spare, to avoid that in the long run – but he took his work and music very seriously. His deep-rooted professionalism, and his memories of the kind of career his gifted father had, made him intolerant of two things in particular – facetiousness and an easy acceptance of the second-best. Much as he liked Gustav Holst, he detested the attitude represented by Holst's maxim 'If a thing's worth doing, it's worth doing badly.' It was his inability to compromise at that level that bedevilled his always uneasy relationship with Beecham, whom in some ways he admired and in others despised. He classed him, not inaccurately, with Delius as another amateur of genius. Geoffrey Toye, Beecham's manager at the Royal Opera House, wrote to Barbirolli at the end of June 'asking if I could see him next week, as both Sir T.B. and himself are *most anxious* that I should co-operate with them in their autumn season at C.G.' John was unable to find time for the

Covent Garden season but agreed to conduct *La Bohème* and *Tristan* on the tour. Rehearsals were held during the Covent Garden fortnight (23 September to 5 October) – this was the season when Beecham passed off the established English soprano Dora Labbette as the 'new find' Lisa Perli to prove that foreign names had more appeal for the public. John described his first rehearsal to Evelyn:

...Did some more *Bohème* and a little *Tristan* with orch: this morning. The latter very necessary as *at least four times* the show nearly *stopped* last night. It was the most disgraceful exhibition by a class company I have ever witnessed in a theatre. T.B. extremely friendly and listened to a lot of my *Bohème* (nearly all), put his arms round me and said 'John, it's grand to hear you conduct again, it sounds beautiful' etc. etc. The boys were asking me afterwards if he wants to marry me!! For the first time in our acquaintance he calls me nothing but John, my dear John, etc., and I went to supper with him after the show, at which he kept me till 2.30 a.m. Had the most amazing conversation with him, far too long to tell you here, but the gist of it is, he cannot (he says) any longer carry on alone with all his enterprises and must have a colleague, and 'My dear John there is nobody but you.' It is all a little puzzling, and as I am in the fortunate position of not caring whether it comes off or not, all rather amusing for the time being. The plan would be that I share his concerts and opera with him and conduct the Phil when he has to be away... T.B. himself referred to the whole show last night as 'the most extraordinary series of sounds I have heard during the last 15 years.' But it is not quite so funny when you realise he can be amused by what was in reality a sacrilege and an agony for any decent musician. What a mixture he is...

There had been lighter relief during August when John attended a summer school at St Andrews, with music in the day and evening, and other pleasures later, as he told Evelyn:

8 August 1935

...Was entertained today by the president of the Royal and Ancient...a very great privilege, and you will be glad to hear, my dearest, that I took my wine (a comprehensive term, this) not only like a gentleman but almost like a sponge. I am beginning to be rather terrified of my prowess. I went to bed at 2.45 a.m. after seeing almost everybody under the table and was cheerily standing Latto [David Latto, secretary of the Edinburgh Concert Society] a glass of Eno's at 7.45. Not so bad!!... The few hours I sleep I sleep well, and it is astonishing how you can go to bed after the most convivial of nights at 2 or 3 and rise perfectly fresh soon after 7...

Streatham, 11 August

St Andrews is one of the most enchanting towns I have been in...also the beautiful evening lights that one gets in the North, which throw into relief the ruins of the Castle and Cathedral which are on the sea front, make an evening walk there something quite magical... There is tremendous enthusiasm and it is rather lovely to see people of all ages (up to 65 or 70) playing away for dear life. One of my violas was a retired colonel (real thing) who weighs 22 stone, who will talk of nothing but string quartets, wine and food. He lives at Elgin and wants me to go and stay with him. We described various 'plats' and vintages to each other with what I can only describe as ravished relish. To hear him say, with a look of ineffable joy on his face, 'Absolutely top hole, my dear feller' was worth going miles for... On the last night I gave a spaghetti party to about 15 people and even the Provost came. I cooked 7 lb. of it in the university kitchens and made tons of sauce and it was a grand success. Even three helpings some had. The Provost toasted the 'cook', and as it was rather late, 1-15 or so, the company sang 'For he's' etc. and cheered *ppp*, a most *dramatic* effect.

Barbirolli's third season as conductor of the Scottish Orchestra began on 12 November 1935. He had carried his point, and the season was extended by two weeks, thanks mainly to the generous patronage of Mrs A. C. MacLeod, a member of the Ladies' Committee, who paid also for some of the expensive international soloists. (Years later her granddaughter, Ann Somervail, played in Barbirolli's Hallé.) Again the standard of soloists was high: the cellist Emmanuel Feuermann in Dvořák's concerto, Alexander Kipnis bass soloist in *Wotan's Farewell* and the *Death of Boris*, Heifetz playing the Brahms and Glazunov violin concertos, Egon Petri in Brahms's B flat and Liszt's first piano concertos, Thibaud in Lalo and Bach, Moiseiwitsch in Rachmaninov, Albert Sammons in Delius's violin concerto, and Gieseking. Evelyn gave the first performance of John's 'Pergolesi oboe concerto' on 17 December. Of the four movements, the first, *Largo*, was arranged from the *Stabat Mater*, the *Allegro* from a set of sonatas for two violins and bass, the *Andantino* from the song *Si tu m'ami*, and the final *Allegro* from another of the two-violin sonatas. Among the other works John conducted this season was Edward German's second symphony, the *Norwich*. He had long wanted to do this last-named work, ever since he had been moved by a letter from the composer in 1934 in which German said to him: 'I will die a disappointed man because my serious orchestral works have not been recognised. This has nothing to do with my lighter works which *have* been recognised. These latter, however, are as serious artistically as my heavier works!' He conducted the symphony first on 30 August 1935, at Eastbourne. He described it to me as 'the sort of symphony Elgar might have written at that date' (1893) and he always intended to revive it with the Hallé. He became friendly with German and also with that other excellent composer of light music Herman Finck, remembered principally for his tune 'In the Shadows.' His admiration for the best in light music – and he had heard much of it from his father – never left him and he detested snobbery about it. How much more inspired it was, he said, than a work like Tovey's opera *The Bride of Dionysus*, of which he remarked: 'It modulates on paper.'

As soon as the Scottish season ended, Barbirolli conducted opera in Edinburgh and Glasgow with Beecham's company from Covent Garden. In *Tristan*, the Isolde was Eva Turner, with Walter Widdop as Tristan, Allin as King Mark and Constance Willis as Brangäne. Eva Turner had been at the RAM with John and had been singing in Italy, under Toscanini's aegis, in the BNOC days. Thirty-six years after these *Tristan* performances she told me that she still remembered the thrill of the breadth and grandeur of Barbirolli's conducting of Act

II. 'You always felt safe with John,' she said. 'He was in complete control.'

At the end of March, after a London concert with Horowitz, he guest-conducted in Holland, and it was from The Hague on 1 April that he gave Evelyn more news of Judson's attempts to obtain for him some engagements in the United States.

> I have had *definite* offer of Minneapolis Dec. 28 to Jan. 24 and New York Phil. Jan. 25 to Feb 21. Scotland have equally definitely declined to release me (and incidentally seem very reluctant to pay me any more, tho' appreciating greatly my services!). There are various ways of looking at this, but I don't feel at all certain I would be altogether wise in pressing for release, tho' to turn down the New York Phil. is almost 'fantastische.' I send you this little item of news that you may turn it round in that good head of yours before I see you to talk to on Friday.

When Friday came there came also on that day, 3 April, a cable to Harold Holt from Judson in his capacity as manager of the Philharmonic-Symphony Society of New York. It said:

> Philharmonic-Symphony New York definitely offers Barbirolli 10 weeks November second January tenth inclusive. Suggest someone go to Glasgow to obtain his release. Immediate action important. Release in Glasgow for entire season seems wise, think I can book from four to six weeks additional Minneapolis. Judson.

In this way Barbirolli learned that he was in line for the coveted musical post left vacant by Arturo Toscanini's resignation from the New York conductorship. It was less than ten years since he had first conducted an opera in Newcastle upon Tyne and eight years since his first London symphony concert. He was taken aback and wrote to Evelyn a few days later: 'I am beset by such conflicting emotions of hope and despair.' He was to have every reason to be.

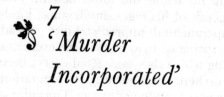

7 'Murder Incorporated'

The New York Philharmonic Orchestra gave its first concert on 7 December 1842. It was founded, as most of the world's great orchestras have been, on the initiative of a few dedicated enthusiasts. Its first English guest conductor was Henry Wood. For the 1909–10 and 1910–11 seasons Gustav Mahler was engaged. After the First World War great new personalities came to the rostrum, Wilhelm Furtwängler, Willem Mengelberg and, in 1926, Arturo Toscanini, then aged fifty-nine. In 1928 there was a merger with New York's other orchestra, the New York Symphony, and its title became the Philharmonic-Symphony Orchestra of New York. (It has now been changed back to New York Philharmonic.)

Toscanini visited New York again in 1927 and 1928, conducting nine weeks of the orchestra's season. He was appointed co-conductor with Mengelberg, but the double harness was doomed to failure, since each man disliked the other and made no secret of it. In 1929–30, he became principal conductor, having decided to end his nine-year tenure of La Scala, Milan, where his open detestation of the Fascists was making his position untenable. He conducted the first and the last seven weeks of the New York season, leaving the central section to guest conductors. The New York public began to idolise him. They had considered themselves at a disadvantage before Boston, which had Koussevitzky, and Philadelphia, which had Stokowski. Now they had the most publicised conductor in the world as well as, in the opinion of most critics and connoisseurs, the greatest. The orchestra's Sunday afternoon broadcasts took his name and music-making into thousands of homes. Legends of his rages, intolerance, kindnesses and general temperamental unpredictability spread like a prairie fire. In the spring of 1930 he took the orchestra on a European tour during which they were fêted everywhere they went. Already the orchestra was earning its reputation for giving a rough ride to every conductor except Toscanini – who terrorised them. When Stokowski went to New York as guest conductor for a fortnight in 1931 there was constant friction between the players and him.

From 1934 Toscanini conducted fewer of the New York concerts. The Depression had affected the box-office returns and the cost of having him as conductor was high. Yet men like Marshall Field and Clarence H. Mackay, president and chairman of the Philharmonic-Symphony Society, would make any sacrifice to keep his services – the Society even paid the tax on his hundred thousand dollar fee for each season. Arthur Judson and Bruno Zirato, manager and assistant manager, were briefed to do everything they could to keep Toscanini happy. Yet not everyone worshipped at the shrine. As early as 1930 a writer in the *American Mercury* said that Toscanini's 'phenomenal capacity for maintaining a persistent tempo with the mechanical rigidity of a metronome' had ruined an orchestra 'which achieved real greatness under Willem Mengelberg.' David Wooldridge in his book *Conductor's World* (1970) takes a dispassionate and cool view of the Maestro:

He combined the jealousy of Furtwängler and the vanity of Koussevitzky with the musical insensitivity of neither, and …successfully turned the musical life of New York over to the tender mercies of commercial exploitation and created of her musicians arrogant and swashbuckling caricatures of themselves.

These 'caricatures' were known throughout the musical world as 'Murder Incorporated', the toughest bunch of players gathered under one roof, perhaps because this kind of temperament can be infectious if it is present on the rostrum. Inevitably there would be a break between Toscanini and New York; the only question was how it would occur. According to Howard Taubman (*Toscanini*, 1951) the break came when Judson failed to consult him in 1935 over the engagement as a guest conductor of Beecham, of whom Toscanini had a very low opinion ('a buffoon'). He told the Society not to count on him for the 1936–37 season, and he refused to be enticed into changing his decision. This was in February 1936, and the Society immediately invited Furtwängler to be permanent conductor. But several members of the Philharmonic board kept alive their hope and belief that Toscanini could be persuaded back before too long.

The Furtwängler announcement provoked abuse and protest in New York. Many of the players were Jewish, and many were refugees from Nazi persecution. Furtwängler was widely regarded as a supporter of Hitler; when the criticisms of his likely appointment were published he sent a telegram to Judson on 15 March refusing the invitation on the ground that he was 'not a politician' and that politics and music were separate. However, Erno Balogh, an American music critic, wrote in the *Washington Sunday Star* of 6 September 1970 that Furtwängler told him in 1954 he had never seen the New York invitation and had not answered it. He was in Egypt at the time resting after an illness and he thought 'it might have been Goering who took care of the correspondence.' Be that as it may, New York was again without a conductor. As we have seen, Judson had been thinking of Barbirolli as a guest conductor in the second half of the season. Now he decided to offer him the first ten weeks and to entrust the last eight weeks to Artur Rodzinski, a protégé of Toscanini who was five years older than Barbirolli and was conductor of the Cleveland Orchestra. The middle six weeks were to be shared among Georges Enesco, Stravinsky and Carlos Chavez.

In England the offer to Barbirolli was a musical sensation. Apart from a minority who sensed and had faith in his artistry, he was regarded by the hierarchy as 'promising'. The BBC had given him several engagements to conduct sections of its symphony orchestra in broadcasts but had never offered him a Queen's Hall concert with the full orchestra – his name was down 'for consideration' at the time of the New York offer. This rankled at first, though he found it amusing later. Scotland, though proud of the honour that had come to 'their' conductor, were sorry to lose him, not least, in the words of a *Scotsman* leader-writer, because of 'his personal relations with the public.'

But no one was under any illusion about what awaited him. Francis Toye, in the *Morning Post*, wrote:

Barbirolli is one of the musicians who command the admiration of professionals more than the adulation of amateurs... And now he has gone to New York to tackle what we all know to be one of the most exacting, not to say ungrateful, jobs in the whole world of music... It may be doubted whether any musician in this or any other country envies him his job!... If all the admiration and enthusiasm lavished here on, say, Beecham, Furtwängler, Bruno Walter and Busch were rolled into one and multiplied several times over, it would not begin to approach the well-nigh fanatical adulation given to Toscanini... All the fierce fanaticism of New York was poured out on Toscanini; and that is why nobody envies Mr Barbirolli...for ignorance and prejudice will combine with genuine knowledge to make it doubly ungrateful.

Typically succinct was Adrian Boult's congratulatory letter to John: 'As I expect many kind people have been quick to tell you, the New York Philharmonic has not too grand a reputation in regard to its treatment of conductors, but I feel sure that you will get the better of them with your absolute knowledge of your scores and your quiet authority and understanding of all the problems involved.'

John had six months before he needed to sail for New York, six months in which to work and to worry, and he did both. In mid-April he took a short holiday in Hove so that he could spend some time in Sussex, walking to Rottingdean and over the Downs to Steyning. During May he began rehearsing the Royal Academy of Music students for two performances of Verdi's *Falstaff* (14 and 18 July) and two of Mackenzie's *The Cricket on the Hearth* (15 and 17 July). He wrote to Evelyn on 27 May:

I forgot to tell you I met Mr. [Walter] Price, one of the New York Philharmonic directors, last Friday at lunch. A dear old gentleman of 70, with a huge 'tummy' and the most delightful face. He was very interesting and helpful... and seemed to like me. One thing he said which was very nice to hear, 'I'm *crazy* for you to win.' Dearest, I wonder sometimes, but it is all part of our job to go through this.

In June, out of the blue, Gaisberg invited him to record the Beethoven and Brahms violin concertos with Kreisler and the London Philharmonic. Landon Ronald, the conductor who recorded regularly with Kreisler, was ill, and arrangements with the Jewish refugee Fritz Reiner had fallen through (Kreisler had in fact been racked by conflict between his real preference for Barbirolli and his fear that if he publicly passed over Reiner, Jewish circles would use the fact in propaganda against him).

The Beethoven concerto recording was begun on 16 June. John wrote to Evelyn that evening:

6 p.m.

...Today has been rather an historic one for me. I have met and made music with a great and lovable man. We have already made 6 sides in duplicate, and he told me it was 'beautiful to play with you.' After the first tutti he also said it 'could not be better.' All this gives me courage just now, dear. More I will tell you another time of his great simplicity and lovableness.

Kreisler and Barbirolli liked each other from the start, and Kreisler remained, for John, a god among violinists. But the admiration was not one-sided. At the time of his eightieth birthday, Kreisler said during an American broadcast in February 1955: 'I cannot tell you too much in praise of Barbirolli. He is the greatest conductor with whom I have appeared. Magnificent – that is the only word for him, and I feel very lucky to have had such great collaboration in my life.' Violinist and conductor shared a similar instinctive feeling for rubato, and this aspect of their mutual understanding is very evident in the two recordings they made together. The Brahms recording was begun on 19 June in very humid, sticky weather. 'We were all feeling exhausted before we began,' John recalled later. 'Going down the stairs to the recording studio Kreisler said: "Never mind. We shall feel better once we begin to play." And we did.' He gave Evelyn more detail:

20 June 1936

...Kreisler was as sweet as ever, he seems so happy playing with me. It is rather lovely, because he is so sensitive to any little thing I do, or that we do together, and looks up and smiles always when we bring off a special bit of 'artistry'. Léon [Goossens] played the solo* most beautifully... Also I must tell you we even made a record, the last, *without* rehearsing. K. said 'it is not necessary, let us just play'...

In the weeks before his departure for New York, John conducted several broadcast concerts. He spent the beginning of September with the family in Brighton, but he was not well although he enjoyed his walks over the Downs with his nephew Dick. He wrote to Evelyn: 'Walked to Falmer, a most delicious little hamlet I had never seen before, then through lovely valleys and farms till we came to the sea at Rottingdean. About 11 or 12 miles in all and not tiring as the turf is lovely to walk on. Ears still troubling me but head is better today. I do hope the ears will improve as it is rather worrying to have that continuous humming like telegraph wires in the wind and sometimes other strange sounds.' This was part of his sinus trouble.

On 21 October (Trafalgar Day, as he would certainly have noticed) he sailed for New York in the Cunard White Star liner *Aquitania*. 'I felt awfully homesick just after leaving the family at Southampton but must resign myself to these things,' he wrote to Evelyn.

I suppose I have come to a very vital moment in my career and the next month or so will decide a lot. I shall hope and try to do well, in fact I will do my damnedest but through it all I think of that little talk we had one evening at Woodingdean, when we walked near to the brow of the hill overlooking Ovingdean and you made me understand to my

* The long oboe solo at the start of the slow movement. Barbirolli had an interesting theory about this passage. He thought the end was weakened by the flute's taking over – obviously because the continuation was dangerously high for the oboe after a long solo. He believed Brahms made this transfer only from necessity, and he wanted to try it with the oboe continuing.

intense joy that you were one with me in understanding and realising that in things like the church at Poynings, and the ineffable peace that falls on our countryside, are to be found the things that matter and that never grow less, and that above all never let you down, but are there to receive and solace you when your need comes... I have worked like a Trojan and memorised (as far as is possible to do this sort of thing) my first programme in case they want any of that sort of nonsense for the first show. Eight hours a day and more have I done. I keep well, the only thing is that I continue very deaf. Do hope this clears up in a day or two.

If his engagement for New York had caused a sensation in Great Britain it had aroused every kind of curiosity in the United States. To the ordinary concert-goer he was probably completely unknown; to the connoisseur his name was perhaps familiar from his recordings. Columns were devoted to speculation about the likelihood of Barbirolli's success or otherwise. The general tone was akin to the thoughts of the Roman audiences who waited for the Christians to be thrown to the lions.

The 'victim' made a good impression at his first press conference on arrival on 27 October. ' "I do not intend to follow in the Maestro's footsteps," he said slowly and forcefully,' the *New York Times* reported. 'No one can do that. Toscanini is unique. His going marks the end of an era for the orchestra. As for myself, I feel that music must go on. I am a simple person who is passionately in love with music. I wish to serve it. I hope you Americans will like me.' He had been met at the boat by Judson's assistant, Bruno Zirato; the press manager of the Philharmonic; the librarian and the orchestral manager. 'They all seem out to help all they can,' John wrote to Evelyn. He settled at Essex House, 160 Central Park South, and soon met the critics for a two-hour session of questions ('I don't think they've met anything quite like me before') and the leader (concert master, in American) of the orchestra, the Russian Mishel Piastro, a superb violinist. (Someone once said to Kreisler, 'What a pity Piastro is *so* gifted but that he's so lazy and doesn't practise.' Kreisler replied, 'Thank God.')

With Zirato, an Italian, and Piastro, John quickly became firm friends. They soon made him aware of the immense influence exerted on the Philharmonic by the society women of New York who were among the orchestra's richest and most voluble patrons – Vanderbilts, Astors, Whitneys, Fields, all the names were there. Most of them had been Toscanini-worshippers and were now gathering round the guillotine waiting for the knife to fall on the sacrificial head of the young man from England who, they had learned with dismay, had only been conductor of a provincial orchestra in Scotland, not one of the main London orchestras. This, and the ferocious reputation of the Philharmonic players, was enough to make Barbirolli apprehensive; he also learned from Judson of the professional jealousy of his compatriot, Beecham, who had *not* been invited to be among the guest conductors. John never forgave Beecham for this conduct and, as will be seen, it was to have its repercussions on his early years with the Hallé.

On the Friday after his arrival the Philharmonic gave a lunch in Barbirolli's honour. Among the guests were Robert and Dorothy Mayer, who had travelled with him in the *Aquitania*. 'On his arrival,' Sir Robert recalls, 'John soon discovered that the majority of the members of the board were against him. At the lunch I sat between two ladies of famous lineage, one of whom was violently pro and the other even more so against J.B.' Neither, of course, could have based her opinion on any practical experience of his work. At 11.30 p.m. on Saturday 31 October, he wrote his first New York letter to Evelyn:

...I have a most beautiful suite on the 30th floor overlooking Central Park, the most beautiful situation in the City perhaps and at this height very quiet. I have had lots of unexpected work to do, as Toscanini had apparently his own music and has taken it with him, so that everything I haven't brought with me has had to be bowed and I have had to sit up each night till about 1 preparing the masters. Piastro the leader I have met. He seems very nice and one good thing, he thinks the programmes 'wonderful'. So many things the orchestra haven't played, yet nothing 'outré'.

Yesterday I made my first speech at a luncheon given in my honour and everyone seemed delighted. The kindness of everyone here is beyond belief. Judson and the office staff are as sweet to me as possible and had a perfect dinner at

Judson's the other night, where I was initiated into the activities, nefarious and otherwise, of the ladies connected with the Society.

The most wonderful news to date tho' is that the hall is already *sold out* for Thursday and that the subscriptions stand *higher* than they have done for *years*.

Now remains the most *critical* moment of all – my meeting with the orchestra on Monday. I hope and pray it will go well and that I shall be able to give all I have to the Society. They badly need a period when it is *Music* that matters and not personalities and under the right circumstances I think I can give them that. You, my love, are a great inspiration to me...and with the strength you bring me I shall go forth with courage and hope.

P.S. Judson told me T.B.'s fury at my engagement unbelievable and that he has letters I would hardly believe possible. This for your private information.

The first rehearsal was on 2 November. For his opening pair of concerts (Thursday evening and Friday afternoon) his programme was:

Berlioz: Overture – *Carnaval Romain*
Bax: Symphonic Poem – *The Tale the Pine Trees Knew*
Mozart: Symphony No. 36 in C Major (K. 425)
Brahms: Symphony No. 4 in E Minor, Op. 98

The Bax was new to America and was probably an unwise, though a loyal, choice in the circumstances. (When John was told in 1966 that it had been recorded he wrote to Millicent Allbrow, secretary of Bradford Record Circle: 'I am surprised it has even been attempted by a semi-amateur body because I have always found it a very difficult piece, not only with English orchestras, but also the best American ones.')

Much has been written about Barbirolli's time in New York, but whatever may be the verdict on it is incontrovertible that he immediately won, and kept, the devotion of the orchestra. His first rehearsals and the first concert on 5 November were described vividly in letters to Evelyn. It is evident that the shadow of Toscanini was across the proceedings:

Monday, or rather Tuesday
12.30 a.m.

...Rehearsal I am happy to tell you was a huge success.
Orchestra most attentive, anxious to give, and sensitive.
Piastro (the leader) was very delighted and happy, and said
it was just 'making music with me.' They loved the Bax
and I wish you could hear the strings play the middle
section (really marvellous quality). There are possibilities
of making a *great* orchestra if all continues well. They have
had a long summer season under various conductors, and
the tone has roughened a bit, but even by the end of the
morning they were already making some lovely sounds.
The Mozart none of them had ever played* and they loved
that too: They seem to like playing in that singing way I
like, and it is an orchestra much more responsive, I should
imagine, to a Latin than a German...

I gather that everyone likes me very much and this
makes me happy rather, for it would be grand to make a
success of this. Some of them came to my room too, to tell
me how much they had enjoyed it, and this is after all a
great tribute from an orchestra that was reputed to refuse
to play for anyone but Toscanini. I had your letter and
your cable in my pocket when I took my stand where just a
short while ago 'he' had stood...

P.S. The orchestra, you will be glad to hear, is all *against*
memory conductors, and tell me they have had some terrible times with some of these gentlemen.

The orchestra as a whole were taken aback by Barbirolli's
youthful appearance. His first words to them were: 'Gentlemen, I may be a good conductor or a very bad one. I know you
to be members of a magnificent orchestra. Are you going to be
with me, for I can do nothing without your friendly co-operation and encouragement? With it, I think I can deliver the
goods.' The principals then rose to shake his hand. His personality had won them over. Three hours later so had his
musicianship.

Carnegie Hall was full for the first concert, which was a
lustrous social occasion and was followed by a party given by
Mrs Vincent Astor, chairman of the Auxiliary (Ladies') Board

* Probably some of them had, under Beecham, 6–8 April 1932.

and a member of the board of directors. John had spent the previous evening looking through his scores and reading a life of Pasteur. He began his letter to Evelyn at 2.30 a.m. on 6 November.

My beloved. Have just returned from Mrs Astor's party and just want to write you a word before going to bed... The concert was a great success. Packed house, lovely audience and a reception they tell me only reserved for Toscanini as a rule. Orchestra played magnificently and I was very happy all through the concert... The orchestra much to everybody's astonishment seem devoted to me, and 'fuss' around me just like my own Scottish. Yesterday morning during rehearsal someone was heard to remark, 'Shut your eyes and you'd think the "old man" (Toscanini) was here.' I don't think anything lovelier could come to my ears...

The critics next day were more favourable than could have been expected, even Olin Downes of the *New York Times*. Downes, a devoted admirer of Toscanini, had savagely criticised Barbirolli's engagement as unworthy of an orchestra like the Philharmonic and was to be a thorn in his flesh for the next seven years. But now he wrote:

Mr Barbirolli makes his orchestra *sound*. His predilection is for a full-blooded tone, and his excitement was felt by the audience. Also evident was a tension and lack of composure very understandable in the circumstances... The best part of the evening was offered by the last two movements of the Fourth Brahms Symphony, where there was exceptional virility, grip and lyrical opulence... In general this was a red-blooded, dramatic and grandly constructed reading.

Lawrence Gilman, of the *Herald Tribune*, stated that by the end of the concert Barbirolli

had won the respect of the knowing ones among the audience... [He] is something better and rarer and finer than a conductor of power and sensibility... He has disclosed himself as a musician of taste and fire and intensity, electric, vital, sensitive, dynamic, experienced...who has mastered not only his temperament but his trade.

Oscar Thompson, in *Musical America*, summed up the audience's reaction thus:

If there was no sensation, certainly there was nothing of frost. Mr Barbirolli was liked, but not altogether 'placed'. If the newcomer was nervous, the signs of it were not to be noted in his demeanour. He came briskly to the platform and went as briskly about the business of making music. A listener who was late in reaching his seat in the middle of one of the front rows, after the intermission, found himself the object of a podium stare that continued until its object had settled into his chair.

What the critics did not know was that the orchestra had sent a telegram to the chairman of the Scottish Orchestra committee saying simply 'Thanks for Barbirolli.'

To read through the names of the hundred-odd players is to realise what a polyglot orchestra it was. Williams, Lucas and Clarke were completely outnumbered by Katz, Fishberg, de Stefano, Dubensky, Schulze, Roelofsma, Schenk, Rabinowitz and dozens more of European emigré extraction. Among them were some great individual instrumentalists: Piastro, the leader, and his assistant John Corigliano (who became leader in 1943); the Russian principal cellist (1936–37 was his first season) Joseph Schuster had been for five years principal of the Berlin Philharmonic under Furtwängler until 1934; two Hungarians, Imre Pogany and Zoltan Kurthy, led, respectively, the second violins and the violas; another Russian, Simeon Bellison, was principal clarinet and the first horn was Bruno Jaenicke, a German who had spent some years in the Boston Symphony Orchestra; the timpanist, Saul Goodman, is regarded by some as the greatest they have heard; first trumpet was Harry Glantz, another Russian, who had gone to America when he was five – he was the hero (or villain) of the celebrated retort to Rodzinski when that conductor was ill-advised enough to ask the orchestra for suggestions which might improve the performance of a Mahler symphony: 'Yep. Send for Bruno Walter.' The principal oboe (since 1918) was an Italian named Bruno Labate, a little man who was fearless enough to have argued with Toscanini about the phrasing in Rossini overtures, insisting that he knew better than the Maestro. He was so short that when he stood up, the other players would shout 'Stand up when you address the conductor.' He could not cope with long words and even abbreviated Maestro to Maestr'. He referred to Otto Klemperer as 'Mr Klemps,' and when Barbirolli arrived at rehearsal on one occasion Labate asked: 'Maestr', we play Moz?' to which the Maestr' replied: 'No, Schub.' Barbirolli inherited from Toscanini a wonderfully large string section: eighteen first violins, sixteen seconds, twelve violas, twelve cellos and nine basses, a total of sixty-seven.

In those days (and with the Scottish Orchestra) Barbirolli had his first violins on his left, seconds on his right, cellos on his left behind the first violins, violas and harps behind the second violins. Basses were at the left rear of the orchestra, stretching across the back row as far as the percussion team. In the woodwind, the front desks were flutes (left), oboes and cor anglais (right), clarinets and bassoons behind them, and horns and celesta behind them. Trumpets, trombones and tuba occupied the penultimate row. He explained in the summer of 1936 in a talk at his second St Andrews summer school why he favoured this system: 'Some conductors like the second violins on the same side as the first violins because, they say, it is much easier for the ensemble. That is true enough, but I find that it is outweighed by the disadvantages when the conductor does not hear the distinction clearly enough when the passages go from the first to the second violins.' He adopted the system of all the violins on his left and the cellos on his right at the front later in his New York period and usually followed this seating plan with the Hallé in the Free Trade Hall.

The Philharmonic pattern was for the two Thursday and Friday concerts to be followed by a 'popular' Saturday (evening) and Sunday (afternoon and broadcast) programme. For his first weekend concerts on 7 and 8 November, Barbirolli kept the Bax and the Brahms but substituted for the Berlioz and Mozart the Purcell Suite which he had arranged for his Chenil Galleries chamber orchestra and Elgar's *Enigma Variations*.

Sunday 12.45 a.m.
[8 November]

...Have just finished my little supper after my 3rd concert since Thursday, and am too exhausted to write but before going to bed just want to tell you we played the 'Enigma' tonight (received with great enthusiasm) and that you, my Evelyn, were so much in my thoughts and in my heart during the performance. I wish you could have heard it. The sound this orchestra can make, and they play as if they loved me, makes it almost unbearable at moments...

Arthur Judson told me that

at that time I was not proposing that Sir John should succeed Toscanini. No matter what young conductor should succeed him there would be no possibility that the public and critics would accept a young man. At that time I intended to propose the engagement of Sir John for concerts in the next season. Before I could do this a member of the board who knew Sir John well asked me when I was going to propose Sir John as a successor to Toscanini. I told this director I had no intention of doing that but would suggest him as a guest conductor. At the next meeting of the board this director proposed that Sir John be engaged as a permanent conductor of the Philharmonic and be given a contract for three years. The board concurred and ordered it done.

However, John's letters to Evelyn suggest that Judson's memory has drawn out events. This letter, for example, which contains the first hint of a permanent engagement, was written *only five days* after his first Carnegie Hall concert:

You will be glad to hear I know that my first week has been a tremendous success and Judson is delighted. I receive letters and telegrams from all over the place and my first broadcast brought me letters and telegrams including a very sweet one from [Eugene] Ormandy. Other colleagues (conductors here) whose names you would not know come to rehearsals and concerts and write to me or wire me, so that at any rate they have better manners than in my own country... The orchestra quite openly clamour for my appointment, and Judson says that he has had men coming to him about me, a thing that has never happened before! Dearest, the following is for your own private ear alone... Judson wants to know if I am entirely free next year as he hopes to offer me the *permanent* conductorship of the orchestra. I have said I am free to come if they want me. I know what this involves, but I really don't feel there is any reason why I should stay in England. Here all the leading musicians and one of the finest orchestras in the world put me in the class of one worthy to lead them and to be the successor to Toscanini. In London I apparently don't even rank with Sargent, Heward and Lambert. I have heard further of T.B.'s doings here regarding me and he is even a dirtier dog than I thought.

All this is of course only what Judson and some others want, but as the orchestra seem to want it too, I hope it will materialise. Those in London who were so sorry for me will now have to change their tune considerably... I am well, though I find this climate very tiring and the concerts exhaust me greatly. It is curious that conducting an orchestra like this is more tiring, because the magnificence and opulence of it seem to affect you spiritually and nervously even more.

Enclose you some notices. *Gilman* is the most important man here and the others Judson is delighted with the tone of them. Just what he wanted, because I gather they are a terrible bunch here. The takings for the first week are nearly 2000 dollars above the corresponding period last year.

Again reflected in John's letters is the way he won over the orchestra.

Wednesday evening 11.45
[11 November]

...The orchestra continues to work splendidly for me, and from outside sources I hear the men are 'crazy' about me. I would like to tell you of one thing that happened today, which did make me rather happy. I had been rehearsing the Beethoven 2nd Symphony, and all through it seemed as if I was shedding rather new light on it for them, but just before the end I asked them to do something which seemed quite natural and simple to me, when, led by some of the wind, the whole orchestra broke out into a 'Bravo Maestro', which I must say, coming from this particular bunch and

their experience with Toscanini, touched me greatly. I also
had to rehearse *very hard* (would you believe it) the *Götterdämmerung* music, and far from seeming to take it
amiss, many came to tell me how lovely and interesting it is
to rehearse with me and how wonderful they think some of
the things I do – which are only what is written, plus I
hope a little understanding...

Sunday morning
[15 November]

...Thursday was a heavy day, and after the concert Judson
very sweetly took me home with him for supper. I did not
get back till after 2, and Friday we had the repeat performance. After that I had to attend a reception in my honour
given by Smith College, where I had to stand and receive
about 5 or 600 females. There was a terrific crush as I
apparently seem to have taken New York by storm and
everyone wanted to be there. I was desperately tired afterwards, so I just took Piastro...out for a meal. We found a
fine old chop house and we had a grand mixed grill and a
bottle of wine.

About the Beethoven–Wagner, this turned out a
triumph beyond my wildest expectations. There I was
really on *his* ground, but even some of the *older* members
of the Philharmonic Committee said they had never heard
such a performance of the 2nd Symphony, and Piastro tells
me the unanimous praise of the orchestra of my Wagner is
extraordinary. Even the German members, who usually
cavil at something, loved it... For your *private* ear: Zirato
spoke to me yesterday and it seems they are toying with the
idea of offering me the permanent conductorship over a
number of years, a thing they have never done before.

He wrote to his fellow Wagnerian, Charles Parker, to tell
him that 'it was a great thrill to do the *Götterdämmerung*...
with the full Wagner orchestra, tubas etc., about 115 all told.
Also I know you will rejoice to hear that after my performance of the "Enigma" we had many letters asking for a *repeat*... So you see I have quietly begun my Elgar propaganda.
We are fortunate people you and I, Charlie, who know and
realise the greatness of this man, for we have been enriched

beyond measure...' John received splendid reviews from both Downes and Gilman for his first Wagner, the latter bluntly saying: 'Here, to the amazement and delight of incredulous Wagnerians, emerged the veritable authentic Wagner.'

The physical strain of these first days was considerable. His attack of deafness had gone but he found sleeping difficult and he was afflicted with severe headaches. No doubt, too, he disliked the social side of New York but realised it was expected of him. As one New York paper wrote: 'John Barbirolli is entering upon the severest test that an orchestral conductor must face in this town – which is neither the critics nor the musicians but the society ladies who pay the bills... Most conductors have to play the society game here if they want to get along.' The 'society game' also involved such journalism as this – about the Smith College Club reception – from 'Simon Snooper' in the *Musical Courier*: 'The only way I could spot him [J.B.] was to search madly in the most crowded corner of the room. At last I spied him knee deep in feminine allure. Girls from the twenties to the sixties were having the time of their lives – and John was enjoying it all excessively. The good humour of that chap is amazing.'

He became a member of the Century Club on West 43rd Street:

I have just dined here alone, the first time I seem to have had a meal alone for ages and I must say I enjoyed it. This is not meant to be ungracious for everyone is so kind, but you will understand. I believe I told you in an earlier letter what a nice place this was. One of the oldest clubs in New York and very old-fashioned, rather like the Athenaeum in London. Members are nearly all old gentlemen, it is very peaceful and all the servants are darling old Negroes. I have had a very simple and excellent dinner, such a dinner as we enjoyed in York, my darling, steak, cheese and a nice half bottle of claret...

Have heard more of T.B.'s nefarious doings here and really he is the limit... When the conductors for this season were announced, would you believe he *sank so low* as to write and say he was 'appalled' at their choice.

Among the works Barbirolli conducted during November and December were Vaughan Williams's *Job* (complete),

Schubert's Second Symphony (for the first time in New York and, it was thought, America), Philip James's overture *Bret Harte* (first performance), and Rossini's overtures *The Siege of Corinth* and *La Gazza Ladra*, the latter having surprisingly never been conducted in New York by Toscanini. For almost all concerts the hall was full, and the Society enrolled new subscribing members. It could not be denied that Judson's faith in Barbirolli was being handsomely justified artistically and financially.

He spent his thirty-seventh birthday on 2 December rehearsing with Heifetz for Sibelius's concerto – 'very difficult work this to make sound' – and was surprised by his first encounter with a ceremony which is now almost *de rigueur*. 'Apparently there is a traditional birthday song here, "Happy birthday to you." Without any signs of anything unusual when I brought down the stick to start the rehearsal, instead of playing the Liszt piece, they played this song for me and then clapped and cheered. So much for their being the "rotters" they have been depicted.'

Five days later, on Monday 7 December, John was able to give Evelyn news of the first official steps towards his permanent appointment.

Monday night

A special meeting of the Executive Council of the Society was called today to discuss my appointment and I heard from Judson at 5.30 it was unanimously decided I be appointed General Music Director and Conductor of the New York Philharmonic for the next three years. This, though, has to be confirmed by the Ladies' Board which does not meet till Thursday. If all goes as is hoped, it will be the most extraordinary thing imaginable and a wonderful victory in a few short weeks. It has been precipitated, I gather, by the request of many people, *unanimous wish of the orchestra*, which was sent to the Board by 4 of their representatives, and the *Box Office*. At the end of my fifth week I am nearly 8,000 dollars ahead of Klemperer last year. The love the men have for me is becoming something really touching, and it is based they say on the thrills they have playing for me... I do work and study hard always to try and be a little worthy of it all. If this comes off it is going to mean a big re-organization of my whole life.

On the 10th the Ladies' Board ratified the appointment.

11 December, 2.20 a.m.

Earlier in the evening I sent you a cable announcing my appointment here, which makes me virtual dictator of the New York Philharmonic till 1940. I have no words in which to express my joy and, I may perhaps be forgiven, my pride in this appointment, for in one of the most difficult situations in the world, and in the face of extreme scepticism, after 5 weeks or so of my work, your John has been *unanimously* selected to direct the destinies of this great organisation. The orchestra played tonight as something I have dreamed of, not, my love, that I forget what the Scottish has done for me, but occasionally with a loveliness of string tone and natural artistry that is rather exquisite... The emotion of the orchestra at my appointment is something too touching for words... I can't believe I am worthy of all this, but you might make me so, as you have already made me do things beyond my power...

The Philharmonic's announcement of the appointment said that it marked 'a new era' and reminded the public that for 1937–38 the orchestra would have a permanent conductor for the entire season for the first time since 1920–21. In Barbirolli they had found 'a young conductor of artistic integrity' who could build for the future and a man 'strong enough to mould the orchestra into a consistent personality and technical unity.' They pointed to 'the amazing growth in attendance' since his arrival. A leader in the *New York Times*, presumably by Downes, pointed out that the appointment 'marks the end of the star-conductor system' and suggested that Barbirolli's engagement for one year 'would have seemed a more prudent course.' W. J. Henderson in the *Sun* was equally doubtful about the wisdom of the appointment. 'Already Mr Barbirolli has been extolled as few other musicians have been in this city and he has also been the cause of perceptible shaking of heads.' But they all wished him luck, with the implication 'he'll need it.'

News of his appointment was in the New York papers on 11 December. On 18 December two of the Philharmonic directors gave a dinner in honour of the orchestra and its conductor. When John arrived home after midnight he wrote at once to Evelyn:

That so soon after Toscanini's leaving, this orchestra could be so bound up in me and...to have heard the toast 'Barbirolli' responded to with such fervour and acclaim by this great orchestra will remain an unforgettable experience... The first horn [Jaenicke] spoke for the orchestra. A magnificent artist and a very serious man. (A German.) He spoke of the various ways they have made music in recent years. Because they were paid; because they were afraid and intimidated; and now 'with Mr B. for the *joy* of making music.' I don't think the greatest orator could have thought of anything more beautiful to say.

At the end of the season he sailed for home in the s.s. *Washington*. The voyage gave him the chance to write to some of his friends, notably his fellow-cellist 'Dot' Mulholland:

16 January 1937 [post mark]

...As you know I have been appointed for 3 years and I must confess I shall not be sorry to leave England. It is a humiliating thought, because I love that land with all my heart and soul, but what I have had to give it musically doesn't seem to have mattered much except to a few very dear people. To those who have understood and believed, I shall ever be very deeply grateful, but I will say this for the Americans, they were not afraid because I was young to accept me.

In spite of this disillusionment, he plunged wholeheartedly into the second half of the Scottish Orchestra's season (the first half had been conducted by Georg Szell, who eventually succeeded Barbirolli as the orchestra's conductor), although he did not, as had been advertised, conduct Walton's Symphony in his first programme on 21 January 1937. For some reason he abandoned this work, which would surely have been ideal for him, and never conducted it (although just before he died he told me he was going to have 'another look at it'). On a guest engagement with the Hallé on 4 February, he conducted the first of the many performances he was to give in Manchester of Elgar's Second Symphony.

For his last weeks with them the Scottish basked in their conductor's reflected glory. Members of the orchestra had greeted him at Glasgow Central Station on his return with 'See the Conquering Hero Comes.' (What they did not know till some weeks later was that he had arrived by an earlier train, but when he heard what was planned he went back to the station and was 'met.') After the Glasgow and Edinburgh series had ended, he took the orchestra on a tour of Scotland. It was a delightful feature of his character that he would put as much effort and artistry into, and derive as much pleasure from, a concert with the Scottish in Elgin as into a New York Philharmonic occasion. His work in Glasgow was a crucial part of his career. He restored the orchestra and its financial situation; and it never looked back. When, in 1950, the orchestra was put on a stronger, all-the-year-round basis as the Scottish National Orchestra, no one was more delighted than Barbirolli. He was glad, too, to be instrumental in 1959 in recommending a young musician whose work he admired, Alexander Gibson, as its permanent conductor and to see him lead the orchestra to new heights and found Scottish Opera.

While Barbirolli was taking the Scottish Orchestra round Scotland, events were happening in New York which were radically to alter the musical climate there. One man in particular had been hurt that no one had notified him of Barbirolli's three-year contract – Toscanini. *He* had never been offered a three-year contract, he complained. Probably he expected Barbirolli's first ten weeks in 1936 to be a failure, and he would not have been human if he had not felt a pang to see 'his' orchestra handed over to this newcomer. At any rate when the critic Samuel Chotzinoff was sent by David Sarnoff, president of the Radio Corporation of America, to Lake Maggiore to tell him of his plan to form, specially for the Maestro, a new radio symphony orchestra, Toscanini agreed to return. Thus it was ensured that Barbirolli would not only have to compete with New York's memories of its idol, but with the idol himself, conducting broadcast concerts to which there was no admission fee.

Towards the end of March 1937, Barbirolli made some more recordings with Heifetz and confirmed his engagement to conduct at Covent Garden during the Coronation season. 'They have offered me £60 a show and to do *Tosca* and *Turandot.* Far better than I expected.' He was also preoccupied with the unhappy business of divorce from Marjorie. In January 1936 she had been granted an order for restitution of conjugal rights. By the end of 1937 John's desertion would have lasted three years, grounds for a decree nisi. It had long been understood between Evelyn and him that they would marry as soon as he was free, and before he returned to New York they had a long talk together in which John again stressed the strength and importance of his love for his family. He followed this with this significant letter:

I put my feelings for my family so strongly before you because I want to be as honest as I can with you... When I say I could not marry you if you did not love them I mean this. If you had not been able to respond to the very great, genuine and deep affection they feel for you, and the simplicity and honesty of their welcome, you would not have been the Evelyn I loved in my heart and I would have feared for the future. But I have no doubts... As for my need of you, I can tell you Evelyn that that is of an entirely *different* nature... I don't even mean always your physical nearness but that wonderful warmth of inspiration that I have known since I first came to love you. What your belief in me means, you well know. I hope it will be given to me to try to repay it, by the dedication to you of such gifts of living and work as may have been granted to me...

After a studio concert with the BBC Symphony Orchestra, Barbirolli began his rehearsals at Covent Garden. 'Met T.B.,' he wrote to Evelyn, 'who was full of "my dear John," drinks and cigars and congratulations. The ******* (think of the worst words you know).' Puccini was still regarded by many London critics of this date as a rather cheap and inferior composer, and Barbirolli's *Tosca* and *Turandot* performances were received with no special insight although they have since become legendary, especially the *Turandot*, of which recordings exist. They preserve the thrill of the singing of Eva Turner and of Giovanni Martinelli (his first Calaf), the fervour of the conducting, the fine playing of the LPO and the poor standard of the chorus. In the first performance of *Tosca*, which Toscanini attended, Martinelli sang Cavaradossi, Gina Cigna was Tosca and Lawrence Tibbett was Scarpia.

This was a brilliant musical season: not only the opera but Toscanini and the BBC Symphony Orchestra, Furtwängler and the Berlin Philharmonic, recitals by Tibbett, Tauber, Gigli, Flagstad and Menuhin, and a Kreisler concert, with the LPO conducted by Barbirolli. But, as everywhere else in the world, Toscanini was the principal attraction. Barbirolli attended one of the concerts and his description of it to Evelyn is worth quoting at length:

May, 1937

...Had lunch with Martinelli [a fellow Venetian]... He is really a dear fellow. We talked a lot about various things and he said how he would love to work with me again, specially if we could have lots of rehearsals as he found lots I had to say about music so interesting and sincere, and because all the artists want to do their best for me. From an old campaigner like that it was nice to hear.

The concert on Wednesday was most interesting, and as always with him [Toscanini], left me food for thought, which as you know is what I like to get from a man of that standard. The orchestra played splendidly, with great enthusiasm but definite roughness of tone, and the wind solos very uneven... They started with the Corelli *Follia* variations, strings only. Here, splendid as the performance was, there was never a real piano, and the forcing of the tone created a roughness that was strangely in contrast with the usual dictates of beauty of sound above all. The Busoni piece [*Rondo Arlecchino*] was really, as far as I could gather, magnificently done. Queer music this, rather arid and sardonic, and I certainly should not like to hear a 2nd rate performance.

The Ravel *Daphnis and Chloë* (beautiful piece) was I suppose good, but I ask altogether different sonorities for this kind of music. It is all quite clear etc., but it sounds rather insensitive to me, and that certain 'shimmering' quality some pages should have was for me entirely missing. The final Dance, which demands energy and climax, of course was splendid, though here again the brass overblew all the time, and the last few pages of the score was all percussion with a little brass audible. I don't think the Toscanini of a few years ago would have been satisfied with this. I am beginning to think that his really great assets are a tremendous rhythmic driving force, a passionate *energy* (not a *lyrical* passion) and at times in the earlier classics (and I should imagine in Beethoven) a fine beautiful line.

Curiously enough for a man of his age an almost complete lack of *serenity*. This I had noticed especially in his *Meistersinger* performance a year ago. I wonder if there is not, behind this, a psychological reason, namely, an intense desire to prove to himself, and of course to others, that he is not getting old. He need not fear, for there are certainly no traces of that, but it seems now as I said earlier on, to drive him to force everything in vigorous and loud playing. Also I would never call him a subtle person. The Coriolanus I have in mind rather darker and more brooding, but it was splendid all the same.

Brahms [First Symphony] was the most disappointing of the evening. Strangest of all he seemed so uncertain of tempo in the first movement, ploughing on unmercifully when a little tenderness and ease would not be amiss, and rather pulling unnecessarily in other places. The 2nd movement I frankly did not like at all. I happened to pick up a *Telegraph* at C.G. today, and reading between the lines I am sure anyone but him, or rather, specially me, would have got it in the neck for some of the things that took place. The 3rd and last were the best, 3rd especially lovely. Finale fine, but again all the timpani and brass forced to the last degree, also be it whispered (for these things I suppose must not be said out loud) he has added *timpani* parts here and there to help the climaxes. That I would not have believed of him...

Gratitude for all I can get from him must not blind me to what I sincerely feel is not the last word in certain things and aspects of orchestral performance. There are certain things he does which sound so inevitable that there is no greater joy than to listen to them, and I like to pay him the tribute of listening with all the mind, heart and sincerity of which I am capable. Spineless adulation must have no place in dealing with such a truly magnificent artist.

I saw him after the concert again this morning. He is always very sweet to me (this rather hurt a bit with what we know) and offered me the parts of the Cherubini (which he has edited) to make a score if I like to play it. But I am glad that at any rate he observes the decencies of professional etiquette on the surface, whatever he may have in mind. Also I suspect he is human enough to enjoy the implied flattery (not that I go there for that) of my being at rehearsal...

The remainder of the summer Barbirolli spent working on New York programmes and studying the scores of three hundred new works. 'To read certain articles in French and other foreign musical magazines,' he wrote to Charles Parker, 'there would seem to be many [new masterpieces], but closer inspection rather finds them dwindling till at last they are non-existent.'

He sailed for New York in October in the *Britannic*. A writer in the *Daily Sketch* rhetorically asked why Britain had let him go and gave as the answer: 'His fault was that he was British and did not belong to the old Royal College tie brigade which controls British music.' In this respect it is interesting to quote from a letter which Eugene Ormandy, conductor of the Philadelphia Orchestra, wrote to Fred Gaisberg of HMV on 16 January 1937:

What do you think of the engagement of Barbirolli? I not only think he is an excellent conductor but I am convinced that he deserved the job. The Philharmonic Orchestra plays better for him than it did for any other conductor outside of Toscanini, and that means a great deal. They all like him personally and musically. Now I hope that his countrymen will feel the same way about him as the Americans do. In music there should be no politics, and they should accept a person for what he is worth; and Barbirolli is certainly worth a good deal.

Even more outspoken had been Francis Toye's letter to John himself (4 December 1936): 'Between you and me, I have always felt that not only as regards yourself but as regards practically all important English musicians except Beecham, my colleagues do not do their duty.'

Barbirolli's first full New York season as the Philharmonic's permanent conductor was important enough in itself: under the shadow of Toscanini's return to start a new orchestra it took on additional stature and excitement. He had arranged an attractive and wide-ranging series of programmes: a feature of his New York period, scarcely appreciated at the time, was the amount of contemporary or unfamiliar music he included, particularly American music. Among the novelties of the 1937–38 season were the first performance of the Purcell–Barbirolli Suite for strings, four horns, two flutes and cor anglais, the first American performances of Bartók's *Music for Strings, Percussion and Celesta*, Poulenc's Double Piano Concerto, Daniel Gregory Mason's *Lincoln Symphony*, Bax's Third Symphony, Elgar's Violin Concerto (with Heifetz), Delius's *Dance Rhapsody* and *Appalachia** and Malipiero's Second Symphony. Among the soloists who played concertos with him were Artur Rubinstein, Gieseking, Josef Hofmann, the eleven-year-old Julius Katchen, Mischa Levitzki, Efrem Zimbalist, Szigeti and Piatigorsky. He conducted an all-Strauss concert, several Wagner concerts with Kirsten Flagstad, Marjorie Lawrence and Charles Kullmann as singers, and great classic works like Berlioz's *Symphonie Fantastique* and

---

* After the performance of the *Dance Rhapsody*, Percy Grainger wrote to Barbirolli (15 November 1937) to praise him for 'such satisfying speeds, such faithfulness of moods. I know Delius's intentions very well in that work as I arranged it for two pianos, and Balfour Gardiner and I used to play it to him in that form very often and noted down his metronome speeds etc. One might wait long to hear such a faithful, sympathetic and inspiring rendering as yours!'

the Beethoven and Brahms symphonies. After his performance of Franck's symphony in November 1937, Arthur Judson, one of the most reserved and undemonstrative of men,
wrote thus to his conductor:

My dear Barbirolli. In the last twenty years I suppose that I
have heard every conductor of note do the César Franck
symphony. The best of these was done by Stokowski until I
heard your performance of it last Sunday. I have never
heard anything to equal that, and I just wanted you to
know it.

It was one of the most successful seasons in the Society's
history, with attendances high and the financial deficit reduced. The critics were generally favourable to Barbirolli. He
received unstinted praise from Lawrence Gilman and won
over Samuel Chotzinoff, a convinced Toscanini-ite, who stated
that fears that the Philharmonic would lose support when
Toscanini returned had proved groundless. (This topic had
been the principal item of press questioning when Barbirolli
stepped off the liner and, whatever his personal misgivings, he
had described the formation of the NBC Orchestra as 'splendid – the more good orchestras there are, the better for music.
The return of a man like Toscanini can do only good for us
all.') Some of Olin Downes's notices in the *New York Times*
read fairly mildly today, and often he bestowed high compli-
ments. Yet some were vicious and there was always an undercurrent of hostility and grudging, rather than wholehearted,
praise. His notice of the Strauss concert upset John, particularly remarks about inaccuracies and poor intonation in the
performances of *Till Eulenspiegel* and *Don Juan*. 'A tissue of
lies,' John wrote in his press-cuttings book, 'the performances
were *technically* at any rate perfect.' To Evelyn he said more:

I suppose I must suffer the fate of some pioneers and I suppose Don J. and Till in their clean and vital guise (if I may
say so) must have sounded strange to them... Even Downes,
in his diabolically clever way, tries to damn the rest, but
admits he has never heard the *Bourgeois Gentilhomme*
sound quite like that... He was the one who wrote nastily
about me before I ever set foot here, and I think it the

E

greatest tribute that the Schubert and *Gentilhomme* articles should have appeared from him. He is obviously safeguarding himself from the day when he knows I will be a power here, and with these things to show, he can always say that, although he may have criticised me, he always 'knew the real quality of the man' (as he has said to a friend of mine). It is significant and curious that either he is rather *nasty* or *marvellous*, a very good sign...

After praising a performance of Brahms's First Symphony given on 29 October, Downes went on:

Weber's Overture was not as edifying. The orchestral prelude to 'Euryanthe' can easily be given a circus effect by rushing the tempo, losing some of the grip of the dotted rhythm, and making a piece which is essentially gallant and romantic a thing of instrumental fuss and whirl. Here was the tendency, sometimes to be observed with Mr Barbirolli, to force climaxes and artificially whip up excitement. Weber can supply a good deal of excitement himself.

Bruno Zirato told me that Downes had a natural antipathy to Barbirolli (although they did not know each other) and this was displayed 'very stupidly' in his reviews. 'If Olin had lived to hear Tita's concerts when he came back...there is no doubt in my mind that he would have admitted and recognised how unfair he was years before and how drastic and unjust were his writings on Tita, writings based on personal feelings and NOT on musical grounds.' Downes told a fellow-critic that he would never accept Barbirolli, presumably because he thought the Philharmonic should have engaged a world-famous name. He also had a personal grudge against the Philharmonic management over a matter that had affected his pocket. But he was merely one figure in the intensely fierce musical-political scene in New York. This ferocity erupted during and after Barbirolli's mid-season break, when he returned to England for a brief holiday between mid-January and mid-February 1938, and the eruption was the result of Toscanini's first concerts with the NBC. The earlier part of the season was comparatively free from worry, but the physical and nervous strain on Barbirolli were considerable, as these extracts from letters to Evelyn show clearly:

Hotel St Moritz, 2.xi.37

Judson was speechless at the Bartók [Music for Strings, Percussion and Celesta], says it's the finest thing the Philharmonic has done for years, and the orch: *themselves* (the darlings) gave me a great ovation for it. They don't seem able to get over the way I beat those sort of things... Brahms 1st symphony I conducted from memory. I have worked very hard at this... Orch. played magnificently again and you can imagine how happy musically I felt, when members of an orch. of that class talk about the joy of playing the Brahms I with any amount of ardour and passion, *but* they say with a *Line* they have almost forgotten... Bartók sounds marvellous, some of it, and surprisingly had a great success with the public. The strain of conducting a work like that (with the concentration needed to keep the orch. on the rails) and *then* the Brahms, is very great. Had a number of sectional rehearsals for the Bartók, and 4 concerts running, with Brahms I three times and Beethoven 7 other times, so that I was completely whacked by Sunday. I am very well really, though I do get much more exhausted than I used, and get rather a pain in my right side in moments of stress.

I was thankful Thursday seemed to go so well for I was really feeling pretty rotten during the concert. Friday I was better and only got pain in the Brahms. Yesterday conducted all day (2 rehs) and was all right. It must be the nervous tension and excitement of big performances upset me a little...

...Four concerts again this week... Don't breathe a word to Mum, but I just hope and wonder sometimes if I can stand this strain. I am supremely confident that I can really, and it is wonderful I feel so well really. Fortunately I am sleeping better so far and that is the *most important* thing of all if I can keep it up.

Hotel St Moritz, 8.xii.37

Despite being so tired last night and going to bed in such reasonable time, I did not sleep till nearly 6. Had to work morning and afternoon and again after the afternoon rehearsal and dinner and concert (Menuhin) to attend this evening. Very interesting. Tremendously gifted boy, but very *Jewish* talent.

A little business which I think will interest you. I have now completed my first 7 weeks (three *without* soloist) and no great names – Gieseking and Rubinstein are not star attractions here – *and* with this we have so far played to *86%* capacity. The highest Toscanini touched was 80%. It is really extraordinary... I am keeping remarkably well really. I have had to take things to make me sleep (quite harmless) and I look well, but this continuous discomfort in my inside and elsewhere is a bit trying at times.

> Hotel St Moritz, 27.xii.37
> 6.45 a.m.

...I must tell you about the rather wonderful happenings of yesterday. Toscanini's first concert was Saturday, so we were rather worried about Sunday. It turned out the 2nd largest audience of the season... Judson, I hear, was in tears at my ovation. I am so happy for him, who gambled all on me, and for Ethel and Rae who talked so much about me to him.

Toscanini's new orchestra had been recruited for him by Artur Rodzinski, whom he had come to know in Salzburg. Rodzinski, it will be recalled, had been selected to conduct the last part of the 1936–37 Philharmonic season, but before his engagements began, Barbirolli's three-year contract had been announced. He was deeply resentful that he was not offered the post, and when Toscanini returned to New York Rodzinski lost no opportunity to denigrate Barbirolli to the Maestro. As Zirato wrote to me: 'Because of some unfortunate misunderstandings Toscanini did not care much for Tita in the beginning of his tenure with the Philharmonic. Rodzinski was much to blame for this.' (Also, John did not like the derogatory remarks which Toscanini made about musicians he admired such as Heifetz, Kreisler, Bruno Walter and Rubinstein.) Returning to New York at the end of January after a brief visit to England, John was delayed by rough seas (he was a good sailor and enjoyed a stormy crossing) and was depressed because he would have to miss his first set of concerts in Carnegie Hall. Also he was afflicted by homesickness. 'I seems an awful long time before we can be together again,' he wrote to Evelyn. '...I don't think, Evie my sweet, I was ever meant to be a very "grand" person, and I am thankful you do not look down on your little "Cockney" Johnny, because for good or ill, a lot of him is to be found there.' How well he knew himself in this respect. To the end of his life he liked to drop into a Cockney accent, especially in intimately amusing moments and when he was sad or depressed.

On arrival in New York he made his first recordings with the orchestra (his Purcell Suite, Debussy's *Ibéria*, Tchaikovsky's *Francesca da Rimini* and Schumann's Violin Concerto, with Menuhin), but he had more disturbing news to tell Evelyn:

> Hotel St Moritz,
> 6 February

...I dined quietly with A.J. [Judson] Friday evening and we had a long talk... He had thought that leaving with that fine success and 4,000 dollars extra in the takings, things would just be quiet till I got back. But no. As soon as I was gone, the Toscanini, Rodzinski, cliques got busy and the lies and innuendoes they spread is something unbelievable. Things like 'that I have ruined the Society by driving all the public away'(?), 'that they would try and buy me out because of my failure' etc., and other pretty things. I won't bother you further with all this muck, but you see, dearest, what a fight it still is. But Evie...they will learn that when you try to put a Briton up against the wall, you sometimes make a mistake... Judson added in final comment 'I am afraid we made two mistakes. I engaged you, and you made a success.' But, with my thoughts of you, beloved, I remain calm and only anxious for one thing, to make my music as well as possible... Some sections of the press have in an insidious way been hinting Enesco would have been the conductor for the orchestra. And it is honestly *bad* conducting. In fact he has no pretensions at being one. Financially too, listen to this. First week of his stay they dropped $250, 2nd week $650, 3rd week $750 and 4th week Menuhin pulled it up with two sold-out houses... I need you to help me keep indifferent to all this dirty, lying treachery, carried to a fine art here by supporters of some of my colleagues... Tonight have to go to the Italian benefit: Tosc. is conducting 9th Symphony. I *have* to go and am interested of course, but these extra revelations of the last few days don't make it more pleasing...

For the remainder of the season his letters speak of 'the dirty intrigue and muck' continuing. However much he pretended otherwise, it depressed him and he had dreadful moments alone when his always insecure self-confidence was further eroded. But he was resilient and found compensation in the orchestra's loyalty, in the audience's ovations and in the music itself, Wagner with Flagstad in particular and the Elgar concerto with Heifetz – though his shrewd comment on the latter was: 'he plays it really wonderfully, though not perhaps with quite enough "hurt." I wonder if he has ever been wounded.' But the concerto moved him to write to Evelyn that night:

I find that it is still a practically unknown, and certainly misunderstood, work here. It brings back so vividly that day when I saw him for the last time and he hugged me and told me how glad he was I had come to see him. I knew then, as I had known before, how much he had felt the lack of understanding in the English people of his work, much public (official!) recognition as he had had. But surely, sweetheart, some day the whole world must know that he was one of the greatest composers of all time...

The genuine admiration of many musicians boosted his morale. 'Orchestra so enthusiastic,' he wrote, 'Evie, I *must* have something to give if all these people feel that way, mustn't I?... I work terribly hard to try and deal faithfully with the music we play... For you and my music I will fight with all my might. The public and many lovely friends are with me, and I will win for you.' The successful financial results of this first season had put him into a seventh heaven by the time he left New York to conduct his first American guest engagements, the lucrative Ford Sunday Evening Hour concerts with the Detroit Symphony Orchestra.

He was encouraged also when a member of the New York audience, Mr H. S. Alexander, sent him a copy of a letter he had written to Olin Downes in reply to an article in which

Downes had suggested that 'Mr Barbirolli should pray to be delivered from his friends.' 'Sad as it may seem, Mr Downes,' Alexander wrote (11 April 1938),

we listeners have become thoroughly nauseated by the type of publicity given Mr Toscanini... The thing that 'gets into the hair' of most of those I know is that constantly repeated line of hocus-pocus about the terrific complexity of score-reading and how Mr Toscanini accomplishes that mental feat, all from memory... Dozens of conductors do it daily without a second thought... The ill effect of your comments will be that a perfectly capable, and I understand a very lovable, gentleman will be put 'in the middle' ... You are quite right when you say that Mr Barbirolli's friends are taking the wrong course in attempting to extol him at the expense of Mr Toscanini, because he does not need that kind of extollation; and I, for one, do not believe Mr Barbirolli would condone such a thing.

Another compensation was the close friendship which developed with his loyal young secretary, John Woolford, who was extremely sensitive to music.

A summer in England (including his first television interview on 29 June) and a holiday in France with Evelyn, then he returned to America in the *Normandie* in the Munich-crisis autumn of 1938 with, as fellow-passengers, Toscanini – 'most charming and very chatty' – and the Russian politician Kerensky – 'funny to think of your Johnny hobnobbing with people like that.' 'I will do my damnedest for you all,' he wrote, 'I only hope it will not be too hard this time.' He had selected an arduous series of programmes (he was to conduct 104 concerts) with several American and British modern works including Griffes's *The White Peacock*, Bax's Fourth Symphony, Vaughan Williams's *Pastoral Symphony*, Delius's Violin Concerto, Elgar's Second Symphony and Lionel Tertis's transcription for viola of the Cello Concerto. He shared a concert with his friend, Nadia Boulanger, and he conducted his own suite of entr'actes from Debussy's *Pelléas et Mélisande*. One concert was devoted to Act II (uncut) of *Tristan**

* This was the first time the uncut act had been performed in New York and the first time Flagstad had sung this version, although she had prepared it for a European performance which was then cancelled.

with Flagstad as Isolde; another to Rossini's *Petite Messe Solennelle*. Heifetz, Rachmaninov, Milstein, Gieseking, Gaspar Cassadó, Rudolf Serkin, Josef Hofmann, Schnabel, Rubinstein, Adolf Busch and Joseph Schuster were among his instrumental soloists.

He enjoyed the social company of musicians, though sometimes he liked to get away from them altogether. But he was never short of good stories about them, as of the time he ended up one evening playing string quartets at a party with Mischa Elman, a notoriously bad chamber-music player, whose Jewish accent and naïve conceit were a source of affectionate amusement to his colleagues: 'Next morning,' John said, 'Elman met a friend of mine outside Carnegie Hall and said "I played with Barbirolli last night. He's a good cellist; when I play solo he plays *quiet*." ' John was a superb mimic with an enviable range of accents – Irish, Scots, Jewish, Cockney, Lancashire and mid-European among them.

In his letters to Evelyn he wrote uninhibitedly about his views on some of the music and musicians of this 1938–39 season (he now had a flat in Hampshire House, Central Park South):

Went to the Toscanini concert [N.B.C.] last night and heard a magnificent performance of Brahms III. It was really the best I have heard from him for a time and so fine in every way. Beautifully played and with wonderful proportions. To be super-critical (and in face of such a performance it seems rather churlish) I might have wished for the ending a little more *peaceful* and *serene*, but a wonderful thing to remember anyway. I came away musically exalted and otherwise terribly depressed and disgusted at the way they run things at N.B.C.... Admission is free and by ticket and it is the strangest sensation-mongering audience with all sorts of theatrical stunts and altogether upsetting. Still I was grateful to be there.

9 November

We are doing the *Berceuse Héroïque* of Debussy, 'In Memory of the Fallen' (Nov. 11th). Evie, this is a most extraordinary piece, and I wish I had words to tell you about it. It is so full of death and desolation, yet a noble spirit broods over it all, as if Debussy were trying to tell the world, with all the sensitiveness of his art, what a tragic futility it all is. It is all very restrained and quiet, and the only 'military' thing about it is a ghostly trumpet call, which made even the orchestra shudder when we rehearsed it. Even that call sounds, in some amazing way, as if it were being played by skeletons in uniform.

8 March

Tonight we played *Tallis Fantasia* (V.W.), Beethoven I and Brahms 2nd concerto with Schnabel. *Tallis* made the most profound impression and it is really a very beautiful work and made me think of the loveliest of our English cathedrals. The orchestra is crazy about the work, which is rather nice, isn't it? The Brahms went splendidly but only after I gave Mr Schnabel the best 'ticking off' he has ever had in his life in front of the orchestra at rehearsal yesterday. Naturally like all would-be bullies he subsided immediately and tonight I conducted the work as a *symphony* with piano obbligato which is as it should be.

16 March

The great hit of the evening was the 'Gypsy Baron' overture. I would love you to hear my boys play this one day. One old Viennese man came to me afterwards and called me 'Herr Johann B'.

20 April

Rather a lovely concert tonight. A beautiful Concerto Grosso by Boyce, Schumann II and Tchaikovsky IV... You will be glad to hear, sweetheart, that the new horn parts and other changes I made for the Schumann really sound... I am glad, for I disagree with this idea of re-orchestrating Schumann but I do think he can be *helped*. What lovely music it is. I would love to conduct the slow movement with you playing in it!

Barbirolli had approached the season, after a long spell of inactivity, in his usual apprehensive state – 'it is always so worrying and trying waiting for the first rehearsal and wondering if there is any music left in me at all' – and he had his intermittent fits of depression, 'but I have sought consolation in work.' Throughout this season he slept badly and his letters are often dated 3 a.m. or even 6 a.m. He spent the sleepless hours bowing parts and marking scores. 'I am really very exhausted physically though I have plenty of energy for my concerts,' he told Evelyn. The demands of social life were considerable, even when they were such pleasant occasions as dinner with the Roosevelts at the White House or a banquet in his honour at the Lotus Club where, on Twelfth Night, he appeared publicly for the first time in America as a cellist, in a quartet with Piastro, Corigliano and William Primrose. Although he said little about it, he was ever conscious of the Toscanini–NBC rivalry, especially when, at the beginning of the season, each conducted Beethoven's Fifth Symphony on successive days. The critic Herbert Roussel awarded the palm to Barbirolli but added, with an eye on Munich: 'The English badly needed a victory of some kind.' It became a matter of comment how many times Toscanini conducted the same work a few days after Barbirolli. The Philharmonic's programmes were, of course, published well in advance of NBC's.

The 'intrigues' continued but seemed to disturb John less. He was, in any case, well established with orchestra and audience, and in February, with another year of his contract to run, he wrote to Evelyn: 'Yesterday at a meeting of the Executive it was unanimously and enthusiastically agreed that when my contract is up I should be re-engaged for a number of years, and A.J. said he could have got a 5-year contract yesterday only he prefers to wait till the time is really up.' Marjorie's divorce petition had been granted on 5 December 1938, and would be made absolute the following June, so that his thoughts now were focused on his marriage and having Evelyn with him in New York. 'Faults I know I have,' he wrote, 'but will you remember one thing, my beloved, that I think may help you to understand what might seem a little difficult at times, and that is a horror I have of hurting others – I have had in my public life to arm myself with a kind of rhinoceros skin to receive the shafts of malice, ignorance and jealousy, but these things leave their mark.'

In March 1939, Barbirolli took the orchestra to play in Boston, with Schnabel as soloist. The *Boston Post* critic congratulated the Philharmonic on their conductor. 'In him one now experiences a sense of security, stability, steadfastness and general satisfaction.' This compensated for Downes's remarks about Elgar's Second Symphony (23 March): 'a lengthy, pompous, bourgeois sort of thing; it reflects the complacency and stodginess of the era of the antimacassar and pork-pie bonnets; it is affected by the poor taste and the swollen orchestral manner of the post-romantics...' If Barbirolli had had no other reason for disliking Downes, this would have sufficed. Downes was director of music for the New York World Fair, and John gleefully reported to Evelyn: 'I am to open the World's Fair with the orchestra on Sunday April 30 (rather tough as I have my own last concert that day) which I am glad of really, as that dirty tyke Downes...had planned for Stokowski and the Philadelphia Orchestra to do so.' The only surviving letter from Downes to Barbirolli is one referring to a programme for the World Fair and ending with a compliment 'on your perfect handling of the baton' – by which he presumably meant just what he said and no more.

For his mid-season break – less than a fortnight this time – John stayed as the guest of Mrs John T. Pratt (of Pratt's oils and petroleum), a member of the Philharmonic board of directors and of the ladies' board and also chairman of the Philharmonic-Symphony League (the orchestra's 'supporters' club'). A widow, Ruth Pratt lived at the Manor House, Glen Cove, on Long Island. John described his sampling of American 'gracious living' to Evelyn:

24 January, 1939

It is the evening of your birthday... I was able to drink a toast to you, my sweetheart, in a very charming Mouton-Rothschild of 1929... Evie, can you imagine your Johnny living in solitary state in a house something like Goodwood? It looks outside like a lovely Georgian English country house and inside is really exquisite. Of course it is large but none of the rooms too much so. A magnificent double staircase greets you as you enter, but somehow it is all very homely... I have had a really grand time browsing in the library and a walk of about an hour each day. We are about 2 miles from the Atlantic (Long Island Sound) and there are lovely walks tho' now it is covered in snow... I am writing to you now in the library sitting in a magnificent Chippendale chair. Nearly all the furniture is English, Chippendale and Hepplewhite, and looks so natural and beautiful in these surroundings. I practically spend all day in this room as it is very cosy with a lovely log fire... I also have my meals in the library... I order just what I want both as regards food and drink. The butler is the real thing just as you see on the stage. He is Scotch, McCullough by name and comes from Perrrth, at least that's how he pronounces it... I think he rather seems to like the fact that I have sherry instead of cocktails... One thing more, I sleep in a four-poster.

He returned there in May, elated by the end-of-season results – deficit reduced, income from radio and recordings increased, attendance at the 104 concerts of 245,658, about eighty per cent of the hall's capacity. At Glen Cove he worked on his next season's programmes and planned the orchestra's first tour of the States for ten years. He also relaxed:

6 May, 1939

I must first of all tell you of today's great thrill when I went riding for the first time... Isn't it funny, darling, that I have always wanted to do this and felt I should be all right somehow. It was really one of the loveliest experiences of outdoor life that I have ever had... There is a lovely gentle horse for me here (Dobbin by name) ideal to learn on... Tonight Mr Hoover (ex-President) has been to dinner.

Fearless and ambitious as ever, he then decided he would start jumping. Result, three cracked ribs, disguised in letters home as 'strained muscles.' He spent the remaining days at Glen Cove in bed, but worked with his secretary, John Woolford.

I completed the first six weeks of programmes... It does seem really an almost impossible job when you first look at that empty sheet of paper and think of what you have to try and do. There is the usual talk about novelties and when you give them nobody seems to want them... But it is wonderful to write all this and to think of you really being here too when it comes to pass...

John's thoughts now were full of his forthcoming marriage and he had views on every detail. For example: 'I think, darling, that to wear grey a rather high colouring is essential, also it is too old a colour for you. What I would love you to have if it could be done again is another frock like your lace one. Do you remember wearing it at a *Meistersinger* performance I conducted for the R.A.M.?' More serious were the feelings he confided to his sister Rosie:

I have learned through bitter experience that certain things are necessary for two people to live together and they are *fundamentals*. Not necessarily the same interests but the same *instincts*. With all my faults I don't think anyone would either call me unkind or a snob...and Evie is certainly neither of those... I do love her, Rosie, and I do think I have (to use a colloquialism) picked a 'winner' this time.

He returned to England in June and they were married at Holborn Register Office on 5 July. John was 39 and Evelyn 28. The best man was Tommy Cheetham, their Lancastrian colleague from the Scottish Orchestra. After the ceremony they and their guests had lunch in the King Edward VII Room of Pagani's and, after a night in Rottingdean, they crossed from Newhaven to Dieppe for a honeymoon in Normandy, staying in and visiting towns which were to be the scene of bloody fighting five years later and discovering among other things the potency of calvados.

They had chosen Normandy because of the need to be able to return to England quickly if the international situation worsened. The threat of war had caused the abandonment of their wish to go to Italy. The imminence of war was to cast its shadow again, when he had to return to New York, on the Philharmonic's insistence, at the end of August and discovered that Evelyn could not go with him because she had no American visa and none were at that time being issued. So John sailed in the French liner *Champlain*, having spent a month in Sussex with his family. At sea on Sunday 3 September, he wrote to Evelyn in language which shows how deep were his feelings for England:

The blow has fallen and honestly sweet I am completely heartbroken. For the past two days I have stuck in my cabin and worked and read till I can hardly see; it seems the only means to hang on to something. I can hardly bear to go on the decks or public rooms, where all the Americans (I am sorry to have to say this) seem to be enjoying life as much as ever... I cannot understand that the only solution, be it of dealing with madmen, races or people, must needs mean the unimaginable and untold suffering of millions of innocents. I wake at night and pray, and pray hard, for I cannot believe *He* wills this... I know your Pete and Rich [her brothers] are not too 'By Gad, Sir' to despise me sending my very real love and affection to my new brothers for whatever is in store for them.

On arrival in New York John's first action was to inform the British Consul that he was ready to return if his age-group was called up for service. He then went to stay with Ruth Pratt at Glen Cove, but his letters disclose that he was finding life difficult in several ways, apart from being concerned to arrange for Evelyn to join him as soon as possible.

19 September

I am strangely unhappy here, for tho' everyone is so kind, there seems a strange lack of understanding of this great thing England is trying to do that taxes my temper and good manners exceedingly. I am a guest here, and they are moving heaven and earth to get you over so I must be patient and control myself but it is hard at times... They say I can't bear criticism of anything we do, and no more can I. This is no time for criticism but for all the devotion and belief of which we are capable. I have even come into rather serious conflict with Ruth on this subject but, darling, I know you would not like me to betray, even in the lightest thought or word, something that I feel now is sacred... I need badly some one of our kind and fibre who doesn't weep at the first bad rumour but who knows in some subtle way (after all it is not by blood I know it) that if England goes, they may as well all pack up... One last word, beloved, I will *wait long* and have you here safely rather than you should be exposed to any undue risk. You *must only* travel on a *neutral* ship.

24 September

The stability and grit of our people are something hard for them to realise here, tho' they read about it occasionally, but they seem to need a daily victory to keep them going. However I think they are gradually beginning to understand that when we are up against it, so to speak, then do the finest qualities of our people come to the fore. To make a rather absurd simile, I said to some friends here the other day: 'If I had turned and run home when I heard the first murmurings of opposition to me here after Mr Tosc. I would have left after two weeks instead of entering my fourth year here.'

He became more and more depressed at Glen Cove and was glad to return to New York for the start of the 1939–40 season. He now enjoyed the friendship of the Venetian conductor, Giorgio Polacco, whom he had first met in his Covent Garden days when Polacco, who was a regular guest conductor of the international season, had casually drifted in to a Barbirolli rehearsal of *Butterfly* and had stayed to the end, deeply impressed by the young man's work. John for his part was entranced by Polacco's conducting of Debussy's *Pelléas*, which he regarded as ideal. Now, in New York, to which Polacco had retired from Chicago, they resumed their friendship and when Evelyn joined John the three had a regular 'date' after concerts at an Italian restaurant, Mama Bronzo's, where they discussed the performances. Polacco, while by no means uncritical when necessary, encouraged John and gave him confidence. Other stalwart friends were the Steinway family, notably Theodore Steinway, the head of the pianoforte firm, and his wife.

John was also enjoying studying a new work dedicated to him and the orchestra by the New York domiciled Czech composer Jaromir Weinberger, composer of *Schwanda the Bagpiper*. This was the *Variations and Fugue on an Old English Tune: 'Under the Spreading Chestnut Tree'*, inspired by the newsreels showing King George VI singing and gesturing to this tune at a boys' camp.

8 October, 10.45 p.m.

I have just written a tuba part for the finale of the Weinberger. I suggested this to him when I saw him Friday and he is going to hear what it sounds like. Also have just thought (and written down) of a few words I feel I ought to say to the orchestra tomorrow. We are all there, every nationality and creed under the sun almost, and I do want it very clearly understood that we are in Carnegie Hall for one purpose only, to make music, and I will not tolerate any political discussions of any kind in the place.

The Variations received their first performance on 12 October at the opening of the ninety-eighth Philharmonic season and were played, according to Howard Taubman, 'with a freshness, accent and brilliance that swept one along irresistibly. The audience thundered its satisfaction.' This, the third season of Barbirolli's original contract, was another set of well-varied and enticing concerts which make the mouth water today. American works were again to the fore: the first Philharmonic performance of Barber's *Adagio for Strings*, the first performances of Bernard Herrmann's cantata *Moby Dick* – the beginning of a long friendship between conductor and composer – MacDowell's Second Piano Concerto and others. He also conducted Bruckner's Seventh Symphony (totally misunderstood by the New York critics almost to a man), and Beethoven's First Piano Concerto with Rachmaninov as soloist – this was the only Beethoven concerto Rachmaninov would play because, so he told Barbirolli, 'the rest are so boring for the pianist!'

Commenting in the *New York Sun* at the end of the season, John wrote of the difficulty of finding new works – 'the public wants to hear nothing but masterpieces.' He went on: 'I heard with almost incredulous astonishment that whenever we announced new American works on our programmes, many subscribers asked to have their tickets changed to the next concerts in which these works were not listed. This can only mean one thing: that they are prepared to damn a new work even before hearing it.' In the 1939–40

season there were 119 concerts, which included 450 performances of 178 works by 71 composers. Of this 71, as high a
number as 25 were contemporary, and of the 25, nine were
American. But were those nine truly representative of the
best available, the critics asked. Since they did not include
Charles Ives, Aaron Copland or Roy Harris, the question was
pertinent.

The tour in November 1939 was the highlight of the season
for John and the orchestra. In the fourteen days from 20
November to 3 December they played in fourteen different
halls in Scranton, Baltimore, Washington, Pittsburgh, Toledo,
Kalamazoo, Chicago, Ann Arbor, Columbus, Utica and
Dayton, and (in Canada) Hamilton, Ottawa and Toronto.
There were no soloists except for the orchestral string quartet
in Elgar's *Introduction and Allegro*. In place of the virulence
or faint praise of the New York critics, the orchestra read
ecstatic eulogies of themselves and their conductor in every
town they visited. It was an invigorating experience, and
especially happy for John because Evelyn was now with him,
having arrived in New York in late October. He spent his
fortieth birthday conducting in Toronto.

Two important events occurred in the 1939–40 season.
First, the first performance, on 28 March 1940, of Benjamin
Britten's Violin Concerto, with Antonio Brosa as soloist. Britten, with his friend Peter Pears, was living in the United
States at this time and was befriended by Ethel Bartlett and
Rae Robertson who drew Barbirolli's attention to the young
composer's remarkable talents. The concerto was a success
with public and press, and remained in Barbirolli's repertoire
for the rest of his life. The second event was Barbirolli's first
and only occupancy of the rostrum at the Metropolitan Opera
House, not, alas, directing an opera but conducting the Philharmonic in a concert in aid of the opera fund. The highlight
of a miscellaneous programme was the performance of the
Love Duet from *Madam Butterfly*, with Jarmila Novotna and
Charles Kullmann.

In February it had been announced that Barbirolli had
been re-engaged by the Philharmonic for the next two
seasons, 1940–42. This was not the five years of which Judson
had spoken some time before, but undoubtedly the possibility
of John's call-up for military service was a governing factor.
For 1940–41, he was to conduct for twenty-two of the thirty

weeks of the season, with Bruno Walter and Dimitri Mitropoulos sharing the remaining eight, as Igor Stravinsky and Albert Stroessel had done in 1939–40. In the summer of 1940 John frankly discussed his future in a letter to Bruno Zirato:

What I write to you now I write as to a brother, for you know that apart from business I think of you as my own. For some weeks now I have envisaged the possibility of my being called for Army service in England and of the attitude I should adopt in that event. In my own mind the thing is perfectly clear. If I am called, I must go, and, without heroics I should go happily to do what I am asked to do in defence not only of my country but, as it is now, my family and *all* that any *decent* person holds dear. You can imagine what these days are for me with constant air raids and the very much worse things which are to follow... What I want to ask you is this. What do you think would be the attitude of the Philharmonic? Is there a chance that they would engage a conductor from season to season and allow me (if I was still there) to fulfil my two years contract when all this ghastly mess was over? I feel sure many, like Ruth [Pratt], Marshall [Field], and [Walter] Price etc. would adopt a very sympathetic attitude. I know A.J. will probably refer to my first papers [of American citizenship] but I am not due to be a citizen till 1943 and the last thing I would dream of doing is to shelter behind that sort of thing. Another factor which weighs heavily is that I cannot refuse to go and face a danger that even my mother and sister (to say nothing of the children) have to face. Financially it would be a disaster because Gibilaro has lost his job and Peter has been called up but we should have to manage as best we could and I have saved quite a bit. The whole damn thing is a tragedy, but there is fast coming a time when it will be worth while facing anything rather than feel you failed to do even a little tiny bit towards helping to stay this disgusting canker that is gaining its festering foothold in the world. England stands alone now. I am proud to be a son of hers, and you will understand.

There could be no visit to England for a summer holiday in 1940. Having been engaged for the famous Hollywood Bowl outdoor concerts in Los Angeles, the Barbirollis had contemplated a holiday in California to visit the eighteenth-century Spanish missions there (which they did later) because they both greatly missed in America the old buildings and traditions. Then came a letter from Rhynd Jamieson, a Scotsman who was music critic of a Vancouver paper, saying that a concert on a grand scale was being planned as climax of the British Columbia Music Festival and inviting John to conduct. The idea of a spell on British soil was irresistible; and there was the bonus of an unforgettable train journey through the Rockies on a train in which one could have a 'drawing room' and complete relaxation, unbroken by the telephone, amid glorious scenery. John and Evelyn fell in love with Vancouver, then largely unspoilt, and its friendly people, and felt at home among so many Scottish and English accents. It was a pleasure, too, to hear the radio news from an English angle, without the anti-British American undercurrent which distressed them in New York. The orchestra was partly amateur and not of a standard which John would have contemplated conducting in the United States, but it amused him to have as horn the man who cut York ham for him in a local shop. Arthur Benjamin (who lived in Vancouver then) was piano soloist in the Franck *Symphonic Variations*, and the concert was a brilliant success.

They went on to Los Angeles in July for John's début at the Hollywood Bowl, where he conducted the *Enigma Variations*, Delius's *First Cuckoo*, and Brahms's Fourth Symphony to an audience of 12,000, one of the largest Friday night audiences in the Bowl's history. John never forgot the complete silence from that vast throng as they listened to the Delius.

August was spent in Chicago conducting in the Ravinia Park festival. The concerts included Sibelius's First and Second, Schubert's Fourth and Ninth and Beethoven's Second, Seventh and Eighth Symphonies, the *Enigma Variations* and some Wagner with Flagstad. The distinguished critic of the *Chicago Daily News*, Eugene Stinson, was deeply impressed by Barbirolli's Beethoven – 'fine inward qualities' – and even more by his Schubert. 'Just as there is no conceivable way in which his musicianship might be caricatured, so there is no just criticism which might seriously be levelled against him,' he wrote. 'He conducts on a more comprehen-

The Barbirollis spent five weeks at North Shore in Vancouver in the late summer of 1940. On 15 September – while the Battle of Britain reached its peak – John conducted the orchestra again in aid of the Canadian Red Cross. It was a delight for him to have Evelyn as soloist at the concert in the Pergolesi concerto. As he had written to her before they were married: '*Nobody* has ever played that like you, and I can hear you now playing the first movement with a poignancy that hurts terribly.' After hearing this performance, Arthur Benjamin made the Cimarosa transcription which has since become well known.

On their return to New York they had a telephone call from Toscanini. 'Why,' the Maestro asked John, 'have you not brought your bride to meet me?' John replied with typical candour that he had grown tired of hearing Toscanini speaking ill of his friends when he 'held court' at his house on Riverside Drive. 'You know me,' Toscanini retorted, 'I am a pig.' So a breach was healed, and Barbirolli and Toscanini saw more of each other during the next two years. (At these Toscanini 'receptions,' often on Sunday mornings, the guests included various sycophants and two wives of members of the NBC who were noted for their gossip. Toscanini enjoyed gossip and would then – often very amusingly but none the less distastefully – disparage his eminent colleagues and members of other orchestras. Because he disliked this so much, John had stopped going to Riverside Drive.) Another great conductor attended Barbirolli's concerts at this time, Otto

Klemperer, who was slowly recovering from a brain-tumour operation. He would go to see John in the conductor's room, help him to change, and sit with him, tightly gripping his hand, as if for reassurance from one artist to another.

The 1940–41 Philharmonic season opened on 10 October with, as one writer said, 'more notables in the audience than you could shake a baton at.' Elgar's *Enigma Variations* and Sibelius's Second Symphony were interpreted by the critics as intentional tributes to the spirit of man. It was another season of first performances – by the Society, in America, or anywhere – and other unfamiliar works, among them John's arrangement of Purcell's Chaconne in G Minor, Bizet's and Chausson's symphonies, the first Philharmonic performance of Elgar's Cello Concerto in its original form (soloist Piatigorsky), Randall Thompson's Second Symphony, Debussy's Rhapsody for Clarinet and Mozart's Clarinet Concerto with Benny Goodman as soloist, Roy Harris's *Three Pieces for Orchestra*, Villa-Lobos's *Descobrimento do Brasil*, Suite No. 1, Eugène Goossens's Symphony, Britten's *Sinfonia da Requiem* (29 March 1941) and D'Indy's *Symphony on a French Mountain Song*. Among the soloists in Carnegie Hall that winter were Kreisler, Rubinstein, Francescatti and Rachmaninov. John spent his January break as guest conductor of the Los Angeles Philharmonic, with whom he revived Elgar's *Carillon*, with Walter Pidgeon as the narrator. The orchestra's leader at this time was Bronislaw Gimpel. The Barbirollis took a house in Beverly Hills and had several delightful evenings of chamber music with the Francescattis, José Iturbi and his sister, the Horowitzes, and Gimpel. An enthusiastic listener, who liked to turn the pages for John, was the actor Edward G. Robinson.

During the summer of 1941, Barbirolli returned to Hollywood for further concerts in the Bowl, with Helen Traubel and Heifetz as soloists. Stravinsky was there to hear his *Firebird* Suite. He was amused because John discovered a mistake in the printed parts which had previously escaped notice. Stravinsky, after long scrutiny, admitted it was wrong, adding: 'That's the worst of my reputation as a modern composer – everyone must have thought I meant it.' For the Philharmonic's 1941–42 season it had been decided to mark the orchestra's impending centenary (7 December 1942) by inviting a representative series of guest conductors to lend variety to the concerts. This was done, with John's approval, indeed at his suggestion. He was to have three periods with the orchestra, and his colleagues were Stokowski, Bruno Walter, Artur Rodzinski, Dimitri Mitropoulos, Fritz Busch, Eugène Goossens, Koussevitzky, Walter Damrosch and, to end the season with six Beethoven concerts, Toscanini.

Barbirolli's programmes in this, his fifth contracted season, were no less interesting for being fewer. Among the works he conducted were William Grant Still's *Plainchant for America*, Vaughan Williams's *Five Variants on Dives and Lazarus*, Castelnuovo-Tedesco's *King John* overture, Pergolesi's *Stabat Mater* and extracts from *Parsifal* and *Meistersinger*. John told a delightful story of Castelnuovo-Tedesco, who was a Shakespearean scholar, coming to him and saying he was inspired to write his *King John* overture for the centenary season when he found the famous passage beginning 'This England never did, nor ever shall, lie at the proud foot of a conqueror...' He declaimed the words with Latin fervour, adding 'How magnificent – it sounds like Churchill.'

Barbirolli spent November and December 1941 in Los Angeles, for concerts at which Heifetz and Horowitz were among the soloists. The first performance of his *Elizabethan Suite*, an arrangement of pieces from the Fitzwilliam Virginal Book which has remained deservedly popular, was given three days before Pearl Harbor. The remainder of the winter before returning to New York he spent conducting in Vancouver, Seattle and Cincinnati. Praise followed him everywhere. One critic asked in astonishment: 'Each appearance of John Barbirolli adds to the difficulty in understanding why musical pundits in the east resort to vitriol-hurling so often in their discussions of what the conductor has done for or to the Philharmonic-Symphony Orchestra of New York.' The coolness of critics like Downes still upset him, and he found comfort in the faith shown in him by Judson's assistant, Zirato, to whom he wrote this letter:

Dearest Bruno. I wept a little just now to think that perhaps, through the modest gifts which Our Lord has given me, I have been able not only to inspire a truly serious and musical spirit in the orchestra but also something which is perhaps even more important, a spirit of decency and humanity which, unfortunately, is all too seldom found. I need not assure you of the sincerity of these inadequate words. There are few things in life of true value. For me they are whatever little I can do for the art which I love so deeply, and a friendship such as you have extended to me with such an open heart. As always, with affection, Your Tita.

When the 1941–42 season ended, Barbirolli's contract with New York expired. It was not renewed, although he was offered eighteen guest engagements in the 1942–43 season. The principal reason for this was Judson's knowledge of John's increasing anxiety about his family in England. He suspected that John would not stay much longer, but he also knew that if he did stay there was one insuperable difficulty: the ruling by the all-powerful Musicians' Union that everyone had to be members of the union to play in American symphony orchestras and that to be a member of the union you had to be an American citizen. This applied to conductors also: after six years they had to become American citizens to hold a permanent post. John never had the slightest intention of becoming an American citizen; in wartime the idea was especially repugnant to him. He had, of course, taken out 'first papers' when he arrived, but this was a formality, a protective gesture with no final commitment. No doubt, also, the return of Rodzinski and Toscanini to the Philharmonic rostrum had re-kindled intrigues and denigration. But it was the question of citizenship that ended Barbirolli's tenure of the Philharmonic rostrum.

Judson knew that as early as August 1941, before the second of the two seasons of his second contract, John had made the first moves towards a visit to England in a letter to his friend the journalist Beverley Baxter.

1591 Sunset Plaza Drive,
Hollywood, California
2 August 1941

...I need hardly tell you that one's thoughts are always elsewhere at this time... I have read from your pen...and other sources with great pride and admiration of the wonderful way my old colleagues and friends are carrying on musically in London... At such moments I feel I would give anything to be able to take a little share in these achievements... I would be very happy to fly over and conduct a tour or series of the London Philharmonic Orchestra or the London Symphony Orchestra, paying my own expenses and of course demanding no fee...

He wrote in similar vein to Herbert Walenn, Adrian Boult, and Stanley Marchant, Principal of the Royal Academy of Music. But his principal ally was his dear friend, the tenor Parry Jones, who went to see A. V. Alexander, First Lord of the Admiralty, and Brendan Bracken, Minister of Information, about obtaining a permit for John to return to the United States and to find some means of his travelling to Britain at a time – the height of the Battle of the Atlantic – when there were no passenger liners and the air services were congested. Apart from the considerable transport difficulties, other matters caused delays in arranging the trip. John had hoped to conduct both the LPO and LSO but, not realising the intensely matter-of-fact, business-as-usual mood of wartime England, he had been slightly 'put out' by the casual tone of a letter from Thomas Russell, the LPO's manager, after which Parry Jones cabled him not to contact the LSO (simply because the LPO was the only orchestra able to organise a tour – they had been doing nothing else for nearly two years). John thought his generous, emotional gesture had been misunderstood, as he explained to Marchant:

13 January 1942

I have never been engaged for a concert by the LPO before,* whereas the LSO gave me my great chance in 1927... I cannot and will not have any part in any musical 'politics' or feuds that may be existing among the London orchestras. My visit would be purely a gesture of affection and goodwill...

And to Parry Jones, about Russell's letter:

21 January

...I must say that this letter gave me and Evelyn the feeling that just to please me and as a great favour they are going

* This was not true.

to try to sandwich me in between Cameron and Sargent and that they might have to take dates from them... Not that I want to be thanked, but I do want to be very sure that I am wanted...

He was still unconvinced that musicians in England had any room for him. Parry Jones knew his John, though, and how to reply:

11 February

...They [the LPO] are delighted at the prospect of playing with you... They are rather tied up with Sargent (clever business man) owing to early war associations. They are doing their utmost to liquidate him, because everyone hates him and his insincerity. But there you are. They have to put up with him for the time being... We are all determined to make your visit something that will make you feel it has been worth while...

The Philharmonic management were very much against John's trip – 'They're hard, the buggers don't understand,' he said – because they thought he would not come back, but they recognised that he was adamant.

There was no possibility of obtaining a passage for Evelyn to accompany him. His air ticket was re-allocated to a Government courier and he had to go by sea. 'For God's sake don't mention a *word* of a sea voyage to anyone of my family,' he warned Parry Jones. 'My poor old Ma would probably die on the spot at the thought of it.' He sailed for England in April in a Norwegian freighter, the *California Express*, which was taking a cargo of bacon to Manchester.

The voyage took twenty-three days – nearly twice as long as was expected – and John missed his first series of concerts. He disembarked in Liverpool and went straight to a refreshment-room where he had 'a pint of warm bitter. It tasted revolting, but I was home!' In thirty-five days he conducted twenty-eight concerts and his two Royal Albert Hall concerts were sold out. Mémé travelled with him, and he was deeply moved to experience England at one of the blackest times of the war – for his visit coincided with the fall of Tobruk – and to conduct for war workers in the factories. He was shattered to see London. It was, he said, like seeing someone whom one loved very much and who had been very ill but was now recovering splendidly. He toured with both the LSO (revisiting Dundee and Aberdeen) and the LPO and conducted the BBC Symphony Orchestra in its wartime home at Bedford Corn Exchange. He conducted in Bristol, Newcastle, Wolverhampton, Streatham Hill and Bradford. A Manchester date was among those cancelled because of his late arrival. A. V. Alexander spoke at his final concert in the Albert Hall on 5 July and before he returned to America John gave a party for the First Lord at the Savage Club. Everywhere he had gone he had been acclaimed and he began to feel that he really was wanted. In addition, Evelyn's letters kept him in touch with New York, where, just after he left, Toscanini returned to the Philharmonic for the first time for over six years. 'Toscanini has behaved like a lamb at rehearsals,' Evelyn wrote (20 April), 'and has told not only Bruno [Zirato] but said to *everybody* that the orchestra is in wonderful shape and it might be the day after he left it etc. etc. so well are they playing now after these years. I'm glad he's saying this, the old bastard.'

He sailed back to the United States in a Fyffe banana boat. On arrival he described the voyage in a letter to Zirato: 'The subs discovered us after two days and a week later attacked in force. We had three ships torpedoed next to us and we must have been missed by yards. It was rather sad next morning to see the empty space, for you become almost like friends steaming along together day by day. The courage of these merchant seamen, some of whom have been torpedoed already five or six times, is truly amazing, for they go on month after month with all that strain and not much glory...'

His first concerts were the Hollywood Bowl series, followed by spells as a guest conductor with the Los Angeles, Seattle and Chicago orchestras. He was not due in Carnegie Hall until 11 February 1943, by which time the appointment of Rodzinski as the orchestra's next conductor had been announced. As usual he included American works in his programmes: Deems Taylor's *Marco Takes a Walk*, Abram Chasins's *Parade* and Toch's *Big Ben Variations*. His greatest pleasure came at the concerts on 18 and 19 February when Kreisler was soloist in his own 'spoof' Vivaldi concerto (which he had first played in Manchester with the Hallé before the

1914–18 war) and in Viotti's A Minor Concerto, No. 22. (Asked some years later how Kreisler played this work, John simply took off his hat and crossed himself.) Having Kreisler as a 'fellow-citizen' had been one of the pleasures of New York for John, although they never achieved their ambition to play the Elgar concerto together. Kreisler had been another source of strength when criticism of John's work was at its height – he had suffered from the critics in his time, too – and the basis of his advice John passed on to others in later years: 'An artist must believe in himself and mustn't be easily swayed. A public man must take whatever comes to him. Read or don't read the critics, but you must not swerve from your own views.' Zirato used to quote to him two of Puccini's verdicts on criticism: 'The most useless occupation in the world' and 'Critics love mediocrity.'

These last New York concerts of Barbirolli's seven years in America were certainly 'atmospheric,' because on the eve of the Kreisler concert, Marshall Field, the Society's president, announced the impending dismissal of fourteen members of the orchestra, including Piastro, Labate and Jaenicke, on Rodzinski's recommendation. When Piastro came on to the platform that evening he was applauded loud and long – applause in which John joined when he came in – and on the following Sunday John himself was the object of a demonstration by the audience which, the *New York Sun* said, 'was plainly meant to convey the affection of these listeners for him.' On 25 and 26 February, John again conducted Vaughan Williams's *Pastoral Symphony*, with conspicuous success.

In his last Carnegie Hall programmes he conducted Strauss waltzes, Skryabin's *Prometheus*, Elgar's *Enigma Variations*, Debussy's rare *Fantasy* for piano and orchestra and, as the final work on 7 March, Tchaikovsky's Fifth Symphony. John described the scene after the symphony, in a letter to Harold Holt (17 April):

After a good ten minutes' applause with the audience and orchestra just sitting and cheering, I made a brief speech during which I said 'Now as I come to the end of my seven-year period in New York' and this was greeted by shouts from the gallery of 'No!' Even after the speech nobody moved and finally the orchestra and audience stood and sang *Auld Lang Syne*. It was really a moving and unforgettable occasion, and people here tell me quite unprecedented.

What the audience did not yet know was that Barbirolli's next post was already almost settled. On 25 February, the day he was conducting the Vaughan Williams symphony, a telegram was sent from Manchester, signed by Robert J. Forbes, the Principal of the Royal Manchester College of Music. It said: 'Would you be interested permanent conductorship Hallé? Important developments pending.' Since his visit to England John had been hoping for a suitable opportunity to return home, even though the Los Angeles Philharmonic were on the verge of offering him their post. As soon as he read this telegram he said to Evelyn, 'This is it,' and cabled back: 'Am always interested to consider a permanent conductorship of an orchestra with as great traditions as the Hallé. Regards.'

With the start of the Hallé negotiations Barbirolli's American period ended. Was it a success or was it, as the London critic Desmond Shawe-Taylor was to say in his obituary of Barbirolli in the *Sunday Times*, 'a flop'? In financial terms and in attendance at the Philharmonic concerts it was a proved and provable success. Artistically? This can be measured only by his effect on the standard of the orchestra and by individual judgment. Harold Schonberg, writing in the *New York Times* of 9 August 1970, asserted that under Barbirolli the orchestra 'lost the tight ensemble that Toscanini had given it... He was too inexperienced at that stage of his career and could not impose his will upon the temperamental virtuosos of the Philharmonic.' That is simply not true, as the foregoing pages should have shown beyond dispute. Erno Balogh, in the *Washington Sunday Star* of 6 September 1970, said that the orchestra 'relaxed too much, and the result was evident in the performances, which lacked the precision and virtuosity that had been developed under Toscanini.' All that these otherwise sympathetic writers are saying is that Barbirolli's approach to music-making was at the opposite extremity from his great predecessor's. Zirato considered that Barbirolli 'was the rightful unsurpassed interpreter of the authentic tradition, and like Toscanini he taught how to understand music and how to be faithful to the score, how to pour out the real essence of the music, how to encourage the orchestra to approach masterpieces with the same humility as he himself did.'

The contrast between Toscanini and Barbirolli was symbolic of the contrast between two generations of conductors and of the altering role of conductors. Toscanini was the supreme autocrat of the old school, ruling by terror, insult, tantrums and his own daemonic drive. Barbirolli, over thirty years younger, was the benevolent autocrat, more democratic, ruling through comradeship with his players, inviting them and the audience to share his own delight in music. The contrast in their philosophy was reflected in their interpretations: Toscanini inspired awe for the music he conducted; Barbirolli inspired love and affection. Their different approaches are crystallised in their respective recordings of Verdi's *Otello* and *Requiem*: the older man relentless, electric, dramatic in the extreme, incomparably exciting; the younger broader, with more humanity, many felicitous touches of detail, and caressing the phrases like a lover. Both are valid interpretations, both are true to the spirit of the music, both reveal different aspects of Verdi's and of their own genius. It is overlooked that Barbirolli not only *succeeded* Toscanini in New York: that would have soon been accomplished, a nine-day wonder. For seven years he conducted almost alongside him, one in Carnegie Hall, the other in the NBC studio. It is a pity that some of the artificial and excitement-craving New York public, egged on by the critics, regarded this as a gladiatorial contest, with Toscanini as the Lion and Barbirolli as the Christian. It is a pity the critics were not broad-minded enough to relish the fascinating contrast of styles that was being laid before them for thirty weeks of the year.

Of course, Barbirolli was not then the great conductor he was to become, for most conductors improve with age, but recordings (commercial and private) show that he was very good and that the orchestra had a rich and sensitive sound. (He himself confessed in his last years that he 'sometimes smiled' at the recollection of his younger interpretations; he constantly re-studied even the most familiar symphonies.) Toscanini was not the man to pay him the compliment he did in April 1942 if he had not meant it – if the Maestro found the orchestra in good shape, we may be sure it was, for he was no sycophant where his colleagues were concerned. Barbirolli did not 'lose' the Philharmonic's Toscaninian drive, for he did not want that kind of playing, but demanded a more spontaneous, inspirational style. To achieve this requires just as much discipline and control over the players. As John Erskine wrote in his history of the first hundred years of the Philharmonic: 'There has been no baton-breaking, score-hurling or bullying since he became head of the Philharmonic-Symphony, yet he has had no trouble whatever maintaining...discipline...' It hurt John deeply that his successor's decisions should have led to a situation where the players voted not to renew contracts unless arbitrators reviewed the cases of the dismissed fourteen, that Piastro should be compelled to denounce the management and Rodzinski for 'intrigue and politics,' and that impartial writers blamed some critics for the intrigues, noting that 'they have been strangely silent' since Rodzinski's advent.

Barbirolli's principal concern was with the orchestra and its welfare. The 'politics' distressed him. 'The trouble with Barbirolli,' a columnist in *Musical America* said in 1943, 'seems to have been that he was wholly uninterested in meeting pompous music patrons and kowtowing to them.' Even so friendly a member of the board as Ruth Pratt told John he should not have social contacts with members of the orchestra and thought he and Evelyn should live 'much more grandly.' Between 1939 and 1941, too, there was a subtle but definite undercurrent of anti-British opinion which resented his occupation of the Philharmonic rostrum; and John would never conceal his patriotism for the sake of expediency. Most of the Philharmonic directors and patrons were Republicans, with a deeply ingrained isolationism which upset him.

His programmes were enterprising and unstereotyped. Yet they were perhaps in advance of New York critical taste. Undoubtedly he conducted too much inferior American music (although, in his defence, it should be stated that he was constantly being pressed by the management to include 'novelties' which the public might like) and he included too many English works. Also, the system of a long season with only one short break was wrong. It must be remembered, too, that at that time he did not conduct the big works like Verdi's *Requiem* and Beethoven's Choral Symphony which he conducted often in his Hallé years. The only Mahler he conducted in New York was the *Adagietto* from the Fifth Sym-

phony. He did not conduct Strauss's *Ein Heldenleben*. He
conducted no Hindemith, no Schoenberg later than *Verklärte
Nacht*, no Shostakovich except *The Golden Age*. There was
scant appreciation of his two outstanding Bartók performances,
the *Music for Strings, Percussion and Celesta* and the *Sonata
for Two Pianos and Percussion*. Nevertheless his Brahms,
Schubert, Ravel and Debussy were held in high esteem; and
the critical acclaim of his work in Boston, Chicago and Los
Angeles suggests the accuracy of Bernard Herrmann's belief
that if Barbirolli had gone to any American city except New
York, Britain might never have got him back.

Much is made of the New York period by those out of sympathy with Barbirolli. It is even suggested that he left
America almost in disgrace, subdued and with his tail between his legs. This idea is preposterous to those who saw the
ebullient little man who arrived in Manchester in June 1943.
Barbirolli was a fighter and it would have taken more than
sour notices from the *New York Times* to make him quit. His
successor, Rodzinski, eventually resigned half-way through a
season, blaming interference by the management – a case of
poetic justice. The great and under-rated Mitropoulos was at
odds with the orchestra and with the critics, whose reviews
were more brutal than anything Barbirolli encountered. It
was even said of the beloved Bruno Walter by one of the
Philharmonic's senior players: 'It took us five years to have
him realise there was nothing he could teach us.' Yet Barbirolli, as will be seen, was invited back in the early 1950s, kept
the admiration and friendship of the players and the affection
of the audience and management, and returned in triumph in
1959 and other years. If this was failure, what may be
accounted success? But undoubtedly the New York years left
a scar on his psychological nature for the rest of his days; and
the stigma of failure, unjust though it was, partially clung to
his reputation in international circles until 1959 when he
reduced his Hallé commitments to give himself more time to
travel.

One comment remains. It is surprising today to read the
constant emphasis on Barbirolli's 'youth' when he went to
New York. True he looked young, but he was thirty-six,
hardly the first flush of youth. It was symptomatic of the attitude to age that prevailed just before the war. Today several
conductors ten years younger than Barbirolli was in 1936 have

held high musical posts in opera houses and concert-halls and the matter of their age has been but cursorily mentioned. But there is one difference: today there are no Toscaninis to follow.

PART TWO

*The
Hallé
Years
1943-70*

'This I feel very strongly,' Barbirolli's cello teacher Herbert Walenn wrote to John's mother at the time of his departure for New York in 1936, 'that music in this country depends much on Tita and this country will eventually claim him.' We shall see how this prophecy came true.

The Hallé Orchestra is the oldest permanent symphony orchestra in Britain and among the oldest in the world. It gave its first concert on 30 January 1858, as a private venture of the German pianist and conductor Charles Hallé, who had settled in Manchester ten years earlier after leaving Paris, where he had been one of a circle of musicians which included Berlioz, Wagner, Chopin and Liszt. For the next thirty-seven years he conducted a season of concerts from October to March, and gained a high reputation as a pioneer of new works. When Hallé died the conductorship was offered to Hans Richter who, after four years' delay, took up the post in 1899, the same year as the formation of the Hallé Concerts Society, which was to run the concerts as a non-profit-making concern. After Richter retired in 1911 came another Wagnerian, Michael Balling. During the 1914–18 war guest conductors, principally Beecham, kept the concerts going, and from 1920 to 1933 the permanent conductor was Hamilton Harty, under whom the orchestra enjoyed a halcyon period. When he resigned, no successor was appointed and, coinciding with a time of unemployment in Lancashire, the concerts went through a lean patch. They survived only because of the agreement reached with the BBC in 1933–34 whereby Hallé players were also employed by the Corporation's Northern Orchestra. This was always an uneasy alliance but it preserved the best players for the Hallé by guaranteeing their income.

For the two years 1939–41 Malcolm Sargent was appointed conductor-in-chief, but the outbreak of war changed the outlook for all orchestras. There was a 'boom' in symphony concerts and the Hallé found itself with more offers of engagements than it could accept – because the BBC refused to release the 'shared' players for any date more than five weeks ahead. Also, because of his close association with the London Philharmonic Orchestra which was touring the country, Sargent's availability to the Hallé was spasmodic. For 1942–43 the majority of Hallé concerts were offered to Leslie Heward, but he was a dying man, and could not undertake such a burden. The last straw came in 1942, when Liverpool, which for nearly a century had drawn on the Hallé for its Philharmonic players, put its orchestra on a permanent basis, with Sargent as conductor.

In December 1942, Philip Godlee, head of a textile firm, became chairman of the Hallé Society. Tall, autocratic, with an artificial leg and an artificial eye as legacies of the 1914–18 war, he was a striking, buccaneering figure, with his incisive wit, his monocle and his high-handed ways in committee. A leader, but an uncomfortable man to oppose. Acting on a suggestion from the Sheffield Philharmonic Society, he was anxious to put the Hallé on a wider basis and to take advantage of the wartime appetite for music. To do this he knew he must break with the BBC, offer the players all-the-year-round employment and find an outstanding permanent conductor. In conversation about possible conductors in February 1943, at the Royal Manchester College of Music, of which Godlee was treasurer, with Godlee and Robert J. Forbes, the Principal, Laurance Turner, the Hallé leader, mentioned the sterling qualities of Barbirolli, under whom he had played in the BBC Symphony Orchestra. Godlee pondered this, and a few days later, while in bed awaiting his morning tea, he rang up Forbes, who knew Barbirolli slightly, and asked him to cable New York. Nothing was said to the Hallé committee at this stage.

Encouraged by Barbirolli's reply, Godlee then advertised in the national press for players to join the 'new' Hallé; the

BBC countered by offering its thirty-five Hallé players more work and more pay. The choice for these players, several of them principals of sections, was simple: security with the BBC, death or glory with the Hallé. There was no doubt that at this date, 5 March, Forbes and Godlee expected the thirty-five to stay with the Hallé. On that same day Forbes wrote at some length to Barbirolli. He explained the background and that whereas the Hallé in 1939 had given about forty concerts a year, now it was proposed to give 'at least two hundred.' He added:

> I don't think there is much doubt that all the Northern players will leave the BBC and come to the Hallé... I hear privately that we shall probably have the choice of some very good people from the BBC Symphony Orchestra, the Scottish, the LPO and the new Liverpool Phil... There are sufficient funds available in the form of guarantees to make the venture a sound one... I shall feel very happy if this first tentative approach results in your coming to Manchester... I am convinced that it would mean the beginning of a new and glorious era for the Hallé.

In later years Barbirolli, without malice, described that letter as 'almost fraudulent.' Only four of the thirty-five BBC players chose to stay with the Hallé; there were no financial guarantees; and there were no good players from other orchestras waiting to join the Hallé. Forbes's letter reached New York at the end of March. Barbirolli cabled asking for an official approach as soon as possible because of 'consideration of important offer here' – the Los Angeles Philharmonic. Then followed some comedy. A panic-stricken cable from Forbes said they had learned from Harold Holt, Barbirolli's agent in London, that John was graded for the American Army, therefore the Hallé had 'felt compelled to explore other possibilities.' In fact they had offered the conductorship to the veteran Sir Henry Wood who, fortunately for them, declined it. Barbirolli told them they had been misinformed and on 5 April Godlee cabled: 'Happy offer you conductorship Hallé Orchestra from July 1st. Suggest guaranteed annual salary £3,500 covering 150 concerts. Additional concerts at agreed rate. Philip Godlee.'
The next day Barbirolli passed this information to Holt,

adding: 'Think offer generous considering conditions but suggest you confer with them as my agent to see if fee can be increased as they will have practically exclusive services. At same time am keenly interested in their splendid project.' A week later Holt cabled: 'Offer now increased to £3,750 with liberty conduct for other interests subject their [the Hallé committee's] consent not unreasonably withheld.' So the matter was settled, and on 18 April Barbirolli wrote the first of many letters to Godlee:

> First of all let me express to you and to the members of your committee my feelings of pride in becoming the conductor of the Hallé. I am very conscious of its great past and I shall hope and endeavour to maintain its traditions at their best. I am arranging with the help of our Embassy to return as soon as possible... I am hoping that you are planning a considerable decentralisation of the concerts, so that one well-rehearsed programme played in Manchester can be played two or three times in nearby districts. Only by constant and detailed rehearsing can an orchestra be led to the heights, and my ambitions for the reconstructed Hallé are high indeed. The higher we aim, the higher we are likely to reach... At the beginning I would like to do all I can myself to get the orchestra thoroughly set. Then I think it would be much more satisfactory, if the right person can be found, to have a permanent assistant. Guest conductors, however distinguished personally, never improve an orchestra; it is generally much the opposite... I only hope that your courage and vision will be rewarded as it deserves.

The previous day Barbirolli had written to Harold Holt:

> ...I cannot tell you how great is my joy, and that of my wife, at the thought of working again in my beloved country with a real permanent orchestra... It will, quite frankly, be rather a financial sacrifice to take the Hallé on. In addition to negotiations which I was having for the season 1943–44 with the Los Angeles Philharmonic, I had already $15,000 [about £3,750] booked for this summer!... You can assure them that I have no intention of running round

the country conducting on every free day I have! I have a big task on hand, and it is one to which you know I will give my utmost devotion... After the thrills of last summer and the feeling I have now that I am really wanted at home, it was hard to resist the appointment... Between ourselves, another factor was the feeling of relief that I can remain a Britisher... By the way, the appointment has made a great impression here, and they are already beginning to figure out when they can get me back!...

From the above can be felt the missionary fervour with which Barbirolli approached his Hallé appointment. It was to sustain him through some perilous moments. He and Evelyn regarded it as an act of God, but Philip insisted it was an act of Godlee.

The Barbirollis sailed from America in a small Portuguese ship, the *Serpa Pinto*. On arrival in Lisbon there was nothing to do but wait for seats in aircraft flying to England. The Barbirollis left sooner than they expected when two seats became available because the actor Leslie Howard wanted to stay in Lisbon for a few more days. So they flew home on a Saturday and Howard left the following Wednesday in the aircraft on which the Barbirollis would have travelled. It was shot down by the Germans and all aboard perished, including a mother and her little girl with whom John, who adored children, had struck up a friendship in the *Serpa Pinto*.

Barbirolli arrived in Manchester on 2 June 1943. He was met at London Road station (now re-named Piccadilly, alas) by Godlee and Forbes. It was raining. He was wearing a wide-brimmed hat and he was rather fat. They whisked him in a taxi to the Midland Hotel 'so that I should see as little as possible of the city.' There the full realisation of what he was expected to do was borne in upon him. The orchestra was booked for a week of concerts at Bradford from 5 July; so he had thirty-three days in which not only to train an orchestra but to find at least half of the players. Immediately he began three weeks of auditions, first a week in London and then a fortnight in a little room in Forsyth's music shop on Deansgate. Because it was in the middle of the war, experienced talent was scarce. As Barbirolli recounted it afterwards: 'I had to find the "slightly maimed"; it didn't matter if they had flat feet as long as they had straight fingers.' He ransacked every possible source, the colleges of music, theatre orchestras, anywhere musicians might be found.

Some remarkable talent emerged: a young flautist, Oliver Bannister, from the Royal Manchester College of Music; Enid Roper, a Keighley schoolmistress who played the horn; Maisie Ringham, RMCM trombonist who played for the Salvation Army; a blonde percussion player, Joyce Aldous, who later became timpanist and a favourite with audiences everywhere; the oboist and cor anglais player Patricia Stancliffe; George Alexander, violist. Also there were those applicants whose enthusiasm outweighed their skill; for instance, the elderly double bass player who played the scherzo from Beethoven's Fifth Symphony without once moving his left hand and was then asked by John to play the solo passage from Act IV of *Otello* which contains the leap from C flat to E flat. The first time he went up a little way. 'Further,' John said. A little higher. 'No, further.' Another try, but no E flat. Barbirolli took the instrument and showed him. 'What,' said the old man, 'oop theer? Ah've never been oop theer before.'

The nucleus of the orchestra, of course, was the number of more experienced players, many ex-Hallé or 1942–43 Hallé, led by the four who abandoned the BBC: Laurance Turner (leader), Pat Ryan (clarinet), Philip Hecht (principal second violin) and Arthur Shaw (principal double bass). In addition there were the veteran harpist Charles Collier; Arthur Percival, Norah Winstanley and Jane Marcus, violinists; Haydn Rogerson, Stuart Knussen and Gladys Yates (cellists); Bert Mitton (bassoon); Arthur Lockwood (first trumpet); Wallace H. Jones (tuba and orchestral manager). Barbirolli had heard Livia Gollancz, the publisher's daughter, with the LSO on his 1942 tour and he engaged her by telephone as Hallé first horn. His old friend from the Scottish Orchestra, Tommy Cheetham, was librarian and percussion player. Intensive rehearsals of the new orchestra began in the Houldsworth Hall on 28 June, the day after the Leslie Heward memorial concert which marked the end of the 'old' Hallé. As in New York, Barbirolli worked nine hours a day and spent most of the night 'bowing' master copies for the strings. Everyone was astonished by his energy and enthusiasm. He gradually welded this mixture of age and experience and youth and inexperience into a team. As the music critic of the *Yorkshire Post* wrote after attending one of the rehearsals: 'The adven-

of what is virtually a new orchestra of great quality would be a rare enough occurrence in peacetime. In wartime such an event can only be regarded as little short of miraculous, but there can be no doubt that the miracle has been achieved with the newly formed Hallé Orchestra.'

Barbirolli had caused a controversy in his first hours with the Hallé. Wartime concerts in Britain were built round piano concertos – usually Tchaikovsky's No. 1, Rachmaninov's No. 2, or Grieg's. Pianists had never had it so good; their success was symbolised by that masterly piece of pastiche, the *Warsaw Concerto* from the film *Dangerous Moonlight*. The organisers of the Hallé week in Bradford had booked five pianists. When John was told this, he exploded. 'How well I recall Godlee and Forbes meeting me on arrival,' he wrote to me in 1963,

and whilst we were awaiting the arrival of the inevitable tea in the Midland hearing the rather ominous remark of 'You tell him,' 'No, you tell him.' I sensed trouble somewhere and finally one blurted out about the pianists. I was a fiery young man in those days and my Italian blood leapt to the surface: 'If I was enticed back from the USA to become a piano concerto accompanist I would return immediately to a more civilised musical atmosphere etc. etc.' I agreed to retain one, and the sole survivor was my old friend Clifford Curzon... Such was the 'power of the pianist' at that epoch that neither Forbes nor Godlee could steel themselves to announce this catastrophic news to Mrs Tillett [of the concert agents Ibbs and Tillett] but it was left to the maestro.

They came from Bradford, too, to plead with him but he was adamant. Barbirolli was, perhaps, still sensitive about the remarks made in New York in 1936 that he had been engaged because he was a good accompanist for famous soloists.*

So, because of this affront to the public's taste, the audience for the first Hallé–Barbirolli concert on 5 July (the Barbirollis' wedding anniversary) in the poor acoustics of the Prince's Theatre, Bradford, was by no means large, though its

* In his first eight months with the Hallé, Barbirolli conducted 138 concerts, of which nineteen were with pianists.

enthusiasm increased after each item. The programme was:

Wagner: Overture, *Die Meistersinger*
Delius: *A Song of Summer*
Tchaikovsky: Fantasy Overture, *Romeo and Juliet*
Brahms: Symphony No. 2 in D

In response to an ovation after the symphony, Barbirolli said: 'I have been entrusted with a very great mission – that the name and fame of this great orchestra shall not, under my guidance, achieve less honour in the future than it has done in the past.' Twenty-five years later, at the end of his silver jubilee season, when he resigned as conductor-in-chief, he recalled this speech and told the Manchester audience: 'Mission accomplished.'

By the Wednesday of that first Bradford week the theatre was sold out and queues were forming in mid-afternoon. The orchestra was not much more than sixty strong, but its achievement and its potential were remarked upon by all the critics. Humphrey Procter-Gregg, then head of the music department of Manchester University, wrote to the *Manchester Guardian* to declare his belief that 'Monday's first concert at Bradford was one of the most satisfying musical occasions I ever remember...the prospects for the success of the new orchestra are, musically speaking, prodigious...the best performance of Brahms's second symphony I ever heard.' Heady stuff, but this was the enthusiasm generated in even so short a time, and nowhere more strongly than among the players themselves. 'Arriving at the theatre one morning,' John said in an interview in July 1943, 'I found the place sounding like a conservatory of music. Entire sections and sub-sections had come down before scheduled rehearsal time and were practising.'

After more rehearsals in Manchester, John took the orchestra for a week to Edinburgh and a week to Glasgow; his popularity from his Scottish years ensured a warm interest in his new venture in both cities. Everywhere the Hallé went in the next eight weeks the pattern was the same: intense public enthusiasm, a good press, mayoral receptions. The Hallé were discovering that they had engaged not only a superb conductor but a master of the art of public relations. On their first visit to Hanley, Staffordshire, in September, an incident occurred which Barbirolli never forgot because it epitomised for him the honesty of the Northerner. In those days he would not see anyone in the interval, but made an exception in the case of a young soldier who wanted his autograph and explained that he would have to rush back to his camp the minute the second half ended. While John was signing, he asked the soldier if he was enjoying the concert. 'Oh yes, sir,' was the reply, 'it's wonderful – so far!' 'So far' became John's watchword thereafter.

The new Hallé's first Manchester concert was not until 15 August. Since 1939 Hallé concerts in the Manchester area had been given in theatres or cinemas in the city and suburbs. The Free Trade Hall had been requisitioned for war uses, but in December 1940 it was destroyed by incendiary bombs and only its Peter Street façade remained standing. John took the Hallé to play in the King's Hall in the amusement park at Longsight known as Belle Vue. Six thousand people went there on that August day to hear orchestral playing 'finer than any we have heard in Manchester for many years,' as Granville Hill wrote in the *Manchester Guardian*. For the next eight years Belle Vue was the venue for the Hallé's Sunday concerts. To most Mancunians it was the home of the circus at Christmas; now it was the home of the Hallé and Barbirolli used the room marked 'Ringmaster'. Acoustics were remarkably good, despite the occasional roar of a lion from the zoo near by or the twittering of sparrows in the roof. It had a wonderful atmosphere not easily explained to those who did not live through those immediate post-war years. When Casals was to play the Elgar, Haydn and Dvořák concertos on 28 October 1945, Barbirolli thought it advisable to warn the great cellist what to expect. Casals listened to a description of Belle Vue and exclaimed 'But, my dear Barbirolli, I *adore* circuses.' Other concerts in the first year were given at the Longford, Stretford, the Capitol, Didsbury, and the Odeon, Prestwich – all cinemas.

If one seeks an explanation for the extraordinary emotional attachment which grew between Barbirolli and his orchestra and between them and their audiences, and which was to last for a quarter of a century, it can partially be found in these early months and years, during and just after the war. For one thing, the whole Hallé adventure was a symbol, in artistic terms, of the feeling in Britain, once the tide of war had turned at El Alamein in 1942, that music and the other arts would matter more than they had, when peace returned. The orchestra at once recognised Barbirolli's powers of leadership, his total absorption in his work, his ability to make them play at full stretch on every occasion, his complete professionalism and his apparently endless capacity for work. Whatever he asked from them, they knew he asked more from himself. It will by now be obvious to the reader that Barbirolli had a re-markable gift for creating this conductor–orchestra–audience rapport. He had done it with the BNOC and in Glasgow and New York. He did it again later in Houston and Berlin. An eloquent tribute to it was paid him in a letter from a col-league, Josef Krips, written in December 1955 after he had conducted the Hallé: 'You have established something unique in Manchester. A sensitive person is quite aware of this from the first to the last bar of a concert. One experiences in Manchester a "one-ness" of orchestra and public with the music which I have never so keenly felt before. And it is due to you.' Barbirolli did not create an instrument solely for himself to play on; the Hallé played superbly for other con-ductors, too.

The rapport between conductor and players was not only achieved in rehearsal and on the concert-platform. It de-veloped in daily contacts, and nowhere more than on long and arduous journeys. There was only strictly rationed petrol for cars in those days, and the Hallé travelled everywhere by train or sometimes by hired buses. The trains were crowded and slow. John shared the orchestra's discomforts and refused any kind of preferential treatment. He stood for hours in draughty or stuffy train corridors, keeping up the players' spirits with his fund of reminiscences. He walked home to his flat in Appleby Lodge, Rusholme, in the early mornings because there were no taxis at the stations. On arrival home, perhaps at 2 a.m., he would begin bowing scores and would usually find Evelyn, who was working for the Hallé and as his secretary, still up, typing. On long winter journeys over the Pennines, he travelled in the coach with the orchestra. He remembered players' birthdays, and once, at midnight on a crowded train, he produced a cake for one of the women players, solemnly presented it to her with a little speech, and led the singing of 'Happy Birthday.' When, in the days of rationing, the cellist Gladys Yates said 'I could just do with a nice pork pie!' he remembered this after the war, and every time the coach stopped in Ripon on their way to play in Middlesbrough he went into a shop and bought her a pie. When he referred to the Hallé as his family, it was no exaggeration. On the rostrum he was the boss; at the lunch break he was in the queue in some café or 'British Restaurant', talking, cheering everyone up. Yet he was not without his own problems, as this note left for Evelyn during 1944 shows:

My darling. I just want very badly to write a word to say how sorry I am for being such a lousy 'marito' just lately. I have no excuse to offer, just this load of depression which seems to have descended on me, though it seems some years since I have had such an unrelieved bout. I know myself of old, and *please* don't think me obstinate, but to keep myself occupied working is the only remedy... God knows I have few other excesses and this is one I am afraid I must ask you to try and bear with a little longer.

There was no depression for the audiences. They were elated. The excitement of those early Barbirolli concerts will never be forgotten by those who attended them. We had heard fine performances before; but these were different. The vitality of the man, his dedication, the feeling he gave you that he was not only demanding the best they could give from his players but also from the audience as listeners, the sense that for the two hours of its duration the concert was the most important thing in the world – all this made a Barbirolli concert exceptional. It had its ritual, too: the short-stepped walk to the rostrum, left arm crossed Napoleonically over his chest, then the National Anthem, conducted, for half its course, facing the audience. He was dynamic, true enough, but he was like the refiner's fire. He sharpened every response. The performances of Debussy's *La Mer*, of Ravel's *Daphnis and Chloë* and of Elgar's *Enigma Variations* were revelations. There was a memorable *Symphonie Fantastique* in Stretford on 30 January 1944, when people stood on their seats at the end and yelled 'Bravo' and Granville Hill, with memories of Harty's great Berlioz stored in his mind, declared it to be probably 'the most vivid playing of Berlioz's music ever heard at a Hallé concert.' In Sheffield, Bradford, Hanley,

Wolverhampton, Leicester and other towns it was the same –
a special bond was forged. The Hallé was as much their
orchestra now as Manchester's. In Sheffield Barbirolli conducted Strauss's *Le Bourgeois Gentilhomme* suite. He sensed
a frigidity in the applause, so he told the audience a little of
the work's history, of what Strauss's writing for the orchestra
meant to him, and he played it all again. At Prestwich on 12
December 1943, he conducted Walton's *Façade* and interrupted the performance after the Swiss Yodelling Song to
rebuke the audience for sitting there like 'a wall of impenetrable grimness.' He would go home if they did not laugh. He
illustrated the jokes, and repeated two of the items. It had its
effect: they laughed and they talked about the Hallé afterwards. It became 'news'.

At the old Eastbrook Hall in Bradford, where Hallé concerts were given from 1944 until the restoration in 1952 of St
George's Hall, he made a special point at the interval of
beckoning to the children perched high behind the orchestra
and chatting to them about the music. As one of them told
me: 'His words of encouragement inspired us to keep listening to classical music, even in face of the sometimes hostile
opposition to it at home.' At Sheffield, too, he had his 'platform kids.' Ronald Stevenson, the pianist and composer, was a
working-class boy in Blackburn in 1943. He wrote in *The
Listener* twenty-seven years later:

> I felt that all the sun which the smoke obscured was burst-
> ing out in the King George's Hall when Barbirolli con-
> ducted Rossini's overtures. In those days he brought light
> to the nightmare of sirens and gas masks. I also remember
> the breadth of bow he drew from the string body: I see
> him now, his left hand throbbing in an imaginary vibrato,
> and I can still hear the sound he produced from his
> players.

That sound gradually and sensationally improved. The
orchestra was soon increased to over seventy, and as the new
players gained experience, the playing acquired freedom and
polish. The programmes were designed to train an orchestra
in flexibility of style, so Strauss waltzes had their place with
Bax, Villa-Lobos and Haydn. William Glock, then writing for
the *Observer*, travelled north in October 1943 to hear the new

orchestra. He was astonished by the discipline, by the four-teen rehearsals before the opening concert of the 1943–44 Manchester season, by the 'verve and strength and tautness' of the strings, by the way the players listened to every part of the score 'with a chamber musician's sense of balance.' Being a critic, he called for 'a courageous choice of programmes' to match the higher playing standards, but the programmes for the first full season were by no means unadventurous for their time, and two of the English works performed, Bax's Third Symphony and Vaughan Williams's latest symphony, the Fifth (first performed in June 1943), were recorded by the Hallé for the British Council. Delius's Double Concerto and Fauré's *Pelléas* incidental music were not exactly everyday fare. But the critic whose every waking hour is concerned with music is inclined to forget that what is commonplace to him is a rarity to others in the audience. In the England of the 1940s, works like Debussy's *La Mer* were an adventurous choice for concerts in Preston, Bolton, Wigan and Newcastle and nothing pleased Barbirolli more than to see crowded and enthusiastic halls for masterpieces of that kind. It is certain that such places had never before heard such carefully pre-pared and scrupulously presented performances.

There were detractors, of course. Not of the playing, but, by some critics, of Barbirolli's conducting. He was good in programme music but the 'logic' of symphonies eluded him, they said; he laid too much emphasis on certain highlights. He broke up the flow. This was true sometimes, but if that was all there had been to Barbirolli's music-making he would scarcely have won the acclaim he did. He was concentrating at this time on creating an instrument on which to play, often with material which, frankly, was below standard; the great maturing of his own musical personality followed. But the conviction with which he carried out all he undertook, the sheer musicality of it all, satisfied most people. True, he intro-duced hesitations into the waltz of the *Fantastique*: and I believe Berlioz would have been delighted. He 'exaggerated' the sudden fortissimi in the *Mastersingers* overture. But did he? They are there, in the score, usually unobserved. The majority of his audience were captivated by his high spirits, the expressiveness of his features, his little touches of show-manship, such as his 'dancing' in the scherzo of Schubert's Great C major Symphony and in Viennese waltzes. At one of his earliest Hallé rehearsals of *Tales from the Vienna Woods*, when the playing was accurate but tepid, he exclaimed: 'My God, you are in the Vienna Woods not the Stockport slums, and you didn't go into the woods to quarrel!'

But not all the Manchester audience were convinced that the advent of Barbirolli was good for the Hallé. There was a core which resented the 'fuss' accorded to this 'fat little Eyetie' with his penchant for publicity, learned in America, no doubt, and his 'big ideas.' This man who cooked his own spaghetti, travelled round with the players, talked to the audience – was he in the Hallé tradition? They missed Sargent, and were by no means convinced that the Hallé had fought hard enough to retain him. Nor was this opinion confined to the general public. Barbirolli had asked Percy Heming to go to Manchester to help on the managerial side, which he did for six months. Writing to him ten years later Heming recalled: 'It seems funny now that I had to work like a black during the first few months with the Hallé to prove and assure everyone in Manchester that Mr Sargent was a joke beside you, and that includes the directors [committee] except Philip Godlee and Bob Forbes.'

An important outcome of these first months was the firm friendship with Godlee. He and Barbirolli had liked each other at once, from the very first evening when John had stayed with Philip and Barbara at Alderley Edge and next day he and Philip had pushed his luggage in a handcart up the hill to the station. Eventually the Godlees moved to Didsbury, nearer to Rusholme, and John played string quartets with Philip and his daughters Elizabeth and Rachel, who later became members of the Hallé Orchestra. John and Philip, though physically contrasted – the giant and the dwarf, yet again – had much in common. Both were living a little out of their time, though they were well able to cope with modern living; both were single-minded in achieving their aims; both were completely possessed by the idea of the Hallé. Godlee believed that his function as chairman was to see that Barbirolli got what he wanted for the orchestra: it was not always easy, but he exercised a benevolent despotism over the committee, letting them talk a subject over and then making sure that his original proposition was carried. Sometimes this involved a display of monocled inactivity. He delighted John by recalling a remark made to him by Lord Stamp: 'You know,

Philip, in my time as an arbitrator I've sat on the fence so often, my arse is like a hot cross bun.'

Godlee had a deep affection for Barbirolli, and thoroughly understood him, warts and all. His faith in him was never shaken, as it might have been at the very first by receipt of a disparaging letter from a member of the British Information Services in Washington whose parents lived in Alderley Edge. 'I'm wondering on what conceivable recommendation this appointment could have been made,' the writer said.

> It is common knowledge that Barbirolli has allowed the New York Philharmonic to fall to about the lowest ebb of its career... Criticisms of Barbirolli in the New York newspapers have been astonishingly frank; they would have been material for a libel action in Britain. I have seen and heard him conduct pretty often in the last few years, and I would say without hesitation that he is not properly qualified to conduct major symphonic works, although he gets good effects with virtuoso pieces... On the other hand I would agree that Barbirolli is quite good 'box office'. He is much liked by the ladies. But I think that your subscribers would scarcely be hoodwinked by his appearance and manners.

Neither was Godlee hoodwinked by the suggestion that the man who had taken a group of inexperienced players and made them, in a very short time, into the best orchestra of its date in England would, only a few months before, have let a great and experienced orchestra like New York's fall into decay. Nor were other people. Barbirolli's return to the English musical scene was generally welcomed. In October 1943 he conducted the LPO at his first Royal Philharmonic Society concert for eleven years. Three months later, on 22 January 1944, he introduced his *Elizabethan Suite* to England at another RPS concert and on 26 May he took the Hallé to give its first concert as a guest of Britain's oldest concert society. He conducted the LSO in a season of Russian music. As could have been expected, the LSO in May 1944 offered him its conductorship for a large fee. It was tempting, but by then he had set in train new plans for Manchester. 'My duty lies with the orchestra it has been my privilege to re-create,' he said, 'I should like to feel we are on the verge of great things.' He was looking ahead to the end of the war, and to a larger orchestra. 'My stay in Manchester will depend on whether my ambitions for the orchestra are reciprocated.' At the next Belle Vue concert he was cheered to the echo. 'I simply can't leave that,' he said to Evelyn.

Already he had realised that, in contrast with the public and with civic authorities elsewhere, Manchester Corporation had little pride in the orchestra – or, if they had, it stopped well short of practical support. Other cities were beginning to vote large sums to support orchestras, but for years Manchester was to drag its feet. In 1943, for the first time, it voted a paltry £2,500 to the Hallé, of which figure £1,000 was to be spent on children's concerts. In a speech at a civic lunch in September 1944 – into which he managed to interpolate his joke about 'that virile monarch Henry VIII and his brilliant if impenetrable daughter' – Barbirolli pleaded for much greater aid and for the city to send the orchestra overseas. 'We shall be ambassadors of trade as well as of art.' 'Unlike Oliver, I would not ask for more, I would ask for a lot more.'

In this way he served notice to Manchester that the Hallé would in future insist on proper recognition as one of the city's finest assets. He sought practical support, not lip service. As he had said in a memorandum to the Hallé committee in January 1944: 'Does Manchester deserve the Hallé? The Lord Mayor of Birmingham, the Mayors of Hanley, Wolverhampton, Rotherham and Sheffield all come to Hallé concerts. Has the Lord Mayor ever been to a Hallé concert? Have the civic dignitaries of Manchester ever shown the slightest interest in the Hallé?' It was to be a long struggle, accompanied by abuse of Barbirolli for his ambitious plans, but eventually it was to end in victory for him and in his becoming a Freeman of the city, the first representative of the arts to be thus honoured in the citadel of commerce. To that shameful criticism of his 'big ideas' he was to give the final devastating retort: 'I agree that if Manchester wants little ideas then I and my colleagues are not the right men for the job.' But the fact remains that if Manchester Corporation had been more generous in the 1950s, the Hallé might have achieved even greater and wider fame and recognition – and kept its players.

Symphony: 'If you don't *love* to play this music you should go out and chop wood.' But he was not one of those conductors who give philosophical lectures on the music at rehearsals: he was businesslike and brisk, but knew how and when to ease tension. The atmosphere of a Barbirolli rehearsal was normally of relaxed concentration. He liked his players to share his own abandonment to music. A young applicant for a position in the Hallé asked him about a pension. He looked at her aghast. 'My dear, if you're worrying about retiring or dying you run along to the BBC. If you want to live and enjoy it, come to my orchestra.'

Barbirolli did not insult individual players – he believed that was not the way to get the best of them. His strictures were made to the room in general. 'Cretins!' was a favourite word of abuse. But when he had castigated them for their errors and omissions he would add: 'Some of you.' This became a byword with the Hallé. Also he would say: 'Now let's hear you play like a *proper* orchestra.' Rumbles of discontent, a few bars of music, then someone would ask: 'Are we playing like a proper orchestra now?' The Italian in him sometimes made him difficult for English players to work with. Some piece of bad playing would cause him to flare in anger and castigate the recalcitrant section – 'playing like *kids*.' A second later, when the less volatile English were still simmering with resentment, he would turn on them a smiling face and ask for some exquisite piece of phrasing. When really angry he would sometimes lapse into virulent Venetian dialect (at one rehearsal an elderly Czech cellist who happened to understand what was being said blushed to the roots of his hair). While uttering his generalisations his eye would rest on one particular player. 'But, Sir, it wasn't me.' 'What! Did I say it was?' 'No, but you *looked* at me.' 'Well, hell, I've got to look somewhere, haven't I? I'm not going to talk with my eyes closed. Now come on, three before K...' A rap on his stand with his stick and off they would go again. Sometimes his repartee was as witty as anything attributed to Beecham: 'Now, woodwind, I want a proper pianissimo here' – peering at the score – 'all of you, flutes, oboes, clarinets, bassoons, pianissimo. Now come on.' 'Clarinets not playing there.' 'What's that? Eh? Let's see. Yes, you're quite right. Well, we'll have a chance of a *real* pianissimo, won't we?' He insisted on constant rehearsal to achieve the pianissimo quality he sought. A friend, much stirred by a performance under Barbirolli of a Tchaikovsky symphony played by combined orchestras, remarked to him afterwards on the thrilling volume of sound. John brushed his remarks aside with 'What about the pianissimi?' And there was the classic remark made before one cold rehearsal at Newport in Monmouthshire, where the Hallé then played in an old chapel. Above the choir in large letters was a text: 'Get right with God.' Barbirolli eyed this and said: 'Get right with God – and get a good A.'

A Barbirolli rehearsal was never dull. Humour, anger, white-hot interest, petulant slaps at the score or radiant joy – any of these might be forthcoming. Teaching a new work to the orchestra he would split it into two sections (strings; woodwind and brass) – 'my sexual rehearsals' he called them, borrowing one of the players' malapropisms – and rehearse each section for three hours and the full orchestra for another three. He was very patient and made them take difficult passages slowly, desk by desk if necessary. Perhaps he enjoyed most working with the strings: perched on his stool, wearing a jacket which might be dandyish or disgraceful, his hair dishevelled, throwing cigarettes to the players and lighting one for himself. The relationship was of easy equality, bordering on the familiar, but in the snap of a finger he could be 'the maestro' if he felt it necessary. He allowed backchat, but everyone knew just how far they could go. Changing from one work to the next, he would drop the score to the floor with a bang, simultaneously announcing the name of the next piece – bad luck for the back desks who couldn't hear him.

His principal concern was for the quality of sound. This mattered more than precision. He forgave wrong notes, missed passages, even bad intonation, but a 'slide' omitted or a *flautando* melody played without quick vibrato and he would blaze out. To the players his methods sometimes seemed 'bitty' and detached, even haphazard, but as the day wore on a pattern emerged, and the orchestra realised they had really learned a work. He achieved his finest performances by his expressive face and by his hands, which could have coaxed music from a slab of concrete. Although his 'stick technique' was second to none, the baton was often merely an extension of his hand, a wand rather than a stick, down which the music travelled to the players. In the exaltation of a sublime passage it might be pointed over his shoulder, but it did not matter: he had the indefinable power of communication, just as Beecham had, the telepathy which is more powerful than any beat. But there was a difficulty with pizzicato. He wanted a particular sound, but the players complained they could not be together if he did not give a strong 'click' beat. 'How can I? If I give you a click beat you'll make the wrong sound.' As Martin Milner put it, he *thought* sound.

He did not belong to the school of conductors who at rehearsal keep something in reserve for the evening: he went flat out all the time and could not understand others who did not. The greatest crime in his eyes was laziness; to see a player with legs crossed, leaning back in his chair, enraged him.

His views on the performance of concertos and on conducting without a score are interesting and were expressed in a talk he gave in his early days with the Hallé. 'I treat a concerto not as a virtuosic display by one individual,' he said, 'but as a collective musical accomplishment and I spare no pains to that end. The great concertos should always be considered part of the orchestral repertoire.' Wherever the geography of the hall allowed he conducted piano concertos with the rostrum on the audience side of the piano. 'I don't like the soloist and my first violins behind my left shoulder,' he said. He rarely conducted without a score on his desk. 'At the outset of my career I did a considerable amount of memory conducting, but I placed on myself the extremely arduous demand that what I conducted from memory I should also be able to write down from memory. As I could not continue to discharge faithfully this onerous conscientiousness, I reverted to scores.' When he last conducted *Die Meistersinger* at Covent Garden he rehearsed it without a score, 'but for the performance something in me said it was more respectful to have the music before me.'

The phrase heard most often at a Barbirolli rehearsal was 'Play at the point of the bow.' In this way string players had to play really softly but also produced fullness of tone. Rehearsing an American orchestra he exclaimed: 'Why are there different ideas in every country on how many inches from the top of the bow the point is? When I say point I mean *point*.' To violinists who were mean in their full use of their bowing arm he would say: 'Did you study the violin in a telephone booth?' The hours he devoted to preparing string parts during his career must have been beyond computation. He marked bowings and dynamics and also special fingerings. From his experience as a cellist he could instruct players how to obtain greater colour and expression by playing in different positions and on unexpected strings. This, and his acute ear for balance between sections, largely accounted for the 'Barbirolli sound' which he obtained from every orchestra he conducted. All the meticulous work that had gone into preparing the performance was followed, at the concert itself, by his ability to inspire the players afresh and to make all his carefully marked detail sound spontaneous. This was the secret of the vitality of his best interpretations. His own description of the sound he wanted was 'a Burgundy sound – like a *good* Burgundy wine, the kind you used to get. I look for warmth and *cantabile* and a working atmosphere where men play beyond the call of duty.'

To this end he would devote hours of his own time to instructing individual players, helping and advising them. When a new oboist joined the Hallé in 1946 who had never played in Elgar's Second Symphony he invited her to his flat and took her through the whole work, beating time with a pencil. It was, incidentally, this player who made a bad mistake in a woodwind entry in Dvořák's 'New World' Symphony at a concert in Portsmouth. She got a fierce glare from J.B.; he brought in the cellos, another glare; then the violas, and she got a third glare – just to rub it in. Afterwards she crept up to him to apologise. He just laughed and pinched her chin. A similar occurrence at rehearsal brought a shout from the rostrum: 'The A string!' One of the women violinists apologised to him afterwards, asking 'Did I use the wrong string?' 'I wasn't yelling at you, my dear,' John replied. 'But as a matter of fact you did.' Once one had been a Hallé man with J.B., said Ifor James, the horn-player, it did not matter where one went afterwards, one remained a Hallé man. In whichever orchestra they played, ex-Hallé men would say: 'The Boss wouldn't have allowed that.' He had the power to interest players in music which was not to their personal taste. Several Hallé players have told me that only J.B. could make Elgar and Mahler tolerable to them: 'He made every phrase live and matter. Somehow, with others, the same phrases are pedestrian.'

It was the same with foreign orchestras. The players invariably went to him, spontaneously, to thank him for the pleasure of working with him and for what he had taught them. The Berlin Philharmonic also enjoyed his broken German. 'You are making the big line but the inside is not right,' he told them. 'It is like a big long Würstel (sausage). It's very long like the big line but before you eat it you've got to cut it up. Schnitt, Schnitt!'

He insisted on absolute silence as he walked into the room to begin rehearsing. If there was as much as a whisper he would let out a great shout of 'Shut up!' as he approached the rostrum. He put this ritual to superb psychological effect in Rome in 1966 when he went to record *Madam Butterfly*. The orchestra thought they knew the work backwards and were in no mood for detailed rehearsal. His recording producer and friend Ronald Kinloch Anderson (who in his youth had attended Barbirolli's Scottish Orchestra concerts) described what happened: *

Before John left his room he said to me: 'They must be silent before I go out. Tell the ispettore (orchestral manager).' It took this poor man a good five minutes but in the end there was quiet. At that crucial moment John (who knew the silence would not last) appeared and walked, followed by me, very very slowly and deliberately to the rostrum by the longest route (and it was very long) in a deathly hush. The orchestra were fascinated by this funereal procession; they had never experienced anything like it; you could have heard a pin drop. The moment of drama created by John completely gripped them. He reached the rostrum, said a few words of greeting and the rehearsal started. He had the orchestra in the palm of his hand and not another sound was heard except when he wished it.

He mellowed over the years, especially when working with choirs. In his early days with both the Hallé Choir and Sheffield Philharmonic Chorus he could be extremely scathing. 'You're singing about Angels and Archangels, not Gold Flake and Players,' was one remark. 'You're not bank clerks on a Sunday outing, you're souls sizzling in hell.' But he could be graphically amusing. Trying to impart the correct note of

* *Hallé* magazine No. 127, 1970–71.

derision to a passage in the Demons' Chorus from *The Dream of Gerontius* – 'What's a saint?' – he sprawled back against the pianoforte, clothes and hair awry, spoke the words 'a saint' with contempt and cocked a double-handed snook accompanied by a fruity 'raspberry'. He made his point. But however much he lashed the choirs they respected him and responded to his enthusiasm. With his gift of words he could make them understand his attitude to a work. After his first *Messiah* in 1951 the Sheffield Philharmonic Chorus thanked him 'for giving us once again a glimpse of that perfection to which in our hearts we would all attain.' When the Hallé Choir sang at the Edinburgh Festival they travelled overnight and arrived, weary and cold, at Princes Street station at five o'clock on a misty morning. All their low spirits vanished when, on the platform, they saw one solitary overcoated figure, with his big hat and his stick, waiting to greet them. It was by actions of this kind, the actions of a thoroughbred professional, that he won the love of all who worked with him. They extended to small, thoughtful details, as when he was leaving the Free Trade Hall after *Messiah*. The bass soloist, Hervey Alan, was some yards ahead and heard John call his name. When John reached him he lifted his hands to Alan's overcoat collar, tucked it round him and said: 'You must always wrap up well after a performance.' Trivial perhaps, but the mark of greatness.

Near the Hewitt Street rehearsal rooms was an old public house, The Boatman's Inn, known to its regulars as 'Old Joe's' after the landlord Joe Bostock, a remarkable 'character', a professed atheist who could quote freely from the Bible and the Koran and knew Shakespeare almost by heart. Labourers and dockers filled the public bar, and there was a cosy little inner room, with a fire, frequented by doctors, barristers, businessmen and some of the Hallé. J.B. soon discovered 'Old Joe's' and ate sandwiches in the public bar while chatting to the dockers. He never said who he was and when Joe discovered his identity he resisted attempts to 'promote' him to the inner room, although later he went there with a few of his cronies from the orchestra, notably Pat Ryan, Tommy Cheetham and Norah Winstanley. He became greatly attached to Joe, and when told of his death from pneumonia hurried to the pub, went up to Joe's room and was found ten minutes later still kneeling beside the bed on which Joe lay.

Six months after his arrival in Manchester Barbirolli told Philip Godlee that he had given the Hallé a first-rate orchestra but they had given him a tenth-rate management. Something had to be done, and that would involve the removal or down-grading of Dick Hesselgrave, the secretary. The committee at this point discovered that one of Barbirolli's weaknesses was that he preferred others to fire his bullets. Nor did he hesitate to use his own importance to the society as a means of bringing pressure to bear. 'Retention or dismissal of manager must be entirely the act of the committee,' his memorandum to them said, 'Mr Barbirolli will not be made responsible for this decision... By April 1st or before he wants to see the proposed schedule for 1944–45 and his decision as to whether he continues with the orchestra will be based on this schedule...'

Hesselgrave resigned and T. Ernest Bean, a former member of the *Manchester Guardian* circulation staff and a WEA lecturer on music, became secretary and general manager in March 1944. He and John took to each other at once, which was just as well in view of what lay immediately ahead, an episode that was farcical, tragic and, as far as the public was concerned at the time, inexplicable and ineptly handled.

When Elgar died in 1934, the Hallé Society elected Beecham to succeed him as its president. The duties of the office were vague and Beecham made no effort to fulfil them, whatever they were. In 1940 he went to the United States where he was the centre of several controversies in one of the least happy and effective periods of his life. Barbirolli's relationship with him had been uneasy since 1929 and Beecham's letters to Judson in 1936 attacking Barbirolli's New York appointment had made matters worse. But when Beecham declared publicly early in 1943 that the New York Philharmonic was 'almost as bad' as one of the London orchestras he had once had to revive, that was the last straw. During 1944 Sir Thomas announced his intention of returning to England and told the Hallé committee that he would be able to conduct the Hallé in one concert in Manchester. Godlee informed Barbirolli, whose succinct reply was: 'If you let that man near my orchestra, you won't see my arse for dust.' He added, for good measure, that the sooner they found a new president, the better he would like it. He didn't care how they did it, but do it they must – without, of course, disclosing the basic reason for their decision. Godlee and Bean decided that, in view of the new policy of involving the city council in Hallé affairs, the Lord Mayor should be invited to become president. This would be moved at the annual meeting in December 1944. Meanwhile, on 17 July, Godlee wrote to Beecham* explaining this position and rather lamely stating that the presidency had been 'allowed to lapse' because of the difficulty of maintaining touch with you.' Beecham soon riddled this feeble argument with holes. At the annual meeting the matter was deferred so that new approaches could be made to Beecham. Already Forbes, who knew him well, had found him conciliatory and willing to meet Barbirolli. Forbes persuaded Barbirolli to write to Beecham what the minutes of the Society describe as 'a cordial letter.' This was not even acknowledged.

On 15 December Ernest Bean went on the intended peacemaking mission to Beecham in Liverpool. He was 'received' at the Adelphi Hotel after a concert and later wrote a magnificent report of the encounter for Godlee. He has also since said (to me) that his role must have seemed to Barbirolli more than a little ambivalent, for while I was partly aware of the unscrupulously Macchiavellian lengths to which T.B. could go in denigrating his colleagues, I couldn't take his villainy all that seriously – off the podium! I knew what a rascal he could be in his professional relationships: but then I

* The letter, and others, may be read in full in *The Hallé Tradition* Manchester University Press, 1960).

knew what a sublime artist he could be when he had only Mozart or Handel or Delius to deal with, and I tended to think that the latter was of more importance.'

The Adelphi interview began with Beecham saying: 'Tell me, Mr Bean, what communication your ridiculous committee has authorised you to make to me.' Without waiting for an answer, he pronounced his opinion that 'the Hallé Society has the manners of a skunk, the spirit of a louse and the conscience of a badger.' This was said [Bean's letter to Godlee continued] 'with flashing eyes and theatrical gestures, his imperial bristling in the air.' So he went on for nearly an hour, an amazing display of invective which he evidently enjoyed. On one matter only, Bean reported, was he in deadly earnest:

He threatened to tell all the newspapers in America what he claims is the common property of everyone in this country 'from the Prime Minister, the Diplomatic Corps, down to the crossing sweepers at the Albert Hall,' namely that the Hallé Society has made itself ridiculous by engaging as conductor 'that upstart Barbirolli'. I used to think that John's dislike of T.B. was unduly strong, even when I knew the good reasons for it, but it's *nothing at all* to T.B.'s stupid dislike of John. It's almost pathological! In the light of all the vituperation he spat at J.B. I am puzzled to explain why he asked Forbes to arrange for a meeting between them.

Beecham admitted to Bean that he loved a fight. The issue of the presidency meant little to him in reality, except the chance to write witty letters to the *Manchester Guardian*. But in his jealousy of Barbirolli, it went deeper. A few days after the Adelphi meeting, the Hallé went to the Western Front and Bean had a long talk with Barbirolli on the train to Folkestone. He wrote to Godlee:

Developments...are extremely sticky. J.B. naturally wanted to know what had happened at Liverpool. The account – even in an expurgated form – caused something like an earthquake. I am afraid any hope of even a face saving reconciliation is gone... J.B. is all for bringing the fight into the light of day – letting it be known what T.B. has said and so finishing the business... He's tired of the intrigue and whispered insinuation and is prepared to leave the public to judge on the merits of the case.

The next move at home was with some of Beecham's supporters in the Hallé Society who told Bean that if, at the extraordinary general meeting, the Lord Mayor was proposed as president they would move an amendment that Beecham should continue in office. They would say that the real reason for Beecham's proposed removal was a personal vendetta by Barbirolli. If they were defeated, as they expected to be, they would give the press a letter from Beecham attacking Barbirolli for this vendetta and the committee for its 'shabby action' in supporting him.

What happened? A glorious English compromise. The committee discovered that the Hallé had had three presidents without there being any provision for the office in the society's articles. So nothing could be proposed and nothing amended. It was proposed that the matter be deferred until a new set of articles was prepared. Two years later a new constitution was presented. It still made no provision for a president, and nobody challenged it.

But the affair simmered in the Hallé committee during the early part of 1945. Some members still wanted Beecham as guest conductor and thought Barbirolli was being 'small' in his attitude. This time he would not budge; he had offered to turn the other cheek once and had it slapped, he would not do it again. The wounds from 1936 were too deep, and he was already too emotionally involved with the Hallé to risk any dealings with Beecham, whom he profoundly distrusted. His attitude was: let Beecham come to Manchester with another orchestra. For years Sir Thomas refused to do this, but eventually he took the Royal Philharmonic in 1948, 1955 and 1959 and informed the press that all the hatchets were buried. When Barbirolli was knighted in 1949, Beecham congratulated him on 'this belated honour.'

In 1970 a friend and colleague who had worked with Beecham and Barbirolli in their opera days wrote to the latter inviting him to contribute to a book of memoirs of Beecham. He added:

I know, and have always been grieved about, the dreadful upset between you and Tommy... Both Forbes and I did our very best to heal it, which Tommy assured me he was more than willing to do as he had no bad feelings about it all. I then made bold to tell him what I believed the trouble was and he seemed surprised and rather taken aback, and explained to me that as far as he could remember, he had said only that, at the time when he was referred to, you had not yet been in full control of such a large and first-rate orchestra as the NYP but that you were a gifted young man and could go far.

Barbirolli replied on 26 May, only nine weeks before he died: 'I cannot accede to your request. Obviously the version you hinted at in your letter has been heavily bowdlerised and is far from the truth.' The truth is as related above.

To more pleasant matters. In November 1943 Barbirolli suggested to Walter Legge, then director of music for ENSA, the organisation for providing entertainment for the Services and civilian war workers, that the Hallé should play to the troops in the Mediterranean theatre of war. The trip was provisionally fixed for the summer of 1944 but transport difficulties prevented its taking place and John himself went for five weeks to conduct Italian orchestras. He also hoped to see Evelyn's brothers Peter and Richard and his own nephew Dick, who were serving in Italy. He was, of course, thrilled at the prospect of conducting for the first time in the 'land of his fathers,' but he found woeful conditions – missing music and missing instruments. His letters to Evelyn give a vivacious account of his experiences:

Naples, 28 July 1944

My darling. What a day! Ensa did not know I was arriving needless to say... As I suspected things are pretty chaotic. All very well for Walter [Legge] to say four rehearsals for each concert. He didn't know, I suppose, they play opera seven days a week and have to fit my rehearsals and concert 'in-a-betweena'. Music there is in the symphony line practically *nothing*, and *no* Tchaikovsky sym. at all. No *Romeo and Juliet*, in fact only Tchaik. available is 1812. They had Brahms II but somebody pinched it. I have been at it all

day seeing people and have fixed to give four concerts next
week with two programmes, the best I cd manage with
what I can find. Orchestra (I heard one act of *Tosca* today,
couldn't stand more) pretty hopeless and most unbelievably awful discipline as it was today. We shall see... Don't
say anything to Walter about the mess. Too late now anyway.

7 August, Naples

I am grateful for two free days before I begin the Bari rehearsals, for it has been gruelling work... I have lost my
voice completely shouting and *singing* at this crowd to get
some sound out of them... Audiences have been simply
terrific... How blind our people were not to send the Hallé
out, we could have played every night to thousands of
music-hungry soldiers and sailors, instead of wasting their
shipping space on *Merry Widow* companies etc... Apart
from the vino (quite good and cheap) I seem to live on
spam and tomatoes...

13 August, Bari

...Orchestra here again not too good... Magnificent leader
and first horn, the rest rather Vancouver Symphony class.
However I got to work and by last night there really was a
transformation... I have been christened by them 'Il Mago
della musica' (the magician of music). Another rather
touching incident was at one of the rehearsals when I finished with the *Traviata* Preludes. To my surprise there
were lots of 'Bravo maestro' shouts, and as I left the orchestra one dear and very old gentleman from the 2nd violins,
with great 'lagrimes',* took me in his arms and planted a
great kiss on me, muttering 'Figlio mio, figlio mio'... A
tribute to my dear Dad, I like to think, from whom I learnt
them.

After two sold-out concerts in Rome, John returned for the
opening of the Hallé season in Manchester for which Bean
had found a venue at the Albert Hall, Peter Street – a Metho-

'Tears.' Barbirolli often used anglicised versions of Italians words in
his conversations with his wife and family.

dist church, too small and resonant, but at least it was central
Here it was possible for the Hallé to give a fortnightly pair of
midweek concerts on the New York pattern, with the identi-
cal programme at each. The popular Sunday programmes
were given at Belle Vue. It was in the prospectus for this
season that John expounded his ideal of 'a great orchestra and
a great public walking hand in hand, treading paths familiar
and unfamiliar, and discovering together in close compan-
ionship, pleasure and at times exaltation.'

The emphasis was on French music – Ravel's *Shéhérazade*
and Left-hand Concerto, Debussy's *Nocturnes* and the *Pelléas*
entr'actes – and on English works like Delius's Piano and
Violin Concertos and Elgar's Second Symphony. For the first
time in his life John conducted Verdi's *Requiem*, at Sheffield
on 21 April 1945, with Victoria Sladen, Gladys Ripley, Parry
Jones and Tom Williams. But the outstanding memory of
that season was the visit to Holland and Belgium in December
1944 to play to the troops, the first time in its eighty-six years
existence that the Hallé had played overseas. They gave
seventeen concerts in fifteen days – seven in Eindhoven, two
in Lille, several in Brussels and one in Ostend. It was an
adventure from start to finish, with many discomforts, but
John described it fourteen years later as 'perhaps the happiest
and most inspiring fortnight the orchestra and I have ever
spent together.' The discomforts began at Folkestone on 20
December when fog prevented the s.s. *Canterbury* from sail-
ing to Ostend. She was packed with troops and there was no
real accommodation for the orchestra, many of whom – including J.B. – slept on deck in the bitter cold. To pass the
time some of the players gave an impromptu concert in space
that was so cramped that, as Barbirolli said, trombonists were
in danger of knocking soldiers' teeth out every time they
played. Music was written on the back of envelopes and held
in front of the players by Barbirolli and other volunteers.

A convey of trucks and coaches took the orchestra to
Brussels for the first concert in the Palais des Beaux Arts. Before rehearsal, John and Evelyn fell off the platform in the
darkness and Evelyn broke her arm. A Christmas Day concert
was given in Brussels and next day the Hallé travelled to
Holland.

Eindhoven was nearly in the front line of Rundstedt's
Ardennes offensive. Digs were found for the players and John

inspected them all. The bassoonist Bert Mitton was found a room somewhat overloaded with religious tracts. John led the way; Bert took one look at this accommodation and said: 'I'm not so bloody sanctimonious as I look.' The concerts were given in the Philips Recreation Hall, which was cold and draughty because it had a large hole in the roof. After one concert the town was machine-gunned by German aircraft. Men just back from the front-line sat in their dirty battledress to listen to the music, demanding encore after encore. The troops travelled miles over ice-bound roads and through dense fog to attend the concerts.

They saw the air battles over Brussels; they travelled miles over bumpy roads; they huddled together for warmth and played in their overcoats. And they all paid tribute to their conductor's leadership, his sharing of all their hardships and his concern for their welfare. Already they appreciated his humanity and perhaps were chuckling over an incident which had occurred soon after his arrival in Manchester. A newspaper's editorial car gave him a lift from Appleby Lodge to the station. The reporter in the car introduced him to the driver, a well-known character named Harry Cater. 'Tell me, Mr Cater,' said Barbirolli, 'do you ever come and listen to the Hallé?' 'Not me,' Harry replied. 'To tell you the truth, Mr Barry-bolly, I'd rather have a pint.' And there was the way he had spent his forty-fifth birthday, just before they left for Europe. He described it in a letter to his mother: 'On taking Tommy and Norah [Tommy Cheetham (percussion) and Norah Winstanley (violinist)], who were in the same hotel, in to dinner with me on Saturday, we were greeted with the news that there was only Spam (cold) for dinner. I immediately walked out, upon which the head waiter followed me and thought they might have some fish. So we had fried fish and chips, and after some more argument, a welsh rarebit. Better than cold Spam, anyway.' There is a gastronomic motif in another of John's choice anecdotes from this period. The Hallé were playing in Liverpool, where Sargent was still conductor-in-chief. Between the rehearsal and the concert John strolled round the city, as he always liked to do, and found a shop selling one of his favourite delicacies, pigs' trotters. The shopkeeper had no wrapping paper so John bought an evening paper and took it back to the shop. The Philharmonic Hall has a rather splendid green room in which there is a

13
'My Great Orchestra'

Barbirolli's association with the Hallé Orchestra lasted twenty-seven years. From 1943 to 1958 he was permanent conductor and musical director; from 1958 to 1968 he was conductor-in-chief and musical adviser, reducing his commitments with the orchestra to about fifty per cent of his availability; and from 1968 until his death he was Conductor Laureate for Life. Within two years of his taking over he had bound himself to the orchestra by the shared experiences of wartime journeys, playing in inadequate surroundings, by the excitement that came from a kind of crusade and from the knowledge that they were fighting for their existence. In his first season they gave 194 concerts and made a profit, without any kind of subsidy; in the second 258. For the next several years the yearly average was well over two hundred concerts, of which Barbirolli conducted the majority.

Of course the strain began to tell; when peace returned and musical life gradually returned to normal, players left the Hallé for the London or BBC orchestras, where pay was much higher and work less arduous. Barbirolli not only trained a new orchestra in 1943: he did it continuously, up to his last season.

It is, therefore, all the more remarkable that the orchestra was so good. Between 1944 and 1946 it had no rival in the land. Later the Royal Philharmonic, Philharmonia, London Symphony, Covent Garden and BBC Symphony Orchestras attained extraordinary heights and were magnets drawing away the best Hallé players. Corporately and in terms of virtuosity they were probably better than the Hallé; they had brilliant individual players, too, but so had the Hallé. In 1963, when Barbirolli had completed twenty years with the Hallé, he sent me a list of thirty-five ex-Hallé players who had become principals or sub-principals elsewhere and this note: 'The riling thing is that when they go to London they are hailed as celebrities; but when they appeared for years in London with the Hallé none of the critics noticed them. Shows what ears they have.'

It would be easy to say that the Hallé was never quite as good as Barbirolli believed it to be if you heard it on one of its bad days – and the same might have been said of Beecham's RPO and Boult's BBC Symphony Orchestra on similar occasions. At its best, Barbirolli's Hallé had a special sound, rich, adaptable, personal; it had the same qualities as its conductor – it was human, not a machine; together, in the music they loved best, they played with a depth of feeling and understanding of the music that transcended virtuosity of execution. A great Hallé performance was an experience in which one seemed to enter the composer's world.

He taught his players style – the style of playing Debussy and Lehár, the Strausses, Delius and Nielsen. If the nineteenth century was his spiritual home, he was also a superb and under-rated Haydn conductor, and he and the orchestra were more at home in the humours and humanity of Haydn than in the sublimities of Mozart. Their performances were positive and had conviction – even when they were not convincing – because they reflected Barbirolli's approach to his work. 'By golly if I'm wrong I'm 100 per cent wrong,' he said to Martin Milner; and to me on another occasion: 'I don't care if you say I overdo something; it's when you say I underdo it that I'll start worrying.' In this respect his defence of the cellist Jacqueline du Pré also applies to himself: 'People sometimes accuse her of giving too much. But I love it. If you haven't an excess of everything when you're young, what are you going to pare off as the years go by?' Fortunately, there are many recordings in which a good deal of the spirit and accomplishment of the Barbirolli Hallé is captured, but no recording can rival live performance, and these of all orchestras and conductors thrived on the living moment, the occasion, the excitement of the hour.

Neville Cardus, lately returned from eight years in Sydney

and hearing Barbirolli's Hallé for the first time at the 1947 Edinburgh Festival, wrote in the *Manchester Guardian*: 'Here is a real orchestra, wanting only a small addition of players to elevate it to European class... The brilliance, flexibility, precision and warmth of the Hallé strings are known far and wide: their reputation has travelled as far as Australia. But no part of Barbirolli's Hallé is greater than the whole: as Szigeti murmured last night as he listened: "They are all, every one of them, playing".' At the same festival a year later Ernest Newman wrote in the *Sunday Times* that the Hallé compensated for poor performances by the Amsterdam Concertgebouw. 'I had not heard Mr Barbirolli for, I think, some twenty years. He has developed into a conductor of the international front rank and has made the present Manchester orchestra an instrument of exceptional sensitivity and polish.'

In the resurgence of British musical life from 1947 until the late 1950s, Barbirolli's Hallé played a major part. Every festival wanted them, and thousands treasure memories of an Elgar or Vaughan Williams symphony played in York Minster or some other noble building. It was Barbirolli who helped to re-establish the Leeds Festival in 1947 when it was revived after a ten-year interval. 'Not since Sir Thomas Beecham was here,' said a Yorkshire critic, 'has one felt the dominance of a single personality so strongly.' The performances of Beethoven's Choral Symphony and Verdi's *Requiem* were also notable as the first appearances in Britain of the great dramatic soprano Ljuba Welitsch, who had sung with Barbirolli in Vienna a few months earlier and been invited to Leeds by him. In the 1947–48 season in Sheffield, over 100,000 people attended the Hallé's concerts and at twenty concerts people had been turned away. Audiences knew that the standard of playing would almost invariably be high; and in Barbirolli himself the rostrum was occupied by a colourful personality about whose interpretations there could be several shades of opinion. Compare, for instance, the reactions of two distinguished critics to his performance of Sibelius's Fifth Symphony:

'It was an inexpressible pleasure,' wrote Ernest Newman in the *Sunday Times* on 5 September 1948, 'to see, for once, a great work gradually taking shape in performance as it must have done in the mind of its creator, developing steadily, logically, from acorn to mighty oak.' But Frank Howes in *The*

Times on 5 October 1950: 'How is it that he cannot see that methods which are right in a tone-poem are wrong in a symphony?... Sibelius's fifth symphony, which is one of the most striking examples since Beethoven of organic growth in music, remained an inconsequential assemblage of over-polished pieces.'

Barbirolli was fully aware of the impact of his musical personality. 'People either adore me,' he said, 'or I nauseate them.' There was also a middle group who were supercili-ously indifferent to him.

He was criticised for what some considered to be his con-servative outlook on music, and from about 1956 onwards it became almost obligatory for critics to snipe at him for his failure to share their enthusiasm for the avant-garde or the twelve-note followers of Schoenberg. He once gave me this description of the 'fragmentary' type of modern music which is familiar today: 'Three farts and a raspberry, orchestrated.' He never closed his mind to new works but he would not conduct anything in which he did not believe nor would he attempt any work without adequate time in which to study it himself and then prepare it with the orchestra. There were many works he wanted to do but which he never conducted because he could not find the time – or the money. But if he believed strongly enough in a work – Berg's Violin Concerto for example, and Chamber Concerto – he would risk failure at the box office. The attacks on his conservatism began when a campaign was mounted to remedy the indisputable neglect in Britain of Schoenberg, Webern and their followers. This coincided with the emergence of a group of young English composers – Goehr, Birtwistle, Maxwell Davies – with whom Barbirolli had little in common. But if the box office could stand it and the right conductor could be found, he was will-ing for these works to be included in the Hallé series. He expressed his own views on these subjects to me in 1963 in a long letter. I had asked him if he agreed that the drawback of a permanent conductor was 'a dictatorship of personal taste':

There can be no great orchestra, with a *style* of its own, without a head of great quality, both as a teacher and as an interpreter, and by style I mean not only a particular characteristic but a suppleness and variety of style that can attune itself to music of all kinds and periods... The Hallé are even taught to play with different kinds of vibrato, for different kinds of music (every 1st class player should be equipped with this quality). There are, of course, different types of portamentos, though few are aware of these, and there is the important question also of *no vibrato* and *no portamento*, which in any case must be used only to stress certain melodic and emotional elements, as Mahler well knew. I cherish a letter from Stokowski who, after a Hallé concert, wrote me that he considered the Hallé *one* of the great orchs. of the world (there is *no* greatest anything) because it had the greatest variety of *style*. As for a dictatorship of personal taste, I don't think Manchester has been unfortunate in having a conductor who has been acknowledged as a conductor of opera (all kinds) and a considerable interpreter of the German classics, the French impressionists, who started conducting Berg in 1924, Elgar, Delius, V. W., Sibelius, Nielsen, Mahler, Bruckner, Bach (Matthew P.), Handel, gave the first performances of the Sinfonia da Requiem and Violin Concerto of Britten, 1st Fricker symphony, A. Benjamin and John Gardner symphonies, all chosen by me. Can't think such a man a great menace to the musical development of a city's public* ...

He many times said that he did not regard Hallé concerts as an 'experimental forum.' He encouraged the public rehearsals of new works which the Hallé occasionally presented, but that was as far as he would go. The twelve years from 1947 to 1958 during which he and the Hallé were the mainstay of the Cheltenham Festival of British Contemporary Music in July was also a period which ended in severe criticism of his choice of works. Symphonies by Alwyn, Wordsworth, Gardner and Arnell were eventually considered to constitute too much of an effort to prolong a declining romantic tradition.

There is much to be said on both sides, for contemporary is not synonymous with avant-garde and the late-romantic has as much right to be heard as the 'wrong-note' man. Also Barbirolli brought forward splendid works by Rawsthorne, Fricker, Iain Hamilton and Alun Hoddinott. But, despite public support, friction developed. John was not temperamentally

* He had conducted Berg's Chamber Concerto in London in the late 1920s. Works by Bartók, Hindemith, Janacek, Prokofiev, McCabe and Martinu were in his repertory.

suited to the Cheltenham selection system of a reading panel which sorted out the wheat from the chaff and passed their 'short list' to him. He did not enjoy having a choice imposed upon him; only if he had found the work himself could he really be prepared to be convinced by it. Eventually, when he began to accept more international engagements after 1958, he let it be known that he would no longer look at works he did not like; and since the festival was moving into a new phase, that was virtually the end of the Hallé association with it, although he returned for one concert in 1965.

However, for most of the 1950s Cheltenham was one of the Hallé's happiest engagements. The new works were thoroughly prepared and no one appreciated this more than the composers themselves. Gerald Finzi, after the first performance of his Cello Concerto in 1955, wrote: 'Adequate rehearsal is a very rare and unusual experience for a composer but the results are so obvious, in a completely secure and digested performance, that I can't thank you and the orchestra enough.' Matyás Seiber, whose *Tre Pezzi* for cello and orchestra Barbirolli conducted in 1958: 'What a joy to watch a conductor whose every gesture is pure music, who obviously *lives* every note, every phrase of the music he conducts. After so many worthy, efficient and deadly dull conductors what a pleasure it is to hear such *inspired* conducting.'

Yet at Cheltenham it was the performances of Elgar, Vaughan Williams, Rubbra, Bax and the romantic classics (Dvořák, Brahms, Tchaikovsky) that stayed in the memory from year to year – and the convivial hours afterwards in the Festival Club, with the orchestra relaxing and John telling his stories and sitting with Vaughan Williams and, on one occasion, solemnly rehearsing Jimmy Edwards and the Hallé trombone section in the bowels of the Town Hall in preparation for a hilarious 'performance' of the *Tannhäuser* overture in the Club at midnight. His imitation of himself that night was superb caricature. He enjoyed those annual weeks and staying on Cleeve Hill at the 'Rising Sun' with its view of the Malvern Hills. For many people those were the halcyon years of the Cheltenham Festival. The musical content may have become superior – at any rate more forward-looking – but the glory departed. Or perhaps we are to be identified with the remark made by John Ireland to Arnold Bax as they sat in benevolent bewilderment listening to a discordant work being rehearsed at Cheltenham in 1950: 'You know, Arnold, there's no room in this world for a couple of romantic old sods like us.'

From 1943 to 1958, Barbirolli and the Hallé earned a permanent place in the history of orchestral music by the variety and standard of their concerts. If together they did little for the avant-garde, they did more for music. Also they played an inestimably important part in the total revival of interest in Elgar and they helped make Vaughan Williams a popular composer in the 1950s. Their achievement should be assessed within the context of a period when municipal authorities were only grudgingly admitting that music was something more than a pastime for the intelligentsia. In helping to bring about this outlook, against the stiffest opposition in the land, the Hallé did more than anyone. Nor was this achievement confined to Manchester, Sheffield and Bradford. They were the Hallé headquarters, but the outstanding feat by Barbirolli, Godlee and Bean was to make the Hallé a truly national orchestra. It visited every part of the country. Edinburgh at Festival time and at other times; Harrogate during a summer week; Newtown during the Montgomery Festival; Buxton's modest but friendly festival; the West Country cathedrals; King's Lynn; Portsmouth; Bexhill-on-Sea; Bristol, where John was given the 'freedom' of that exclusive gathering the Bristol Savages; the industrial towns of Preston, Blackburn, Bolton, Wolverhampton, Leicester, Nottingham – all had their regular visits from the Hallé and Barbirolli. They had friends and fans everywhere, and they earned more money in box-office revenue than any other British orchestra. What gave Barbirolli special pleasure was that the big audiences were for the orchestra and him, thereby justifying his 1943 policy of refusing to rely on soloists. Typical was a concert in Gloucester Cathedral on 24 May 1951, when between four thousand and five thousand people filled every available inch of space and hundreds were turned away. People sat on the floor, on steps, and stood in the centre of the Choir.

But as a result of this popular success, there were drawbacks:

It has always appeared to me [he wrote] that my orchestra was penalised for being so successful. The more we earned ourselves, the less we received by way of financial support –

support that would have enabled me to enlarge the orchestra and create better conditions for the players... Slowly but surely progress has been made, and though my own city has always given me less financial support than other cities offer their orchestras, they have never failed to give a sympathetic hearing to our pleas.

That was a diplomatic statement made for public consumption. Privately he was more likely to refer to Manchester City Council as 'those miserable skinflints' and he fulminated to friends about the lack of generosity of Manchester's private patrons, citing a remark made by Philip Godlee when asked if it was worth approaching the members of the Hallé committee for contributions towards some venture: 'Waste of time – meanest lot of bastards in Christendom.'

Why, it may be asked, did Barbirolli stay in Manchester rather than accept a post with one of the big London or European orchestras? Was there the fear of another deep scar to be added to the one left by New York? Probably he would not have admitted this even to himself, if indeed he was conscious of it, but knowledge of his inferiority complex, his lack of complete confidence in himself until he was actually on the rostrum in front of the orchestra, and the misgivings that preceded his visits abroad (even to orchestras where he had already been acclaimed), leads inevitably to the supposition that in Manchester he felt not only artistically satisfied but emotionally safe. When, at the memorial service in Manchester Cathedral, Sir Geoffrey Haworth spoke of Manchester as 'the rock' on which Barbirolli built his international career, he was making a particularly shrewd diagnosis.

In a letter to me, John explained something of the satisfaction he found in Manchester:

I suppose some may be right who regard me as a fanatic as far as music is concerned... To begin to feel, after conducting it for 30 years, that you understand something of, and can communicate to others some of the might of, Beethoven 9 is to feel life is worth living after all. And it seems to me that Manchester must be good for fanatics, i.e. workers who can be oblivious to surroundings provided they are content in their work, for you have produced some great ones in M/c... But another very potent factor must be the loyalty, affection and trust the people of this great city and all over Lancashire have shown me. I think it can all be summed up in what I said to Evelyn at Belle Vue soon after I had refused the offer of the conductorship of the BBC Symphony Orchestra: 'If I had accepted, I could never have faced these people again'.

When, in 1958, he was made the 62nd Honorary Freeman of the city in a memorable ceremony in the great Town Hall, he was genuinely touched. He characteristically recalled how he had, only twelve years earlier, watched Churchill receive the same honour. It was on this occasion that John said he counted himself blessed in his Franco-Italian–Mancunian–Cockney heritage and declared that he would never leave the Hallé 'for my heart is ever with my children of the orchestra and the people of this great city.' He meant it. Whatever frictions arose between the Hallé and Manchester Corporation, John retained the friendship of many members of the Council. On those rare occasions when he attended civic receptions or functions in the Town Hall he invariably gave the evening a 'lift.' No one who met him there, or on any similar occasion, such as a party after a concert, in any city or town, could have had an inkling of the doubts and depressions which were a large part of his nature. He was courteous, amusing, delightful; no one left his company without feeling better for it.

Of Manchester's affection for him personally, especially in his later years, he was never to be left in any doubt. It was demonstrated at nearly every concert and it was particularly strong during four great seasons: in 1951–52, the first years of the rebuilt Free Trade Hall; in 1957–58, the centenary year; in 1963–64, his twenty-first season; and in 1967–68, his twenty-fifth. The Free Trade Hall will ever remain haunted by him while anyone lives who saw him there: the drawing aside of the curtain as he came on to the platform; the nods and smiles as he bowed from the rostrum before silencing the applause with the Anthem; his unforgettable mannerisms while conducting, face radiant as he turned to the violins in broad melodies, left thumb expressive beyond words; the quick little step to the edge of the rostrum to bring out some special point from the second violins; the sweeping, all-embracing gestures to the brass at some majestic climax, his hair, head and body vibrating, his whole being inviting the biggest possible response; his habit, after a concerto, of standing among the violins, talking enthusiastically while the soloist took the applause; making a special fuss of a beautiful woman soloist; stopping for a chat with the back desk of cellos as he walked off. In so many works, memory will continue to provide the counterpoint of the groans which were wrung from him by the intensity with which he conducted.

Then there were the speeches on particular occasions. He was a good speaker, with a fluent command of words, but emotion was near the surface and until he got into his stride there would be much coughing and clearing of the throat; it was part of the fun that he should pay himself some ingenious and ingenuous compliment, and never did he fail to refer to the Hallé as 'my great orchestra' and the audience as his dear friends. On these occasions the warmth that kindled his conducting flowed from the platform to engulf all but the stoniest heart. His room up the stairs behind the platform is haunted too. There he had a shelf across the width of the room on which he kept photographs of special significance to him. In earlier years he had a small bust of Charles Hallé on his table. There, too, he saw friends and 'hangers-on,' his overcoat flung loosely round his shoulders, often looking utterly exhausted until some remark about the music would bring him to life and to his feet. As I write I can feel the way he would push or grip my arm to make some telling point; and then, if he wanted to retail a bit of scandal or tell a supposed secret or a risqué story, would draw me into the little washroom and conspiratorially close the door. There was something very Italian about him at such moments, as if he was a character out of a Verdi opera and the plot had reached Scene 2 of Act II.

But whether Manchester fully appreciated what an exceptional musician was working in its midst, I sometimes wondered; and so did he. Perhaps he was taken for granted; perhaps a natural English reticence held back the fullest acknowledgment of his work; or perhaps there were more lukewarm (what he called *Manchester Guardian*-ish) people in the audience than one thought, people who were resistant to the emotional aura which surrounded him. At any rate compared with the ovations which he received in Berlin, those in Manchester sometimes seemed reserved, or with reservations. His friend the surgeon W. R. Douglas said in a letter to the Hallé violinist Audrey Napier Smith in September 1964: 'Manchester never seems to be able to appreciate his real worth. They will only realise it when he puts down his baton for the last time.' On the other hand, for very many individual members of the audience he remained what Nikisch had seemed to the young J. B. Priestley: 'almost demonic, producing what seemed to me an astounding effect of verve, brilliance, white fire.'

The very real affection of the majority of the Hallé players for him is evident from the large number who, despite the temptation of better-paid and lighter work elsewhere, stayed with him for many years. The Indian violinist, Mehli Mehta, on leaving the Hallé summed up what perhaps many felt: 'Every concert with you left me not only completely exhausted but also divinely transformed – and God bless you for it.' Or, on another level, there was Pat Ryan: 'Your amazing courage during the last few days has surely put us all to shame,* but for the Holy Mother of God, *take it easy*.' Barbirolli was generous in his encouragement of members of the orchestra to appear as soloists at Hallé concerts. One particular individual was much disliked by Wally Jones, the burly tuba player who was also the orchestral manager; when this person was chosen to play a concerto in the Manchester series, Wally knew that he would find it hard to stomach the eulogy of the performance which would be sure to issue from Barbirolli immediately afterwards. He tried to keep out of the way, but failed. As Barbirolli walked to the conductor's room he saw Wally and called to him: 'Yes, Wally, I know he's a so-and-so, but didn't he play beautifully?'

He was fortunate in his two leaders: for the first fifteen years Laurance Turner, the opposite pole to him in temperament but loyal and 'like a rock,' as John described him; then from 1958 onwards Martin Milner, a young man whose training had been in a drier, more classical style than Barbirolli's romanticism. Again, the mixture of temperaments worked. Barbirolli looked upon Milner as a 'son.' Sometimes they clashed, and Martin would patiently and distantly wait for the thundercloud to disperse. On one of these occasions, after all

* This was when J.B. had tripped over a recording cable in the Free Trade Hall and fallen from the platform into the body of the hall. Only his light weight saved him, but he chipped a vertebra and, despite severe pain, conducted *Gerontius* on the day of Elgar's centenary (2 June 1957) in Manchester and a few days later in Dublin.

was peaceful again, John said to him: 'You know how to handle me, don't you?'

In later years, when John spent a lot of time away from the Hallé, this friendship was invaluable because it was based on unstinted admiration for Martin's musicianship. He trusted him to start rehearsing works for him, though he would send him a stream of instructions from abroad. At a deeper level was a letter written from Houston late in 1962 when Milner was contemplating resigning for personal reasons:

> Completely unselfishly I am trying to prevent you making in any sort of haste an irrevocable decision... You are a superb Leader in the best sense of the term and the finest I have ever had in a fairly long career. I am in the dark as to what has prompted your decision...but I can tell you this... any artist of your gifts and potentialities who deliberately thwarts the fulfilment of the gifts God has given him will never in the end find peace or contentment of any kind. This is the most important thing I have to say to you and I say it with all the force a loving father would have for a favourite son.

The crisis passed. 'Ah were proper wurried,' wrote the 'father'.

Many other orchestral players went to him for advice or help and were never refused. He had his critics, of course, as strong personalities are bound to have, those players who thought him a show-off or considered that he took all the glory to himself. They delighted in an anecdote of his reading at rehearsal a letter of congratulations from a composer whose work they had played: 'I would like to thank *you* (fortissimo) and (sotto voce) your fine orchestra...' Or there was the time he was annoyed during rehearsals of Bach's *St Matthew Passion* by a man in the choir who kept his hands in his pockets. At last he said: 'The gentleman with his hands in his pockets – I think he should remove them, out of respect for God, and for Bach, and, come to that, for the conductor.' 'Crikey,' said one of the orchestra, 'he's got them in the right order.' But Daniel Barenboim has perceptively pointed out that if there was anyone from whom one could learn the difference between being a showman and a show-off it was Barbirolli.

One of the most emotional and widely publicised landmarks of Barbirolli's years with the Hallé was his refusal in 1948 of the conductorship of the BBC Symphony Orchestra. The affair was typical of his attitude to the Hallé. It is unlikely that he seriously contemplated acceptance, because the idea of working for an organisation in which a committee selected the programmes for the conductor was anathema to him. He would not have tolerated it for five minutes. But he was also fully alive to the use that he could make of the offer by capitalising on the already deeply rooted feelings that it would be disastrous for the Hallé were he to leave. So for three weeks the press in the North, and elsewhere, was full of 'Will he, won't he?' stories, and John maintained a dramatic silence, breaking it only to emphasise how tempting the offer was and how much consideration it needed. Meanwhile he gave the Hallé committee the conditions on which he would stay: that the orchestra's minimum pay should be raised to that of the BBC Northern Orchestra; that principals should receive salaries nearer to those obtaining in London; that as soon as the Free Trade Hall was rebuilt, the orchestra should be increased to its pre-war strength of ninety-six; and that there should be a foreign tour every year. He sought no pecuniary advantage for himself. These conditions were met and the BBC offer was refused.

His decision was highly praised, particularly by those who deplored the drain of talent to the South of England. Six months later he was knighted. So, before his fiftieth birthday, he was now Sir John Barbirolli, committed to the Hallé, he said, for as long as they wanted him. There can be no doubt, apart from the deeper considerations mentioned earlier, that he drew strength from the orchestra's long history. To quote his words: 'I have always been deeply conscious of a Hallé "tradition," though it would be difficult to define exactly what I mean by it. I have always been a traditionalist by nature but that does not imply being an enemy of progress; and if tradition means a re-kindling of past greatness in the terms of our own times, I can think of nothing finer.' It was a strange relationship, his with the Hallé, with an element of 'love–hate' about it. Not all of them loved him, but even those least impressed by his 'public image' could not, in performance, resist the power and inspiration of this little man, and they played their hearts out for him.

14 Behind the Scenes

'Hardly a committee meeting passed without a demand from him for the performance of an exacting and expensive work, or the undertaking of an ambitious and also expensive tour abroad. He was a scourge and a goad to us and we loved him for it.' The words of a Hallé chairman, Sir Geoffrey Haworth, in Manchester Cathedral. No business or organisation can be run without management, and in his early years with the Hallé Barbirolli took the closest professional and personal interest in every aspect of affairs. He attended some committee meetings, he kept a watchful eye on finance, he checked the programme-notes – nothing escaped him. For several years he worked closely with Ernest Bean, whose admiration for Barbirolli – 'he was like an electric dynamo' – knew few bounds.

One man in particular, on the managerial side, was to play an important part in Barbirolli's life for twenty years. Kenneth Crickmore was born in Manchester in 1921. Although he won two scholarships from elementary schools his family were too poor to afford the extra expense which would have been incurred by his going to a grammar school. They moved to London in 1934 and the following year Ken started work as an office boy with a small cinema chain. At sixteen he was manager of a theatre. In his spare time he studied the history and appreciation of music; and by the time he volunteered for air crew duty in the RAF at the outbreak of war he had run a club showing cinema classics and become booking manager for some news theatres in London. He was on continuous active service in fighters and bombers until December 1943, when his aircraft hit a tree in fog. He was seriously injured and invalided out of the RAF, returning to his old job. But this soon palled and he decided on a career in music. In 1944 he was appointed to the new post of chief administrator of the Sheffield Philharmonic Society. Sheffield's policy was to work closely with the Hallé, and so Crickmore and Barbirolli soon came to know one another. Crickmore was then twenty-three and he was astonished and pleased because Barbirolli was 'the first business associate I had had to that date who made no comment on nor appeared surprised by my youthfulness... He treated me from the outset as a fellow professional.'

Very quickly Barbirolli came to admire Crickmore's encyclopaedic knowledge of the repertoire and his knack of programme planning; he recognised his ability in the field of 'appreciation' and in organising support for the orchestra among young people; he liked his views on the business aspects of music. Also he had an understandable, and perhaps sentimental, regard for Crickmore's background and a patriotic admiration for his war record. After about two years he asked Crickmore to be his personal manager and gave him considerable freedom in his business affairs. Ken Crickmore was an enigmatic figure, not easily knowable. He had a very likeable, kind and amusing side to his personality; his ability was indisputable. But there was something about him – a certain brash or slick aspect to his demeanour – which some people instinctively and immediately disliked and distrusted. Suspicion of Barbirolli's motives in many a situation, and later of the Hallé Society's, among other musical organisations and individuals, was engendered by distrust, whether justified or not, of Crickmore. He had the born publicist's knack of popularising – his enemies would have said vulgarising – musical events. Barbirolli shared his view that music was no longer the exclusive preserve of the leisured class and co-operated fully with him, thereby confirming the worst fears of some of the Hallé committee and Manchester intellectuals that Barbirolli's 'cheapness' was not quite the thing for the Hallé.

This was on a public level. On a more personal level, there was the ambivalence of Crickmore's attitude to Barbirolli which he revealed to a few people. This came as the bigger surprise considering the frequency of Barbirolli's eulogies of

Crickmore's achievements. One could talk to Crickmore about Barbirolli and after a time realise that what was being said was not an objective assessment – for if no man is a hero to his valet, no conductor is likely to appear in that guise to his manager – but a subtle piece of character-assassination. What was said was usually true in essence, but the edges were blurred, the picture tilted off-centre, so cleverly that a caricature emerged, a rather horrid one, which dwelt on Barbirolli's insecurity and inadequacies. Perhaps there was a pathological jealousy here, or perhaps there were causes which one can never know. What is certain is that if one had attempted to convey one's unease to Barbirolli, he would have exploded in wrath and written one off as an enemy of Crickmore with an axe to grind.

As the association with Crickmore grew in the late 1940s, so Barbirolli's trust in Bean's 'Civil Service'-type policy on Hallé finance correspondingly dwindled. Bean, for his part, found it well-nigh impossible to reach Barbirolli because J.B. was 'screened' by Crickmore. The Hallé committee divided into two factions, one pro-Barbirolli under Godlee and the other pro-Bean under Leonard Behrens. Godlee and Behrens were inimical, in any case, and the whole situation became almost farcically impossible. The situation was resolved when Bean was appointed general manager of the Royal Festival Hall, London (opened in May 1951). Barbirolli at once told Godlee that Crickmore should be the next Hallé manager, and Godlee, despite opposition from Behrens, persuaded the committee to appoint him. Had this course not been followed Barbirolli would have left the Hallé. This was the one time when his threat was wholehearted, as is evident from this extract from a letter to Godlee:

I have not yet signed my contract, and I do assure you and the committee that I have no intention of doing so until I know what your decision is likely to be in the matter of choosing the man with whom I shall have to work in close co-operation for many years to come, I *hope*. Consequently I must hope that this will not be long delayed, for obviously we cannot publish the prospectus till it is known whether I am to be here next season or not... We have never had secrets from each other, Philip, and they do not fit in *our* scheme of things.

In later years John acknowledged that he had been unjust to Bean; and it is pleasant to record that the two men remained friends, with a deep mutual admiration. Crickmore at once justified his appointment – one which he personally would have preferred to forgo. He took over when the Hallé faced bankruptcy and with the City Council in an extremely critical frame of mind towards further subsidies. By a series of brilliant and businesslike moves, Crickmore converted near-disaster into profit and achieved his ambition of persuading the City to give the Hallé a direct grant, with which it could budget ahead, instead of Bean's preference for a guarantee against loss. Nothing can rob Crickmore of the credit of having saved the Hallé at the moment when, for the first time for twelve years, it had its own concert-hall, the Free Trade Hall, as a home again. Ironically, there might have been a hall and no orchestra. The memory of all this, twelve years later, intensified the effect of Crickmore's tragic betrayal of John's trust and affection which broke up their partnership and caused John deep suffering, affected his health, exposed the vulnerability of his lack of security, and added to the strain of his last years.

In twenty-seven years at the head of the Hallé – and a musical organisation is never the most harmonious of bodies – John was fortunate to have congenial colleagues with whom to work in management and committee. For Sir Geoffrey Haworth as chairman, John developed a regard almost as warm as he had had for Godlee. Yet even those who admired Barbirolli the man less than Barbirolli the musician allowed no personal antipathy to affect their attitude to his achievements. Behrens, when he became chairman in 1952, wrote frankly to him: 'We have disagreed in the past and we may disagree again, but nothing can ever extinguish in my mind my gratitude to you and my admiration for the immortal (that is the right word) services you have rendered to all of us.'

This admiration also extended on all sides to concern for Barbirolli's health. In 1950 John wrote to Philip Godlee: 'The colossal and continuous physical strain of rehearsals and performances, week after week and month after month, is about as much as I can stand, and unless I can feel more secure and serene as to what goes on behind me, I should have no alternative but to give up, as you can see from my present state of health.' He had been injured in a car accident during 1948 but made a complete recovery. In February 1949 he had to rest because of 'nervous gastritis' and in August of that year, after his holiday in Sussex, his doctor, Billy Douglas, was shocked by his condition and persuaded him to cancel all except Hallé engagements for the next twelve months. Over 250 concerts a year for six years, one meal a day, little sleep, heavy smoking and constant studying of scores had begun to take their toll. On top of this, he had had whooping cough which weakened his chest.

In February 1951, while in Melbourne, he had severe gastro-enteritis and ran a temperature of 103 degrees but refused to cancel any concerts. On his return to England he looked ill and drawn and had lost weight – the tubby J.B. had gone, never to return. The upshot was an operation for appendicitis in Manchester on 13 March in which Billy Douglas, a renowned cancer surgeon, also took the opportunity for 'a good look round' but found nothing amiss. He insisted, however, on a seven-weeks convalescence to which John reluctantly agreed, but only on condition that he could spend the time studying Handel's *Messiah*. He had long wanted to conduct it, but would not approach it as run-of-the-mill. He wanted to look at the original and at various editions and to devise his own 'compromise', somewhere between the purists and the nineteenth century.

Never again was Barbirolli as robust as he once had been, and in 1955 and 1956 he again looked desperately ill. At the Cheltenham and King's Lynn festivals in July 1956 he was in acute abdominal pain and the heart 'murmur' which he had had since birth was slightly more in evidence, though a specialist declared it to be 'no more serious than grey hairs.' He struggled on to the holiday month of August. From Brighton he wrote to Audrey Napier Smith: 'I am really being good. The warning from the old "ticker" must perforce be taken notice of. I stay in bed doing bowings till at least 11.30, have a little stroll before lunch, and a read, and a spot of cello (just for fun) after.'

Later that month he returned to Manchester for an operation by Billy Douglas for removal of a non-malignant intestinal obstruction caused by adhesions from the 1951 appendix operation. His friendship with Billy was one of the most cherished personal relationships of his Manchester days. With his own knowledgeable interest in medicine, and with Billy's sensitivity to music, they had everything in common. Both were short in stature and came from humble origins. Sometimes John went to watch his friend perform some complicated cancer operation. After one of these occasions he wrote: 'I can only say it from instinct, but I know I saw a Master and an Artist at work and the sight was both gladdening and deeply moving... You are a great man, Bill, great in your skill, your knowledge, but above all great in your wisdom, humanity, kindness and powers of imparting to others something of what can only be acquired with infinite patience and pain.'

So he had complete faith in Douglas where his own health was concerned and even, though not without a struggle, accepted his ruling that he must have a long convalescence. Evelyn had written to Billy: 'The truth is that *nobody* wants John back till he can come back as a normal man, and be talked to and dealt with as an ordinary person, NOT (as has been the case for at least the last year) as a semi-invalid on the verge of breakdown who must never be upset.' While he was in hospital John worked on the programmes for the Hallé centenary season of 1957–58 and began a thorough and exhaustive study of Bach's *St Matthew Passion*. He decided to convalesce in Italy ('I would be less bored there than anywhere') but as the prospect came nearer it became less appealing.

On 5 October he wrote to Audrey from London:

We were due to leave for Italy tomorrow but I have been so very depressed at the thought of this ominous 'orrible idea of 'oliday that I cld not face it and yesterday decided to put it off for a bit... I shall probably have to face it and go a little later, and now that there is a real prospect of an Italian tour next June it won't perhaps be quite so bad, as I have been commissioned to see various agents etc. on behalf of Hallé...

And on 14 October:

...I cannot in truth think of the trip without that 'sinking feeling' in the pit of my stomach, but it may be better when I get there. Anyway I will try hard & make the best of it... I am still feeling far from well, and in my heart of hearts know I cd. not start active work yet... Have spent quite a time re-bowing and revising the Bruckner 7th this week. A really lovely work in which I find a great affinity to Elgar. Not in actual music, of course, but in loftiness of ideals and purpose, richness of melodic line and harmony, and even an affinity of defects. The over-development sometimes to the point of padding, the sequences etc., but all *very lovable,* and to me easily tolerated and forgiven in the *greatness* of it all... Your Schweitzer books have been of tremendous help with the *St Matthew*... I certainly don't feel half so frightened and unfitted to tackle that mighty work as I did.

He was little better when he reached Naples:

26 October 1956

...I fight hard against this deepening gloom which of course is not restful, and the only real refuge I have is to get to my work. These last few days I have memorised the choral finale of Mahler II (for next season) and that is another little job done. Occasionally the clouds seem to disperse a little and for a few fleeting moments I feel alive again.

On 4 November he wrote to me from Venice:

At 1 a.m. this morning I finished what I will call the 'first draft' of an entirely new edition of the *complete* St Matthew which retains all the original phrasings which have come down to us and such dynamics (very few) that exist. It has been an absorbing and at first a terrifying task to contemplate, but aided by friends, Elgar, *Schweitzer* (particularly), Sanford Terry and Parry I gradually took heart. Anyway it has proved a real refuge during these difficult weeks.

His bout of depression was cured by a Hallé financial crisis. The mid-1950s were the nadir of Manchester's financial aid to the Hallé. There were councillors whose attitude was summed up by the statement of one of their number in a 1951 debate on Hallé aid: 'I have read that Sir John Barbirolli may leave. I would say to Sir John that Manchester City

Council has no responsibilities in this matter and the sooner you get your skates on and travel the sooner you will be satisfied.' A Hallé tour of America on which Barbirolli had set his heart was cancelled in 1956 because the Government would not contribute to the fares. Nor was he convinced that the Hallé committee were doing enough in the matter and he reminded them, through Crickmore, that he himself sub-sidised the orchestra by conducting the Hallé for one-third of the fee paid him for other British concerts and one-quarter of his overseas fee. His Hallé salary had not altered since 1943 and he refused anything extra for himself now, but insisted that the 'saving' on his fees should go towards foreign tours and towards helping him retain key players. 'You have be-come used to being tailored by Savile Row at Burton prices,' he said. 'I will help you to retain this illusion as long as I can, but cannot guarantee to do so until further notice.' When it seemed that plans for the centenary might be jeopardised by lack of adequate funds, he flew from Italy to meet the City Council in private and successfully pleaded for a special grant.

'I was in Manchester a day or two for meetings with Cor-poration and committee,' he wrote to Audrey Napier Smith from Palermo, 'where I let all have a good piece of my mind which I think did me good. I would have loved to see you a moment but it didn't seem possible and I am *so bad* on the telephone, the damn thing still terrifies me.' At Palermo he conducted again, the first time for nearly five months. 'Evelyn says I seemed to start again as if I had never left off.' His courage in combating illness was frequently to be seen hence-forward to the end of his life, yet as far as his work was con-cerned he would not have regarded his dedication as courage. 'I'll be all right when I'm on the box' – and he always was. 'I think I would feel rather lost without an ache or pain some-where these days!!' he wrote in February 1957. Most of the pain for the next twelve years came from stones in the kid-neys, the cause of most of his severe backache. 'Feel rather exhausted at times,' he wrote to Audrey on one occasion, adding: 'However, it will pass. Literally, I hope!' He was as tough as nails, and his literally broad shoulders could carry all the burdens laid upon him.

One may marvel, too, in regarding the constant struggle to make ends meet at the Hallé, that he kept his promises in

15
Katie

Barbirolli enjoyed the company of beautiful and intelligent women, and they enjoyed his. Of the women who played important parts in his life, his mother came first. He adored her and also was in awe of her. She alone could make him do as he was told, and even as a man of sixty he was a little frightened of her if she was critical of him. For example, he never dared to tell her that he had lost while sea-bathing the signet ring which she had given him when he was in the Army in 1917. In several press interviews up to the 1960s he referred to the ring which was so well known to concert audiences as a gift from his mother, whereas in fact it was one he had bought for Evelyn in Finland in 1935. They decided it was more suitable for a man so she gave it to him. He had a true Italian respect and devotion for Mémé as head of the family. As Evelyn realised, if you wanted John you had to take Mémé as well. Delightful person that she was, she was an extremely strong character, dominating and possessive, and her grip on her elder son's affections was absolute. When she died he said: 'I feel that half of me has gone too.'

His love for Evelyn was fortified by a lasting and genuine admiration for her as a musician. He would speak of her achievements with touching pride that never slackened. After some performances together in 1950 he wrote: 'Numbers of people have *raved* about your broadcast... I thought it was wonderful, too, but I don't suppose you believe this. Secretly tho' I think you do. Lovely to look after you in the concerto. I think I do help a little.'

They knew each other for forty years and were married for

thirty-one. Like all marriages theirs had its rocky moments – but it withstood them because they truly loved each other. They had no children (though both loved them) from choice, first because a wartime world did not seem an inviting place into which to bring them and later because John knew how torn he would be when leaving them for long periods while he went abroad.

He was capable of conceiving a 'grand passion' for a woman but was not interested in casual affairs. He was even slightly prudish. As a young man he had refused to visit a Parisian show in which nudes appeared because he considered it degrading for the women concerned.

With two women members of the Hallé he was on especially friendly terms. Norah Winstanley was highly attractive to Barbirolli, a gay companion who was much liked by his family and spent several Brighton holidays with him and Evelyn. Audrey Napier Smith became another of his confidantes, to whom he wrote many letters (for which readers of this book have cause to be grateful). When abroad he looked forward to Audrey's letters, especially when she practised Italian, with which he assisted her. She had been a friend of Evelyn from the years when they were at the Royal College of Music. During the war she served in the WRNS and she shared John's admiration for Nelson, which was why many of his letters to her were signed: 'Admiral John.'

One woman was in a category of her own – Kathleen Ferrier, 'my beloved Katie,' as he invariably called her. She was one of two immensely gifted women musicians whose tragic and untimely deaths within a period of four years had a profound effect upon him. The other, and the first to die, was the French violinist Ginette Neveu. From his first encounter with Neveu, John recognised her as one of the elect – 'destined to be in the succession of Ysaÿe and Kreisler.' On that occasion they played the Brahms concerto and at rehearsal 'played the whole work through without a pause and without a word, for there was no need to speak... I experienced an inward glow of musical satisfaction I had not known since I last played it with Kreisler.'*

* From the introduction Barbirolli wrote to *Ginette Neveu* by Mme Ronze-Neveu. In his last years he likened only two performances to Kreisler's, both in America, one of the Brahms by Francescatti and the other a Mozart performance by Henryk Szeryng.

When Ginette Neveu played with the Hallé she travelled in the bus with the orchestra, and going to Sheffield John would arrange for the driver to take the more picturesque route over the Snake Pass so that she could enjoy the moorland scenery. In October 1949 she played the Sibelius concerto ('They don't know him in France,' she said, 'and they don't want to know him') and I have not since heard her equal for physical excitement and fiery spirituality. A few days later, on 28 October, she died in an air crash at the age of thirty. In her memory John conducted Verdi's *Requiem* in Sheffield and at Belle Vue. 'Never shall I forget the silence of those 5,000 people assembled in Manchester as I went forward to conduct the *Requiem*,' he wrote. 'Rain was falling in torrents all through the performance and although quite audible the sound did not seem to disturb but rather to intensify the feelings of all of us.'

His first musical contact with the contralto Kathleen Ferrier was less auspicious than was the Brahms with Neveu. In 1945 he began to study Elgar's *The Dream of Gerontius* before conducting it for the first time. As he has told in a memoir he contributed to a tribute to Kathleen Ferrier published in 1954, some of the Hallé players who had heard her broadcast urged him to engage her for the part of the Angel. This was only three years after her first London recital and she was by no means the household name she was to become.) He asked her to sing Elgar's *Sea Pictures* at Sheffield. Her competent and cold-blooded' performance of a work with which she had no sympathy disappointed and distressed him. The rehearsal also happened to be one of the occasions, comparatively rare, when he flew into a rage and threw a score, narrowly missing Kathleen. He was often in a bad temper in the City Hall, Sheffield, because of its appalling acoustics, which he once likened to 'playing in a bale of cotton wool.' However, he persevered and, with *Gerontius*, there began a close musical and personal relationship. In the 1948–49 Hallé season Kathleen sang Mahler's *Kindertotenlieder*, the first time Barbirolli had conducted this work since his 1931 performance with Gerhardt. The next year she sang Berkeley's *Four Poems of St Teresa of Avila* and Brahms's *Alto Rhapsody*. For the 1950–51 season Barbirolli planned some special Ferrier occasions, concert performances of Gluck's opera *Orfeo* in Sheffield, Manchester and Hanley, and a revival of Chausson's song-cycle *Poème de l'amour et de la mer*, in which he had played when it had its first English performance at a Royal Philharmonic concert on 29 May 1919. This latter work was chosen because he was disturbed that Kathleen's voice seemed to be deepening and that she might become merely an 'oratorio contralto,' since she was in great demand for oratorio work. Kathleen protested that it was too high for her but she worked hard at it. By now she was almost one of the Barbirolli family:

9 October 1950

It is always such an experience to make music with you and I count myself so wonderfully lucky to be able to do so. I should lay me doon and dee were I ever to let you down... Now I am looking forward to *Orfeo* and the Chausson, and I hope to come back from Paris with all my 'des, les et mes' put right!... Much, much love to you and Evelyn — safe journeying for you in the Southern Hemisphere.

John returned from Australia very ill, as already related. 'I collapsed after my first rehearsal and was told by my old friend and great Manchester surgeon Billy (W.R.) Douglas that I should have to be "carved up".' His one fear was that he would have to miss the Ferrier concerts and Douglas agreed to 'keep him going' until they were over.

'I can't ever forget that you put off your "appointment" with Billy Douglas until *Orfeo* and the Chausson were over,' Kathleen wrote to him. 'Those ten days — working and being with you — were inexpressibly wonderful... It is the loveliest time I ever remember and I keep on re-living it, and purr with pleasure every time I do so.'

Not long afterwards the first signs of the cancer that was to kill her put Kathleen in hospital for an operation. While she convalesced, she and John discussed his editing of *Messiah* and it was because she told him of the difficulty she had in 'bringing to "O thou that tellest" the easy light phrasing the music demands while the orchestration forced her to..."pump it out"' that he returned to the original scoring for strings only and realised the figured bass. When she returned to the concert platform after a Sussex summer holiday with John and Evelyn, she again sang the Chausson (Ernest Bean delightfully described the effect of her performance of this romantic music as 'like living in sin with Kathleen') at the Edinburgh Festival and at Nottingham:

In train, 4 Oct. 1951

...I think the old Chausson is growing a bit now, isn't it? I enjoyed it really for the first time last week and now feel I'm getting away from a *Messiah*-like sound. As for the banquet, luv!!! Well!! Words fail me. It *was* so good and so beautifully served – you're a ruddy wizard.

It was at Edinburgh, where Kathleen gave a Lieder recital with Bruno Walter as accompanist, that Walter told John how much 'freer and easier' her voice had become, sufficient justification of his experiment.

In November 1951 the rebuilt Free Trade Hall was opened in Manchester and the Hallé returned at last to its traditional home. At the opening ceremony in the presence of the Queen there was a short concert of which the never-to-be-forgotten climax (John's idea) was Kathleen's performance of 'Land of Hope and Glory.' As Norman Shrapnel wrote in the *Manchester Guardian*: 'It was fine and it was right, but lovers of this tune will fear that never again can they hope to hear it in such glory. There were few dry eyes, as notices of such events used to say.' Kathleen stayed the weekend with the Barbirollis at their Appleby Lodge flat and John took her to see some of his favourite Cheshire haunts, in particular Gawsworth which he loved to show to people who thought that all the best English villages were in the South. She attended the Hallé's first public concert in the new hall, at which William Primrose played Walton's Viola Concerto and there was homage to Berlioz – long associated with the Hallé concerts – in the *Symphonie Fantastique*. Neville Cardus wrote in the *Manchester Guardian* that 'Sir John conducted as if possessed by the music. He has come into his own, and the audience's acclamation let him know, and everybody else, that they honour him and appreciate his value.'

At Sheffield on 8 December 1951 Barbirolli conducted his first *Messiah*. Kathleen was unable to be among the soloists because she was having further X-ray examinations, but she wrote on the day to John: 'I think Mr Handel will revolve in pride and peace tonight instead of whizzing round in be-

wilderment at the strange things done to his heart's outpouring!' Later, she sang in several performances, and the strange
surroundings of Belle Vue became hallowed while she sang
'He was despised' with a poignant intensity that has not since
been approached let alone equalled. In fact 1952 was a miraculous year for Ferrier, a year snatched from the hastening
approach of death in which her art blossomed and matured as
though she knew, as indeed she must have known, that she
had to concentrate the rest of her career into a few months.
Several performances in that year were given with Barbirolli
and the Hallé in various British cities; they included
Mahler's *Das Lied von der Erde*, Brahms's *Four Serious Songs*
and a series of *Gerontius* performances about one of which –
in London in June – Cardus wrote that 'it came as close to
faultlessness as could be wished.'

At the memorable 1952 Edinburgh Festival Kathleen sang
Mahler with van Beinum and the Concertgebouw Orchestra,
the Brahms *Liebeslieder* waltzes with Seefried, Patzak and
others, and *Gerontius* and *Messiah* with the Hallé. This was
not merely a musical miracle, it was a medical one: a Harley
Street specialist gave as his opinion in May 1952 – the very
month she went to Vienna to record Mahler's *Das Lied von
der Erde* with Bruno Walter – that it must be unique for a
patient undergoing X-ray therapy for numerous skeletal
lesions at the same time to appear on the concert platform. It
was this knowledge that impelled Barbirolli to try, before it
was too late, to consummate their artistic love affair with some
Covent Garden performances of Gluck's *Orfeo*, in which
Kathleen had appeared at Glyndebourne seven years earlier.
Thanks mainly to the courage and generosity of the Royal
Opera House's general administrator, David Webster, who,
knowing the risks involved, was still prepared to put everything in motion, the new production was announced for
February 1953. Kathleen and John practically retranslated
the opera – it was to be sung in English – and the closeness of
their relationship at this time is apparent from this letter:

1 December '52

Tita darling. This is just to bring you all my love in
boundless measure on this your birthday, and to say that all
my thoughts and dearest wishes are with you – now and

always. I hope you are not too weary, my darling, though it would seem difficult for you to be otherwise with all the work you have done and are doing – but if unceasing and loving thoughts can speed through the air and reach you in gloomy Sheffield, then, perhaps, a little of the burden of your work may be lightened. You have helped me so unbelievably these last 18 months that I feel sure that such thoughts *can* aid and heal and bless, and with each meeting we have added more treasures to our store of memories, both grave and gay, haven't we, love? Look after yourself, beloved Tita – many, many happy returns – you have all my love. God bless you, from Katie.

Whenever they had a free moment John and Evelyn would go to Kathleen's Hampstead flat and play trios for cello, oboe and pianoforte with her. Also there were intimate supper parties at which Kathleen would convulse the guests with one of her delightfully bawdy 'cabaret turns.' At one such gathering, on New Year's Eve 1952, the toast at midnight was Kathleen Ferrier, CBE. Her gift of swift Rabelaisian repartee gave John immense delight; for example, when she heard that two male musicians were setting up house together: 'And I suppose they'll call it "Homo sweet homo".'

Orpheus was staged on 3 February 1953. The producer and choreographer was Frederick Ashton, the scenery and costumes were by Sophie Fedorovitch (who died tragically almost on the eve of the performance), the principal dancers were Svetlana Beriosova and Alexander Grant, and the two singers besides Ferrier were Adèle Leigh (Amor) and Veronica Dunne (Eurydice). On the eve of the performance Kathleen gave John a set of blue-enamelled cuff links and evening dress buttons with this note: 'For my beloved maestro! With my devoted love and oh! so many thanks for making an Orpheus dream come true – and for many other blessings spread over the last three years. Katie.' He wore her gift regularly and with great pride. On the first night, Kathleen sang marvelously and looked strikingly beautiful. Yet so brittle were her bones because of the cancer that shortly before the end of the second performance on 6 February her hip splintered and she realised she could not move. Thanks to the static nature of the plot, she was easily able to conceal this from the audience by leaning against a stage prop, but John, in the pit, realised that

H

something drastic had occurred. His agony can be imagined: few conductors can have experienced such a situation. Yet, as always, professionalism on the stage and on the rostrum en sured that the end was reached without disaster. Though in severe pain, Kathleen sang without stinting. At the end, the audience threw flowers on to the stage at her feet while she took her bows with Adèle Leigh and John literally propping her up between them. When the curtain had descended for the last time, she was taken to her dressing-room. Asked if there was anything she wanted she replied 'Yes, get a stretcher.' She never sang in public again.

It would be impossible to deduce from the criticisms of *Orpheus* that a moving and heroic drama had been enacted, although the nature and inevitable outcome of Ferrier's illness were widely known. Her singing was highly praised – even her movements were held up as examples to the ballet, which delighted the crippled woman herself – but the general attitude to conducting and performance was cool. 'Bugger the critics,' Frederick Ashton wrote to Barbirolli, 'the public has responded.'*

During the eight months of life that remained to Kathleen, John spent every possible moment with her, in hospital or at her home. He spoke to every doctor he knew, and he knew many, about the hope of finding some 'miracle cure.' In February 1964, over ten years after Kathleen's death, he recalled his efforts in a letter to Audrey Napier Smith, who had told him of a visit she had made to a mutual friend in the Christie Hospital and Holt Radium Institute, Manchester:

Mention of Christie's again brings back tragic memories. After my last big 'op', Billy [Douglas] called to take me for a drive and we passed Christie's. B. said shall we pop in for a moment and that was the end of the drive!! However whilst there one of his pupils was doing an adrenalectomy Complete removal of the adrenals, a thing impossible before the arrival of Cortisone, for one cannot live without the adrenal secretions, which can now be artificially sup plied by the cortisone (or some by-product). I mention this because I had read in an American journal of some quite

* In 1970 when Barbirolli congratulated Ashton on becoming a fellow CH, Sir Frederick replied: 'I always remember our wonderful but tragic time.'

remarkable results in advanced cancers by a noted American surgeon with this procedure. I dared, because of my beloved Katie, to suggest such a procedure for her and of course was ridiculed by her medicos. Billy was *not* amongst them. However some 18 months later (much too late) the very surgeon who initiated the procedure was in London and he saw her. He said at this stage she had but a 50-50 chance but by all means try. She made spectacular improvement for a very short while but it *was* too late. And now it is regular procedure!! Such is the fate of all pioneers. Lister, Semmelweiss and others have had to see so many die before they are vindicated.

Just before she had this operation John visited Katie. She had had a preliminary small operation, and John reported to Billy Douglas: 'Her first words to me when I asked her if she was not too uncomfortable after the minor "do" were "No, I'm fine. Farting freely." What a girl!!'

Barbirolli and others have told of Ferrier's classic courage in her last days, though he was not able in his lifetime to print this example of how she worried more about others than herself:

5 May 1953

...How are you my beloved adored wizaldric maestro? Working too hard, I know, but I won't bully you – I know it's no good! But you are precious to us all, my darling, and to me in particular – so just remember that, won't you love, when you are debating whether you can crowd in a morning concert in Llanelly as well as a matinée in Cork and a *Tristan* at C.G. in the evening!?

It was probably only Barbirolli's medical knowledge and interest – which eliminated any squeamishness his emotional nature might otherwise have felt – that enabled him to sustain the sight of Kathleen almost disintegrating before his eyes. Not long before she died, as she lay in her hospital bed he sang to him the opening phrases of the Chausson song-cycle 'in a voice with all the bloom and tender ache of spring in it...the glory that was hers remained untouched.' She died on 8 October 1953, aged forty-one. A few days later John wrote to Billy Douglas:

I loved her very dearly and I know I meant a deal to her. We had moments of radiant happiness in our work together and I shall ever be grateful that it was given to me to be so close to her. She was perfect to the end, Bill, and her last words to me, affectionately and simply Lancashire, were 'Goodbye love'.

Never again, to the day he died, did John hear Kathleen' voice on her recordings. When I asked him how he managed to avoid them when listening casually to the car radio or to programmes like *Desert Island Discs*, he replied: 'I have a sixth sense.' But he knew he had to continue conducting works in which she had sung with him; and here he was helped because he had had to find substitutes in her lifetime when she had been ill. He had the highest respect for the singing of Gladys Ripley, but she, too, was dying of cancer, so for the Angel in *Gerontius* he turned to Constance Shacklock and later to Anna Reynolds, Norma Procter and Kerstin Meyer. With Miss Meyer he also again performed *Das Lied von der Erde* and Chausson's *Poème de l'amour et de la mer*

In 1964, when he recorded *The Dream of Gerontius*, John began his association with the second of the two great post 1945 interpreters of the role of the Angel, Janet Baker. Her range and repertoire were wider than Ferrier's and she sang not only Elgar with him – including the *Sea Pictures* – but Mahler, Berlioz's *Nuits d'été* and Verdi's *Requiem*. Although no one took Kathleen Ferrier's place with him, Janet Baker carved her own place in his affections and admiration. He once said: 'Of course, Janet is by far the greater *artist*.' His professional honesty forbade him to say otherwise.

Orpheus was one of several operas which John conducted when he returned to the Royal Opera House as guest conductor in October 1951, for the first time for fourteen years. It was widely rumoured that he would be appointed musical director in succession to Karl Rankl, but no such full-time post was contemplated. He returned for three seasons, 1951-52, 1952–53 and 1953–54, conducting on some of the provincial tours in addition to the London season. His first opera date was 22 October 1951 – *Turandot*, with Gertrude Grob-Prandl as the Princess and James Johnston as Calaf. In the same season he conducted *Aïda*, with Gre Brouwenstijn as Aïda, Hans Hopf as Radames and Edith Coates as Amneris

Opinions among the critics differed on Barbirolli's effectiveness. He was not short of people to remind him that 'the critics hate success' and that his success, in particular, was anathema to some musical circles in London where he had never been accepted and where Beecham's word 'upstart' was still bandied about. But Harold Rosenthal in *Opera* (December 1951) said simply: 'Here at last was what Italian opera at Covent Garden has needed for the last four years... Italian music excitingly played and sung, carefully prepared and rehearsed; may we have lots more like it.' Others found Barbirolli 'too much the star of the show.' Various cast changes in *Aïda* over the next two seasons meant that on one occasion, in Coronation week, he conducted Maria Callas in the role – he thought her magnificent and enjoyed working with her – and on several occasions Joan Hammond, whose portrayal he considered to be much under-rated. An additional personal pleasure in conducting at the Garden was that his brother Peter was in the viola section of the orchestra.

Later he conducted revivals of *La Bohème*, of *Madam Butterfly*, with Lenora Lafayette, and of *Tristan und Isolde*, with Sylvia Fisher as Isolde and Ludwig Suthaus/Wolfgang Windgassen as Tristan. The *Tristan* performances were outstanding for the lyricism, poetry and beauty of detail which Barbirolli drew from the score. Whatever reservations some critics had, the public as a whole relished his return to opera, and for John himself the acclaim of old friends meant most. In the 1950s, to quote Cardus, he was 'doing the work of six horses and two Trojans', and his friends' letters urged him – in vain – to ease off. Well-meaning though they were, they did not understand that for John there could be no easing-up. It was not within the scope of his temperament. This was not because of any personal ambition but simply because he was a servant of music and the idea of taking a day off from such a task amounted almost to blasphemy. There was always some little extra job to be done; and if it involved some former colleague who had endured illness, as in the case of Albert Sammons, the violinist, he would expend every drop of energy to make sure that a testimonial concert was a success. It was sufficient reward to receive a letter afterwards: 'I shall never forget our Elgar and Delius concerto performances... All my heartfelt blessing to yourself for your wonderful effort on my behalf. Your devoted friend.' People who said that

was about 1964). Afterwards he sat exhausted, obviously profoundly moved, and hardly able to speak. Evelyn and I were standing near him and we began to speak of something else to relieve tension. John joined in and seemed to have regained composure. Suddenly, he gripped Evelyn's forearm with one hand, and mine with the other, tears filled his eyes, and he said with frightening intensity: 'God, I love that music.' His body was shaking as though swept by forces he could not control.

'Any friend of Elgar's is a friend of mine' was a favourite saying of his. But it was not until 1946 that he conducted *The Dream of Gerontius*, at Sheffield on 26 April. The soloists were Kathleen Ferrier, Parry Jones and David Franklin. He had studied it for months beforehand: 'I began to realise for the first time the great delicacy, imagination and subtlety of much of the scoring.' The intensity of his interpretation shook the composure of so experienced a professional as David Franklin. In the next twenty-four years he conducted it many times, not only in Britain, but in Dublin (with Our Lady's Choral Society), in Rome, in Perugia, in New York and in Houston. Both as a musician and as a Roman Catholic he felt more meaning in it than he could easily express in words.

English audiences were fortunate in the twenty years after the war in being able to hear such individually superb performances of Elgar's masterpiece as Boult, Sargent and Barbirolli offered. One does not attempt to say which was 'the best.' Each great conductor gave of his best to the music, and the results were in each case memorable. Because Barbirolli began his career conducting *Butterfly* and *Trovatore*, some English criticism always tended to assume that his approach to choral music was inevitably dramatic, blood-and-thunder, hell-for-leather. ('They think I'm a passionate ignoramus.') Yet this was far from being the case. Drama he certainly found in *Gerontius*, *Messiah*, the *St Matthew Passion* and Verdi's *Requiem*, but it was a true, spiritual drama, not applied theatricality. His recording of the Verdi *Requiem* is notable for its reverence and restraint, above all else for its treatment of the work as *religious* music; and in *Gerontius*, too, while he vividly pointed up the brilliance of the orchestration and made the most of the Demons, his interpretation generally was notable for its breadth, its sense of the work's inhabitation of an other-worldly sphere, and its self-renewing imaginative insight. Sometimes he lingered with excess of affection, seemed perhaps too finicky over details so that the broad sweep was in danger of being lost, but not for long. He described the work as 'written in a constant white heat of inspiration,' and this was how the best of his performances sounded. The rather slow but majestic tempo for the Prelude set the mood; in it he made the pauses after the big climaxes just that fraction longer, so that the awe of the moment was magnified (just as, in a lesser context, he held on a fraction longer than anyone else, with superb effect, to the last chord of the *Carnaval Romain* overture).

Of *Gerontius* performances, two in particular remain in my memory. One was at Hanley on 2 November 1950, perhaps the greatest account of the work I expect to hear, and the other was a performance with the BBC Symphony Orchestra at the Royal Albert Hall on 19 February 1947. In both, the Gerontius was Parry Jones, who was not only Barbirolli's close friend but was much admired by him. 'Not a great voice,' he said, 'but a great singer.' His account of the exacting role on these occasions was extraordinarily fine. Jones himself wrote to Barbirolli the day after the 1947 performance:

I'm still bowled over. It was a very great and moving musical and spiritual experience. And I bless you for giving me the great opportunity of singing it with you. I have never seen so many people after a performance so moved. That tough nut Paul Beard [leader of the BBCSO] said to me afterwards: 'God! what a performance. You don't realise what a tonic he is to us. I never, in my position, especially after all these years, make any quick conclusions, but I think he must be the finest conductor in the world...'

When Parry Jones died early in 1964 John wrote to his widow: 'His singing of "Thy rebuke" [from *Messiah*] and the opening of the *Dream* have never been equalled, let alone surpassed.' From about 1950 onwards, Richard Lewis was John's Gerontius whenever he was available, and Ronald Dowd in later years identified himself with the part magnificently. Of the Angels much has already been said. In the bass part, after David Franklin there came Norman Walker, Marian Nowakowski, Kim Borg and David Ward. John was much criticised for his use of foreign basses, but his principal concern was for a real bass quality.

On 29 September 1958 John conducted Part I of *Gerontius* with the Dublin Choir in the presence of Pope Pius XII at Castel Gandolfo, only a few days before the Pope's death. 'I have often wondered,' he wrote, 'what the feelings of Newman and Elgar would be if they could know that the last music [the Pope] heard had been Elgar's setting of Newman's words "Go forth upon thy journey, Christian soul".' As Barbirolli knelt before him, the Pope said: 'Figlio mio, questo e un capolavoro sublime' ('My son, that is a sublime masterpiece'). This historic event had been arranged by the then British Ambassador in Rome, Sir Ashley Clarke, who became a close friend of John and Evelyn. He had written to them in February: 'I have just heard that the Pope has caused the Irish Ambassador to be informed that he will receive the Irish Choir and they may sing for 10 minutes but no more!! What an unlucky man the I.A. must be (not for quotation, please). Marcus Cheke and I must now see if we can perform a rescue operation.' Which they did. Sir Ashley also helped to arrange, in Elgar's centenary year 1957, the first broadcast performance in Italy of *Gerontius*, in Rome with the RAI Chorus and Orchestra. 'Longing to tell you of the wonderful performance of the *Dream* they gave me here,' John wrote to me. 'Chorus was absolutely incredible, and I don't think I have ever heard it sung better.' He held to that opinion, and it was supported by his friend William Walton who happened to switch on his radio in Ischia, thought how fine a performance it was, and could not imagine which English choir could be singing with such superb diction! The next September, at the Sagra Umbra festival in Perugia, John conducted the Dublin choir and Maggio Fiorentino orchestra in *Messiah* and the first public performance in Italy of *Gerontius*. When the tiny English contingent, occupying a box in the lovely Morlacchi Theatre, observed tradition and stood during the Hallelujah Chorus, the astonished Italians, not to be outdone, encored it.

So much has been said about *Gerontius* because of its crucial significance for Barbirolli himself. When his recording was issued in 1965 he wrote to me: 'I sometimes can hardly believe it has all come to pass. How I wish our great and beloved E.E. could have heard it, for I like to think in my old age that I have brought more and more people to a realisation of his stature.' To another friend he said simply and without affectation: 'I wanted to leave it as a kind of testament of my faith.'

His capacity to find new delights in the music he loved was one of his chief attributes. Recording *Sea Pictures* with Janet Baker, he telephoned me from the hall simply because he wanted to share with a fellow-Elgarian his bubbling enthusiasm for the scoring of the first song. I can hear his voice still: 'He makes you *see* the sea lapping over the beach, you can almost feel the pull of the tide, don't you agree, Mike, dear boy?' Dear John! This, too, on a postcard from Monte Carlo in 1969: 'I hadn't done the *Enigma* for some time and was completely overwhelmed by them again.' And in July 1966 he wrote to me from King's Lynn:

Last week I recorded with New Phil. all the 5 Pomp & Circ. Marches, *Froissart* (lovely piece, almost first manifestation of the great Elgar), and the string *Elegy* and *Sospiri*. The orchestra arrived all in rather facetious mood, saying they had brought Union Jacks: but after the 1st march, I think it was No. 3, there was a unanimous 'Must admit it's a bloody good tune' and they ended captivated by *Froissart* and the smaller pieces.

His marked scores for the Marches show how much care he took with them; nothing was left to chance. Above the first page of No. 5 he wrote: 'In the existing record [by another conductor] the soft percussion parts are completely *inaudible*. Pity, for they are typically E.E. and should be very effective.'

Of the two Elgar concertos, he conducted that for cello more frequently, for it is shorter and easier to fit into a programme. Also, more cellists are successful in it than are violinists in their concerto. Strangely, he did not admire his revered Casals's performance, because he considered that he phrased the long theme of the first movement 'all wrong.' But with Pierre Fournier, André Navarra, Jacqueline du Pré, Amaryllis Fleming and others, he gave many fine performances. It is instructive to compare the slower tempi and broader conception of his recording with du Pré with the more lyrical and possibly more idiomatic 1957 recording he made with

Navarra. He was constantly looking for a violinist for the concerto to match Kreisler, whom he heard play it, and Sammons. He thought the true tragedy of the music was missing from Heifetz's technically superb performance. A performance in Manchester in 1964 with the Hallé leader, Martin Milner, satisfied him as much as any.

Somehow Barbirolli overlooked the tone-poem *In the South*, Elgar's portrait of Italy. Determined to remedy this omission, I implored him to study it, pointing out that of all Elgar's works this, the Anglo-Italian one, was made for an Elgarian Anglo-Italian conductor. In April and May 1970, he conducted three vibrant performances. As could easily have been predicted, he went to the heart of the music. But again, how typical it was that he would not tackle even so comparatively short a work until he had studied it 'properly.' So it had been in 1954 with the symphonic study *Falstaff*. When he first conducted this complex work for the Hallé audiences in Sheffield and Manchester, he preceded the performance with a long 'spoken programme-note,' in which he went through the 'plot' of the work, with over forty short illustrations by the orchestra. Some sobersides complained that they did not go to the Hallé concerts for a lecture, but probably most people were grateful for this aural introduction to a difficult piece instead of having to try to follow a complicated printed analysis.

There remain the two symphonies, each of which he recorded twice. In his approach to them can be discerned the special insight which stemmed directly from his un-Englishness. Elgar's music, although 'typically English' in many ways, is remarkably un-English in its brilliant colour, freedom from emotional inhibitions, its violent changes of mood and combination of reticence and rodomontade. It was perhaps because Barbirolli himself had no English blood that he was paradoxically English to the core in his patriotism, love of tradition, nostalgia for the past, and understanding of all the cosmopolitan as well as the English elements in Elgar's music. I have heard him rail, in lurid language, against those evasions and reticences of English taste and outlook which also enraged Elgar. That perhaps is why some English temperaments were uncomfortable with Barbirolli's Elgar. I remember a performance of the Second Symphony at Cheltenham in 1957 after which the music critic of *The Times* left the hall snorting like an outraged Colonel Blimp. The tender of the sacred flame of all that is most English in English music had clearly been offended to hear an English masterpiece conducted with a cosmopolitan comprehensiveness of technique and emotion. But if anyone should doubt that Barbirolli's Hallé was a great orchestra, I would only say that they should have heard it in Elgar. Here the benefits of long association, of careful rehearsal, of the inspiration of the moment, communicated by the flash of an eye or the raising of an eyebrow, were apparent. Conductor and orchestra were as one, unified and not just playing but living, recreating the music. Cardus said that 'Sir John and the Hallé serve Elgar as once on a time the Vienna Philharmonic and Bruno Walter served Bruckner.'

It is difficult to say in which of the symphonies Barbirolli was the more effective. In No. 2 there was greater scope for the defects of his qualities, and his interpretation altered considerably over the years. As he grew older and as its personal nostalgia for him – memories of his London youth and of playing it in memory of Philip Godlee – intensified, he tended to draw out the first movement beyond even its power to sustain an unbroken span through many episodes. Rhetoric replaced eloquence. One best-forgotten performance in London took seventy-one minutes. But that was exceptional. His 1964 recording inclines to linger too long in the first movement – yet, in some moods, it is perfect – but the performance and interpretation of the three other movements are so fine that one is happy to indulge Barbirolli's indulgence – so sincere and heartfelt, in any case. Nevertheless his earlier Hallé recording is, for me, a truer representation of his interpretation of this work at its peak. It was with this symphony that he opened the Elgar Festival in London on 30 May 1949 in the presence of the Queen (now the Queen Mother). On being presented to Her Majesty he remarked how much he admired Elgar's music. She replied: 'I agree, but it isn't at all the thing to say these days, is it?' By the time Barbirolli died it was very much the thing to say, no small thanks to him.

In his later years he tended to conduct No. 1 more often, and here he generally kept near to Elgar's own performance. His ability to make an orchestra produce a true full-toned pianissimo lent a special beauty to his performance of the Adagio, just as he imparted the 'English Mahler' touch of fantasy to the airy raptures of the second movement. His special joys in the first movement were the horn harmonies in the opening bars and the cello solo just before cue no. 31. He was delighted when Basil Cameron wrote to him in 1958, after his first recording was issued, to say that he was 'especially thrilled to hear you expand this horn phrase [at cue no. 17] just as Nikisch did (and of course Henry J. [Wood] adopted it at once!). I shall never forget the moment when (after playing it several times under Elgar the first time *he* conducted) Nikisch first came to this spot in the symphony and got the horns (headed by Alf Brain) to blaze this passage out. Thanks for a fine piece of music-making, John!' Barbirolli saw visions in Elgar and he communicated them to his listeners more strikingly than any other conductor. In the performances of the First Symphony in the last week of his life there was, in addition to the usual grandeur, a by no means unintentional elegiac tenderness.

History might almost have arranged matters specially for Barbirolli in that the Elgar centenary (2 June 1957) and the Hallé centenary (30 January 1958) fell so close to each other and enabled him to play and record so much Elgar in 1957–58. He opened the 1957 Edinburgh Festival with an Elgar concert which pleased all the critics; after the ovation for the First Symphony he held the score aloft and kissed it. He chose this symphony as the climax of the Hallé Centenary Concert in Manchester when the late Colin Mason wrote that the performance was 'not four movements but a single symphonic poem, haunted all through by the tempo and mood of the opening march theme. It may be doubted whether Richter himself did better for the work than this.' This was the right choice for that occasion, not only because the work had had its first performance under Richter at a Hallé concert fifty years earlier, but because it symbolised the special bond between Barbirolli and his audience. Taking a tip from Beecham's method of handling the public, he had in 1945 challenged the Manchester audience to 'fill Belle Vue' (six thousand people) for his first performance there of the Second Symphony. And of course they did. Elgar was not 'box office' then, but Barbirolli's Elgar was. No doubt he was specially pleased by Colin Mason's appreciation of that centenary performance, because in the 1950s (though he revised his opinions later) Mason showed little sympathy for Elgar's music. This gifted and knowledgeable critic took over on the *Guardian* in Manchester from Granville Hill in 1951 when he was twenty-seven. His first notice caused a considerable stir. It had an acerbity that had been lacking in Hill's criticisms (urbane and witty though these were, as re-reading them has reminded me), although it was not particularly savage, merely a complaint about Belle Vue's acoustics and some uncomplimentary remarks about a less than usually good Beethoven performance. But one might have thought the Holy Grail had been violated, so affronted were some of the Hallé's aficionados.

John did not like the *Guardian* as a newspaper and did not take it – he saw its notices only when they came from the cuttings agency or when friends showed them to him. Unfortunately there were those, in the orchestra and outside it, who pandered to his vanity by surrounding him with sycophancy, and they were there in full force on the Monday Mason's notice appeared, which happened to be the day of acoustic tests in the new Free Trade Hall, a particularly emotional day for John. They did not let him read the notice but gave him garbled extracts which exaggerated its language. He was furious. 'Who is this little whippersnapper? I'm not going to be told how to conduct Beethoven by some young upstart on a newspaper' and this, that and the other. Perhaps the name Colin was too near to Olin for comfort, and stirred unhappy New York memories. At any rate the initials C.M. on a *Guardian* notice were enough to raise hackles all round.

Mason was not happy in Manchester; he disliked provincial musical life and its revolving round one fixed star. His criticisms of Barbirolli at times had an unpleasant personal edge but were much less severe than the legend insists. He was a champion of the avant-garde and the Hallé programmes were altogether too conservative for him. He did not want Elgar, Mahler, Bax and company, nor the Cheltenham composers, and he said so. On the other hand, Barbirolli and the Hallé considered that he took no account of the extremely precarious financial position of the Society in the 1950s; while the orchestra was fighting for its life was no time, in Barbirolli's view, to be playing Schoenberg, Webern and Messiaen, even if he had wanted to, to audiences the majority of whom did not want to listen to them. Perhaps – and Mason would have said no doubt – this financial pressure towards conservatism was not entirely unwelcome to Barbirolli, or at least not very strongly resisted. But when Barbirolli began to make plans for the Centenary Season he invited Mason to join Crickmore, himself and me on a committee to ensure that as wide a selection of music was played as was practically possible. Mason accepted, and helped to put together one of the finest sets of programmes ever heard in Britain – although it was perhaps a pity that the (then new) work he particularly championed, Tippett's difficult Second Symphony, was unceremoniously abandoned by Barbirolli at rehearsal as being 'not worth the effort involved.'

Here, at any rate, is Mason on the 1951 Hallé:

> The orchestra played…as near flawlessly as any conductor could wish, as fully realising Barbirolli's intentions as he the composers'. At any time there is little fault with the orchestra in romantic full-orchestral tuttis… Each phrase grew out of the last and into the next so perfectly that the line was unbroken from beginning to end. They were such performances as one may rarely hope to hear bettered.

The performances were of Brahms's First Symphony and Vaughan Williams's *London Symphony*. As with Elgar, so Barbirolli felt a special affinity with the music of Vaughan Williams. He had conducted it for most of his career; and his return to Britain in June 1943 coincided with the first performance of V.W.'s Fifth Symphony. Barbirolli loved this work from the first and recorded it within a year. He always described it as 'like a benediction.' He wrote in 1967: 'We played V.W.5 in Sheffield last night to a house that could have been sold out four times over, they told me. What a work it is. Strange that our two most beloved E.E. and V.W. in the closing bars of the slow movements of V.W.5 and E.E.1 give us in music a glimpse of "our God in Heaven" vouchsafed to no one else except perhaps the great J.S.B. in the penultimate quartet and chorus of the Matthew.'

Likewise, when the Sixth Symphony appeared in 1948, Barbirolli and the Hallé at once took it up and played it throughout the country, 'making it their own,' as Capell said. Their performance at Cheltenham in July 1948 was broadcast and brought John a letter from the composer:

> The first movement was wonderfully clear, as also was the third. I liked the slow opening of the slow movement.

The only thing I find not quite happy (and perhaps that was only the wireless) was the reiterated trumpets. I originally put dots over the notes and that made them sound too perky altogether, so I changed these to stress marks and now that seems to have taken some of their fierce quality away. I do not quite know what the solution is.

It was at a rehearsal of this symphony in the Sheldonian, Oxford, on 2 June 1949, that the friendship between Barbirolli and the composer began in earnest. V.W. was particularly impressed by the performance of the scherzo. He wistfully remarked to John that 'Malcolm says it needs another tune,' but Barbirolli told him: 'You leave it alone, it's all a question of tempo.' Thenceforward they saw much of each other – and V.W.'s affection for John disconcerted some who thought that there could be no common ground between them. Vaughan Williams was thrilled by the vitality, colour and breadth of John's interpretations of his music.

When in 1950 the Royal Philharmonic Society awarded Barbirolli its Gold Medal, the highest distinction in British musical life, his pride was further enhanced when he learned that V.W. would make the presentation. 'It had not even remotely crossed my mind,' he wrote to Norah Winstanley, 'and I feel very moved and very humble.' The Gold Medal concert – at which Vaughan Williams's Sixth and Sibelius's Second Symphonies were played – was on 13 December 1950, in the Royal Albert Hall in the presence of the Queen. Vaughan Williams described Barbirolli as 'one of those wizards who can take the dry bones of crotchets and quavers and breathe into them the breath of life... I think part of Sir John's magic lies in the fact that he can always spot the melody – however unpromising sometimes.' In his speech of acceptance, one of the best he made, John mentioned the 'particular happiness' of receiving the medal standing in the midst of his Hallé, and ended with Sachs's words in the last act of *Mastersingers*: 'Friends, words, light to you, bow me to earth. Your praise is far beyond my worth.'

The Hallé gave many performances of Elgar and Vaughan Williams during the 1951 Festival of Britain. Barbirolli's principal tribute to V.W., however, was the inclusion of the existing six symphonies in the first Hallé season in the new Free Trade Hall as a prelude to the composer's eightieth birthday in October 1952. When V.W. heard of this, he wrote to John on 12 September 1951:

This seems to me a good opportunity to overhaul them, and I have already started doing this. Do tell me quite frankly any points either in construction, orchestration or anything else that occur to you which want alteration or revision. With all your experience you must know rather more about it really than I do... Please be quite frank about it. I am much too old to have my feelings hurt.

The revisions of the symphonies were fairly extensive and John made the invited comments. Most interesting were his remarks about the violent Fourth Symphony which he had taken up on a friend's insistence in 1950 and of which he gave several exciting performances:

3rd movement (scherzo). I think the metronome marking *too fast* for clear and accurate performance. A slight reduction to ♩. = 120, which is about the speed at which I find I get best results, would, I think, be helpful. 4th mvt. Here again I think the metronome just that bit too fast to make *good strong* playing almost impossible especially at the splendid passage between (9) and (10). I play the movement at about ♩ = 116–120 (except for the Epilogo (con anima) which I take at a good ♩ = 130) and at that speed the passage can be played as it stands (it would be a shame to alter it) and sounds very exciting. However after much experimenting I have only found it possible with the following bowing [which he then detailed].*

In reviewing the Hallé performance of this symphony on 15 February 1952, Colin Mason mentioned London critics who 'last year objected to Sir John's restrained tempo for the scherzo, but no one could have desired it (if indeed it were physically possible) faster, lighter of tread or more full of humour than on this occasion.' Barbirolli, like Beecham, often proved that by playing a work slightly slower to enable

* An interesting point in Vaughan Williams's reply referred to the tuba tune in the scherzo: 'I put the bassoons in just to steady the tone of the tuba, but they can be left out if you prefer it and have a bare solo for the tuba.'

correct articulation it sounded faster. The only symphony in which the composer made no alterations was the *London* (1914). He wrote to Barbirolli on 6 October 1951: 'The *London* Symph. is past mending – though indeed with all its faults I love it still – indeed it is my favourite of my family of 6.'

Soon the 'family' was to be increased. During 1951–52 V.W. revised his projected *Sinfonia Antartica*, based on music he had written for the film *Scott of the Antarctic*. He wrote to John on 12 March 1952: 'If by any chance you thought well of it, it would be a great honour to me if you could conduct it at one of your next season's Hallé concerts.' Rayson Whalley, the Hallé pianist, played this elaborate score through *on sight* when V.W. visited Manchester later that month to conduct the Hallé Choir and Orchestra in his *Sea Symphony* in Manchester and Sheffield. In Sheffield, to the old man's intense delight, John played at the first desk of cellos in the evening performance. 'I shall never forget that,' he wrote to John. In 1911, Kreisler had played in the orchestra under V.W. at the Three Choirs. 'Now I can boast that Barbirolli has played for me too,' Vaughan Williams told his friends.

The first performance of *Sinfonia Antartica* on 14 January 1953 was a major event in Hallé history. V.W. declared it to be the finest first performance he had had in over fifty years, and that night a famous sobriquet was born when he wrote on Barbirolli's copy of the programme: 'For glorious John, the glorious conductor of a glorious orchestra.' There was much public interest in, and much critical head-shaking over, the wind-machine, but the best joke about it was known only to those who attended rehearsals. It was thought that, on the Free Trade Hall's steeply-raked platform, the sight of the player, coat tails a-flying, turning the handle of this contraption might prove irresistibly comic to the audience so he was enclosed in a little canvas 'shelter.' On which, of course, a wag in the orchestra immediately hung a sign – GENTS. John took great care with the balancing of the off-stage women's voices which wail bleakly on the Antarctic wind. When rehearsing the work in Melbourne in 1955, he told Norah Winstanley, he 'had a job getting them to *moan*, so in desperation I said to them "I want you to sound like 22 women having babies *without* chloroform." It did the trick.'

Just over a year later, in September 1954, R.V.W. told John that he again had 'symphonic rumblings – it may be something or it may be nothing at all.' It proved to be Symphony No. 8 in D minor. In April 1955 John was shown the score of the work that was to be dedicated to him. 'I have had a good look,' he wrote, 'and can quite honestly say that I am greatly intrigued by it; although absolutely authentic V.W. it has touches of most charming originality both in harmony and orchestral texture as well as some very lovely music.' In February 1956 the symphony was given a private play-through in the Free Trade Hall. R.V.W. wrote on the 10th: 'Dear Glorious John. I expect it was really your magic, but if you approve I propose not to scrap the symphony.' The first movement is a set of variations. After each variation Barbirolli made a slight pause. This was so effective that at one of the early rehearsals someone suggested to V.W. that he should indicate these pauses in the score. He replied: 'No. Everyone else will make them too long. John does them just right – and how can I indicate what he does?' The symphony had its first performance in Manchester on 2 May 1956, and the composer wrote on the manuscript score 'For Glorious John, with love and admiration from Ralph.' Colin Mason, writing for the *New York Herald Tribune*, commented: 'During these last 13 years Barbirolli has given himself completely, heart and soul and every physical nerve and fibre, too, to the Hallé, which owes him not only the prestige of these two Vaughan Williams first performances, but also the entire restoration of its pre-war reputation and every inch of its high national and international standing.'

Barbirolli conducted the Eighth Symphony wherever he went. It was a symbol to him of a precious friendship, of happy days at the Cheltenham Festival and especially of the 1958 festival, when on one warm July evening the Hallé gave a luxuriant performance of the *London Symphony* and the audience stood as the great composer, white-haired and stooping, took his bow amid the players. That evening R.V.W. and his wife Ursula – whom he had decided to marry after they had attended one of John's 1953 performances of *Tristan!* – dined at Cleeve Hill with John and Evelyn and my wife and me. The sunset over the Malvern Hills was Wagnerian in its rich intensity of colour; and John never forgot the sight of the wonderful old man gazing over the English landscape in that particular setting, nor, a few weeks later, the sight of him lying dead in his home in Hanover Terrace – 'like the effigy of a mediaeval prelate.' He wrote to me in 1962: 'You and I have lived with history and history which will remain immortal. V.W. 5 and 6 next year and Elgar violin. How rich our lives are that we love and understand these things.'

It was ironical – and it amused Vaughan Williams – that a composer whose music brought the best from Barbirolli's art and personality was Mahler, of whose work the Englishman had such a poor opinion. Yet only those of pigeon-hole mentality hold the view that it is impossible to admire with equal fervour the music of such contrasted composers as Vaughan Williams and Mahler. For Barbirolli the problem did not arise: both were great composers, both fascinated him. Yet there is perhaps a clue to his special gifts as a conductor in the success he achieved with Elgar, Vaughan Williams, Mahler, Bruckner, Nielsen, Delius and Sibelius. Each makes a strong *personal* appeal – people in general either like them or loathe them. Barbirolli's music-making was also extremely personal and idiosyncratic; and his ability to identify himself with these composers was almost certainly a result of this individuality of temperament.

With Mahler, too, one finds further proof of Barbirolli's intellectual qualities as a conductor – though he was never a conductor for intellectuals. Notwithstanding the emotional fervour of his performances they were not inspired improvisations, but superb, coolly planned combinations of heart and brain. In one of his notebooks Barbirolli wrote a quotation from Bertrand Russell which is particularly apposite to his approach to Mahler: 'Nothing great is achieved without passion, but underneath the passion there should always be that large impersonal survey which sets limits to actions that our passions inspire.' Barbirolli conducted all the Mahler symphonies except the reconstructed Tenth and the Eighth (though he prepared the score of the latter). Before each of his first performances he worked for months on the score, bowing the string parts, meticulously writing into his own copy accurate translations of Mahler's detailed instructions. He thought, talked and dreamed of nothing but the symphony he was learning: it is ironical that the effort of composing the symphonies shortened Mahler's life; interpreting them certainly put an enormous strain on Barbirolli in his last decade, for they are gigantic works, the shortest lasting an hour and most of them nearer to ninety minutes, and require a huge orchestra. Both men were possessed by a daemon. Undoubtedly Barbirolli found in this music not only a marvellous and satisfying challenge to his musical temperament, but he recognised in it the complex humanity of the composer which paralleled his own intricately wrought and volatile nature. There was something almost Hoffmannesque about Barbirolli in his last years. The frail frame, greying hair, deep-set eyes, dark yet bright, his pallor, the expressiveness of his face, and the increasing prominence of his nose: he seemed to grow to resemble the music in which he excelled, romantic and on a grand scale with profound emotional depths.

'The art of conducting,' Mahler said, 'is that of being able to play the notes that are not there' – in other words, to reach the inner significance of an outpouring of the human spirit for which crotchets and quavers are but the outward and visible symbols. Art of this kind is especially needed in Mahler's music. Barbirolli was fifty-four before he conducted a complete Mahler symphony. He had conducted the *Adagietto* from No. 5 in Glasgow and New York; and he had conducted *Kindertotenlieder* and *Das Lied von der Erde* (his first performance of the latter, with Catherine Lawson and Parry Jones, was in Manchester in the 1945–46 season). His exploration of the symphonies, therefore, was confined within sixteen years. In them he found the satisfaction which every artist needs – to do something new to prevent stagnation. He could not find this in contemporary music, try as he might, because he did not find it 'great.' As he said in an interview in *Die Welt*,

Mahler had so much to say...and much of what he wrote strikes one in its language as new music... Today no really great music is written, but good music, very interesting music that one should hear and know... If you want to conduct Mahler well his music must be under your skin and in your bones. Because I subsequently spent two years studying one of the scores, I have, as it were, enriched myself in doing so, and it is a joy to me in my advancing years that I have found something which, apart from the connoisseurs, is new to people and is also of such mighty dimensions... Of course it does not take me two years to read these scores, but if you prepare for a journey through such immeasurably wide musical spheres, you must know exactly where the musical ideas begin and where they end, and how each fits into the pattern of the whole. In Mahler's symphonies there are many highlights, but only one real climax, which one must discover. To do so needs less a simple study of the score than an all-embracing aesthetic reflection.

Barbirolli was led to the Mahler symphonies by Neville Cardus, who had long championed the composer's cause. Recalling in the *Manchester Guardian* on 4 October 1952 Harty's Hallé performance of the Ninth Symphony in February 1930, Cardus said: 'It is the ideal work for Sir John Barbirolli to conduct. Why has he not been drawn to it these several years?' The answer came on 19 February 1954, when, after nearly fifty hours of rehearsals, Barbirolli conducted No. 9 in Bradford and later in Sheffield, Manchester, London, Edinburgh and many other cities and towns which had never heard it. The standard critical response to Mahler in England then was typified by Richard Capell who, when I told him of the amount of preparation the symphony had had, expostulated: 'What an example of misapplied effort.' But a younger generation – William Mann, Donald Mitchell, Deryck Cooke – was following Cardus in appreciation of Mahler's virtues. Other conductors besides Barbirolli had discovered him, too, of course, and one of them, Walter Süsskind, wrote a generous letter after one of the earliest Barbirolli performances: 'I have known this symphony intimately for 25 years and have conducted it twice in Scotland and 11 times in Israel recently. I've also heard many performances of it under Walter, Talich and Mengelberg. But all these recede into a grey background after your almost unbearably moving interpretation.' After a performance of the same symphony in New York in December 1962 another eminent conductor, William Steinberg, later the conductor of the Boston Symphony Orchestra, wrote to Barbirolli:

Not on any other occasion have I heard a work of Mahler's so completely – it was indeed one of those gripping occasions when one is hardly aware of the performance as such... I don't wish to burden you with a catalogue of the many details that impressed and excited me – for example, right near the beginning, the careful and fastidious distribution of weights and accents across the 1st & 2nd violin parts with the telling extra gentle emphases from the clarinet. What I am so grateful for is the grasp of the whole work, or even more than that, the faith in this music. It was the identification with Mahler that gave us the reading that was so completely Mahlerian... It was wonderful to be able to experience things that hitherto I had had to take for granted from the score only – that the angelic descent of the flute at the end of the first movement can be truly "schwebend" [hovering]; above all, the motionlessness of the barely inflected lines on the last page of all – the idea of "Abschied" [Farewell] was not just a phrase from programme notes but an agonising experience of an immediacy to leave one shaken. Altogether, your performance was something against which to measure the rest of one's experience...

A remarkable letter, from a colleague whom Barbirolli hardly knew.

Next, in 1955, he tackled the First Symphony. He conducted it in Manchester a few days after Beecham's triumphant concert in the Free Trade Hall with the RPO – and he was determined that no unfavourable comparisons should be made. As Colin Mason recorded: 'The orchestra played like an immense chamber orchestra, all soloists yet completely at one under the conductor, they giving every detail of the score its proper colour while he made the colours into a composition. The work does not always sound like that and...this magnificently coherent performance will do Mahler's reputation good.' Following Mahler's instructions to the letter, Barbirolli insisted on the horn players standing up at the triumphal climax of the finale (cue 56) where they have to be 'louder than anything else, even the trumpets.' When the Hallé played the symphony at the Festival Hall on 22 November 1955, a critic of *The Times*, ready as ever to criticise Barbirolli's 'theatricality,' asked if it was 'really necessary' for Sir John to ask his horn players to stand up 'like jazz musicians'. Barbirolli made it a rule – which he observed – never to answer critics except on a point of fact. This was too good a fact to miss, and he wrote to *The Times* on 29 November drawing the critic's attention to Mahler's directions. The printing of the letter brought him a gleeful note from Paddy Hadley (then Professor of Music at Cambridge) which included a splendidly bawdy but unprintable limerick on the critic's name. 'I sit opposite Howes at lunch at the RCM each Tuesday,' he added, 'there was a spot of merriment that day.' (Frank Howes was not the critic concerned, but was chief critic. *The Times* notices were still unsigned then.)

Steadily over the next few years Barbirolli added other Mahler symphonies to his repertoire: the Second ('Resurrection'), the Seventh, Fourth, Sixth, the surviving movement of the Tenth, the Fifth and Third. The Fifth he first conducted in England at concerts in Manchester and London to mark Cardus's fifty years in journalism – a unique tribute from conductor and orchestra to a critic. Between 1960 and 1970 he conducted Mahler all over the world, notably, as will be seen, in Berlin and even in Italy. Public and critics alike acclaimed his interpretations. Four of these (Nos 1, 5, 6 and 9) are fortunately recorded, while two radio recordings exist of his superb interpretation of No. 3, the final Adagio of which was perhaps the most moving of his Mahlerian voyages. Criticism tends to stress the emotion in Barbirolli's performances, perhaps because his slower tempi focus extra attention on the beauty of the slow movements, but so eminent a Mahlerian as Deryck Cooke laid special emphasis on his ability, in the diffuse No. 7, to make the structure of the work cohere. Nor must one regard Mahler's symphonies merely as exercises in nostalgia; one of their characteristics is the love of life which they convey and this is especially strongly reflected in Barbirolli's recording of No. 5, a very great performance indeed, full of wonderful examples of his insight into the music, insight made explicit by scrupulous care for the texture, the subtlest nuances of phrasing, by spaciousness and by the acute sense of contrast – magic and mystery one moment, joy another, nightmare the next. He seems to read Mahler's mind and to persuade the orchestra to create the variety of mood as if it were instinctive. The fact is he often had difficulty in coaxing out of British string-players – even, as in this case, those of the New Philharmonia – enough of the unfashionable portamento he and Mahler required. 'It's not immoral,' he would tell them; 'anyway I'll pay the fine for indecency.'

Characteristically, Barbirolli selected the 'Resurrection' symphony as the climax of the Hallé's centenary season. 'After all, I resurrected the orchestra,' he said. In 1959 he conducted it in La Scala, Milan, with Emilia Cundari and Stefania Malagu as soloists. It was inevitable that his devotion to Mahler should have overshadowed his work for Bruckner, yet with this composer, too, he had an affinity, stressing always the Schubertian rather than the Wagnerian aspects. The Seventh Symphony was perhaps his favourite – how beautifully he phrased those ascending opening phrases on the cellos – but he also conducted the Third, Fourth, Eighth and Ninth, giving four memorable performances of the Eighth shortly before he died. Again, it was his ability to teach the orchestra the composer's idiom that marked him out as a great conductor. As Cardus wrote after a Hallé performance of the Fourth Symphony: 'It would be comforting to think that any German or Austrian conductor could do as much justice to, say, Elgar, as Sir John did to Bruckner.' Barbirolli was a democrat, but he took a proper and admirable pride in his honours and decorations. That he received the Medals of both the Mahler and the Bruckner Societies gave him particular pleasure. The Bruckner Medal was handed to him in the Brangwyn Hall, Swansea, on 7 October 1959, by Harry Neyer, the American vice-president of the society who said that during Barbirolli's 1959 tour of the United States 'the American critics finally realised what the public always has known, that Sir John was and is a great conductor.' The Mahler Medal was presented in 1965.

Three composers' names head this chapter because they were significant to Barbirolli musically and personally. But there were others – apart from Brahms, Schubert and Verdi – with whose music he achieved considerably more than routine success: Nielsen, for example, and Sibelius; and in the Fifth and Sixth symphonies of Rubbra he brought all his care for texture to bear where it was most needed. In Berlioz's *Symphonie Fantastique* poetry and wizardry were combined. He was a sympathetic interpreter of John Ireland and Bax, and a friend of both men. For Delius he had instinctive sympathy and in his later years, with the shadow of Beecham removed, he found something new to say about it. The care he lavished on small works was as great as on a symphony: his recording of Sibelius's *Valse Triste* and Delius's *Irmelin* prelude prove that. His very last recording, of Delius's *Brigg Fair*, captures the essentially tragic nature of the piece, and his *Appalachia* was sheer magic. Again, perhaps it was the foreigner in Barbirolli which ensured his insight into this most un-English of English composers. Nor will thousands easily forget the *joie de vivre* of his famous Viennese programmes, waltzes, polkas, marches, all played with zest and brilliance. Manchester audiences had the pleasure for a few years of dancing to his conducting of the Hallé on New Year's Day at the Hallé Ball, waltzing to Lehár's *Gold and Silver* while J.B., covered in paper streamers and bombarded by balloons, presided like everyone's favourite uncle.

One work, however, outside the nineteenth-century–early twentieth-century repertoire in which he excelled, should end this chapter: Bach's *St Matthew Passion*. The Hallé Choir presented him with the 1854 Leipzig Gesellschaft edition on the occasion of his fiftieth birthday and knighthood in 1949. This, no doubt, planted a seed, but first he wanted to conduct *Messiah*. This was a remarkable interpretation, but not as successful as his *St Matthew* because although he threw a revealing light on beauties which had become slovenly routine, he also overdramatised parts of it, and his odd liking for a shouted final 'Hallelujah' in the chorus, though thrilling the first time, soon palled into a mannerism (or so I thought). One performance, at Easter 1956, was described by Colin Mason as 'electrifying,' and of a kind 'to rouse the audience for once to appreciative *critical* admiration of the performance on a purely musical level, and this moreover without encroaching on their enjoyment of it as a religious work.' The soprano on that occasion, Margaret Ritchie, wrote to Barbirolli: 'Your conducting is everything a sensitive singer dreams of and longs for and enjoys, it seems, once or twice in a lifetime only.'

He had completed his study of the Bach masterpiece by the end of 1956 but it was to be over four years before he conducted it, mainly because of the expense involved. It was, in fact, the constant putting-off of this project because of lack of money that caused him to flare out in 1960 and threaten to resign unless there was a full inquiry into Arts Council and municipal support of British orchestras. He won his point.

What a study he embarked upon! He read everything about the Passion on which he could lay his hands; he annotated several vocal scores, one with Schweitzer's notes, another with the cuts and alterations made by Vaughan Williams; and his big presentation score is a collector's piece of a conductor's art – every dynamic pencilled in, the bowing marked, and throughout pencilled description of the action ('the procession sweeping on amid increasing lamentation,' in the opening chorus, for instance) and, above the arias, pithy extracts from various commentators on the score. He decided to perform the work (in German*) in its entirety down to the last *da capo*, with harpsichord continuo and obbligati for viola da gamba and oboe d'amore. His first performance was in Manchester on 26 March 1961, and in his foreword to the programme he wrote: 'The more dramatically it can be sung the better – providing that the dramatic conception is a profound one... It is offered in fervent humility and devotion.' Anyone who expected an *operatic* performance was soon disabused. Indeed, the outstanding feature of the four performances which Barbirolli conducted in Manchester between 1961 and 1968 was the restraint, even sometimes the austerity, contained within the framework of the drama. It was the Bach Passion According to Sir John, an act of musical and spiritual devotion and scholarship which in some ways marked the beginning of the great climax of his artistic development and maturity.

* Although in his youth a protagonist of opera in English, in later years Barbirolli preferred to conduct works in their original language. His concert performances of operas in Manchester were sung in Italian.

Even in the period from 1943 to 1958, when Barbirolli spent most of his time with the Hallé, he went abroad each year as a guest conductor and also took the Hallé on several tours. His Ensa visit to Italy in 1944 was followed by a visit to Hamburg in September 1945 to conduct the Sadler's Wells company in *Madam Butterfly*. 'Orchestra (the Hamburg Phil – Karl Muck's old orchestra) is excellent,' he wrote to Evelyn, 'and I have already got them to the *point of the bow* and "gliding". They seem very happy playing for me...they know *Butterfly* well so I can really spend time on detail. Singers not bad, but by God what a state this crowd have got into.' In August 1946 he conducted at the first post-war Salzburg Festival and made his first Vienna appearance in November of the same year. His second visit the following April was for two *Aïda* performances and two of Verdi's *Requiem* (both with Ljuba Welitsch as soprano), in the Theater an der Wien. One critic wrote of 'a splendour not known since Toscanini's legendary days.'

On his first day rehearsing the *Requiem* he was horrified by the poor playing of the cellos in the Offertorium. The Vienna Philharmonic, like many foreign orchestras, has a pool of players, and since Barbirolli was a name new to them he had been given what could be called 'the second eleven.' He invited the Intendant to hear them, and then gave an ultimatum: 'Better players or no concert.' But before he did so, he took one of the cellos and played the passage himself, to general astonishment. The 'first eleven' were then produced.

This story is a reminder that as far as Europe was concerned in 1947, Barbirolli had his name to make. England was still not regarded as a natural breeding-ground for musicians, and the war had overlaid whatever was known or remembered about Barbirolli's elevation to New York in 1936. In Italy his name endeared him to audiences from the start, and on a visit to Rome in January 1947, he not only had successful concerts but saw his eighty-year-old Uncle Libero, one of the few non-musical Barbirollis, a former 'inspector of railroads,' no less. In the last twelve years of his career when, as will be seen, he spent much of his time abroad, the affection and admiration for him on the part of foreign players was very real. At breaks in rehearsal they gathered round him to talk, for he was never aloof, and they worked willingly for him. In 1965 one of his visits to Berlin coincided with the Cleveland Orchestra's visit. A group of its players tracked him down to his hotel where they begged him to 'come and conduct us in Cleveland one day.'

The Hallé's first post-war overseas tour was to Austria in the summer of 1948, a hastily reorganised trip in place of a projected visit to the Prague Festival which was cancelled because of the Communist take-over of Czechoslovakia. Innsbruck, Graz, Salzburg and Vienna were visited, with Evelyn giving the first performance of the newly discovered Mozart Oboe Concerto in the Mozarteum at Salzburg. John wrote to Philip Godlee on his return: 'When I started to thank the British Minister in Vienna for his party to the orchestra he interrupted me with: "No, I have to thank you, for you have achieved in five days what I couldn't do in five years." The public, press etc. were all obviously taken aback at the quality of the playing, and knowing the Viennese public as I do it was a triumph won note by note.' For their part the orchestra discovered what a superb 'guide, philosopher and friend' their conductor was on a foreign tour. He was tireless, always knowing of some place of interest the players would like to see, always whiling away the boring parts of travelling with his supply of anecdotes. He was genuinely thrilled to see them playing in the beautiful architectural surroundings of some overseas halls and theatres. It is necessary, in order to present a rounded portrait of Barbirolli, to show his inner misgivings and depressions, but he hid these from all but his intimates. The impressions that remain of him with most are of his wit and humour, his delight in simple incidents, his powers of observation of some amusing situation and his inimitable artistry as a raconteur, with a robust relish of the bawdy and an appreciation of elegant repartee.

He took the Hallé abroad twice in 1949, to Holland in the spring, where Ginette Neveu played Beethoven with them, and to Knokke-le-Zoute, Belgium, in August. In November 1950 they went for thirteen days to Portugal, a visit which ended with Barbirolli playing the cello in a Haydn string quartet performed during a Mass in memory of the cellist Suggia. He himself visited Cannes and Rome that year and toured Australia in January 1951, where he was much impressed by the young violinist Carmel Hakendorf, who later played concertos with him and the Hallé in England. In 1952 he went in August to Lucerne, where Clara Haskil played Mozart with him. This followed the first Hallé season in the Free Trade Hall and he wrote to Norah Winstanley: 'The last week in M/c will ever remain one of the most memorable of my life. To say I was deeply moved by it all is to say nothing. It went far deeper than that. The playing of my orch: was indeed a reward for the years I have given them, the spontaneous tributes of affection from my audiences showed me too *how right I was* not to desert you for the BBC.' In June and July of 1953 the Hallé went to Bulawayo, Rhodesia, for the Rhodes Centenary Festival. They encountered startling variations of temperature, including freak frost at night. John described conducting in the Theatre Royal (an unheated, uncomfortable aircraft hangar) as 'like standing on the top of Everest in evening dress.' After the Hallé had returned home, he went back to Rhodesia to conduct the Covent Garden Company in *Aïda*.

His guest conducting in 1954 was in Scandinavia and Italy; Scandinavia (twice) and Australia in 1955; and Paris (with the Hallé) in October to play Brahms's First Symphony. Barbirolli's interpretation impressed René Leibowitz enough for him to write of the symphony's being 'stripped of the encrustations of tradition.' In 1956 he conducted in Switzerland, Scandinavia and Italy, returning to Denmark and Sweden in February and March of 1957.

Bergen, 19 March 1957

[To M.K.]

...Just *between ourselves* my stone trouble has been
rather a nuisance as the constant discomfort and attendant
backache at times gets somewhat wearisome. However,
good old Music comes to the rescue... Most rewarding, one
of the orchestras even sent me flowers thanking me for the
rehearsals. Good God, what are we coming to! I shd think
an almost unique event. Some of the old Hallé sweats wld
have a fit! One rather amusing incident, and I must stop
and go to reh: The King of Denmark (conducting one) cd
not come to the concert, it being his birthday that day, and
he was conducting a military band performance of Beet. V
as a treat so he came to a rehearsal instead. We were reh:
the Haydn oboe with Evelyn (who by the way has quite
stunned them with her playing) when he arrived, and
during a short break afterwards he said to me 'What's it
like conducting for your wife? Can you keep her well
under your thumb?' This last sentence with appropriate
gestures. It has caused intense amusement to any Danes I
have related the incident to, as apparently he (by nature
very open and friendly) is kept in very good order at home
by HER majesty!!

Bergen, 19 March 1957

[To Audrey Napier Smith]

My very dear Wren Audrey – ...What a charming people
the Norwegians are. After the last concert we were entertained in a lovely old wooden house in the mountains, all
log fires, candles, champagne, brandy and good company.
'Very melting and affable indeed' (almost a Shavian quotation). Their taste in modern art I find a little more debat-
able, a sense of query our ambassador here shares. In the
concert hall, which is the Great Hall of the University, there
are most disturbing (in an *unpleasant* sense) frescoes dedicated to the worship of the Sun, verging on the indecent. It
perhaps explains my reticence to bask in its rays!!* The
other morning whilst doing some shopping had a look at the

---

* Barbirolli disliked sunshine and while everyone else lay in it he
would shut himself in a room with the curtains drawn and study a
score.

21

21 *With Vaughan Williams at a rehearsal of* Sinfonia Antartica, *January 1953. On the right is Eslyn Kennedy*

22 *Rehearsing in Bergen, 1963, for the King's Lynn Festival. Martin Milner, J.B., Sydney Errington and Evelyn Barbirolli*

23 *With Pierre Monteux and Charles Münch, Boston, 1959*

24 *After-dinner raconteur. Press dinner in Manchester, October 1963*

25

26

25 *Sixtieth birthday toast with Evelyn in the Free Trade Hall, Manchester, 2 December 1959. (In the background is a bronze head of Kathleen Ferrier)*

26 *Working in the plane on tour with the Houston Symphony Orchestra, 1964*

27 *Rehearsing in Bucharest,*
September 1958

28 *Interviewed at 5.30 a.m. on arrival at Kingston, Jamaica, 1963*

29 *Cellists' duologue. With Mstislav Rostropovich, at a party in Berlin, 1969. In the centre background is David Oistrakh*

28
29

30 *With Sir Neville Cardus, Manchester, 1966*
31 *At EMI, 1967, with Jacqueline du Pré
and recording producer Suvi Raj Grubb*

30

31

*32 Returning from Houston to conduct
a seventieth birthday concert
in Manchester, December 1969*

33 *Contemplating a problem with Martin Milner in York Minster, July 1969*
34 *J.B. rehearsing the New Philharmonia at the Bishopsgate Institute, London, 28 July 1970, a few hours before he died*

33

34

New Town Hall (in Oslo this is). Very modern but not without a sense of design – rather like one of the least objectionable Cheltenham works!!! However even there this vague sense of the indecent seems to persist. In the courtyard there are a series of pictures or scenes in coloured 'Bas Reliefs' representing various aspects of nature, one being of a young woman watering flowers etc. All very laudable and correct, but she manages to convey the impression that she is doing it from her own water generating system (I had almost written urogenitalating). Pas très commode!!... Not long before Wolverhampton now, and I hope I will find you all in grand form... Ever your devoted Sir John, Admiral.

In June 1957 the Hallé played at the fifth Ravello Festival. 'I shall die of shame,' John wrote to Norah Winstanley, 'if after Ken and I succeed in bringing the orch: to this paradise on earth, anyone starts moaning about tea and fish and chips!!' The concerts were given in the open on a platform built over a seaward precipice. Near by was the garden where Wagner composed some of *Parsifal* and which is known, therefore, as Klingsor's Garden. Because of the heat rehearsals were held at 5 a.m. After the final programme (a Wagner concert, with Sylvia Fisher) the townspeople were so enthusiastic that John conducted, with enormous zest, an impromptu concert of Strauss waltzes in the main square at 10 p.m., culminating at midnight with drinks all round and flowers for the maestro. He was back in Italy in November for the *Gerontius* performances mentioned in the previous chapter.

24 November 1957
[To A.N.S.]

...You would have been amused to hear me translate the Devils' Chorus for them into very lewd and obscene Neapolitan dialect. The result was electrifying!!... One of the older members of the orchestra said 'You are the only Italian maestro left with the true Italian spirit'... Am so happy about the *Dream*.

The period from the autumn of 1957 to the summer of 1958 was one of the peaks of Barbirolli's life. He had for years

I

looked forward to the Hallé centenary – anniversaries meant
a great deal to him – and something of what it signified can be
gauged from this letter to me, written in January 1958:

> I did not have an opportunity to tell you properly last
> night what your beautiful letter about the Centenary has
> meant to me, or what it will continue to mean during all
> the years I may be spared to remain on this earth. You, my
> dearly beloved friend, are one of the very few, I think, who
> really knows what my music-making costs me, and your
> understanding and generous appreciation (poor word) of it
> all, are a great source of inspiration and a means of *gather-
> ing strength* to continue.

The season, triumph that it was, was clouded for him by the
discovery that Crickmore had cancer, which necessitated am-
putation of a leg. This meant that Crickmore could not accompany the orchestra on its centenary tour of Europe in May and
June during which the Hallé for the first time played behind
the Iron Curtain, in Poland and Czechoslovakia. The tour had
opened in Germany, in Hallé's birthplace, Hagen; and at
Linz, in Austria, birthplace of Bruckner, John conducted the
Fourth Symphony. In August he spent his usual time in Sussex
with the family – the 'orrible 'oliday, as he described it to
Audrey, complicated by an arm injury to his brother Peter.

Brighton, 14 August '58

[To A.N.S.]

…You can imagine that added to the fearful fits of depression that seem to settle on me at this time of dreaded holidays, things have been rather difficult for me. I have sought
the usual refuge in work and since there was a great deal to
be done, in view of recordings, 8 or 9 hours a day have
mercifully been accounted for. You know I am not proud of
this, I only wish I was made differently. It seems I am getting
worse as the years go on; I only manage to sleep fitfully and
always wake with this pall of gloom over me. It seems such
a shame that after that wonderful centenary season for
which *I am so grateful*, so very deeply grateful, I cannot
seem to find any rest. I try so hard to reason with myself and
fight it all I can (and of course put up a show for the family)
but it is all so very exhausting. Perhaps I shall be better

when we start... Glad to hear you have been practising. Plenty of *slow* scales I hope (nothing better for intonation) with every note dead on, and nice slow tunes with a nice juicy vibrato.

At the climax of the centenary season, just before he received the Freedom of Manchester, Barbirolli announced that he was resigning as permanent conductor of the Hallé and becoming conductor-in-chief, reducing his schedule with them to about seventy concerts a year. In the previous fifteen years, apart from the 1947 visits to Vienna and a visit to the Berlin Philharmonic in 1950, he had not conducted any of the major European orchestras, despite numerous invitations. There would come a time, he well knew, when he could not continue to say 'No' because he would no longer be asked. Judson had for years been pressing him to return to the United States, and he had said that he would go only if he could take the Hallé. But this dream was as far as ever from realisation. He was nearing sixty and he perhaps felt that he had not even yet completely fulfilled himself. Evelyn would have liked him to have reduced his Hallé commitments a few years earlier, but he would not. Throughout the 1950s he had admired Crickmore's campaign to put the Society on its financial feet – the engagement of George Weldon as associate conductor in 1952 to take charge of industrial concerts and others, the 1955 contract with Associated Television (ill-fated, but full of promise at first, notwithstanding the shocked attitude of some Hallé sceptics), the growing number of foreign tours. Nor could he bear to leave his audience, his supporters in the Hallé Club, his friends in all the Hallé towns. Nowhere else would he be able to achieve a properly prepared *St Matthew Passion*. Yet he was conscious of what he had sacrificed for the Hallé – he was not well represented on recordings, and his new contract with Pye, for which he had severed an association with HMV of over thirty years, was not proving to be as satisfactory as he had hoped. So he decided to keep Manchester as his base, but to give himself the chance of conducting orchestras as illustrious by international standards as the New York one he had left fifteen years before. He really enjoyed the experience of teaching new orchestras to play in the way he wanted: that was his element.

He also enjoyed visiting towns and cities. He had always

been an 'explorer'; when he and Evelyn arrived at their hotel, while she unpacked John would wander off to find a delicatessen or a good place for 'vino' and to size up the architecture. So in 1959 he began the busiest decade of his career, for he travelled incessantly and still conducted more concerts for the Hallé than other conductors-in-chief conducted with their respective orchestras. These were the years, too, of increasing ill-health: stone trouble for which, when the pain was particularly severe, he took Pethidine tablets (he was extraordinarily resistant to drugs and also quite amazingly stoical about pain), neuritis in his arm, deteriorating eyesight and eventually heart trouble. In addition he had for years had a left inguinal hernia which he refused to have treated because it would have meant two months away from the rostrum. On the rostrum, in fact, he gave the impression of unbounded vitality and youthfulness. The most important features of the years from 1958 to 1970 were his return to the American scene and his association with Berlin. These will have chapters to themselves. Meanwhile here are Barbirolli's accounts of some of his other travels, told in letters to Audrey Napier Smith.

Madrid, 22 November 1959

We were taken to Toledo yesterday (first free day for ages, it seemed), a most lovely old town and free from tourists at this time of year. Saw some wonderful Grecos and churches and visited his house. Most wonderful of all, though, through private influence we were able to visit the apartments of the Duchess of Lerma who possesses his last great unfinished picture and his *palette*, with the various mixtures as he prepared them... Orchestra most interesting here...a most enchanting and beautiful violin sound once I had got them out of the anaesthetic (which didn't take long)...

In May 1960 John conducted the Czech Philharmonic Orchestra in Prague in Mahler's First Symphony. This was a performance he never forgot. The correspondent of the *Musical Times* reported: 'Sir John had a reception that had to be seen to be believed, and this from a people who – in Central Europe at any rate – are regarded as somewhat staid and phlegmatic.' From there he went to Israel.

Tel Aviv, June 1960

...Orchestra [Israel Philharmonic] has a great potential in many ways and in need of much orchestral discipline (tech nical, not in personal behaviour) which *they are getting*... Beautiful violin sound, as I also found in Budapest. The 3 orchestras have been all excellent in their various ways. Best wind in Prague, best strings all in all here, as is also the brass, but Budapest fascinating for me in their intense musicality; one of the most *musical* orchestras I think I have ever conducted anywhere.

British Embassy, Rome
14 November 1960

Am lying on my bed in our sumptuous apartment here with a frightful backache (result of Mahler 9 yesterday in Florence, I hope...) This is really an astonishing country for things and buildings of quite ravishing beauty. Yesterday, for instance, whilst waiting to go on and do Mozart 34...I looked out of a little window in what was my dressing room and my gaze fell on the exquisite Perseus statue of our old friend Benvenuto Cellini... The Florence Orch: gave me a fine show of Mahler 9. They had never played it and really loved it, rather to my surprise, as did the public ... One lovely thing is that I seem to have much to teach all these orchs and they are *grateful* for it... Tonight we leave on the night train for Turin, after the concert, and I start on Mahler 9 again.

During 1961 the Hallé made two tours abroad with Barbirolli, to Switzerland in April (Locarno, Eva Turner in the audience) and in August to Greece, Turkey, Cyprus, Jugoslavia and Italy. All the concerts were played in the open. At the Dubrovnik Festival John brought off a neat diplomatic coup. For an encore, in what until 1918 had been part of the Austro-Hungarian Empire, he played *Tales from the Vienna Woods*. After the first bar the whole audience rose and applauded. As he walked back to his hotel the town band followed him, playing lively music, and the crowds cheered him. A British visitor, Philip Glass of Glasgow, congratulated him on the encore. John winked and said: 'Was I right?'

In the early summer of 1962 the new Coventry Cathedral was consecrated and John conducted the Berlin Philharmonic Orchestra there on 6 June in Vaughan Williams's *Tallis Fantasia*, Haydn's 98th symphony and Brahms's Second Symphony. He then flew to Jerusalem, whence the next letter to Audrey Napier Smith:

King David Hotel, 17 June 1962

Exactly a week ago I started my work here (in Israel) with 3 rehearsals...and have had a real Hallé schedule... The drive here from Tel Aviv is not very pleasant, hot, arid and dusty, but there was one most charming and compensating sight, a mare with her foal. A most adorable and enchanting sight... Since there is no real news from here I might tell you something about my concert with the Berlin Phil. in Coventry Cathedral. First about the church itself. It is undoubtedly impressive in many ways; and whether one is completely won over to it or not, it is impossible not to pay due tribute to Basil Spence for at least an attempt to create something imaginative, of our time, and not unworthy of the name of architecture. On the credit side: the fine proportions of the Nave; the Roof, which might be described as an austere modern version of medieval Fan vaulting (do you happen to know that noble example of this in Cirencester?). Very impressive in its deeply rich colouring is the great Piper window, and in fact all the glass. For me (and for E. too) here the virtues cease.

The great (only in size) Sutherland tapestry we both found quite hideous. Crude in colour, and the figure, as I told some of the church dignitaries (much to their amusement), resembles a bearded Edwardian maidservant with a badly ironed apron on. The canopies over the choir stalls meant to be a motif of thorns, just look like a cloakroom awaiting its coats and hats. The last and most ludicrous thing of all is the so-called spire, which looks like nothing more than an elongated wireless aerial on the top of which some large bird has rather untidily nested.

As for the concert itself it was a most moving occasion the orchestra gave me a wonderful welcome and played most beautifully for me with such generosity and devotion ... There are, Audrey, a few compensatory moments in the years of struggle and groping for understanding of the never-ending mysteries of the great works in our art, and this was one of them. Another that comes to mind is the devotion with which my own Hallé helped me with the *Passion*.

Venice, 27 June 1962

...The Israeli silver jubilee festival came to a triumphant end last Saturday with a charming orchestra party afterwards at which the chairman of the orchestra officially told me that whenever I wanted it, or would honour them by accepting it, the conductorship of the orchestra was mine. I suppose in naval terms this would make me a kind of C-in-C Mediterranean. But at my age I have no such ambitions. I remain content with my C-in-C Manchester Ship Canal!

We arrived here Sunday about midnight and had almost a free day Monday which I *actually enjoyed*. Went to a place called Chioggia, a fishing port down the Adriatic, about 2 hrs. on a slow boat, which my Dad had often told me about, and which I had always wanted to see... A completely unspoilt large fishing village you might call it, with humble little fish restaurants dotted about, all first-rate I shd imagine if the one we chose was any criterion.

At this date, not only was Barbirolli C-in-C Manchester Ship Canal, he had taken on a new commitment as conductor of the Houston Symphony Orchestra of Texas.

Return to America

After he had sailed from New York in 1943 Barbirolli was not forgotten by his American friends. In December 1952 Bruno Zirato, the Philharmonic's assistant manager, sent him a telegram asking him, at the unanimous request of the board of directors, to take over the orchestra for three weeks because Mitropoulos was ill. 'We all hope you will be available and willing to come back to your old orchestra in this emergency.' He could not go, but the invitation pleased him. His ambition was to take the Hallé. In the early 1950s negotiations went near to completion but foundered on the question of fares. During 1954 Crickmore went to New York to meet Judson. Nora Shea, Judson's secretary, wrote to John on 6 October of that year bringing an old skeleton from the cupboard.

> Dearest Tita... You know how happy I would have been to have you come here for any one of the really numerous offers you have had, but I had some misgivings about Downes. He is so fuzzy-minded and has come to feel so oracular that I think he perhaps consults his old files when an artist returns so that he may stick to his viewpoint... His confusion in reviewing Prokofiev's latest symphony was pitiable (there is small doubt that the poor old thing signed up with 'the party')...

'I was very amused with our old friend Olin Downes's various problems,' John replied. He did not really like the critics. In his copy of Richard Strauss's *Recollections and*

Reflections, he wrote against a disparaging sentence about them: 'Today, tomorrow, yesterday, the conceited bastards will never vary (with few exceptions).' As he used to say to the orchestra, 'Some of you!'

In 1958, however – by which time Downes was dead – he accepted Judson's offer of a tour of the leading American orchestras (something he had been unable to undertake in his New York years). He left London at the end of November to conduct in Winnipeg, Detroit, Washington, Philadelphia, New York (sixteen concerts), Boston, Cincinnati, Los Angeles, San Francisco and Vancouver. He took a strong English repertoire, the eighth and ninth symphonies of Vaughan Williams (when he heard of the existence of the ninth he had written to the composer to say 'eager hands will be clutching for the score'), Walton's *Partita* and Violin Concerto, Holst's *Planets*, Elgar's *Variations* and *Gerontius* and his own *Elizabethan Suite*. In Detroit, Washington and Philadelphia there was a warm welcome for him, but it was the next city, New York, that mattered most. He spent Christmas in Philadelphia.

Christmas morning

A happy Christmas, Mémé, and my dear ones all, specially you Rosie... We shall spend the day very quietly by ourselves thinking of you all and be happier so. I suppose you will be having your Christmas dinner (visions and smells of Mémé's turkey stuffing and boiled turkey wings) at 7, so we will drink your health at 2 p.m. here... Have had a wonderful time with the Philadelphia Orchestra... Rarely have I found an orchestra so ready, anxious and willing to do all I want and of course this makes me very happy, for it is the greatest compliment a conductor can be paid.

Christmas here seems a real 'racket'... I can hear Pete's comments when he knows we have even refused a big country house party with a millionaire, which on this particular day would have driven me 'nuts'... You will be amused at our Christmas menu. To be on our own we are having it in our room and one of the Italians in the orchestra took us shopping at a place just like Bomba in the Italian quarter. We have got Carcioffini al' olio, green and black olives, tonno, real imported salami, mortadelle and a lovely slice of baked Virginia ham (*without* cloves)... The turkey etc. we can have in March!!

But it was not only being away from home at Christmas that kept him in his hotel room – he was in a state of terrible apprehension about his first New York concert on 1 January. He need not have worried. The orchestra, which included thirty of his 'old boys,' were thrilled to have him, retired members and widows of others came to see him, and his first programme (Elgar's *Introduction and Allegro*, Brahms's Second Piano Concerto with Gina Bachauer and Vaughan Williams's Eighth Symphony) pleased all the critics. One of those who had been active in 1936–43, Irving Kolodin, noted 'changes, refinements, mellowings... Where the old (that is to say the young) Barbirolli endeavoured to accomplish his intentions by sheer force and an over-production of effort, the new (which is to say the older) Barbirolli does it with full confidence in the sense and validity of his musical ideas, plus a mature technique in the art of persuasion.' But what pleased John most was a sentence in the *Herald Tribune*: '...a golden lustre absent from the Philharmonic's string section for fully fifteen years.' At the end of the first week John wrote to Mémé: 'Am very tired but *very happy*... Going to our old Venetian restaurant with Polacco tonight and that will be a lovely ending to our first week here.' Polacco was now eighty-six. The restaurant, like much else in New York, was changed for the worse, but staunch friends remained the same, particularly his former secretary, John Woolford, who abandoned his work to 'look after' his old boss.

On 11 January he conducted Mahler's First Symphony in Carnegie Hall. 'His widow Alma Mahler came to both rehearsal and concert,' he told Mémé, 'and said: "It was just like seeing and hearing my great husband again." You can imagine how happy this made me.'

New York, Sunday 18 January

[To Mémé]

...Yesterday I had a very moving afternoon with my beloved Fritz Kreisler. I was rather dreading going in a way for everyone was saying how changed he was, but though he is now quite blind and very deaf (though he can hear music on the radio very well) he still looks the noble figure he always did and was so very sweet. He was very happy to be with me and chatted away, telling stories of Richter, Strauss and Bruckner, and obviously he is mentally quite himself and I gather has an enormous appetite. He is thrilled at my triumphant return here, and Mrs Kreisler (89) was telling Evelyn how fond he is of me and always says 'Barbirolli is like a son to me'.

One of the stories Kreisler told John on this occasion was that of Bruckner saying he had been praying that one day somebody, somewhere, when speaking of the three Bs, would say 'Bach, Beethoven and – Bruckner.'

The Barbirollis were fêted in New York – dinner with Eleanor Roosevelt, with Danny Kaye, with Judson, and a reception given by the Philharmonic president. It was truly a case of 'Ritorna vincitor'; and although John did not convert the American critics to a proper appreciation of *Gerontius*, the four performances were richly satisfying, and were given to packed audiences. Next came Boston.

Boston, Sunday 1 Feb.

[To Mémé]

Have now conducted the 3rd of the Big Three (as the NY, Philadelphia and Boston are known) and this Boston orch. is perhaps the greatest of the lot... The other day after I had rehearsed the 2nd Brahms symphony the whole orchestra stood and cheered me for quite some time, and they have done the same at both concerts... It was lovely, too, at the first concert to have both the present conductor, Münch, and one of the past conductors, Pierre Monteux, both there.

All three had a memorable dinner together afterwards.

Vancouver, 22 Feb.

[To Mémé]

In San Francisco saw a lot of Danny Kaye who was doing a show there too. He is really a dear... Came to my reh: and the afternoon concert and we went to his show that eve:

He conducts his band in it, and gave a terrific impersonation of some of my gestures... He is just as amusing off the stage as on, & so sweet and *affezionato*. You will be interested to know he is pure Russian by blood & this perhaps explains his facility in imitating languages.

John gave Danny Kaye a lesson in starting Beethoven's Fifth Symphony, one of the most difficult for a conductor in this respect. That evening the band at Kaye's show kept playing the opening bars of the symphony, whereupon Danny turned round and called out: 'Was that all right, Johnny?'

After celebrating his sixtieth birthday on 2 December 1959 by conducting Bach, Brahms and Bartók in Manchester, Barbirolli returned to the United States in January 1960. His first engagements were with the Kansas City, New Orleans and St Louis orchestras. While in New Orleans he spent a morning in the famous Charity Hospital watching operations, of which he wrote a detailed and critical account for Billy Douglas.

St Louis, 26 January 1960

[To A.N.S.]

A really superb principal cello here [Leslie Parnas] who turns out to be the boy to whom I helped to award the Casals prize in Paris two years or so ago. He was very keen to find out something about the Elgar concerto which he did not know, curiously enough. Although played all over Europe it is practically unknown here. He got a copy and I took him right through it for tempos and interpretation. Would you believe that he *read* it and played it including all the difficult passages better than many I have heard who have studied it for years. As my dear old friend Adolf Busch used to say 'It is not to believe'... With much love, John.

P.S. Now retired from the Navy and taking an interest in Music!!

Atlanta, 26 February 1960

[To A.N.S.]

It has all been very interesting, and standards in the main high. To keep up the flow of good string players seems to be their main difficulty, particularly violins, but have come across a very good crop of really excellent young cellists. I have had to do a lot of *teaching*, for none of them seems to have a real orchestral discipline of bowing, ensemble etc... Big programmes in Toronto: *La Mer*, Elgar II and Tchaik 5... *La Mer* was with the Symphony Orchestra, and as usual when I broke down the string passages (1st line 2nds alone etc.) found, as I had even in Philadelphia, that they hadn't a clue. For this I blame their conductors... These Americans, to whom I am really grateful for all their goodness to me, are really an extraordinary mixture. Their *un*reticence in certain respects is really rather appalling. Every hotel room has a television set, so when we are in, in the eves: having a bite in our room, we have a look in. Some of their commercials, particularly relating to female hygiene, almost made *me* blush; and nothing is beyond them. They even advertise 'Kosher Bacon'... I forgot to tell you, in the Toronto orchestra there was the prettiest young cellist I have ever seen, complete with 'nez retroussé', my downfall!! [This was an intimate joke for friends who knew how enchanted he was by *retroussé* noses and how he laughed about it with Evelyn, whose nose is *un*retroussé.]

He did not visit New York on this trip but had his biggest success in Houston and in Chicago, with Mahler's Ninth. During relaxation after rehearsals of the Mahler in Chicago he played chamber music with some of the principals, one of whom exclaimed, 'Boy, can that man play cello!' In Houston, where Stokowski was musical director, the language of the leading critic, Herbert Roussel, became lyrical: 'The concert...was a magnificent music lesson... The evening provided a revelation of what a first-rate symphony orchestra should sound like... The devotional and vastly accomplished artistry of one of England's supreme orchestra masters was the beginning of miracles in the Music Hall.' It had happened again – orchestra, audience and conductor 'clicked' at first sight and sound. Houston went mad about him. It was obvious, when Stokowski resigned at the end of this 1959–60 season, that an offer would be made to Barbirolli. This was put to good publicity value in England, as was his subsequent refusal. Then came the rumpus over orchestral subsidies, the threat to resign from the Hallé, the improvement in Arts Council aid followed by withdrawal of the threat and, two days later, the announcement in October 1960 that Barbirolli *would* succeed Stokowski but that it would not affect his position with the Hallé. His schedule for the next few years ran to a pattern whereby he opened the Hallé season in Manchester in October, went to Houston, returned for December and January, returned to Houston, back to the Hallé mid-April and May, summer shared between the Hallé and the continent, and visits to Berlin, Italy and Scandinavia fitted in whenever possible. Now at last, at sixty-two, he was living the life of an international conductor, accepting instead of rejecting.

His first concert as principal conductor at Houston was on 16 October 1961, opening with the *Carnaval Romain* overture and closing with Brahms's Second Symphony.

Warwick Hotel, Houston
28 October 1961

[To A.N.S.]

...Wonderful welcome at first concert... The apartment in the hotel is charming (rather old-fashioned hotel for the States, with chandeliers etc.) overlooking a big park on one side and two lovely churches on the other and v. quiet. The schedule will work out at roughly 3 concerts and 5 rehs: a week. People are very kind about acceding to our request of *not* being asked out much so I can work at my Mahler 10 and Bruckner 9 quietly in my spare time. Have also just finished marking the masters of the *complete Daphnis* which we [Hallé] are to do in April. I think you will love this and it will need all your most super portamentos, nearly all indicated by Ravel himself.

Houston, 14 November 1961

[To M.K.]

My dear Mike. Just a brief word to give you a little news from here... Apart from the orchestral scene, chamber music really flourishes here, with large audiences and most interesting programmes of all types. The 3 main groups are drawn almost entirely from the orchestra. A very healthy situation. It seems a very vital and one might even say dedicated community. For instance they have magnificent hospitals, and I am told on good authority that the medical centres of research etc., especially cancer, rank as among the finest in the States at the moment. The Texans are very different from other Americans we have known so far. Rather gentle, very courteous and warm and affectionate. The skyline of the city is quite attractive in its own way, and the residential districts very beautiful. Rather in the old Colonial style... There is also a very live theatre situation. Saw a really first-class perf. of Shaw's *Misalliance* the other night. Am deeply immersed in Mahler 10 at the moment. An amazing piece, that 1st movement, it might easily have been of the greatest...

The Houston musical scene had its 'socialite' aspect as New York's had done, but at this stage of his career there was little need for John to do more than show the usual courtesies. He quickly saw that those who ran the orchestra were determined to make it better and better known, and this 'building' atmosphere was the one in which he thrived. He keenly looked forward to the next stage of the season (and fitted in a visit to California first, where he enjoyed seeing Bernard Herrmann and his wife):

Los Angeles, 9 February 1962

[To A.N.S.]

...Many of the orch. here are old friends of mine over many years and we have a very nice mutual bond (both musical and personal). They have played superbly for me, almost sounding like my own Hallé at times... A real triumph for our delicious and wonderful old friend Haydn. You remember how we sat and looked at his entrancing, enigmatic and surely mischievous smile from all angles in that statuette presented to me in Budapest [which depicted Haydn without his wig], well, we opened with the 98 in B flat last night and this afternoon (the one with the slow movt. that begins with the National Anthem) and the audience cheered and clapped as if it was the end of a concert. I confess it gave me the greatest pleasure. To sadder things, our beloved Fritz [Kreisler] has gone, but he will be with us, and all those of us for whom Music means Beauty, as long as a civilised world remains (which I sometimes fear may not be long)...

Houston, 22 February 1962
6.30 a.m.

[To A.N.S.]

...Sleep having eluded me almost completely this last night
got up at 3.30, did various chores, washing drip-dry
pyjamas, handk's., dress ties, reading and feeling more
wideawake than ever!*... I was most interested you managed to see the TV film [about the Hallé] and that you
found it so good... My 'ballet' episode I am afraid you must
put the blame on Dvořák's rhythms for... Very good public
library here and I have found an excellent biography of
Irving I had not previously read.

Houston, 18 March 1962

[To A.N.S.]

...This has been a heavy patch with out-of-town concerts
and big programmes to prepare including Mahler 2 for the
final pair of concerts. 17 days in all without a free day.
(Touch of Hallé here.)... I am becoming a very expert
laundryman with all the nylon, and do handk's quite
beautifully, dried on the bathroom tiles. Your bits of silver
must give you the same quiet pleasure, I am sure, as my
glass does sometimes in moments of stress†... I finish here
Tues. eve. and fly to Prague Wed. aft., arriving there
Thurs. eve. Record‡ Fri., Sat., Sunday and fly to London
Monday...

Before he returned to Houston, the event he had long
dreaded occurred. He had once told Norah Winstanley that
he hoped he would die before Mémé, but on 2 October, on
the eve of her ninety-first birthday and the opening of the
Hallé season in Manchester, she died in her Streatham flat
while watching television. He had seen her the previous
night, after he had recorded Sibelius's Second Symphony with

* One 'chore' he regularly performed when unable to sleep was to clean
everybody's shoes! He found it very satisfying.
† The Barbirollis had a fine collection of seventeenth and eighteenth
century glass.
‡ Franck Symphony with the Czech Philharmonic.

the RPO. Her death was a blow from which he never fully recovered, for the bond had been more than usually strong, but the Hallé concert had to go on (Brahms's Second Piano Concerto and Beethoven's Seventh Symphony). Afterwards John wrote to the Orchestra:

4 October 1962

My dear friends – I was very conscious last night that your superb playing was an expression of sympathy for me in my moment of grief, and I feel I must send you my profound and heartfelt gratitude. She was a wonderful 'young' lady and was very fond of you all, and all you did to help me achieve what we have. Great occasions like the opening of the Free Trade Hall and the Centenary were unforgettable moments in her long life and no one was prouder of you than she was! – Your devoted J.B.

A practical consequence of Mémé's death was that he took even less holiday, for the August month in Sussex had been mainly for her benefit when he enjoyed cooking with her and 'pottering about.' As at so many other times of trouble, work was the antidote.

Word had already gone round the United States from soloists about the quality of the Houston Orchestra (from 1962 to 1963 Barbirolli had the title of 'conductor-in-chief and musical adviser'). The following is from a letter to me from Evelyn:

Houston, 11 November 1962

Wish you could hear the orchestra now. John has enlarged the strings a bit and re-made the cello and viola sections and the horn section, so the slight weaknesses there were are no more... The head of Columbia Concerts [Kurt Weinhold] came from New York to hear the orchestra and wants to take them on tour all round America and is really thrilled with the quality. The big-time agents are pretty hard-boiled so we take this as a compliment... They have had so many conductors here doing their war horses that it's easy to do really first-class first performances – others such as Nielsen 5, Mahler 9 etc. We continue to like the people greatly and though we would certainly not want ever to live in America these 6-week periods are happy and rewarding. Ken Crickmore is over here now – poor chap has another abscess on his stump. He's doing the round of U.S. doctors.

John became very good friends with Tom Johnson, the general manager of the orchestra, and his wife Kathleen; he also soon became well-known in the Houston shops, where he was recognised as a connoisseur of food. Kathleen Johnson discovered that an old southern recipe for cooking ham almost exactly resembled the way Mémé had cooked it. She prepared this dish for John, who was overjoyed and departed with the remains of the ham tucked under his arm.

In New York he conducted the Philharmonic during the inaugural festival of the Lincoln Centre. Whatever the New York critics had said about him in the past, they were united in their praise during this visit, particularly for the performance of Mahler's Ninth Symphony which has already been described. 'I am fortunate and very grateful for the recognition I am getting in this very difficult and sophisticated city,' he said, with some feeling.

In the second half of his 1963–64 Houston season, the fiftieth in the orchestra's history, the projected twenty-three-day American tour materialised, including concerts in New York.

Houston, 8 February 1964

[To A.N.S.]

Excitement is mounting for they have never been east before, and it will be their first appearance in cities like New York and Washington... It is going to be pretty strenuous... Just room for a word about the £800 paid by Sadler for a Lupot [violin]. Really the prices paid for instruments today are staggering, especially over here. I suppose the Lupot will be on sale at about £1,000 which seems absolutely ridiculous. In the 20s they were regarded as a kind of minor Vuillaume and prices ranged between £60 and £80... I enquired of some people 'in the know' what they thought my Gagliano (Januarius) would fetch over here and they said at least £10,000. I nearly had a fit.

26 February 1964
In the air between Brunswick
(Georgia) and Columbia (S. Carolina)

[To A.N.S.]

The towns are hideous. Blackpool I would say was gracious in comparison. E. says the food v. expensive and *terrible*, but you can just eat it if very hungry which she always is, bless her... We played in Jacksonville near where Delius came in 1884 to his orange plantation... Although he was there only 2 years, when they heard the little house he lived in was in danger of becoming a ruin a great admirer of his, a Florida lady, bought it and presented it to the Music Dept. of the University of Jacksonville... Isn't it a splendid effort?

2 March 1964
After Washington

[To A.N.S.]

N. and S. Carolina both v. disappointing (and cold) except for some nice old plantations outside the so-called towns which are all alike and miserable. Sad to think we are now emulating them and all our adorable country towns are being sacrificed to the motor car, supermarket etc. I do feel this very deeply for I do love England and no amount of the fiercest taxation wld. ever make me live out of it. The Washington concert was really a triumph... The President and Mrs Johnson were there... The inside of the White House is also v. lovely with some of the loveliest Waterford chandeliers I have ever seen. Touched by the light they seem to radiate the subtlest shades of rubies, emeralds and sapphires... The lunch was interesting. Just 6 of us besides the President and his Lady. He is obviously a very astute politician and has a natural eloquence of his own which, without being of great distinction, is at any rate preferable to some other politicians' meaningless mumblings... But, between us, I did not feel any element of real greatness there. It was all a little too highly professional.

When the orchestra performed in New York, John fulfilled a long-standing wish to appear there with a visiting orchestra.

He hoped it would be with the Hallé, but Houston got there instead. He included two symphonies in his Philharmonic Hall programme – Vaughan Williams's Sixth, which had not been played in New York since 1949, and Beethoven's Seventh – and was delighted when Harold Schonberg, in the *New York Times*, called the English work a masterpiece, adding:

> Sir John led a strong performance, handicapped only by the physical resources of his orchestra [94 players]. More weight of tone was needed... But these defects did not show up in the Beethoven...there was a leanness, a rhythmic snap, that was most welcome. Sir John's ideas towards Beethoven always were sturdy and essentially uncomplicated. Even as a young conductor with the New York Philharmonic he never attempted to give us a shined-up, fancy-fancy Beethoven. Last night his performance was as remembered – clear, logical, musical, strong and direct.

Surely, by now, the ghost of Olin Downes was laid. It is unlikely, however, that such a thought occurred to John, who was usually looking ahead to the next concert.

17 March 1964
[To A.N.S.]

We got back from tour last Thursday and immediately plunged into choral preparation of *The Dream* [*of Gerontius*]... How rightly you divined my touring travelling habits. In these days I have bowed the whole of Mahler 6th [an eighty-minute work] and begun an intensive study of it. But it is a godsend to have this work to do, for tho' I have kept pretty well I have little appetite (tho' I *do* try) and I suppose the continuous little sleep helps to create a general depression and sadness during the long nights in spite of all the public triumphs. How little the public know. E. (a severe critic) thinks I am conducting better than ever... Perhaps it has to come the hard way... I am *so* looking forward to my Band again.

This 1963–64 season was as arduous in England with his 'Band' as in Houston, for it was his twenty-first in Manchester and he had made it a celebration. But there was another orchestra now with which his relationship was close and deep – the Berlin Philharmonic. Their acceptance of him as a maestro in the great tradition was one of the joys of his last decade, yet he could scarcely believe it.

Barbirolli first conducted the Berlin Philharmonic in three concerts at the 1949 Edinburgh Festival. He had just been ordered by Billy Douglas to rest, but no one could have made him cancel this engagement since he had been prevailed upon to give up his first Berlin appearance in February 1949. From the first note of the first rehearsal conductor and orchestra liked each other; indeed, it is no exaggeration in writing of this relationship to describe it as a 'love affair' between Barbirolli and the Berliners. Their performance of the *Enigma Variations*, for example, was as great a revelation as that by Toscanini and the BBC Orchestra. He was immediately again invited to Berlin as a guest conductor and went there in April 1950, when his interpretation of Brahms's Fourth Symphony divided the critics but won him rapturous acclaim from orchestra and public. Thereafter, although he was invited back, illness or other engagements prevented his going, and his 1956 operation caused him, to his undying regret, to miss an engagement to conduct *Gerontius* in Berlin with the Dublin Choir.

He did not return to Berlin until January 1961. By then the orchestra – of which Herbert von Karajan had become principal conductor – had a new Intendant (general manager), Wolfgang Stresemann, himself an erstwhile conductor and sensitive musician who had been in America while John was in New York. Stresemann admired him and had been determined to obtain him as a guest conductor. At the break in the first rehearsal on 17 January, several players went to

Stresemann and said: 'Please engage this man as often as you can.' Stresemann told me that this has happened on very few occasions in his experience. The Berlin Philharmonic Hall had not then been built and the concerts were given in the Musikhochschule. At his first concert – the first of seventy over the following ten years – John conducted Sibelius's Seventh Symphony, Beethoven's Third Piano Concerto, with Wilhelm Backhaus as soloist, and Brahms's Second Symphony. 'A really lovely orchestra,' he wrote to Audrey, 'with the most beautiful sound, who last night played themselves to a standstill for me and then proceeded to outdo the audience in applauding and cheering me. I must say it gave me a very warm inner feeling for they tell me it is an unheard of thing for them to do, and it was after Brahms II. Curiously enough the same thing happened in Boston, and they gave me an ovation too after the Brahms reh.' John was not exaggerating. For an English conductor to inspire a German critic to say that he had not listened to Brahms with such interest and pleasure for many years was no mean achievement.

He returned in December 1961, when he conducted one of the rare Berlin performances of Dvořák's D Minor Symphony and Haydn's 98th Symphony. Members of the Berlin Philharmonic have since told me that they regarded him as one of the great Haydn conductors – 'the moment he began rehearsing Haydn with us we knew that he ranked among the exceptional, really musical, conductors.' The players recognised at once his thorough professionalism and musicianship. 'He gives us freedom to express ourselves, yet he gets exactly what he wants'. They roared with laughter at the delicious inaccuracies of his German, learnt from Mahler's voluminous indications in his scores, with some Wagnerianisms called upon too. A greater triumph awaited him in January 1963 when he conducted Mahler's Ninth Symphony. Mahler was not often played in Berlin, and the orchestra frankly confess that they do not particularly like his music – 'but,' said one of the principals, 'Sir John made us love it as much as he did himself and we played it as he wanted.' So well, indeed, that a leading Berlin critic wrote: 'Not since Furtwängler have we heard such human warmth and soul combined with superb musicianship.'

The orchestra themselves asked that Barbirolli should record this symphony with them, the first English conductor to record with the Berlin Philharmonic since Beecham in 1937. During the cold January of 1964 this famous recording was made in the Jesus-Christuskirche, in the suburb of Dahlem. On this visit also, John conducted three public concerts, each repeated, in the new Philharmonic Hall. His programmes included Haydn's 92nd Symphony, Mahler's Fourth Symphony (with Irmgard Seefried), Brahms's Fourth Symphony, Vaughan Williams's Eighth Symphony and Berlioz's *Symphonie Fantastique*. After the final concert, ending with the Berlioz, the audience applauded for thirty-five minutes, refusing to leave the hall and crowding up against the low platform to greet Barbirolli and even to touch him. But it had been like that, too, after the first concert, as he told Audrey:

Hotel Steinplatz, Berlin
9 January 1964

The orch: seems to feel so easily what I am after... Concert last night Haydn's 'Oxford' symphony, 4 exquisite Mahler songs and Mahler IV. Completely sold out and ovation even for the opening Haydn. At the end it was quite overwhelming and continued long after the orch: had left the platform. Stresemann...a rather shy, reticent but dear man, told me later at supper it is quite extraordinary what I have come to mean to these v. sophisticated Berliners in such a short time. Such *atmosphere* and scenes are never seen except when I come, and I was v. touched when he said I have somehow created at a Berlin Phil concert a kind of 'family' feeling that has not previously existed. Don't think there is any conceit in this, my music takes far too big a toll of me.

Earlier in this letter he described the new hall:

...Like all these modern halls and theatres very cold and clinical looking. Makes me feel I shld enter with aseptic clothing and a sharp knife instead of a baton. The shape is rather interesting with the orch: almost centre and *surrounded* by the audience; when the hall is full it does create a certain intimacy which is quite attractive. At rehs: I was rather disappointed in the sound, rather Festival Hall-like, very clear and dryish, but it was definitely much better with the audience there... Not the most inspiring surroundings for music-making. The two halls in Israel are much the same. Strange what this generation seems to be seeking in art in general. With all the problems that surround us in the world, you wld think they wld seek something a little more of a consoling nature.

Quotations from the Berlin critics during this visit are eloquent testimony to the impression John made: 'Mahler's Fourth Symphony was interpreted in all its heterogeneous structure... Nothing was felt of the irregularity of the form and of the *absolute* musicality which so often prevents the proper understanding of Mahler's music.' 'With Barbirolli on the rostrum, one can hear what accuracy and dynamic delicacy the Philharmonic is capable of, what rich and yet sensitive sound can be produced by the strings.' 'The personal concentration of the conductor and the power of his passionate and at the same time intellectual musicianship inspired the orchestra to such a degree that the performance attained utmost perfection.'

Each time he returned to Berlin, John experienced agonies of apprehension: 'I feel it can't last.' But it always did. On his next visit, early in June 1965, he conducted three performances of Mahler's Second Symphony, with Janet Baker as one of the soloists and the Choir of St Hedwig's Cathedral, and two performances of Elgar's Cello Concerto, with one of the orchestra's principal cellists, Ottomar Borwitzky, and of Bruckner's Seventh Symphony. John wrote in his engagement book: 'Wonderful, treasured evening with my beloved Berlin Phil and Bruckner.' Stresemann recalls this occasion: 'He returned from the rostrum (in spite of the tremendous ovation) visibly bewildered, trembling and almost moved to tears. He was not certain whether he had done justice to Bruckner or to the orchestra. It sounded almost like a confessional when he declared that it had been his first Bruckner performance in Germany.'

In January 1966 he conducted Vaughan Williams's Fifth Symphony, Brahms's D Minor Piano Concerto, with Daniel Barenboim, Beethoven's *Eroica* Symphony and Mahler's Sixth (which he had conducted for the first time exactly a year earlier, in Leeds). Of the *Eroica*, not exactly unknown in

Berlin, the critic of the *Morgenpost* wrote: 'It is sufficient to say that it is many years since I heard so blissful and thrilling a performance, with a near-ideal balance of tension, intelligence and emotion. The orchestra was brought to life by Sir John...one could hardly believe it was the same orchestra which recently played this work so particularly badly.' In September he returned to conduct Mozart's 40th Symphony and Bruckner's Ninth Symphony in commemoration of what would have been Bruno Walter's ninetieth birthday, and in May and June of 1967 his Berlin programmes included Debussy's *La Mer*, Hindemith's Cello Concerto, and Schoenberg's *Pelléas et Mélisande*. While he was in Berlin at this time the Arab–Israeli War began and his departure for concerts in Israel was delayed. So, at the request of Hellmut Stern, the Berlin orchestral manager, he conducted Beethoven's Ninth Symphony in aid of Israeli victims of the fighting. The following October he returned to conduct Strauss's *Don Quixote*, a performance that Stresemann remembered as one of his greatest. 'It is like playing on a wonderful cello or piano for me,' John wrote to Audrey. 'Stresemann said afterwards that *Don Quixote* has never hitherto had a success with the public here.' Barbirolli used to say of *Don Quixote* that it was not Strauss's greatest work but it contained his greatest music. On this visit he also conducted Haydn's 83rd Symphony and Elgar's *Enigma Variations*.

He gave three more sets of concerts in January 1968: a Brahms programme (Second Piano Concerto and First Symphony), Mahler's Fifth Symphony and two performances of Verdi's *Requiem*. By now the critics referred to his seasonal visits as 'the Barbirolli Festival.' Writing of Brahms's First Symphony, the critic of *Der Tagespiegel* said: 'Never does he try to distort the music by emphasising specially brilliant passages or to break the general structure by impressive details. Who else is able to interpret this symphony so absolutely free of any artificial virtuosity as Barbirolli does again and again?' The Mahler was likewise acclaimed, and concerning the *Requiem* the critic of *Der Tagespiegel* asked: 'What kind of mystery is it which surrounds Barbirolli with an invulnerable aura of something apart from everybody else? There is hardly any conductor who is loved so much as he... It may be his spiritual incorruptibility and mental discipline that put him far above many of his colleagues.'

For the tenor part in the *Requiem* John had engaged the young British singer David Hughes, whose career he had done much to foster. Hughes had made the difficult transition from the world of popular music to opera, and John well knew the kind of coolness of which the English musical world was capable in such a case. After the Berlin performances Hughes wrote to him: 'No one in the musical world has shown as much faith in my singing as you have done, and because of this many other people are beginning to take notice of me... It is impossible for me even to be able to repay you for your kindness except by trying to sing better and better.'

Throughout his week with the orchestra in September 1968 John was suffering agonies from kidney stones. 'Took my "stuff",' he wrote, 'even the new one doesn't make me doze!! and it certainly helped the pain... Took more Pethidine and rested till the concert. My dear Berlin lads didn't think I looked too well and rewarded me with some really magnificent and beautiful playing' – in Britten's *Sinfonia da Requiem* and Beethoven's Fifth. Six months later he returned to conduct two performances of Mahler's Third Symphony, in which Lucretia West sang the solo part and the chorus was again that of St Hedwig's. His conducting of the final Adagio, Stresemann said, was 'almost unbelievably restrained and yet filled with the utmost emotional intensity.' He wrote to Brenda Bracewell, his 'carissima segretaria,' that the orchestra was 'as lovely as ever, and the welcome from them and the public if anything greater than ever. Very touching this for me as I sometimes wonder how long it can possibly last!' Like 'the smell of lilac in Russell Square in the springtime' of childhood days.

In September 1969 he was delighted to have one of the orchestra's viola leaders, the Venetian Giusto Cappone, as soloist in the Walton concerto and, as he wrote, 'I played *William Tell* overture (which they had never played before) because of the wonderful cello section, and the famous 1st violin passage was really exquisite. The most touching little tributes are paid me by little groups of rank and file, such as "Meister, it is always a feast of music-making when you come to us".' The last 'feast' was in February 1970 when he introduced Nielsen's Fourth Symphony to Berlin, accompanied Pina Carmirelli in Mendelssohn's Violin Concerto, and conducted Haydn's 99th Symphony ('a marvellous one even for

him, full of his inimitable sly little smiles'). This programme
was given three times, and his second set included a Mozart
piano concerto, Vaughan Williams's *Tallis Fantasia* and Mahler's First Symphony. He was to have returned twice in the
1970–71 season to conduct more Haydn (No. 95), Strauss's
Bourgeois Gentilhomme, Dvořák's G Major Symphony and
Mahler's Seventh Symphony, but instead Barenboim conducted Mozart and Bruckner (No. 7) in two concerts dedicated to Barbirolli's memory – a rare tribute to a foreign conductor.

The above detail has been given because it is impossible to
overestimate the significance to Barbirolli of those ten years
with the Berlin Philharmonic. For the first time since New
York, and in spite of his misgivings (which he called 'my usual
"worrying" state'), he achieved close and prolonged musical
rapport and personal affection with one of the undisputed
leading orchestras of the world (the best, in his opinion), and
also with the Berlin public and, to his wonder, with the
critics. The long ovations he received were quite extraordinary, lasting sometimes, as we have seen, over half an hour,
the audience refusing to leave even when the hall lights were
extinguished but recalling him again and again. No wonder
the receptions in Manchester and London sometimes seemed
reserved by comparison. Of the orchestra's playing – 'It is all
so beautiful and so *generous*,' was his summing-up; for their
part they were equally fond of him as a man – several could
imitate him as accurately as any of their British colleagues –
and they brooked no argument about his stature as an artist.
'Like every true musician,' Stresemann wrote of him after his
death, 'he was not a specialist. He was an heroic interpreter of
heroic music. He always plumbed the inner depths, and the
all-embracing humanity of his musicianship was somehow
imparted in an almost overwhelming manner to all the
people with whom he came into contact.' It was not only John
F. Kennedy who could say 'Ich bin ein Berliner.' The *Morgenpost*'s headline over the announcement of John's death
was to sum it up: 'The hearts of the Philharmonic and of the
Berlin public beat for him.'

20
Darkening
Days

'What a fine orchestra is the Hallé when Sir John Barbirolli conducts it!' 'O for the Barbirolli touch! Never could
he words "routine performance" be written for anything per-
ormed under his baton.' These are typical extracts from pro-
incial non-Mancunian notices in 1963–64 when the differ-
nce in the Hallé between its 'Barbirolli sound' and its sound
nder some other conductors was frequently remarked upon.
)ne of the Hallé's most successful ventures with Barbirolli
vas its tour of Scandinavia in June 1963, when it played Sibel-
us (and Mahler) to the Finns in Helsinki and Nielsen to the
)anes in Copenhagen, emerging laurel-laden from both im-
»ertinences. Peter Davies of the British Council in Helsinki
vrote to John afterwards: 'After your second concert Jussi
alas [son-in-law of Sibelius and himself a fine conductor]
aid to me. "We Finns ought to be ashamed that it takes a
}ritish orchestra and a British conductor to show us how to
lay Sibelius".'

The opening of 1963 marked Barbirolli's return to HMV
or EMI as it was now known) with a contract to record with
ther orchestras besides the Hallé. For the first time, there
'as a real opportunity for his major interpretations to be pre-
erved, and he began his new association by re-recording
'aughan Williams's Fifth Symphony with the Philharmonia
)rchestra. He enjoyed recording; he was very experienced in
t and he liked working with the technicians whose contribu-
ion to modern high standards is so great. And they enjoyed
is reminiscences of the 'prehistoric' days of records: of play-

ing *The Broken Melody* and *O Star of Eve* on the cello
accompanied by Rosie, for Edison-Bell at the age of eleven; of
making his fingers bleed by rehearsing cello pizzicati with
Ambrose Gauntlett for an early recording of Arthur Bliss'
avant-garde work of the 1920s, *Rout*; of recording *Madamina*
from *Don Giovanni* with Chaliapin, with Sacha Guitry listening, and Chaliapin, armed with several kinds of pills and a
bottle of brandy 'to stimulate the voice'; of making the famous Tchaikovsky Piano Concerto records in 1932 and the beginning of a lifelong friendship when Artur Rubinstein exclaimed after the first few bars: 'What a man! At last I can
play this concerto'; of the *Abscheulicher* with Frida Leider in
1928, recorded by 'landline' at the Kingsway Hall, when after
recording it twice and being satisfied, Gaisberg found that the
landline had failed and not a note had been captured (Gaisberg hired every taxi in sight, rushed singer, conductor and
orchestra to the Small Queen's Hall, and started again); and
of the day in 1935 when, just back from Russia, he recorded
Vieuxtemps's Fourth Violin Concerto with Heifetz that afternoon never having seen the work until he studied the score
with its fiendish one-in-a-bar scherzo, over lunch in the
Berkeley Hotel.

He had old friends at EMI, too – among them David Bick-
nell, who had witnessed his signature on his first contract with
Gaisberg, and Victor Olof, who had been in his Chenil string
orchestra. He made new ones, in particular Ronald Kinloch
Anderson, who was to be the producer of most of his recordings between 1963 and 1970 and in whose sterling musicianship he had absolute confidence. There were Anderson's colleagues Peter Andry and Christopher Bishop, too. It was
Bishop with whom he was working at the Abbey Road Studio
on a day at the height of the Beatles' popularity. As John
arrived he saw the famous four and their retinue. 'Is that the
Fuzzy Wuzzies?' he asked Christopher, 'because we'd better
close the door – in case they *charge*.' He worked also with Suvi
Raj Grubb, with whom he shared a passion for cricket. In a
pub near Kingsway Hall John demonstrated Woolley's cover
drives to Grubb, remarking that 'they don't make 'em like
that any more.' To a customer who chipped in with 'I agree'
at this point, John said genially, 'Of course you do, any
reasonable chap would.'

The casual observer could not have imagined clouds on

John's horizon at this point of his career, any more than he could have suspected the depressions which preceded a day's impassioned work in the rehearsal-room or the recording studio. Yet they were gathering. But first there was the excitement of his twenty-first season with the Hallé, at the start of which – at a concert on 29 September 1963 – he received the gold medal which the Hallé Concerts Society presents to members of the orchestra who have served for twenty years. He asked that it should be presented to him by the leader, Martin Milner, after he himself had presented medals to four survivors from his 1943 orchestra who, as he put it, had 'served their time.' Milner's happy phrase for his chief was 'a Kreisler among conductors'; and the Lord Mayor later described him as 'Manchester's greatest citizen.' It was an emotional evening – the programme was a repetition of the first he had conducted in Manchester in 1943 – with cheers and tears, the bust of Hallé on the platform, and a superb performance of Tchaikovsky's Fifth Symphony in which, at the point in the finale where the motto-theme returns in triumph, John laid down his baton, put his arms to his sides and conducted by nodding his head and, of course, with his eyes, as Richter was said to do. It was as if he were listening to the achievements and the memories of two momentous decades of music-making. Few conductors have created such a bond with the public and been so accessible personally.

Barbirolli was by now what the British public takes to its heart – 'a character.' He had always been that, of course, as a black-haired, enthusiastic youngster, but with the spread of television and radio, millions knew him where only hundreds had in earlier days. They knew his sardonic humour, his unmistakable and often imitated voice (imitated most faithfully in my experience by Alexander Gibson); they knew his nostalgia for the past which expressed itself in his purchase of an old street gas lamp to be re-erected in the garden of his house, Walton Lodge in New Hall Road, Salford, where he had lived since 1960, and in his admiration for an interior such as that of Liverpool's elegant town hall; they knew his English passion for cricket which he followed with Italianate fervour, having Test Match scores brought to him regularly at rehearsals. Although in later years he gave himself little chance to watch cricket – except on television, when his comments and advice to the captain were juicy – he was extremely knowledgeable about it; a schoolmaster who sat next to him at Lord's in June 1949 remembers him as a very shrewd and percipient student of the game.

Many knew, too, of his vivid admiration – as if they were his contemporaries – for two historical figures, Lord Nelson and Henry Irving. He was by now looking rather like Irving, with his gaunt face and intensity of expression, though his flamboyance was of an altogether less histrionic kind. On great occasions he liked to end his speech with the words Irving often used at the Lyceum: 'Ladies and gentlemen, I am your most humble and obedient servant.' He never let a Trafalgar Day go by without drinking a toast to 'the little Admiral' and on the nearest available free day to 21 October he would have a small private dinner party for which he wrote out the menu, with such specially devised dishes as 'La douceur d'Emma,' 'Frutti di Mare Brontë,' 'Poularde en cocotte Horatio' and, best of all, 'Hearts of (artich)Oke.'

This was the Barbirolli who, despite his curious affectation from the day he was fifty that he was 'an old man,' remained young at heart, taking delight in 'silly little things' – 'What fun we get out of them, don't we?' he said. Fun, but also there was something very touching about his reverence for the past, as when he sent a picture postcard from Vienna to my wife and me in December 1967, while he was recording the Brahms symphonies there. It said only: 'In a tiny room in this house died our beloved Schubert: and my thoughts immediately went to our mutual feelings about this adorable and very great man.'

The public also recognised in him an entire absence of 'side' or snobbery. Although he rejoiced in the honours which began to be showered upon him – honorary degrees, Italian Knighthood, other foreign decorations – he was in no sense an 'Establishment' figure, as that term is generally if imperfectly understood. Dr F. A. Iremonger when Dean of Lichfield in 1951 summed up what Barbirolli meant to many when he thanked him for taking the Hallé to play in the Cathedral: 'To have given up so much of your precious time to a hazardous venture such as we made last week and to have entered into the spirit of it all with the simple friendliness you showed ...'

If he could not find young composers who excited him, he found many young executants. After Frederic Cox became

Principal of the Royal Manchester College of Music in 1953, John regularly conducted the College orchestra – 'with tonic effect,' Cox said. The soloist on one occasion was a student pianist, John Ogdon, whose career from that date accelerated to international renown. Alan Schiller and Daniel Barenboim among pianists, the cellist Jacqueline du Pré, Anna Reynolds and Elizabeth Vaughan among singers, these are merely representative names among a new generation who were helped and admired by Barbirolli. He conducted the students' orchestra at the Royal Academy of Music, too, on one occasion in *Gerontius*.

From his television appearances and similar occasions the public learned, too, that Barbirolli's natural charm gave an extra fillip to the most unpromising circumstances, even to *This is Your Life*, the television programme in which an unsuspecting celebrity is confronted with an array of his friends who wax effusive and nostalgic about their memories of him. John listened to it all with chuckling amazement – the more amazed because he had no idea what the programme was supposed to be. Part of his secret lay in his prowess as a public speaker. One would have thought this was a natural gift but as a child his speech was hesitant and when he was at school he found, when reading aloud, that he had great difficulty in starting, especially with the letter L. (He confessed in maturity that he disliked 'Ladies and gentlemen' for that reason, and usually substituted 'My friends.') Fortunately he had a sensible English master who, one day when John stood silent on being asked to read aloud, let it pass and sent for him afterwards to discover if the reason lay in something more than wilful naughtiness. John explained about his impediment, and the English master, by selecting special passages for reading aloud, helped him to overcome it almost completely. No wonder, then, that John was proud of the evening in June 1954 when his speech at a dinner of the Cricket Writers' Club brought him the written compliment from his boyhood hero C. B. Fry that it was 'quite one of the most successful one has enjoyed during quite a lot of years.' Fry probably did not know that the speech was 'sprung' on John just before the dinner by the chairman, Neville Cardus, who blithely wrote in apology afterwards: 'It never occurred to me to warn you, for whenever I have heard you speak at dinner in the past you have done it after the manner born, with ease and wit, as in fact you spoke last night.'

One of his most amusing speeches was during his Hallé Gold Medal season when the press, radio and television journalists of Manchester gave a private dinner in his honour to acknowledge the courteous and frank way in which he had dealt with the press for twenty years. No other public figure in the city had hitherto been honoured in this way. The only date he could give was *after* a Hallé concert (which, incidentally, had included *La Mer* and Elgar's Second Symphony, no lightweight labour) so the reception began at ten p.m., the meal was served at about eleven, and by the time other speakers had finished it was one-thirty a.m. when J.B. began. For an hour he kept his audience of seventy hard-bitten journalists in fits of laughter at racy anecdotes from his career, a *tour de force* of after-dinner speaking. He then signed everyone's menu, joined them for drinks and went home at about four a.m. At nine-fifteen he was at Manchester Airport en route to Houston. The evening is already a Mancunian legend, the tape recording of his speech jealously preserved.

An immediate consequence of his return to EMI was the beginning of a seven-year association with another great orchestra, the Philharmonia. He made his first public appearance with them in London on 24 March 1963, in a performance of *Gerontius* which *The Times* described as 'blazing with glorious conviction...every moment is as real as truth to him, impossible of exaggeration. One could regard Elgar's careful markings as restrictive; Sir John understands them as spurs to the imagination.' In August of that year he took the Philharmonia on a tour of South America. 'The orchestra has played splendidly,' he wrote from Buenos Aires, 'and is improving every day. They rehearse with great enthusiasm and goodwill but despite some very fine instrumentalists (some have just joined for the trip) it is *not quite my Hallé*... Last night a man came to the dressing-room and in a lovely Cockney voice said: "I wish I 'ad me Union Jack 'ere".'

Twice during 1964 he conducted in Italy, visiting Florence and Venice in July. He liked to walk round the cities at night:

[To A.N.S.]
The only tragic thing about Florence is that in the daytime the traffic and those bloody awful 'Lambrettas', nasty little

Italian motor bikes without silencers, make life an absolute misery, for the noise is frightful and in some of the lovely narrow cobbled streets they even mount the pavements regardless of pedestrians. The Italians at their worst... So with my lack of sleep I did see the city at its best for a few hours, for apart from a few policemen (and, I fear, pansies) I saw no one... Venice is really a marvellous place (tho' of course it wld take *months* to explore it properly) with superb examples of architecture of all the great periods... It is a joy here just to walk to the exquisite theatre and our ancient eating house (Trattoria) as opposed to restaurant... You might like to conjure up a picture of your Maestro doing his scales by candlelight in the conductor's room of the Fenice, surrounded by the original posters of the first performances of *Traviata* and *Rigoletto*.

He was practising his scales at the Fenice, which he conidered to be the most beautiful theatre in the world, in preparation for the King's Lynn Festival where for several years he had not only conducted the Hallé each July or August in the beautiful St Nicholas's Chapel but played chamber music in an ensemble with other members of the Hallé (Laurance Turner – succeeded by Martin Milner – Sydney Partington, Sydney Errington), Evelyn, sometimes Lionel Tertis and, as the pianist, the instigator of the festival, Ruth Fermoy (Lady Fermoy) who became a close friend of the Barbirollis. Nothing would make John miss King's Lynn. He planned his summer schedule round it, with Hallé visits to King's College Chapel, Cambridge, Ely or Lincoln en route. If, as in 1964, it meant interrupting a foreign tour to fly home, that was no matter. After King's Lynn he returned to Italy where, at Taormina, he gave classes of interpretative studies for young conductors from all over the world.

I have never done anything like this before (the classes are also with orch:) and am quite enjoying it, but it is rather pathetic to see young people without any real gift wanting so passionately to *conduct*. Only one with any real gift at all – a funny little Chinese girl (22). Very musical and quite a personality... This week I have had to get well stuck into my 'homework' for next season. It has been a *godsend* though, for I have been v. depressed these last weeks. Poor

old Ken to be sentenced in the prime of life after all he has
been through. He is taking it magnificently... He has developed a new inoperable malignancy in the abdomen. It
has been a great shock for we have been very close for 20
years and in spite of certain 'funninesses' of his own he has
always had a tremendous loyalty and affection for me.

Crickmore had given up the Hallé directorship in 1960
and handed over to Clive Smart. He went to the United States
as agent for Barbirolli and to make arrangements for a Hallé
tour. While there he married Rosalind Booth, who had been
John's secretary for many years. John returned to the United
States in October 1964, for his Houston season and also for
some very successful concerts with the Boston Symphony
Orchestra. ('V.W.6 very well received,' he wrote to me, 'except for one young critic who I gather is a disappointed atonal
composer. What a combination! !') While in Houston, where
Evelyn broke her wrist, they learned that Crickmore's mother
and stepfather, who were caretakers at their Salford house,
which had originally been bought by Crickmore, had left
without warning. Other developments followed, succinctly
described in a letter from John to me after Crickmore's death
in April 1965: 'We discovered...that my late manager had
been "helping himself" liberally to my cash and at 66 I have
practically to begin again... Evelyn and I are suffering greatly
but we keep our heads up.' He added: 'I had to record *The
Dream* soon after the awful discovery, so you can see it has not
affected my music.' The *Gerontius* recording, on which he
had set his heart, was made in the Free Trade Hall just after
Christmas 1964, and only this work, perhaps, could have sustained him through the worst weeks of his life, when he was
morally shattered. He was also rehearsing the Hallé for his
first performance of Mahler's Sixth Symphony. Other
troubles piled on him at this time: he trapped his finger in a
car door, injuring it badly; he was disturbed by the increasingly serious illness of Billy Douglas; and he was depressed by
the death of Churchill. From Battle Creek, Michigan, in
March, after hearing of Billy Douglas's death, he wrote to
Audrey:

He had nothing left to live for and was happy or, rather,
glad to go. We loved him dearly and were greatly touched

and moved when we heard that just before he died, with exquisite thoughtfulness for us, he wrote a little message: 'Thank you both for a glorious friendship'... I work incessantly on the journeys, studying my *Siegfried* and other works I want to do next season, including the reconstructed Mahler 10th. A remarkable achievement by Deryck Cooke*... We have not got very far in the unravelling of our affairs, but what has been revealed so far is far worse than we ever dreamt... The strain these last months, and I am afraid it will continue for many more, has been v. great. The tour is strenuous enough, plus all I have to study, and to be bereft of sleep (the nights are pretty grim) and fight on is, at times, v. hard... Strangely enough I am always well, poised and calm when working.

The affair hung over them throughout 1965 while preparations were made for a claim in California against Crickmore's estate. His widow counter-claimed for over £80,000, alleging that conduct by the Barbirollis had aggravated her husband's illness and speeded his death. Extracts from John's letters to Audrey Napier Smith during this year give a vivid picture of his anxiety and how he fought it. He conducted at the Sibelius Centenary Festival in Helsinki in May and took the Finnish orchestra on a tour of Europe. He spent August in South America again with the New Philharmonia (astonishing them with his tireless energy), returning to Houston from Manchester in October, well supplied with antibiotics to try to throw off a stubborn virus which caused diarrhoea.

Houston, 22 October 1965

...In the throes of preparing Bruckner 9. I feel v. tired today (free day) so have decided to stay in bed and start work seriously on studying Mahler V. It will be nice to get on with it... My warmest greetings to your Papá... Incidentally, when you refer to your parent in Italian you must put the accent as above, otherwise you will have elevated him to the Papacy and I don't think it would please him greatly to become 'His Holiness'! !

* He changed his mind about conducting this, because, much though he admired it, he felt that something essentially Mahlerian was missing.

Houston, 8 November 1965

...Our 'affairs' out West don't seem to make much progress... You can't wonder, Audrey, that when I have long sleepless nights there are dark and depressing thoughts, especially when two people on whom I lavished such affection and trust have led me to this impasse. Fortunately our lawyer is to be here next week and we can ask him some blunt questions...

Houston, 12 November 1965

...I am a bit better, curiously after a completely sleepless night. I read for a bit then was so wide awake that I started on Mahler 5 at 2.15 a.m. so in the last 24 hours I have done at least 18 on it. But it is beginning to bear fruit, I think. It is the *vast* design of these works apart from the technical complications that makes the most intense study of them imperative.

Houston, 10 February 1966

Have had to spend 6 hours reading through what our lawyer aptly calls 'legalese' amounting to at least 100 pages or more... Beastly to have to re-live that disgusting business... Splendid opening concerts (*Eroica* strangely enough) but I had to work v. hard getting the orch: back to its real shape. Strange how the *Eroica* exhausts me these days. It may well be because I am really beginning to plumb its depths. It is really a tremendous piece, isn't it?

Houston, 10 March 1966

...Spent the whole afternoon on more depositions refuting untruths, always a sickening business... Mahler 5 is very taxing for me emotionally, physically, and requiring at the back of it all an ice-cold concentration and control.

Houston, 17 March 1966

Yesterday another blow fell which upset me greatly. We heard from our lawyer that the verbal depositions I told you about have to be given in Los Angeles, so on the 6th instead of flying to Manchester I have to fly to L.A. (with E.) and after 3 days of questioning fly to N.Y. and then N.Y.-M/c where, D.V., I shall arrive Easter Sunday... It is not the physical side that bothers me but the mental strain is great and the only way I can keep my head above water is to work still more, and to help me have started on Mahler III.

Boston, 30 March 1966

These have been hectic days, 12 Mahler Vs in just over three weeks, journeys, programmes for next Hallé and Houston seasons to be made. The prelim: drafts for both of these are finished, as also the bowings for the huge Mahler III (next season)... In spite of all my difficulties in seeking some mental repose...all the band keep telling E. what 'wonderful form the old man is in.' The Lord is truly kind and good to me... Wednesday we leave for the 'ordeal'.

The case dragged on for nearly another twelve months. In March 1967, in San Francisco, an out-of-court settlement was announced whereby £35,000 was to be paid to the Barbirollis out of the Crickmore estate, all counter-claims being dropped by Mrs Crickmore. 'Strange,' John wrote, 'that though we are of course greatly relieved, even our brilliant counsel, who has become a dear friend, cannot feel jubilant, it was all so revolting to the end.'

The mental strain on Barbirolli from this unhappy affair – from December 1964 until March 1967, nearly two and a half years – was acute and on several occasions, combined with physical illness, it affected his conducting. He developed a habit of stamping on the rostrum and beating time with his baton on his desk, as if he was at rehearsal, when the orchestra was not responding as he wished. Some of his interpretations were erratic and several performances well below standard. His gestures sometimes amounted to a bizarre self-parody. In Manchester even some of his most loyal admirers, not knowing what lay behind his behaviour, wondered if he had stayed too long, and if his often-expressed determination never to leave the Hallé might not prove to be an embarrassment. Yet, in works such as the Mahler and Elgar symphonies, he would recover all his old brilliance and banish any doubts. On a tour of Russia in January 1967 with the BBC Symphony Orchestra, for instance, he had conducted a performance of Elgar's Second Symphony in Leningrad which had moved the Russian audience to a tumult of appreciation. And he had brought all his customary enthusiasm to the opening of Houston's new hall, the Jesse Jones Hall, in October 1966. He wrote these letters to Audrey Napier Smith:

Houston, 5 October 1966

The hall, though contemporary in some ways, is very warm and intimate tho' large (just over 3,000). Lovely warm round sound and all the players say what a treat to be able to hear each other. The walls all of teak wood, rather gorgeous red upholstery (is that right?) and carpets and even the top tiers of seats sloping down to stage level. Of course full evening dress everywhere, and I dread to think what the poor husbands paid for their spouses' dresses... Programme turned out splendidly... Finished with Suites I and II *Daphnis* with full chorus. Wonderful facilities for that here as the orch: pit goes down to Bayreuth level and holds 95 players. I put the chorus right down there and the effect was magical as no one could see them... E. and Brenda [Bracewell, John's secretary and manager] are out all day practically today, and I am having a good day at my Mahler 3... I have refused all social invitations and E. and B. are deputising for me, guzzling caviar and pâté de foie gras...

Houston, 13 October 1966

The actual pair of concerts opening the season went well... V.W. *London*. Considering they never play this kind of music (except with me)...it is quite extraordinary how quickly they grasp the spirit and significance of it all. What a lovely piece it is, with a kind of Whistler aspect of London, pastel and greyish at times, but with the underlying inner heart of my old London still there with its humour and its passion too.

In Houston, four months later, in February 1967, came the first serious warning that the left ventricle of his heart was affected:

> Houston, 10 February 1967
> Between rehearsals

> ...Concerts going magnificently; E. came to Brahms I the other night and seemed overwhelmed (which is quite something for her). I have not really been too well again. I know you would not like me to keep things from you, but you must *tell no one*. I am afraid I had a 'black-out' for a moment at rehs: (before Brahms) and fell on the platform but recovered quickly and went on without leaving the platform. Rested all afternoon and was all right for the show and very steady 'on me pins'...

> Houston, 16 February 1967

> ...I persevere with all my pills and I do think they do help, especially some to take in the morning when I wake with this awful veil of dark depression. But don't worry too much about my little black-out. There are various explanations and I was examined immediately afterwards and blood pressure etc. seemed quite all right and have done some strenuous conducting since with no ill-effects.

He refused to see a doctor, except for one who went to the hall and found his blood pressure normal. 'I just pray that it was the effect of the blood pressure reducing pills,' Evelyn wrote to Audrey. 'It seems they *can* cause black-outs and their effect would be triggered off by an empty tummy... Otherwise he is up and down, more down than up. One lovely afternoon and evening here [San Francisco] when he was happy we went on the old cable cars, wandered around Fisherman's Wharf etc. and had a meal in an old Italian restaurant. It was a great joy to see him his old self.'

Just after this 'black-out' John took the orchestra on a tour of the West Coast, as a farewell gesture, for he had decided to give up his conductorship at the end of the 1966–67 season. 'You know,' he wrote to me in November 1966:

I have for some time hinted to you I would be doing less here some time and I have chosen the end of my present 3-year contract to make the break and become Conductor Emeritus. It is really now one of the great American orchs: and accepted as such by all the great cities over here, and I feel now my main job is done. They are rather heart-broken, poor dears. They are very lovable and kind... I promise you *In the South* will be a first priority when I get home.

His main reasons for his decision were that he wanted to make more recordings and to return to opera. It was because of his recording of *Madam Butterfly* with the Rome Opera that offers to him began to arrive from opera houses; and it was after the success of that recording that he seemed to put his unsettled spell behind him and to enter upon a new and greater phase of his career, a phase that was to be a race against time, but was to yield performances of increased depth and intensity as though he was exploring each masterpiece afresh.

house down' and is already going the rounds of the town. It was to the effect that some of them played pizz. rather as if they were scratching their navels, *but without enthusiasm*... I had a word with Ronnie Anderson in Rome. He is doing my *Butterfly* and has been recording something else there. He sounded completely worn out already, saying that recording with Italian orchestras and singers etc. is like trying to superintend an asylum for advanced homicidal maniacs... Have been rather depressed these days but mercifully have had some days to tackle Mahler 3 in earnest – 11 to 12 hours a day I have done.

I have described in an earlier chapter how Barbirolli won the respect and discipline of the Rome Opera Orchestra for the *Butterfly* recording. This was his first large-scale opera recording (a year earlier he had recorded Purcell's *Dido and Aeneas* with Victoria de los Angeles) and he was absorbed in it. 'The most difficult parts in *Butterfly* are the ones nobody notices,' he said; and he spent half an hour rehearsing the little scene in the first act where Goro presents Butterfly's servants to Pinkerton and an equally long time on the scene with Prince Yamadori. The result was a recording of remarkable beauty, a revelation of the genius of Puccini's score and, in my opinion, the most movingly Barbirollian interpretation we possess. Every bar brings him to mind. The scene between Butterfly (Renata Scotto) and Sharpless (Rolando Panerai) in Act II is an outstanding example of the way the whole performance is tended and guided with subtlety and insight. The orchestra began the fortnight bored stiff with *Butterfly*, which they played several nights a week at the Baths of Caracalla, but they later told John he had shown them the music's true stature. At the end of the sessions they gave a party for him – an unprecedented occurrence – to claim him as their friend; and many of them also attended the two concerts in which he conducted the Santa Cecilia Orchestra in the Basilica of Maxentius, Rome's open-air concert-hall. The director of the Rome Opera invited him to return as soon as he could to conduct any opera he liked, with any number of rehearsals.

With his *Butterfly* recording made, with the Crickmore affair settled, and with his twenty-fifth season with the Hallé ahead of him, the world suddenly smiled on John. Not that he could throw off his depressions or his misgivings, not that he

could turn back the clock and repair the damage he had done
to his physique by the demands he made on himself – 'I ask
rather a lot of J.B.,' he had said over thirty years earlier – but
the years brought pleasant anniversaries. While his friend and
solicitor Lionel Biggs had been Lord Mayor of Manchester he
had celebrated in December 1961 the fiftieth anniversary of
his first public appearance by a dinner in the Town Hall. In
April 1967 came the fiftieth anniversary of his first engagement as a cellist by the Royal Philharmonic Society. A particularly nostalgic event was his visit in December 1967 to
Padua, the home of his ancestors, where he spent his birthday.
With Evelyn as soloist (when she had a temperature of over
101°) he conducted the Marcello Oboe Concerto with a small
string orchestra, the Solisti Veneti. There were many
thoughts on that day of Lorenzo Barbirolli. From Naples a
few days later he had another family connection to report
amusingly to Brenda Bracewell: 'A most gorgeous looking
creature came to the artists' room after the concert speaking Venetian and turned out to be a cousin. Bless her.'

In June 1967 he conducted twelve performances of Beethoven's Choral Symphony in Israel just after the Six Days
War. 'The Ninth proved very suitable for their victory mood,'
he wrote,

which is also a *peaceful one*... Studied *Otello* and did all
other work (Smart and co.) in bed, far too hot to go out...
Yesterday [2 July] went to the Old City of Jerusalem and
saw much evidence of heavy fighting but no Holy places
touched. Had the score of the *Matthew* with me as I know
the road well and all rather dull. But extraordinary to go to
all the actual places in the Passion with the music vividly in
my mind... For me the loveliest thing was the Garden of
Gethsemane, far the least spoilt, and peaceful.

He was proud that he, who was not Jewish, had been honoured in 1965 by the naming of an estate in Netua, Upper
Galilee, after him by the Jewish National Fund in recognition of his services to the Israeli Philharmonic Orchestra.
This tribute was later marked by a concert and dinner in
Manchester, at which Vladimir Ashkenazy was the soloist and
the speakers included Edward Heath and Harriet Cohen. He
had been in Berlin when the Six Days War began and there

was no means of communicating with the Israeli Philharmonic management. But the orchestral officials met every plane which reached Israel because they said they knew Barbirolli, unlike some others, would not let them down and be afraid to come. Evelyn and he arrived in time to attend the wedding of Daniel Barenboim and Jacqueline du Pré.

For the past few years the Barbirollis had had a tiny *pied à terre* in London at 45 Huntsworth Mews, just off Gloucester Place. This was a convenient home for him while he made recordings. In the summer of 1967 he re-recorded Vaughan Williams's *London Symphony* with the Hallé and made a rich crop with the New Philharmonia – Mahler's Sixth, Strauss's *Metamorphosen*, Berlioz's *Nuits d'Eté* with Janet Baker, Schoenberg's *Pelléas and Mélisande* and both the Brahms piano concertos with Barenboim. After a public performance of the Schoenberg work he received a heart-warming letter from that expert Schoenbergian Hans Keller, who wrote: 'May I thank you for your stunning performance – no, interpretation – of Pelléas. Incidental things which went wrong didn't matter at all. It was by far the most musical, the most warm-hearted build-up of the work, the clearest articulation of its structures, the biggest line in it I have heard in my life: it all took a second. I was quite shaken – at last one could exclaim, instinctively, "What a piece!" Can there be a greater compliment?'

In September 1967 John returned to Manchester to launch his jubilee season. This, he determined, was to be the climax of his Hallé years. He set aside more time with the orchestra than he had given it since 1963. The programmes were a review of most of his favourite music and in the three weeks between 12 April and 2 May he conducted three great works in which Janet Baker was one of the singers, Mahler's *Das Lied von der Erde*, Verdi's *Requiem* and Bach's *St Matthew Passion*.

For the end of the season, on 16 and 18 May, after days of intensive rehearsals and weeks of preparation, he achieved the ambition of a lifetime by conducting Verdi's *Otello* for the first time. The two magnificent performances in the Free Trade Hall and one in Sheffield were the true culmination of his work in the city. Yet when it was over he was plunged again in depression, as Evelyn, who missed the first performance because she was adjudicating in Prague, well knew he would be when she wrote: 'You do so deserve that all should go well and I pray that it will and that you can have a little *happiness* when it is over, even if only a little, *tesoro*.' The jubilee season demonstrated his indispensability to the Hallé. He was its priceless asset, in Manchester and even more outside it. The very fact that a musician of his stature had been content to live and work outside London for a quarter of a century was of incalculable value to the cultural life and pride of the North of England. In those twenty-five years he had grumbled about conditions, gambled on his own importance by threatening to go but only once had he really meant it, and he had stayed, fighting, working. He liked Manchester, anyway. But he knew he had to make some sort of break and to allow Clive Smart time to try to find a successor. For some time he had pondered the situation and while in Houston in the spring had made his decision. He wrote to me:

Houston, 18 March 1968

Dearest of Friends. Very privately and confidentially I am sending you a copy of a letter just sent to the Hallé chairman. It is for your eyes alone (and of course our beloved Eslyn's too). Evelyn and I have thought much and long over this, and we both feel that after 25 years (and approaching the allotted span) there are some things I must do before it is too late. But you will see I cld not bear to part with my Hallé, but my régime must come to some climactic closure, and yet remain your Papá. I doubt if anyone will ever guess how much of my 25 years with the Hallé they owe to you, beloved friend. Your affection and *understanding*, sensitive beyond words, of what my dedication to music has unceasingly led me to try and do, have often sustained me in moments of doubt which must come to all of us. This is being posted at the same time as the letter as I could not bear for you to hear of it in any other way. Much love to you both. Ever, John.

In his letter to Sir Geoffrey Haworth, the Hallé chairman, John said:

It has been my privilege and honour to lead the Hallé to its pre-eminent place amongst the orchestras of the world. To achieve this position for our orchestra, I have had to reduce considerably, or renounce altogether, many offers from all the greatest orchestras of our time. Now also invitations from the great opera houses to return to my old love – opera – are becoming more and more insistent.

But, he emphasised, it would be 'distressing' to separate completely from 'my beloved orchestra.' He would still be available, if they wished, for important concerts, foreign tours, broadcasts and recordings. Of course they wished it, and they conferred on him the unique title of Conductor Laureate for Life. It was a brilliant choice, the word Laureate with its Elgarian and Tennysonian overtones for this man who was glad that he was born in 1899 because he could call himself a Victorian and because it was the year of the *Enigma Variations*. Thus this twenty-fifth season ended in an atmosphere of intense emotional feeling toward him; as Gerald Larner wrote in the *Guardian*, 'the only man who could replace Barbirolli is another John Barbirolli.' Possibly, too, now that his artistry could be heard with other orchestras, some Mancunians began to realise what he had sacrificed by devoting so much of his life to an orchestra in which – though he was loath to admit it – some of the players were less good than he deserved. A superb Mozart performance with the London Symphony Orchestra in 1969, for instance, showed by comparison that the Hallé was sometimes unable technically to rise to its conductor's heights.

For six weeks in June and July of 1968 John took the Hallé on its most extensive and ambitious overseas tour, to Latin America and the West Indies, where it played in Mexico City, Puebla, Caracas, Port of Spain, Kingston, Lima, Santiago, Buenos Aires, Porto Alegre, Sao Paulo and Rio de Janeiro, a total of twenty-three concerts in forty-two days, all conducted by Barbirolli. Before they left they gave a 'bon voyage' concert in Manchester on 29 May, which was also the evening on which, at Wembley, Manchester United were playing Benfica for the European Cup. John had a transistor radio off-stage and went off between each item to hear the score – he was hoping to be able to announce the result at the end of the concert but was thwarted by extra time. United's manager, Matt Busby, had started his career in the city only a year or two after John. When Busby was made a Freeman of the City John wrote to him: 'When we met we chatted about the similar type of job we have both been given here and the difficulties and problems and eventual success. You have done a magnificent job for your boys and for the prestige of this great city.'

The Latin American tour was arduous and successful. But there was a disturbing concert in Mexico City when John gave several wrong leads to the orchestra and seemed to be so out of touch that the players wondered if he was sober. He himself was puzzled and went to a doctor, who pointed out that the altitude of Mexico City affected people with high blood pressure and with heart trouble. Thereafter oxygen was provided. In his programmes John included Elgar's Second Symphony, Vaughan Williams's *Lark Ascending*, Walton's Violin Concerto and Britten's *Sinfonia da Requiem*. As an encore during the tour he performed Elgar's *Pomp and Circumstance* March No. 1 and used it with particular effect on the evening of the second concert in Caracas, Venezuela, given in the university. He was just about to walk to the rostrum when a crowd of students marched into the hall, shouting slogans and waving banners. The orchestra had no idea whether this might by some chance be an anti-Hallé demonstration and become violent. John was concerned also about the instruments and ordered the orchestra off the platform. Then the students – who were demonstrating against nothing more terrible than bad food in the canteen – made more speeches, sang their national anthem and departed. After the concert the Elgar march was played twice –'no makeweight extra,' said Alan McLean of the British Council, 'but an electrifying and deeply felt rendering.' Later, at a British Council official's house (where John insisted on cooking his own bacon and eggs just as he wanted them) McLean asked why he had selected that particular encore. 'Those fellows had their turn at the beginning,' he replied, 'and I thought now it's our turn to make a bit of noise and show them what we can do.'

For this anniversary-loving conductor 1968 was a vintage year! It marked the 125th anniversary of the New York Philharmonic, and they had invited their old chief back to conduct four concerts (one programme) in April. He chose two symphonies, V.W.'s *London* and Dvořák's D Minor. 'There is never a time when his interpretations are anything but broad, relaxed, musical, natural-sounding,' Schonberg wrote, 'and for this kind of musicianship one would give a year's total product of all the young neo-Toscaninians rolled together. The Philharmonic last night played as though it enjoyed making music, with Sir John ever a genial, warm-hearted and full-blooded leader.' It was to prove to be his New York epitaph, and he would not have wished for a better.

He recorded *Otello* in Walthamstow town hall during August, after King's Lynn, with Gwyneth Jones as a radiant Desdemona, James McCracken as Otello and Dietrich Fischer-Dieskau as Iago. '*Otello* went wonderfully well,' he wrote to me, 'and up to schedule (to everyone's intense surprise), the great choral scenes, trumpets at different distances etc. Cast *really a team* and worked superbly for me. Fischer-Dieskau's Iago I think will be a revelation (but keep this to yourself for now).' Although not as uniformly satisfying as *Butterfly*, this proved to be a splendid recording and, as might have been expected, the orchestral detail was lovingly captured – the horn before Iago's dream, the evil sound of the Credo, the subtleties of the writing in the jealousy scene between Otello and Iago, to give only three examples. Overall, Barbirolli's grasp of the structure, his skilful dovetailing of its transitions and his instinct for tempo, although the reverse of Toscanini's driving energy, are equally valid and artistically secure. He remembered his father's telling him of Verdi's insistence on the right tempo for 'Ora e per sempre addio,' which is marked *allegro assai ritenuto*. EMI, to mark the fortieth anniversary of his first record for them, gave him a hat bought from the branch of Borsalino's where Verdi bought his hats. It was made to Verdi's specifications of crown and brim, and John wore it with pride.

Most of the 1968–69 winter he planned to spend abroad, with brief spells with the Hallé. Almost everywhere he went he conducted Mahler symphonies, which physically and mentally took every ounce of his strength. He had also returned to the two early works by Britten which he had championed in New York, the Violin Concerto and the *Sinfonia da Requiem*. 'It gives me the greatest pleasure,' he wrote to the composer, 'to think I have "fathered" these two magnificent works, but oh! I do wish for another purely orchestral work from you. Is there any hope?' Britten replied: 'One day I really *will* write another orchestral work and I promise to let you know once it has started brewing!' During 1968 Barbirolli acceded to a plea to musicians by Rafael Kubelik not to conduct in countries which supported the Russian invasion of Czechoslovakia. By this splendid gesture he deprived himself of the chance to conduct the recording of *Die Meistersinger* which EMI had hoped to make with the Dresden company in East Germany.

Henceforward John's life was an intensifying battle against increasing ill-health. He would not, could not, rest and he would not give up any engagements, no matter who pleaded with him. Since 1966 his doctor in London had been Michael Linnett, who had prescribed the pills to help his depressions, which medical science now recognised as an illness. Linnett grew to love and understand Barbirolli; moreover, since he had studied to be a pianist and was deeply musical, there was an additional bond. But even his persuasiveness – 'a little *rallentando* in your own programme' – fell on deaf or unwilling ears. John had fought all his life and did not know the meaning of giving up. His physical and moral courage was that of a tiger and it needed to be, for quite apart from his rupture, his sinus trouble and his stones, his periods of suicidal depression grew worse and more frequent. To fight these took all his powers. It was frightening to see him when he was in their grip: he looked grey and his already deep-set eyes seemed to have receded further and had a haunted look. If he was asked 'Can you not think that you will come out of it, that later in the day there will be music and public acclaim?' he replied 'No, when one of these clouds is over me all I can think of is the dark tunnel I'm in, and all I can do is to work and work because if I didn't I might do something irrevocable.' In his copy of Lord Moran's book on Churchill he underlined without comment Churchill's remark: 'Death is the greatest gift God has made to us.'

But in spite of the refuge of hard work the effect of his depressions in his last years was that his life-tempo slowed down notwithstanding drugs. It was no wonder that by taking these 'pills to purge melancholy' he gave uncharitable, malicious people the impression that he was drunk, an impression fostered by the knowledge that he always carried a flask of whisky and a bottle of soda water with him (also by the indistinct speech caused by his stubborn refusal to wear his dentures, and perhaps, too, by his tremulous hands – in fact a hereditary Barbirolli trait: Mémé would say scornfully, when he took her a cup of tea with most of it in the saucer, 'Not *my* side of the family.') He liked his 'little nip,' as he called it – though soda and whisky would often have been a more accurate description of what he drank – and he frequently took it on an empty stomach, because of his lack of appetite for food. In no pejorative sense of the word, however, was he a drinker: he could not have undertaken his work if he had been. The reality of John's condition was far more serious than nips of whisky. Not only were there the drugs for the depressions and the pethidine for the pain from the stones but, worst of all, inexorably creeping up on him was the generalised arterio-sclerosis which affected the left ventricle of the heart, sometimes causing the brain to be starved of blood and eventually causing, first, short 'black-outs,' and later longer spells of unconsciousness when the heart almost stopped. The wonder is not that there were a few inconsistent performances during his last years but that there were so many superb ones. For, miraculously, though he now looked to be ageing rapidly, he seemed to be transformed when he got 'on the box.' Frail and tired before and after the concerts; but while on the rostrum vigorous, absorbed, his usual self. He seemed now to be looking far beyond the notes to try to achieve some ideal which eluded his grasp. He was easier at rehearsals, sometimes letting errors pass upon which he once would have pounced, sometimes less watchful with a soloist, but the results he achieved 'on the night' were more penetrating than they had ever been, as his recordings testify, notably those of Mahler's Fifth Symphony and Verdi's *Requiem*.

In October 1968, his first season as Conductor Laureate, he took the Hallé to play in Switzerland, Austria (Vienna and Salzburg) and Germany. In Venice in November he taught the Britten *Sinfonia da Requiem* and Mahler's Fourth to an orchestra which had played neither work before. In December he went to Rome and thence to Paris to conduct the recently formed Orchestre de Paris and to record some Debussy with them. 'Magnificent orchestra. Great musical and personal treat for me,' he scribbled in his diary; this was yet another example of immediate rapport between him and a body of players. 'Programme includes Nielsen 4 which I am sure the Parisian audience will hate,' he wrote to Audrey, adding: 'After the second day's work with me the whole orchestra asked that, if possible at all, I should become

Münch's* successor. I must say I feel very touched because you know their reputation here.'

In January 1969 he at last accepted an invitation to conduct the Concertgebouw Orchestra of Amsterdam. 'I was a little disappointed at first,' he wrote, 'but by the interval something had clicked and it was a bit like the Kiss of Siegfried (piccolino maestro) having awakened Brünnhilde (the orchestra) from their long sleep!! They played very beautifully last night (especially strings) and so *very musical* and sensitive, tho' by no means all perfect (specially brass).' By the end of the week he found them 'as happy as Berlin to work with.' Thence to Stuttgart: 'The orchestra, which is really the opera house orch:, is first class. Well routined, enthusiastic and musical, which is just as well as we have Mahler 9 (the most difficult of them all) to prepare in 4 rehs:'.

In Hamburg he discussed plans to conduct *Tristan* and *Otello* at the opera. 'Kerstin [Meyer] is a member of the company, reputed one of the best in Germany, and it was lovely to have her at my concert.' That was at the end of February. He returned to England to conduct Verdi's *Requiem* in honour of the centenary of his old friend Henry Wood with four young soloists – Anne Evans, Oriel Sutherland, Stuart Kale and Brian Rayner Cook – flew to Houston to conduct Mahler's Second, had a spell with the Hallé and in Berlin, and on 1 April arrived in Rome for a month to conduct several performances of *Aïda*, his first opera in the opera house for fifteen years. He had been invited to record it but did not approve of the cast EMI had chosen. Now he had Gwyneth Jones as Aïda, Fiorenza Cossotto as Amneris and Gianfranco Cecchele as Radames.

On Easter Sunday he wrote to Audrey from Rome:

God bless my very dear Audrey on this Holy Day... It seems almost incredible that this time last Sunday I was still at Streatham. The flight on Arab Airlines was very good, except that I had two little 'black-outs' during it. May have been altitude, but glad to say they had the oxygen all ready by the time I came round. There were no after-effects and by the time I got home here about 9.30 or so enjoyed a very nice plate of 'tagliatelle'... Already I have done a lot. Al-

* Charles Münch, first conductor of the new orchestra, had recently died.

ways 2 rehs: a day, twice this week *4*. For I like to supervise everything besides music, such as staging etc. Excellent cast, which is beginning to take shape. There is little discipline or sense of style in Italy today, for it appears there are no Maestros with the power of enforcing it. Some of my older colleagues here are so happy for they say I have brought back something which has been missing for so long...

Friday, 11 April

[To A.N.S.]

Today is a free day so have decided to stay in bed and do my work (Walton Partita, new Britten Ov. for Orch: and Chorus)* from there, as I realise I must rest the 'machinery' now whenever I can. The rehearsals have gone very well, a fine company and everyone in the theatre doing their very best for me. It is very interesting and heartening for me to have soloists and orchestra who have sung and played *Aïda* for years saying what a revelation it is for them. I heard from back stage sources that the orchestra, who played at least 16 perfs: in the summer at the Caracalla (old Roman Baths) are saying 'he has performed the feat of making *Aïda* rehs: really an interesting experience.' Dress Reh: is tomorrow night & 1st perf. on Monday. A really historic day for your piccolino, for it will be my first opera performance in Italy.

18 April

[To A.N.S.]

...It has really been a fantastic success. Public, press, orch: and artists, everything. Phrases such as 'seemed a new opera', 'the aristocratic dignity of *Aïda* has been restored to it by Maestro B.'... Lovely, too, that the artists have loved it and collaborated splendidly... E. is out sight-seeing but of course I have no time to go, with this schedule I *must* rest when I can & I really feel the need of it now, tho everyone is amazed at my energy etc.

* Overture, *The Building of the House*, of which John gave several Hallé performances.

His poetic approach to the great work, especially its orchestration, was, as he said, generously appreciated by the Italian critics. The final performance was on 29 April and he proudly told Benjamin Britten: 'I left Rome at 1.30 a.m. and at 3 p.m. was in the Festival Hall rehearsing your Violin Concerto.'

So it went on, recording Mahler's Third Symphony for the BBC with the Hallé in May, after a brief visit to Prague, Sibelius symphony recordings for EMI with the Hallé, then for a week to Puerto Rico to conduct Sibelius and Mahler symphonies at the Festival Casals – and to see Casals himself. At rehearsal and while working on scores John wore his glasses on a long cord so that when he did not need them they hung across his chest. It was while they were in that position that Casals hugged John with such ferocity after a rehearsal that one lens was broken. It remained broken, as a memento of the great cellist's embrace.

On 14 June, in the Queen's Birthday Honours, it was announced that Barbirolli had been made a Companion of Honour. The congratulations poured in, but he left almost at once for Genoa. 'We have now tackled Mahler V (which they have never played) and it is rather a grim business. Have rehearsed all day and at last a glimmer of light has appeared, but am desperately tired. I ache in every inch of my body,' he told Brenda Bracewell. Genoa was not a good orchestra, but he loved the city and some friends there and the little fishing villages. So often sentiment played a part in his choice of engagements – with the Dublin Choir, for example, even Houston and the Hallé. Had he been more exacting he might perhaps have conducted at Bayreuth or the other major festivals; but it was not in his personality to exclude the human touch. More Mahler, the Second, in York Minster in July, and he recorded the Fifth Symphony in Watford Town Hall later that month. Then in August he recorded Verdi's *Requiem*. 'Just a word before I go into the thick of it tomorrow,' he wrote to Audrey on 17 August. 'As usual I feel rather depressed and full of anxieties about the *Requiem*, probably because I know it will be my first and last, *and it is such a wonderful piece.*'

He went in September to conduct the Scottish National Orchestra at the Edinburgh Festival and was pleased to find what a good Orchestra Alexander Gibson had made it. 'The ironic gods,' Neville Cardus wrote, 'have left it to the Scottish National Orchestra in collaboration with Sir John Barbirolli and Claudio Arrau to elevate orchestral concerts at this year's Edinburgh Festival to truly international stature.' They played the Chopin E Minor Concerto, 'conducted,' Cardus continued, 'as I have never before known a Chopin concerto conducted... Sir John transformed the usually colourless and anonymous orchestral scoring of Chopin to an integral part of the concerto and...after Chopin, proceeded to conduct the Fifth Symphony of Sibelius with a greatness and grandeur of span seldom achieved in my experience.' Lunching with Alex Gibson, John complained: 'What have they been up to in Glasgow – they've pulled down all my favourite courting spots.'

Still he would not relax. Berlin, *Heldenleben* with the LSO and, in Manchester on 23 October, Mahler's Second Symphony. During the first movement, at a point where the conductor's control is needed most critically, the playing suddenly faltered and Barbirolli could be seen mechanically beating time and frantically turning the pages of his score as if lost. The moment passed and the performance regained its momentum. He said afterwards that he had no recollection of the incident; it was another minor black-out, caused by his heart, but by some miracle – perhaps through superhuman will-power because he was at a public concert – he did not fall. But, for the first time, an audience sensed that he was not indestructible. Not he himself though; and a day or two later he was introducing his recording of *Otello* in the Lesser Free Trade Hall, 'conducting' it and telling the audience: 'If that bit doesn't melt you, nothing will!' On 31 October, on the eve of a flight to Los Angeles, he was invested by the Queen with the insignia of his CH.

1 November 1969

[To A.N.S.]

Just a last little *parolina* before we depart for Los Angeles. A long flight, but direct. For the first time we shall be flying over the Pole (I don't know which it is, North or South, 'ignoranto' that I am) and tho' it is purely a magnetic point somewhere it is quite a symbol. I remember so vividly when the news of the heroic tragedy of Scott burst on the world. I would be about 11 and was standing outside the Marchmont Street post office when the news men and boys started rushing by with their posters and shouting the news... Thursday arrived here about 4.30 p.m. and spent the rest of the time with my two doctors 'Griff' [Dr Ivor Griffiths] and Linnett. Griff is a very dear old friend, we spent a very interesting and useful hour together and he reported all well, which was v. satisfactory. Linnett gave me a thorough going over and he seemed pleased that at any rate as far as he could read the cardiograph there has been no deterioration since the last time, but handed out the usual warnings. Rather amusingly he made this simile: 'No vehicle was ever constructed to stand such strains, and the blackouts on the plane and platform are indications that the motor misses fire for a moment or two.' Griff put it very sweetly, remarking on my powers of recovery, in broad Welsh, 'Johnny boy, don't take advantage of it'... Had a lovely time with our dear Queen this morning. The equerries etc. told me it wld only take a very short time, and were very surprised that I was with her (alone) for nearly ½ hr. The Order itself is most lovely... She handed it to me reading the inscription on it 'In action faithful and in honour clear'. It was all rather moving, the two of us alone in a charming smallish drawing room...

(The Queen would have appreciated another typically British tribute to him at this time: a racehorse was named after him, and it won – but not on the day he backed it.)

He liked working with the Los Angeles orchestra, some of whom had played with him when he first conducted it thirty years earlier. Five performances of Mahler's Ninth lay ahead of him; and in Los Angeles, too, was one of his former Hallé violinists, Mehli Mehta (father of the conductor Zubin Mehta) who himself had taken up conducting. The following incident was typical of John's friendship with former colleagues:

Los Angeles, 10 November

[To A.N.S.]

A very heavy day yesterday. Reh: a.m. concert at 3, then I attended Mehli's concert *miles away*, with the American youth orch. E. didn't want me to go (I was nearly dead beat) but I am glad I did, for dear Mehli was magnificent. Made those children 12 to 22 play really quite splendidly, and laid it all down to his 'Hallé training with the greatest of them all.' Then there was a supper in his honour and I took care to give him his full due. I was really thrilled and impressed.

They stayed in Los Angeles with Tony Jackson, who had been their lawyer in the Crickmore case, and his wife and family. Even in such happy surroundings John had several bouts of depression and sleepless nights: 'always the case when things turn out so successfully,' he told Brenda. 'Linnett says that this is the result of the great effort it involves.' He went on to Houston to conduct two pairs of concerts (each given three times).

On Thanksgiving Day he wrote to Audrey:

We were invited out of course by a dear family and some of the orchestra but I cldn't face it. I have been so depressed of late, I cldn't bear the idea of being 'all cheerful like' from 6 to 11. I pleaded indisposition, if tiredness and horrid depression can be called that. E. has gone and I know will enjoy it greatly... I have stayed here & studied. We are doing 'Harold [in Italy]' and 'Fantastique' as our Berlioz Celebration Concert... I have a magnificent new life of Disraeli here [by Robert Blake] but can only skim through it, but one glorious quote I must give you, made on his death-bed an' all. Asked if he might like the Queen to visit him he replied 'No, it is better not. She would only ask me to take a message to Albert.' It is one little thing that has lifted the darkness a bit...

The final Berlioz concert was on 2 December. It was his seventieth birthday. In the previous sixteen months he had travelled thousands of miles and conducted 142 concerts. In addition there had been hours of rehearsals and recording sessions. He told the Manchester journalist Arnold Field, an old friend, 'If anyone thinks that just because I'm seventy I'm going to take it easy they're greatly mistaken.' His financial position after the Crickmore affair – let alone his temperament – would not let him 'take it easy.'

22

Adagio

Barbirolli returned to Manchester to conduct *Messiah* and a seventieth birthday concert – Elgar's *Introduction and Allegro*, Vaughan Williams's Sixth and Beethoven's Seventh Symphonies – and for the third time within a year he had to answer a mountain of letters. 'First it was my 25th season,' he told Evelyn, 'then the C.H. and now this birthday. The next lot are the condolences, and they're *your* job!' He had grown attached to Walton Lodge, where there was room for their glass and other treasured possessions to be properly displayed. Not only did he have the old gas-lamp which he had bought from Salford Corporation when they removed it from New Hall Road, but he now had another on the corner of the house. This had been presented to him by Liverpool. 'It welcomes me home like a beacon,' he told the town clerk, 'especially when I come back very late from long distances.' John and Evelyn lived on the first floor and overlooked trees. Brenda Bracewell had an office on the ground floor and would go upstairs while John, in old dressing-gown and slippers, dictated. He was punctilious about letters, and took especial pains with those from people who were seeking advice or help. Some letters set him off on a reminiscence and out would come his best stories, told with actions and accents. On such a day perhaps fewer letters than usual would be answered, but he would say: 'We've had a hard morning, haven't we dear?' Brenda had tape-recorded the various birthday tributes – *Music Magazine*, etc. – which he had missed while in America and arrived in her office one morning to find a letter on her typewriter, written at 6 a.m. and typical of his thoughtfulness and appreciation:

29 December

My very dear Brenda. Last night we were able to listen properly to the tapes and I cannot begin to thank you for this joy you have brought me now and one that I know will grow with the years. My life *as you well know* is so full that I rarely have the opportunity to sit back and begin to realise that perhaps after all I do mean something to all these dear people. Above all I want to thank you with all my heart, first for the lovely and so kindly thought that made you do this for me and *also* for the excellence and professionalism of the whole business! ! Bless you, dear.

He was seriously ill over Christmas with bronchial pneumonia, the culmination of years of chest trouble. For some time he had had no doctor in Manchester but now Neil Campbell Brown went to see him, prescribed new antibiotics and prevailed upon him to give up some recording sessions before he left in early January for Milan, Rome and Turin. There, in Milan, the colossal Mahler Second Symphony, of all works, awaited him, with an orchestra who had never played it before.

Rome, 13 January 1970

[To A.N.S.]

...Managed my two 6 hr-a-day rehs: on arrival in Milan. Tuesday was a free day and stayed in bed in view of the Wed... I had hoped the Tues. rest might help but halfway through the morning reh: on Wed. began to feel v. queer. Finished the Reh: and then, I am afraid, collapsed with a temp. of 101–2 and the old ticker playing a very good imitation of Woolliscroft's solo in Nielsen 5th.* Went straight to bed and lay there shaking like a leaf. It was just a complete relapse. Had all my anti-biotics with me

---

* Eric Woolliscroft, principal percussion player in the Hallé. In Nielsen's Fifth Symphony the side-drummer is requested to improvise and overwhelm the rest of the orchestra.

(Brown, my new doctor, having provided against such a contingency) and calmed down towards eve. Of course I cancelled the rest of the day's work as the only hope of appearing Thurs–Fri my last 3 rehs: and the perf. I must really be tough for I was *there*. One good thing, my mind was absolutely clear and very much master of myself, and E. said no one wld have known anything; but the one thing that worried me a little was my 'povere gambe' [poor legs]. Another 20 bars or so and I think I wld have been 'grounded'... Won't try to write any more now. Am tired and have 4 hrs. Schoenberg [Pelléas] to face tonight. Your loving Johnny.

On he went to Turin, to conduct Mahler's Fifth, and returned to London where Dr Linnett made him cancel a visit to Houston because X-rays showed a pneumonic patch on one lung. After a fortnight in bed he flew to Berlin, where the usual affectionate greeting awaited him, back to England for concerts with the Hallé, and then to Vienna to conduct the Vienna Symphony Orchestra and to Frankfurt on 16 March where he had two concerts (Mahler's First). On Good Friday, 27 March, he gave a dinner-party in Manchester for ten Hallé players who had played over five thousand concerts under his régime.* After Easter he returned to Germany for a performance of Mahler's Second Symphony in Stuttgart on 5 April with Helen Donath and Birgit Finnila as the solo singers. This was to be the last time he conducted a Mahler symphony. The performance was attended by a friend of Wolfgang Stresemann who said: 'It was as if the great old man was trying to shake the gates of eternity from their hinges.'

John went from Stuttgart to Munich to conduct the Bayerischer Rundfunk orchestra in Brahms, Vaughan Williams's Sixth Symphony and Walton's *Partita*. He was thrilled by the virtuosity and musicianship of this orchestra. On Sunday 12 April he had his final concert with them in the morning and went that evening with Evelyn to see *La Bohème* at the opera house, where it was extremely hot. What followed he himself described next day:

* Arthur Percival, Eric Davis, Phyllis Greenhalgh (violins); Sydney Errington, Audrey Napier Smith, Donald Shepherd (violas); Gladys Yates, Joseph Richmond (who was unable to attend the dinner) (cellos); John Sullivan (double bass); Charles Cracknell (bassoon).

Munich, 13 April 1970

[To A.N.S.]

...I was not allowed to go to Hamburg today following a rather severe 'ticker' attack last night. We are playing it down very much in the English Press... I had my last session (Brahms–Haydn) yesterday morning. Exquisitely played for me, came home for a sandwich, feeling almost too tired to eat it, meant to do some letters in the afternoon (gave it up) before going to *Bohème*. Leaving the theatre it was pouring with rain and no taxis to be found, so I suggested walking slowly home (not too far away) when the pain started, and the next thing I remember was a sudden increase of pain, then I must have collapsed, for 2 charming elderly gentlemen had lain me up against the walls of the Opera House while poor E. was getting help. I was taken immediately to hospital, where they took a cardiograph and allowed me home only on condition that their top heart man wld see me in the morning, and in any case there was no hope of my going to Hamburg... Sorry, my love, to give you these occasional shocks, but there we are.

He had been unconscious for about four minutes. On return to Manchester he saw a heart specialist on 18 April who confirmed his 1963 diagnosis of arterio-sclerosis, with sclerosis of the aortic valve of the heart. The pain in Munich was caused by angina pectoris. Electro-cardiographs showed his heart action as surprisingly normal in view of the increasing seriousness of his condition, which also included cardiac asthma. By 22 April he was rehearsing the Hallé for concerts in Leicester and London and preparing for three end-of-season concerts in Manchester at one of which he was to conduct Elgar's *In the South* and Bruckner's Eighth Symphony. Ill as he looked – he had had another minor attack on his return to Walton Lodge – it was impossible to believe that his days were numbered, so life-giving was his music-making. The Elgar performance was incandescent, and rarely had he conducted Bruckner better, with such nobility and structural control. Gerald Larner of the *Guardian* described the Elgar as ' a great performance... It was a superbly calculated interpretation, every tempo change made for a good structural or expressive reason (usually both). The magnificent opening passage and its several reappearances were alive with such energy that their pulse was still felt to throb even throughout the lyrical and scenic episodes which intervene and which, in many performances, prise the construction apart into unwieldy lumps. This is not to say, however, that the quieter sections were lacking in poetic contrast to the hurly-burly rest: Sir John phrased the melodies with his very happy instinct for the Elgar line and the Elgar sound.'

Every Manchester appearance John made now was the signal for a long and affectionate ovation. For these concerts he had an improvised dressing-room at the back of the Free Trade Hall platform to save him from climbing the stairs to his own room. There, at the interval and after the concert, he saw a few friends. He sat in a chair in his overcoat, the sweat showing on his forehead, his hands cold to the touch. He seemed withdrawn, conserving himself for the next big effort, but still talking and looking ahead, still under the spell of the music and deeply moved by it. On 3 May he conducted Sibelius's Sixth Symphony and, at the interval, made a presentation to Arthur Percival, the former sub-leader from his 1943 Hallé, who was retiring. His speech was witty and endearing, spiced with anecdotes, and the family atmosphere of a great Barbirolli–Hallé night was created in all its potency. After the interval he conducted Ravel's *Ma Mère L'Oye* and Stravinsky's *Firebird*, works in which he and the orchestra understood each other perfectly. Another ovation at the end, as he smiled and waved and nodded, tears glistening in his eyes, gave his usual final wave to the side-circle, walked briskly off and was gone from Manchester's music for ever.

Although the specialist had implored him to reduce his engagements he flew to Dublin on 4 May for a heavy programme of rehearsals, with his favourite Our Lady's Choir for performances of *Gerontius* and Verdi's *Requiem* in the choir's silver jubilee year. A writer in *Hibernia* attended the choir rehearsals in the overcrowded Carmel Hall. Barbirolli, she said, 'looked round at the assembled ranks with an eye as lively as an old but wily parrot, bent over the score and said... "Now I want a sound like John McCormack used to make. My late father gave him his first engagement and bless his heart he never forgot it. All eyes on me please. I'm not much to look at, I know, but make the best of it".' He enjoyed working in Dublin, where his friend Father Andrew Griffith was such good company; and on this visit, on 9 May, in a chapel at the Archbishop's House, Fr. Griffith privately performed the religious wedding ceremony for John and Evelyn which their register office marriage in 1939 had of course denied them – in the eyes of the Roman Catholic Church they had not been married, nor, of course, did the Church recognise his first marriage. Another attraction of Ireland was the chance to spend three days in the beautiful eighteenth-century house of Herman Lindars, his friend since they had been at the Royal Academy of Music. Lindars had been an 'infant prodigy' organist, and although his successful professional life was spent in the steel industry he remained active in music as chairman of the Sheffield Philharmonic Society and as a conductor skilled enough to direct the Hallé in Stravinsky's *Rite of Spring*.

This was a difficult time for Evelyn and those near to John. They knew that he would literally work himself to death (and it was right that he should be allowed to die in harness) but with so much planned for him – *Otello* at Covent Garden in May 1971; operas elsewhere; and recordings of Verdi's *Falstaff*, the *St Matthew Passion*, and Puccini's *Manon Lescaut* with Montserrat Caballé and Carlo Bergonzi – it seemed imperative that he should give up some of the less important engagements. The trouble was, he regarded every engagement as important, whether at Solihull or Stuttgart. He hated letting people down. Evelyn and Clive Smart had one tempestuous morning with him at Walton Lodge, talking him into reducing the scope of his next American tour, talking him out of conducting any Sunday concerts in the 1970–71 Manchester season. Eventually he exploded: 'This is all a bloody waste of time. Why don't you two go to Kensal Green and start digging the hole and I'll just wait here till you're ready for me.' A day or two later the possibility of a future Hallé tour was mentioned. John waited till he was alone and rang Clive: 'Now, let's see how I can manage it. I can switch this date here, and fly from...' He was incorrigible, indomitable. He worked happily with Clive, and with the concerts manager, Stuart Robinson, sending them voluminous instructions and comments from Houston, often in light vein as, for example, in 1968 when Clive told him they were engaging a former naval officer, Gerald Temple, as orchestra manager. 'Sounds splendid,' John wrote, 'and only hope he will not prove too magnificent for us. May have to wear my foreign decoration buttons at rehearsals now ! ! !' If in his last years he tended to put off making decisions till the last minute, Clive understood and realised that patience would eventually be rewarded.

On 20 May he repeated *In the South* and the Bruckner Eighth for a Royal Philharmonic Society concert. So his last London concert was for the 'grand old Society' which had helped him in his early career. Six nights later he dined with Neville Cardus at the Garrick Club, in sparkling form, absorbed as a schoolboy in the portraits on the staircase of great actors and actresses of the past. At the end of the evening, while they were preparing to depart, John, to Evelyn's dismay, began slowly to climb the stairs again, leaving her and Neville without a glance. They watched him to the top. He stood, silent and intent, gazing once again at the bronze head of Henry Irving. Two days later, while rehearsing the New Philharmonia at the Bishopsgate Institute, he collapsed on the stairs on the way back to the rostrum and was unconscious for several minutes. He was taken to St Bartholomew's Hospital where the doctors attributed the collapse to a 'Stokes Adams attack,' a condition of cardiac arrest when the heart almost stops beating because the electrical impulses within the heart are interrupted. On returning to Huntsworth Mews he had daily visits from his friend the Cockney greengrocer, Sam Oddy, 'my mate,' as John called him, with whom he liked to talk in the richest Cockney. Sam's company was a source of real pleasure.

It was about this time, when he returned to Manchester by train, that he found himself in the same compartment with Sir William Mansfield Cooper, then the Vice Chancellor of Manchester University, who had been a friend for several years. John, in dark glasses on a blazingly hot day, was working on the score of *Manon Lescaut*. 'He clearly wanted to work but was a trifle suspicious of me,' Sir William records. 'To silence my desire for conversation he thrust into my hands a copy of the *Musical Times* and instructed me to read something about Music and Charles Dickens. I was not interested and I quickly fell asleep. Immediately I was so, J. decided *he* wanted to talk and vigorously woke me – and all the way to Manchester he poured out comment and reminiscence, all of it fascinating.' At Piccadilly Roy Braithwaite – Roy and Mary Braithwaite were the Barbirolli's caretakers at Walton

L

Lodge for whom they had a great affection – met him with their four-year-old daughter Donna, a special favourite, and Brenda. 'Kisses all round and the child clutching his knees,' Mansfield Cooper added. 'So mine was a happy farewell.'

On 8 June John flew to Copenhagen to conduct one concert. 'Still a most attractive city,' he wrote to Brenda, 'but prices! – a city of Robbers. Even the Americans are complaining. I would love you to see it but advise you to defer the pleasure till you can land a very handsome millionaire worthy of you.' A week later he conducted in Zurich, with Geza Anda as soloist in the Brahms B Flat Concerto. At a party afterwards at the Andas', John was the life and soul. He was in equally happy mood a few nights later at Walton Lodge when my wife and I dined with Evelyn and him and he prepared a special dish in our honour, as he always did, and we sat for hours talking music, cricket, politics, nonsense – it was the old John, relaxed, at ease, the best host in the world. On the 28th he went to Rome for two concerts. He and Evelyn again stayed at the British Embassy with their friends Sir Patrick and Lady Hancock. He rehearsed on the morning of 1 July and returned to the Embassy for lunch:

British Embassy, Rome
Saturday, 4 July 1970

[To A.N.S.]

First concert last night in that lovely setting with a huge audience and most fervid ovations. Good concert, too, *Semiramide*, *Firebird* and Beethoven 7th. But a little drama before that, I am afraid. Went to my first rehs: and had a really rapturous reception from the orchestra. Worked very hard and had really detailed reh: of *Firebird* (as we do at home) each line separately in the passages, which was received with much enthusiasm. For 30 years they have scraped through this and it was well due for a clean-up. Second rehs: splendid, the detailed work had told its tale, on other things as well. Went home to lunch (Pat and Beatrice, 'Their Excellencies', have been adorable) and washed etc. and was to meet them for a drink. With us they nearly always use their flat rather than the official rooms but I forgot and went down to the more official drink room. I seemed a long time arriving so E., thinking I might have gone down by mistake, came to look for me and found me, alas, once again unconscious on the floor. This is the 3rd time, poor dear, and of course a shock. The Embassy doctor was called (very efficient), gave me an injection at once and wld not move me for a couple of hours. Later he called in a 'heart man', took a cardiogram etc. and was a little later put to bed. Felt much better and was allowed a little light supper.

Both said I must not do the concert, and then the 'battle' began. I said I must, for another collapse story wld have been the very devil. We compromised and I forsook the first rehs: giving out to the management it was a recurrence of my 'stone' trouble. Anyway the story does not quite end there. After a splendid performance of *Semiramide* went off to take calls and someone had carelessly placed 2 chairs (laid down on the floor). Of course I tripped over and rather damaged myself. Not seriously but of course quite a shock and rather painful. Have a beautiful black eye and a very stiff shoulder and right arm. They sponged my face down and we went on to *Firebird*. At the interval my own doctor arrived, found my pulse, as he put it, 'acting crazy' but I did not feel too bad. Was given another injection and on to Beethoven 7 which E. said was really terrific. Came home, enjoyed a drink and my supper, and this morning the doctor found everything normal. I had been given good dope for the night and was well rested... Well, my love, only hope the next few days pass without any more incident. By the way I tore my trousers badly, but fortunately I did not notice it till after the concert or I would have been rather self-conscious!!

John had been unconscious for thirty-five minutes in the Embassy. He thought later that he might have had a slight black-out when he tripped over the chair. The Italian doctor, who expected him to die, could not believe his ears or his eyes when he heard and saw the vitality and energy of the Beethoven performance.

In his letter to Audrey, John had added a postscript: 'Am still not unduly worried about myself, but that it is tough for those near me I can well see. Ma andiamo avanti e speriamo.'

He was fearless and fatalistic. 'I'm going on till I drop,' he told Martin Milner. 'If I never come out of one of those attacks it's a nice way to go.' He dreaded a disabling stroke. Home in Manchester, he went again to the heart specialist on 14 July. It was a distressing interview. He had to be told that if he did not stop working he would soon die, even might die on the rostrum in front of an audience. 'You cannot beat this thing, Sir John,' he was told, 'it will beat you.' But John, though shaken for the first time, did not want to know, and bluntly refused to give up his work. On the way home all he said to Evelyn was: 'Silly ass. I shan't die on the box.'

Throughout his last months his sense of humour was keener than ever. His Stuttgart reheasals for Mahler's Second were full of jokes – in German, too – and on one occasion he mordantly corrected some sloppy Hallé playing with the remark: 'Come on, it's me that's supposed to be half-dead, not you lot!'

But he did give up a few Hallé concerts so that he could concentrate on Harrogate, where he was conducting Delius's haunting *Appalachia* before he recorded it. He had several performances of his beloved First Symphony of Elgar scheduled, too, and the King's Lynn Festival was not far away. He began recording *Appalachia* in the Kingsway Hall on 15 July. Just before the afternoon three-hour session on the 16th he collapsed unconscious in the body of the hall. This time he was 'out' for only about five minutes and came round to find Audrey Napier Smith and Gerald Temple beside him. Temple called to somebody: 'We've sent for an ambulance.' 'Ambulance,' John snorted, 'I'm going on with the Delius.' A doctor arrived whose every suggestion was brushed aside. Eventually John was carried to his dressing-room and Dr Linnett was telephoned. While they waited, John sat immobile, his eyes brooding, his thoughts unfathomable. He turned his head a fraction to look at Audrey and raised his eyebrows in the most minute shrug of resignation. The telephone rang and he was out of his chair like a shot to speak to Linnett, playing down the whole affair. But he went home to rest, and returned next day to complete *Appalachia* and then to record *Brigg Fair*. On the 18th he returned to Walton Lodge and during that weekend telephoned me to report: '*Appalachia* is in the can, despite a little setback, but don't let's talk of that.' He was not usually the man for an extended phone conversation but this time he wanted to chat about how well Lancashire were doing in the county cricket championship and what a fine captain Jackie Bond was. Could I not go to Ely the next week? – 'We're doing V.W. Tallis and Elgar I, and it's the most wonderful setting. Do come, Mike.'

I drove to Ely on 23 July, a glorious day. The two English masterpieces were performed with supreme beauty. John was happy and we talked animatedly of Vaughan Williams and Elgar as we had done hundreds of times before. He took my score of the symphony and marked some of his favourite passages. He seemed in spirit to be the same John I had known when he came from New York, yet I also knew what the specialist had said. As we walked back to our seats before the symphony, Evelyn said to me: 'I feel sure now that he thinks every performance might be his last.' After the concert he was buoyant and we went with Martin Milner for a few minutes to the Lamb Hotel where he told us a joke about Richter I had not heard before. I waved to him as his car left for King's Lynn and I drove home with my mind full, not of Elgar's music, but of the certainty that I had said farewell to my old friend.

The two King's Lynn Festival concerts on 24 and 25 July were the final concerts of the Hallé season before the orchestra went on holiday. The first was an Elgar programme, with Kerstin Meyer singing the *Sea Pictures*. As John walked with her into St Nicholas's Chapel for rehearsal, he fell. He was not unconscious, but the 'motor' had missed again. He let Martin Milner take the first work but insisted on rehearsing the rest. The whole concert, his last Elgar, was recorded by the BBC. Next evening he ended the programme with a rejuvenating performance of Beethoven's Seventh Symphony.

On Sunday 26 July John and Evelyn drove to Huntsworth Mews. They were to fly to Japan in August where he was to conduct the New Philharmonia in Osaka and Tokyo as part of Expo 70, but first he had three days of rehearsals with them at the Bishopsgate Institute. On Monday he rehearsed Mahler all day, the First Symphony and the two song-cycles *Kindertotenlieder* and *Lieder eines fahrenden Gesellen*, with Janet Baker. 'That last afternoon held no sort of shadow,' Janet wrote to me a few weeks later.

That this was the last one didn't begin to cross my mind. The whole three-hour session was 'special' from the first moment J.B. toddled towards me, and as he kissed me in greeting he said 'Now, here I am. Your favourite Yorkshireman.' We had a joke – I refused to give Lancashire all the credit for him – and some time ago decided that he was, for me at least, an adopted Yorkshireman. He used to laugh at this. Anyway, we rehearsed *Fahrenden Gesellen* and *Kindertotenlieder* as I have never heard them rehearsed. With such meticulous care. At one point he leaned over the desk and whispered 'I've got every single breath you take marked in here!' He kept calling me up to hear his latest story and altogether was on his very best form. At the close of the session he looked out of those bright eyes and said 'Good-bye, sweetie.' I said to Keith on the way home that it had been one of the best rehearsals of my life.

It was the same the next day, too, when he rehearsed Britten's *Sinfonia da Requiem* and ended with Beethoven's *Eroica*. He held a press conference and photographs of him at work were taken. His last words to the orchestra were: 'We'll take the Sibelius [Second Symphony] tomorrow.' He left the hall, chatted to a journalist in the street, shook hands with the caretaker and went home. 'I really was in tremendous form today,' he told Evelyn. He was happy, and wanted kippers for his supper. He read till after midnight and went up to bed. Evelyn was awakened by him later: he thought he had had a nightmare or perhaps a little 'attack' in his sleep. She sat by his bed and he said: 'Anyway I can have a good rest in the morning, there's no rehearsal till 3.' He went back to sleep but Evelyn, apprehensive, lay awake reading. A little later she heard him knock the bell by the side of his bed and heard his laboured breathing. He was unconscious but in the throes of a major heart attack. Whether he died in the little mews house or in the ambulance no one can be sure.

He was cremated on 31 July and his ashes were buried in his parents' grave at Kensal Green, whence Chesterton's Englishmen go to paradise. He had asked that at his funeral three of his recordings should be played: of Evelyn playing the slow movement of the Marcello concerto, of Elgar's *Nimrod* and of Janet Baker singing Mahler's *Ich bin der Welt abhanden gekommen* with the Hallé. This wish was carried out, at the crematorium and at the memorial services in Westminster and Manchester Cathedrals in September. At both services music-loving friends of John officiated – Father Andrew Griffith at Westminster and Dean Alfred Jowett in Manchester.

In Manchester, on 27 September, the Hallé performed *The Dream of Gerontius* in his memory, conducted by his associate, Maurice Handford. At the end, where the Angel sings

> *Farewell but not for ever! brother dear,*
> *Be brave and patient on thy bed of sorrow;*
> *Swiftly shall pass thy night of trial here*
> *And I will come and wake thee on the morrow*

Janet Baker's voice broke and she stood, head bowed, the tears streaming down her cheeks, while the orchestra continued until she whispered her last words. He would have been so touched.

23
John

The power to produce great art is often, though by no means always, associated with a temperamental unhappiness so great that, but for the joy which the artist derives from his work, he would be driven to suicide. We cannot, therefore, maintain that even the greatest work may make a man happy, we can only maintain that it must make him less unhappy.

Barbirolli knew the truth of these words of Bertrand Russell. The crest of every wave was followed by a deep trough and by the onset of a 'depression.' He was not self-pitying about these dark moods, which he knew had also afflicted Puccini and many other men. When he read Lord Moran's book on Churchill in 1968, he was fascinated to learn that Sir Winston had suffered from the same 'black dog,' as the great man named it. 'Not putting myself in his class,' John wrote, 'it does seem inevitable that anyone who is completely dedicated to a task which is almost unrealisable must suffer for it.' Here he was thinking, perhaps, not only of his medically explicable depressions but of his insecurity in the face of great masterpieces, his misgivings when visiting a great foreign orchestra. Maybe this insecurity was partially the result of the high standard demanded of him in his childhood by his loving but hypercritical mother, but it certainly derived from an innate humility and an almost overpowering conscientiousness. His artistic ideals were lofty; and solely on the practitioner's level he knew that it is much harder to stay at the top than to reach it. From the age of seven or eight, he dedicated his life to the art and practice of music, a life that as it unfolded seemed to him sometimes like a dream but, as he said in 1961 after his public career had lasted fifty years, 'in terms of sheer hard unrelenting application towards achievement has sometimes seemed a nightmare.' What effect his depressions had on his conducting it would be impossible to discover with any accuracy. It was probably very small, although perhaps they gave him extra insight into the psychological complexities of Mahler, Elgar and Puccini. I detect – and this is an entirely personal view – a hint of what it was like to peer into the abyss of gloom in his recording of Elgar's tragic little masterpiece *Sospiri*.

People who knew only the public Barbirolli might easily have not suspected what he was really like. Some were embarrassed by his boasting, unselfconscious – and usually truthful – though it was. 'They'd never heard Brahms properly till I went there.' 'I can make any orchestra in the world sound as I want it to in two rehearsals.' Others, Cardus for example, found it endearing and naïve. It was psychological over-compensation for the doubts that tortured him. One thing it was not was any form of complex caused by his lack of inches. He was not in the least concerned about being small – and both his marriages were to tall women.

He had his share of little vanities and of conductors' occupational egocentricities. He did not like to admit he was wrong. Not many do. He was partial to flattery, as distinct from praise, but in the cold light of morning he well knew one from the other. To mention his faults is only to emphasise that he was intensely human.

He was a man of principle. If he gave his word it could be relied upon, which was why he would not commit himself to conduct a work unless he knew he could fulfil his obligation to the composer in full, in letter and spirit. In a profession where it is rife, he had no time for double-dealing. Loyalty was the virtue he perhaps valued above all others: he expected it and he gave it. He never forgot his friends; and some of them remained white in his eyes long after they should have been black, or at least a shade of grey. It took much for him to realise that someone was no longer worthy of his friendship, and when eventually he convinced himself he was savagely hurt. If he thought musicians were working hard and were loyal, he would forgive much in their playing, even when they perhaps were past their best. He provided an outstanding example of loyalty to an admired colleague when Hugo Rignold's contract as conductor of the Liverpool Philharmonic Orchestra was not renewed in 1950. John told the society's officials that they were making a mistake and demonstrated his belief in Rignold by handing over the Hallé to him for a Liverpool concert (31 December 1950) which he himself was unable to conduct. Illustrious though John's career was, it might have been still more illustrious had he been ruthless and cut himself loose from those to whom he felt bound by shared experience. But had he done so he would have been that much less himself and that much less the artist.

Orchestral players, especially principals of sections, who appreciated his practical knowledge, rejoiced above all in his sensitivity to the fine artistry of other musicians. A particularly beautiful piece of playing by one of the orchestra during a performance would be rewarded by a smile or a nod. He identified himself with his players and delighted to give dinners or parties for them on certain anniversaries and occasions, as when they received the Hallé gold medal. His closeness to them is well illustrated by a note he sent in 1970 to Sydney Errington, his principal viola in the Hallé, who had been with him since 1943. Errington had retired through ill-health while John was away, but John had set his heart on Sydney playing the beautiful solo viola passage in Elgar's *In the South*: 'I cannot bear to think of you not playing that, because as I studied it, I could see your fingerings, your vibrato and your bowing arm.'

This sensitivity was combined with a severe insistence on standards. He deplored any tendency to lower standards among the young. If he was involved in adjudication for any award, particularly for cellists, such as the RAM Piatti Prize or the Suggia Gift, he strongly opposed making an award if nobody really merited one. Not everyone could be a great soloist, he said, but such prizes should go only to someone capable of becoming a member of a first-rate quartet or the principal of an orchestral cello section.

I met him first when he came to Manchester during the war. More than any other conductor, he made music more important, more moving, for me. Even when my head did not wholly agree with his interpretations, I knew that if I had been a conductor my heart would have led me to the same approach. The tragedy of his life, as far as I am concerned, was that he did not conduct more Wagner in the theatre. What a *Ring* and what a *Parsifal* he would have given us.

One evening in the 1950s my wife and I went to his flat. When we arrived it was clear that some family crisis was raging and John, as male head of the family, was deeply concerned. He spoke on the telephone to one of the family in London and, in emphatic and voluble Italian, he was laying down the law. In the midst of this outpouring, and as though standing outside himself, he put his hand over the mouth-piece, gave us his most conspiratorial glance and said: 'Now you know why I can conduct Verdi.' He then returned to the fray. For those who shared his almost physical identification with music he was an inspiration from the very first. He made you feel, if you were in sympathy with him, that each phrase of a work was like a living organism. That was his magic.

Our friendship never wavered, even though I was a professional critic in Manchester for the last twenty years of his life. Here I can do no better than quote from an article in the *Yorkshire Post* by its music critic, Ernest Bradbury, written shortly after John's death:

Critics and artists do not easily mix; and a critic makes friends with a performer at his own risk – one bad notice and there's a beautiful friendship in ruins. But Barbirolli was friendly with three critics, Sir Neville Cardus, Michael Kennedy and myself: three writers not averse to giving John a 'cool' notice now and again (for no conductor, as the old adage might have said, 'is at all hours wise'), but three who, by nature and temperament, were on his wave-length. Really loving music – that I think was the key to our understanding; that we could all make mistakes, but music was greater, and more important, than any of us.

Ernest Bradbury himself was once the object of one of John's most endearing gestures. It was at Cheltenham in 1956 when John was in acute abdominal pain. After the morning rehearsal we were with him in his room and Ernest looked in, too. John was insisting that he must be well enough to play his cello at King's Lynn, whereupon Ernest remarked that he had never heard him as a solo cellist. 'Well, you shall now,'

John said, and, ill as he was, played a movement from a Bach suite to his audience of three.

He was at his best at home as host to one or two friends. He would prepare a special dish with all the concentration he brought to Mahler. 'I went to the market myself at six a.m. to get this fish,' he would tell you, and you could imagine how much he had enjoyed himself there, probably haggling over the price. He would begin some dishes before the concert, sometimes even in the morning. Many a soloist invited back to dinner has been told at rehearsal: 'I've already started cooking the supper!' He would take his creation, when ready, to each guest in turn, standing by them, urging them to eat while it was hot, and waiting for some reaction. Pleased, he would attend to the next, and eventually bring something quite different and much less exotic for himself.

Then the talk would begin in earnest: we ate at Walton Lodge in the kitchen or in the little dining-room adjoining it, and he liked to stay at the table after the meal, believing the atmosphere was broken if you moved into another room, though he himself was up and down like a jack-in-the-box, fetching objects to be admired, or a book in which to track down a favourite passage, or a score in which to point to a great moment. His conversation was brilliant, wide-ranging, but not in any oracular, self-conscious way: he was just full of interest in so many subjects. To emphasise a point, he would thump the table with his hand until the pots jumped up and down. His laughter was a chuckle. If he was discussing some mutually admired passage in music, he would sing it in an unmusical but effective voice and his body throbbed as if he was on the rostrum. At such times, his face alive with changing expressions, his eyes alert and shining or tear-filled, he was the John one loved – not exalted by his musical achievement, not belittled by petty irritation, not fussed or domineering or boastful, but kindly, witty, simple-hearted, a unique and irreplaceable friend.

The most English thing about him was his sense of humour. His private woes he successfully concealed or forgot in company. There were usually smiles or laughs wherever he went; he invariably had a good new story to tell. His outlook was sunny, if sardonic, not morose, although he viewed the state of the world and the ugliness of much modern art with scepticism and dislike. In the music of Delius and Elgar he

found escape from that kind of reality. He relished amusing
extracts from the biographies that were his main literary diet.
'Glad you enjoyed my Lytton Strachey tit-bits,' he wrote in
1968, 'and apparently not a great deal of "tit" about it as far as
he was concerned.' He read little fiction, except Agatha
Christie, and told me once that the only Hardy he could read
was *Under the Greenwood Tree* – 'the rest are so bloody
miserable.' He missed little from other people's conversation,
even when working. 'I hear what I want to hear, things that
interest me catch my ear. I let the rest go.' This was a knack
he learned as a child, while studying among a large family
living at close quarters.

His place is with the legendary conductors. In England he
was perhaps taken for granted, especially in Manchester. The
esteem in which he was held abroad was sometimes forgotten,
and it has been an aim of this book to remind readers of the
extent of his worldwide reputation. Nevertheless what he did
for music in the North of England cannot be exaggerated. No
future conductor of the Hallé, however gifted, is likely to
excel the devotion which Barbirolli lavished on the orchestra
in twenty-five years and especially in his first fifteen-year
tenure. It should never be forgotten, on a purely material
level, that he conducted the Hallé for fees well below those he
commanded elsewhere and was content provided that the
money thereby saved was spent on foreign tours or bettering
the orchestra. A remarkable tribute to his influence was paid
by Carlo Maria Giulini, who never met him, in a letter after
he had spent ten days with the Hallé as a guest conductor in
1968:

> I have had the opportunity to discover another side of your
> outstanding talent – that of teacher, of leader. Everything
> and everyone in the Hallé bears your stamp. Rarely have I
> had occasion to work in an atmosphere where the levels of
> courtesy, professionalism and humanity have reached such
> heights. This is due to you – to your constant intense and
> inspiring work of years and years; and it has been wonder-
> ful for me to see this all for myself.

He belonged to the romantic tradition, but, like Wilhelm
Furtwängler, he was a law unto himself. He was the Barbirolli
tradition, all of it, the best and the worst. As an artist he was a

mixture, with inconsistencies and heights and depths. No conductor can be all things to all men or to all composers. But he never sanctioned a shoddy performance, was never untrue to himself. Music mattered to him more than anything in life – in the end more than life itself.

Shortly before he died, he set out one morning on a long car journey. He was tired and ill and had had a sleepless night. He was wrapped in a thick coat and wore his 'Verdi' hat. He settled into his seat, took a score from his briefcase and began to mark it. No one spoke, hoping that he might drop off to sleep for a little while. His companion looked out of the window and kept very still, then, after a few minutes, glanced at him. He was in tears; and pointing to a little phrase in the viola part he said: 'Isn't that beautiful?...'

26 September 1970–24 March 1971

Sir John Barbirolli's
Honours

Companion of Honour
Knight Bachelor
Fellow, Royal Academy of Music
Freeman, City of Manchester
Conductor Laureate, Hallé Orchestra
Commendatore, Order of Merit, Italian Republic
Grand Star and Collar of Commander 1st Class of White
    Rose of Finland
Officer, Order of Merit, French Republic
Officer, Arts and Letters, French Republic
Honorary Doctorates of the Universities of Manchester, Dub-
    lin (Trinity College), Sheffield, London, Leicester, Keele
Fellow, Trinity College of Music
Honorary Member, Royal Manchester College of Music
Honorary Academician, Accademia Nazionale di Santa Cecilia
Honorary Freeman, Worshipful Company of Musicians
Honorary Liveryman, Worshipful Company of Dyers
Freeman of the Borough of King's Lynn
Freeman of Houston, Texas
Estate in Netua, Upper Galilee, named after Sir John
Awarded Gold Medal of the Royal Philharmonic Society
    Gold Medal of the Hallé Concerts Society
    The Bruckner Medal
    The Mahler Medal

I should like to express my grateful thanks to the following, for without their ever-ready assistance the compilation of this discography would have been impossible:

Anthony Pollard (Editor of *The Gramophone*); Michael Kennedy; Mrs G. Platford, George Port, John Watson (all of EMI Ltd); Miss Jane Friedmann (CBS Records: Columbia Broadcasting System, Inc.); Lady Barbirolli; Ian Cosens; Charles Haynes (Concert Hall Record Club); Eric Hughes (British Institute of Recorded Sound); Hallé Concerts Society; Miss M. Scott Mampe (Mercury Record Corp.).

Since this discography was compiled, details of further recordings have come to light. These are listed in chronological order at the end of Part One (pages 397).

August 1971   MALCOLM WALKER

❧ *Abbreviations*

Recording companies

A	Angel Records (USA)
AC	CBS Records (USA)
AGS	American Gramophone Society (USA)
BIRS	British Institute of Recorded Sound
Cap	Capitol (USA)
CBS	CBS Records (UK)
CH	Concert Hall (UK)
Col	Columbia (UK)
E	Edison Bell (UK)
El	Electron (Edison Bell, UK)
Elect	Electrecord (Rumania)
F	Fontana (UK)
GH	Electrola (Germany)
H	His Master's Voice (UK)
HSP	EMI Special Pressing (UK)
IPL	International Piano Library (USA)
Mer	Mercury Records (USA)
MFP	Music for Pleasure (UK)
NGS	National Gramophonic Society (UK)
P	Pye Records (UK)
Pea	Pearl Records (UK)
R	Rococo (Canada)
RCA	RCA (UK)
RD	Reader's Digest (UK and USA)
Sera	Seraphim (Angel Records, USA)
Sp H	Spanish HMV
Sup	Supraphon (Czechoslovakia)
V	Victor (USA)
Van	Vanguard (USA)
VdP	Italian HMV
Voc	Vocalion (UK)
WRC	World Record Club (UK)

Type of disc

m	denotes mono 33⅓ rpm record
MD	denotes mono disc
MT	denotes mono tape
s	denotes stereo 7-inch 45 rpm record
SD	denotes stereo disc
ST	denotes stereo tape
*	denotes automatic 78 rpm coupling
†	denotes export number only
bold number	denotes stereo 33⅓ rpm record

italic number denotes mono 7-inch 45 rpm record

bold italic number denotes stereo 7-inch 45 rpm record

Key signatures in capitals denote major keys, those in lower case minor

Orchestras, instruments and voices

Augusteo	now known as the Orchestra of the Accademia di Santa Cecilia, Rome
bar	baritone
contr	contralto
ECO	English Chamber Orchestra
fl	flute
HO	Hallé Orchestra
JBCO	John Barbirolli's Chamber Orchestra
LPO	London Philharmonic Orchestra
LSO	London Symphony Orchestra
m-sop	mezzo-soprano
NGSCO	National Gramophonic Society Chamber Orchestra
NPO	New Philharmonia Orchestra
ob	oboe
OdP	L'Orchestre de Paris
orch	orchestra
pf(s)	piano(s)
Philh	Philharmonia Orchestra
PO	Philharmonic Orchestra
PSONY	Philharmonic-Symphony Orchestra of New York (now called New York Philharmonic Orchestra)
ROH CG	Royal Opera Orchestra, Covent Garden
RPO	Royal Philharmonic Orchestra
SO	Symphony Orchestra
SoL	Sinfonia of London
sop	soprano
ten	tenor
vlc	cello
vla	viola
vln(s)	violin(s)
VPO	Vienna Philharmonic Orchestra

PART ONE
Commercial disc recordings

Acoustic recordings

1911 *October*

VAN BIENE. Broken Melody
John Barbirolli (vlc), Rosa   E VF1131
Barbirolli (pf)   E Winner 2148
WAGNER (arr. ?). Tannhäuser.
O Star of Eve
John Barbirolli (vlc), Rosa   E VF1131
Barbirolli (pf)   Pea m GEM105
THOMÉ. Simple Aveu
John Barbirolli (vlc), Rosa   E VF1132
Barbirolli (pf)   Pea m GEM105
PERGOLESI (attributed). Tre Giorni
John Barbirolli (vlc), Rosa   E VF1132
Barbirolli (pf)

1925 *June*

MOZART. String Quartet in d,
K421; String Quartet in E flat,
K428 – Menuet
Kutcher String Quartet (Samuel   Voc K05190–3
Kutcher and Max Salpeter, vlns;
Raymond Jeremy, vla; John
Barbirolli, vlc)

GIBBONS. Fantasias nos 3, 9, 6, 8
  Music Society String Quartet   NGS NGS29–30
    (André Mangeot, Boris
    Pecker, vlns; Henry Berley,
    vla; John Barbirolli, vlc)
GOOSSENS. By the tarn;   NGS NGS28
    Jack o' Lantern   NGS NGS30
  Music Society String Quartet

December
McEWEN. Peat Reek
  Music Society String Quartet   NGS NGS52
VAUGHAN WILLIAMS. Phantasy
    Quintet for Strings
  Music Society String   NGS NGS54–55
    Quartet with Jean Pougnet (vla)

1926   *February*
PURCELL (ed. Mangeot and
    Warlock). Fantasia Upon One
    Note
  Music Society String Quartet   NGS NGS53
PURCELL (ed. Mangeot and
    Warlock). Fantasia in c
  Music Society String Quartet   NGS NGS51
PURCELL (ed. Mangeot and
    Warlock). Fantasia in Three
    Parts
  André Mangeot (vln); Henry   NGS NGS52
    Berley (vla), John Barbirolli
    (vlc)

Electrical recordings
1927   *January*
CORELLI (ed. Frank Bridge).
    Concerto Grosso in g,
    op. 6/8, 'Christmas'   NGS NGS69–70
  NGSCO   NGS NGS69A & B
DEBUSSY. Danse sacrée; Danse
    profane
  Ethel Bartlett (pf), NGSCO   NGS NGS70–1

DELIUS. Summer Night on the
    River
    NGSCO   NGS NGS72
WARLOCK. Serenade for Delius's
    60th Birthday
    NGSCO   NGS NGS75

October
ELGAR. Introduction and Allegro
    for Strings, op. 47
    NGSCO   NGS NGS94–5
PURCELL (arr. Barbirolli). 'Suite for
    Strings'
    NGSCO   NGS NGS96–7
MARCELLO (arr. Barbirolli).
    Allegretto
    NGSCO   NGS NGS97

November
HAYDN. Symphony no. 104 in D,
    'London'
    NGSCO   NGS NGS98–101
MOZART. Cassation no. 2 in C,
    K99 – Andante
    NGSCO   NGS NGS101

December
HUMPERDINCK. Hansel and Gretel –
    Overture
    SO   El X520
WAGNER. The Flying Dutchman –
    Overture[1]
WAGNER. The Mastersingers – Prelude
    to Act 3
    SO   El X521–2
MASCAGNI. Cavalleria Rusticana –
    Santuzza's aria (in English)
    Lilian Stiles-Allen (sop), orch
PUCCINI. Madame Butterfly – Love
    duet (finale)
    Lilian Stiles-Allen (sop), Dan Jones
    (ten), orch   El X523

[1] extract from this recording on Argo **ZPR122-3**.

1928   *January 28 and July 13*
MOZART. Serenade no. 13 in G,
   K525, 'Eine kleine
   Nachtmusik'
   JBCO   H C1655–6
                                    V 9789–90
                                    V 36283–4

February 20
VERDI. Don Carlos – O don fatale;   H DB1158
   Il Trovatore – Condotta ell'era,   H unissued
   Stride la vampa
   Maartje Offers (contr), orch

March 1
HAYDN. Symphony no.
   104 in D, 'London'
   JBCO   H C1608–10/C7228–30*
                                  V 35981–3

March 28
CASALS. Sardana
   London School of
     Cellos   Sp H AF207
                              H m ALP2641(SLS796)

MOZART (arr. Barbirolli). Die Zauberflöte, K620 –
   Possenti numi
   London School of Cellos   Sp H AF207

May 8
BEETHOVEN. Fidelio –
   Abscheulicher! . . . Komm,
   Hoffnung
   Frida Leider (sop), orch   H D1497
                                   V 7118
                                H m COLH132

May 11
GLUCK. Armide – Ah! si la
   liberté
   Frida Leider (sop), orch   H D1547
                                AGS AGSB26
                                H m COLH132

MOZART. Don Giovanni, K527 –
Don Ottavio! son morta . . .
Or sai chi l'onore
Frida Leider (sop), orch   H D1547
                                   AGS AGSB26
                                   V m LCT6701
                                   H m CSLP503
                                   H m COLH132

WAGNER. Wesendonk Lieder –
Träume
Frida Leider (sop), orch   H DB1553
                                   V 7708

May
VERDI. Otello – Dio! mio potevi
scagliar; Niun mi tema
Renato Zanelli (ten), orch   H DB1173[1]
GLUCK. Orfeo ed Eurydice – Che farò
senza Eurydice
HANDEL. Serse – Ombra mai fù
Maria Olczewska (m-sop), orch   H D1490
                                   V 7115

June 19
MOZART. Don Giovanni, K527 –
Madamina!
Feodor Chaliapin (bass), orch   H DA994
                                   V 1393

July 12–13
HAYDN. Cello Concerto in D
Guilhermina Suggia   H DB1186–8 (not used)
(vlc), SO   H D1518–20

July 13
PURCELL. The Married Beau –
Hornpipe
JBCO   H C1656
                                   V 9790
                                   V 36284
                       H m ALP2641(SLS796)

---

[1] This coupling number was also used for Zanelli's 1929 Milan/Sabajno recording. This 1928 version uses the matrix numbers CR2094/5.

August 24

WEBER. Oberon – Ocean! thou
 mighty monster
 Florence Austral (sop),   H D1504
 ROH CG   H m COLH147

August 27

BRAHMS. German Requiem –
 Ye that now are sorrowful
 Florence Austral (sop),   H DB1540
 ROH CG Chorus and   H m COLH147
 Orch

SULLIVAN. The Golden Legend
 – The night is calm
 Florence Austral (sop),   H D1506
 ROH CG Chorus and Orch
WAGNER. The Flying Dutchman
 – Senta's Ballad
 Florence Austral (sop),   H D1517
 ROH CG Chorus and Orch   V 7117
                                  V m LCT6701
                                  H m CSLP503
WAGNER. The Flying Dutchman –
 Spinning Chorus
 Nellie Walker (contr), ROH CG   H D1517
 Chorus and Orch   V 7117

August 28

ROSSINI. Stabat Mater –
 Inflammatus
 Florence Austral (sop),   H D1506
 ROH CG Chorus and   H m COLH147
 Orch

September

ELGAR. Caractacus – Leap,
 leap to light
 Peter Dawson (bass-bar), orch   H C1988
ELGAR. Caractacus – O my
 warriors!
 Peter Dawson (bass-bar), orch   H C1579
                                  H m HQM1127

November 28
VERDI. La Forza del Destino – Son
    giunta! . . . Madre, pietosa (a)
                                            H DB1217
VERDI. La Forza del Destino – Pace,
    pace, mio Dio
    Dusolina Giannini (sop), orch and   H DB1228
    in (a) chorus

December
MOZART. Die Entführung aus dem
    Serail, K384 – Overture
    JBCO   H unissued
                                            (Cc12485–86)
PUCCINI. La Bohème – Che gelida manina
MASCAGNI. Cavalleria Rusticana –
    Mamma, quel vino è generoso
    Joseph Hislop (ten), orch   H DB1230

1929   *January 18*
HANDEL. Messiah – Comfort ye,
    my people . . . Ev'ry valley
    Walter Widdop (ten), orch   H D1620
                                            H m HQM1164
HANDEL. Messiah – Thou shalt
    break them
HANDEL. Judas Maccabeus –
    Sound an alarm
    Walter Widdop (ten), orch   H D1886
                                            H m HQM1164
                                            R m 5250

January 28
ELGAR. Introduction and Allegro for
    Strings, op. 47
    JBCO   H C1694–5

April 15
BACH. St Matthew Passion –
    Du lieber Heiland
    Maartje Offers (contr), orch   H DB1761

ELGAR. Sea Pictures, op. 37 – Where
    corals lie
    Maartje Offers (contr), orch   H DB1761

April 24
VERDI. Un ballo in Maschera –
Eri tu che macchiavi
Giovanni Inghilleri (bar), orch   H D1823

May 15
MESSAGER. Fortunio – The Grey
House
RACHMANINOV. To the children,
op. 26/7
Joseph Hislop (ten), orch   H B3154
TRADITIONAL (arr. Gibilaro).
Turn ye to me
TRADITIONAL (arr. Moffat). O' a' the
airts the wind can blow
Joseph Hislop (ten), orch   H B3155

June 7
DELIUS. A Song before Sunrise
New SO   H D1697
                                                   V 4732

June 21–22
BIZET. Carmen – Habañera; Mon
coeur s'ouvre
Irene Minghini-Cattaneo (m-sop), orch

                                                   H DB1303

SAINT-SAENS. Samson et Dalila –
O aprile foriero; Amor! I miei sini
Irene Minghini-Cattaneo (m-sop), orch

                                                   H DB1332

June 19
PUCCINI. Tosca – Tre sbirri, una
carozza; La povera mia cena
Giovanni Inghilleri (bar), Octave   H D1701
Dua (ten); ROH CG Chorus and
Orch
ROSSINI. Il Barbiere di Siviglia – Largo
al factotum
Giovanni Inghilleri (bar), ROH CG   H D1698

June 22
VERDI. Otello – Inaffia l' ingola
  Giovanni Inghilleri (bar), Octave   H D1698
  Dua (ten), Luigi Cilla (ten),
  ROH CG Chorus and Orch

June
ROSSE. The Merchant of Venice –
  Suite
  JBCO   H C1731–2
  Doge's March only   H m ALP2641(SLS796)

July 1
BACH. Sonata no. 1 in G
  for Cello and Piano,
  BWV1029   NGS NGS133–4
TRADITIONAL (arr.
  Bartlett). Three
  Irish Melodies
  (Golden Slumbers;
  Ancient Lullaby;
  My Love's An
  Arbutus)
  John Barbirolli (vlc),   NGS NGS132
  Ethel Bartlett (pf)
  Golden Slumbers only   H m ALP2641(SLS796)

July 3
WAGNER. Lohengrin's Narrative (in
  English); The Mastersingers –
  Prize Song
  Joseph Hislop (ten), orch   H DB1351

July 10
PUCCINI. Tosca – Recondita armonia;
  E lucevan le stelle
  Joseph Hislop (ten), orch   H DA1062
LEONCAVALLO. I Pagliacci – Recitar! . . .
  Vesti la giubba; No!
  Pagliaccio non son
  Joseph Hislop (ten), orch   H DA1062

BIZET. Carmen – Flower Song
  Joseph Hislop (ten), orch   H unpublished
                                       (CR2445)
December 4
VERDI. Falstaff – Your honour!
  ruffians!
  Arthur Fear (bar), orch   H C1822
WAGNER. The Mastersingers – Elders'
  scent grows
  Arthur Fear (bar), orch   H C2072

December 10
LUIGINI. Ballet Russe
  ROH CG   H C1948–9

December 11
GRIEG. Symphonic Dance no. 4, op. 64
  ROH CG   H C1928
WALLACE. Maritana – Overture
  ROH CG   H C1927

December 18
VERDI. Otello – Otello's monologue;
  Otello's death (in German)
  Lauritz Melchior (ten), New SO   H D2037

December 19–20
TCHAIKOVSKY. Violin Concerto in D,
  op. 35
  Mischa Elman (vln),   H DB1405–8/DB7057–60*
  LSO   V 8186–9/M79

1930   *April 11*
GLAZUNOV. The Seasons, op. 67 –
  Autumn: Bacchanale
  Les Ruses d'Amour – Ballabile
  ROH CG   H C1930
                                     V 11442
May 29
WAGNER. Rienzi – Allmächt'ger Vater
  Tannhäuser – Dir Töne Lob!
  Lauritz Melchior (ten), LSO   H D2057
                                     V 7656

LEONCAVALLO. I Pagliacci – Recitar! . . .
  Vesti la giubba (in German)
MEYERBEER. L'Africaine – Au
  paradis (in German)
  Lauritz Melchior (ten), LSO   GH EJ582

July
MUSSORGSKY. Song of the Flea
  (in English)
  Peter Dawson (bass-bar), orch   H C1579
            MFP m MFP1144

September 23
GOUNOD. Faust – Selection
  ROH CG   H C2055
BIZET (arr. Gibilaro). Carmen –
  'Potpourri'
  ROH CG   H C2056

December
JOHANN STRAUSS II. Die Fledermaus,
  op. 362 – Finale to Act II
  (Brother dear and sister dear . . .
  Oh! what a feast)
  Members of the British National   H C2107
  Opera Company, LSO

1931   *January 8–9*
CHOPIN. Piano Concerto
  no. 2 in f, Op. 21
  Artur Rubinstein (pf),   H DB1494–7/DB7074–7*
  LSO   V 7404–7/M110

January 9
MOZART. Piano Concerto
  no. 23 in A, K488
  Artur Rubinstein (pf),   H DB1491–3/DB7217–9*
  LSO   V 7609–11/M147

May 11
HAYDN. Die Jahreszeiten – Schon
  eilet froh der Ackersmann
MENDELSSOHN. Elijah–Herr Gott
  Abrahams

Friedrich Schorr (bass-bar),   H DB1564
   LSO   H m HQM1243
                             R m 5260
LOEWE. Fridericus Rex
HILL. Herz am Rhein
   Friedrich Schorr (bass-bar), orch   H DA1224

May 16
WAGNER. Die Meistersinger
   von Nürnberg –
   Selig, wie die Sonne
   Elisabeth Schumann   H D2002
   (sop), Gladys Parr   V 7682
   (contr), Lauritz   V m LCT1003/*WCT4*
   Melchior (ten), Ben   H m COLH137
   Williams (ten),   H m ALP2641(SLS796)
   Friedrich Schorr (bar),
   LSO
WAGNER. Die Walküre –
   Winterstürme wichen
   Lauritz Melchior (ten), LSO   H DA1227
WAGNER. Die Meistersinger von
   Nürnberg – Morgenlicht
   leuchtend
   Lauritz Melchior (ten), LSO   H DB1858
                              H m *7P350*

May 18
WAGNER. Tristan und Isolde –
   Mild und leise
   Frida Leider (sop), LSO   H DB1545
                               V 7523
               V m LCT1001/*WCT2*
                   H m COLH132
WAGNER. Parsifal – Ich sah das
   Kind
   Frida Leider (sop), LSO   H DB1545
                               V 7523
               V m LCT1001/*WCT2*
                   H m COLH132
WAGNER. Wesendonk Lieder – Schmerzen
   Frida Leider (sop), LSO   H DB1553
                               V 7708

June 26
MASSENET. Manon – O dolce incanto
   Beniamino Gigli (ten), orch   H DA1216
                                       V 1656
                              H m ALP1681
                              A m COLH118
SULLIVAN. The Lost Chord
TOSTI. Addio (in English)
   Beniamino Gigli (ten), orch   H DB1526

September
MASCAGNI. Cavalleria Rusticana –
    Intermezzo
   LSO   H C2292
PONCHIELLI. La Gioconda – Dance of
    the hours
   LSO   GH EH835
WAGNER. (arr. Gibilaro). Tannhäuser –
    selection
   LSO   H C2293

December 2
BACH. Violin Concerto in E,
    BWV1042
   Mischa Elman (vln), CO   H DB1871–3

1932   *April 1*
WAGNER. Die Walküre – Die alte
    Sturm, die alte Müh!
   Friedrich Schorr (bar), Emmy   H DB1720–1
    Leisner (sop), LSO   V 7742–3

June 9–10
TCHAIKOVSKY. Piano
    Concerto no. 1 in b
    flat, op. 23
   Artur Rubinstein (pf),   H DB1731–4/DB7242–4*
    LSO   V 7802–5/M170

September
BACH. Piano Concerto in f, BWV1056
   – first movt only

M

HAYDN. Piano Concerto in D – third
    movt
    Yvonne Arnaud (pf), string orch   H C2455
SAINT-SAËNS. Valse caprice, op. 76
    Yvonne Arnaud (pf), string orch   H C2456
                                         HSP m RLP10
RAFF (arr. Gibilaro). La
    Fileuse, op. 157/2
    Yvonne Arnaud (pf),   H C2456
      string orch   HSP m RLP10
                  H m ALP2641(SLS796)

September 29
NEVIN. The Rosary
GOUNOD. Nazareth
    Richard Crooks (ten), orch   H DA1288
                               V 1634
                            H *7P333*

ADAMS. The Holy City; The Star of
    Bethlehem
    Richard Crooks (ten), Hubert   H DB1798
      Dawkes (organ), orch   V 7854
                              H *7P249*

1933   *March 20*
LEONCAVALLO. I Pagliacci – No!
    Pagliaccio non son
    Beniamino Gigli (ten), orch   H DA1312
                            H m COLH144

HANDEL. Serse – Ombra mai fù
    Beniamino Gigli (ten), orch,   H DB1901
      Herbert Dawson (organ)   V 7194
                        H m ALP1681
                      A m COLH118

DONIZETTI. L' Elisir d' Amore –
    Una furtiva lagrima
    Beniamino Gigli (ten), orch   H DB1901/
              DB3906/DB4592
                              V 7194
                      H m ALP1681
                      A m COLH118

COTTRAU. Santa Lucia
    Beniamino Gigli (ten), orch   H DB1902/DB3907

May 4
JÄRNEFELT. Berceuse
    SO   H B8112/DA4399†
                                        V 4320

July 20
AUBER. Fra Diavolo – Overture
    LPO   H C2644
QUILTER. A Children's Overture, op. 17
    LPO   H C2603
                                       V 36370

TCHAIKOVSKY. Swan Lake – Ballet,
    op. 20 (4. Waltz; 9. Act II:
    Introduction; 13. Second Dance
    of the Queen of the Swans; 14.
    Dance of the Little Swans; 24.
    Czardas)
    LPO (Antonio Brosa, vln)   H C2619–20
                                     V 11666–7
    Nos 4, 9 and 14 only   H *7P222*

October 18
SCHUBERT. Rosamunde – 'Ballet' no. 2;
    Marche Militaire no. 1 in D,
    D733
    New SO   H C2637

October 19
JÄRNEFELT. Praeludium
    SO   H B8112/DA4399†
                                        V 4320
BALFE. The Bohemian Girl –
    Overture
    SO   H C2635
                        H m ALP2641(SLS796)
GRIEG. Peer Gynt – Suite no. 1,
    op. 46
    SO   H C2640–1
                              V 11834–5/M404

October 23
GRIEG. Piano Concerto in a,
    op. 16

Wilhelm Backhaus (pf),   H DB2074–6/DB7560–2*
New SO   V 8232–4/M204

December
BACH. Concerto in C for Two Pianos
    and Strings, BWV1064
    Ethel Bartlett, Rae Robertson   H C2648–9
    (pfs), CO

1934   *February 23*
MOZART. Violin Concerto
    no. 5 in A, K219
    Jascha Heifetz (vln),   H DB2199–202/DB7692–5*
    LPO   V 8601–4/M254

March 28
GLAZUNOV. Violin
    Concerto in a, op. 82
    Jascha Heifetz (vln),   H DB2196–8/DB7696–8*
    LPO   V 8296–8/M218

May 2
MOZART. Piano Concerto
    no. 27 in B flat, K595
    Artur Schnabel (pf),   H DB2249–52/DB7733–6*
    LSO   V 8475–8/M240
                                 H m COLH67
June 29
D'ERLANGER. Midnight Rose
GRIEG. Sigurd Jorsalfar – Suite, op. 56:
    Homage March
    SO   H C2711
DELIBES. Sylvia – Suite (Prelude; Les
    Chasseresses; Intermezzo; Valse
    lente; Pizzicato; Cortège de
    Bacchus)
    SO   H C2695–6

1935   *March 14*
SCHUMANN. Cello Concerto
    in a, op. 129
    Gregor Piatigorsky   H DB2244–6/DB7742–4*
    (vlc), LPO   V 8518–20/M247
                             V m LCT1119/*WCT1119*

March 18
VIEUXTEMPS. Violin
   Concerto no. 4 in d,
   op. 31
   Jascha Heifetz (vln),   H DB2444–6/DB7857–9*
   LPO   V 8913–5/M297
SAINT-SAËNS. Introduction and Rondo
   Capriccioso, op. 28
   Jascha Heifetz (vln), LSO   H DB2580
                     V 14115
WIENIAWSKI. Violin
   Concerto no. 2 in d,
   op. 22
   Jascha Heifetz (vln),   H DB2447–9/DB7866–8*
   LPO   V 8757–9/M275

May 25
ROSSINI. Il Barbiere di Siviglia – Una
   voce poco fa
   Lily Pons (sop), orch   H DB2501
                     V 8870
MOZART. La Flûte enchantée, K620 –
   Ah! je le sais
   Lily Pons (sop), orch   H DB2502
                     V 8733
BISHOP. Clari – Lo! here the gentle
   lark
   Lily Pons (sop), Gordon Walker (fl),   H DB2502
   orch   V 8733

June 6
MOZART. Piano
   Concerto no. 22 in
   E flat, K482
   Edwin Fischer (pf),   H DB2681–4/DB7692–5*
   CO   V 14089–92/M316
               V m LCT6103
July 8
CHOPIN. Piano Concerto
   no. 2 in f, op. 21
   Alfred Cortot (pf),   H DB2612–5/DB8658–61*
   orch   V 15449–52/M567

October 23
BELLINI. Norma – Casta diva
    Ina Souez (sop), chorus and orch   H DB2720
                                            V 36286

1936   *June 16*
BEETHOVEN. Violin
    Concerto in D, op. 61
    Fritz Kreisler (vln),   H DB2927–32/DB8210–5*
    LPO   V 14168–73/M325
                                  H m COLH11
                                  WRC m H101

June 18 and 22
BRAHMS. Violin
    Concerto in D, op. 77
    Fritz Kreisler (vln),   H DB2915–9/DB8127–31
    LPO   V 14588–92/M402
                                  H m COLH35
                                  WRC **SH115**

December 27: live performance
CHOPIN. Piano Concerto no. 2 in f,
    op. 21
    Josef Hoffman (pf), 'orch'   IPL m IPL501
    (actually PSONY)

1937   *March 25*
TCHAIKOVSKY. Violin
    Concerto in D, op. 35
    Jascha Heifetz (vln),   H DB3159–62/DB8282–5*
    LPO   V 14401–4/M536

April 5
CHOPIN. Piano
    Concerto no. 1 in e, op. 11
    Artur Rubinstein (pf),   H DB3201–4/DB8290–3*
    LSO   V 14717–20/M418

April 9
SAINT-SAËNS. Havanaise, op. 83
    Jascha Heifetz (vln), LSO   H DB3211
                                          V 15347
SARASATE. Zigeunerweisen, op. 20/1
    Jascha Heifetz (vln), LSO   H DB3212
                                          V 15246

May 5: live performance at Royal Opera House,
Covent Garden
PUCCINI. Turandot – Signore,
    ascolta; Non piangere, Liù;
    In questa reggia to end of
    Act II; Nessun dorma
    Eva Turner (sop: Turandot);   H unissued
    Mafaldo Favero (sop: Liù);   (TT2352/1–7)
    Giovanni Martinelli (ten:
    Calaf); Octave Dua (ten);
    Giulio Tomei (bass), ROH
    CG Chorus, LPO

May 10: live performance at Royal Opera House,
Covent Garden
PUCCINI. Turandot – as May 5
    Eva Turner (sop: Turandot);   H unissued
    Licia Albanese (sop: Liù);   (TT2353/1–7)
    Giovanni Martinelli (ten:
    Calaf); Octave Dua (ten);
    Giulio Tomei (bass), ROH
    CG Chorus, LPO

1938   *February 7*
PURCELL (arr. Barbirolli). Suite
    for Strings, Four Horns,
    Flute and Cor Anglais
    PSONY   V 15328–9/M533
                                   H DB3729–30

DEBUSSY. Images – no. 2: Ibéria
    PSONY   V 14955–7/M460
                                   H DB3661–3S

February 9
TCHAIKOVSKY. Francesca
    da Rimini Overture,
    op. 32
    PSONY   V 15595–7/M598
                    H DB3658–60S/DB8597S–9*
                    RCA m LP reissue during 1972

RESPIGHI. Ancient Airs
    and Dances – Suite
    no. 3: Arie di corte
    PSONY   V 17558
                              H DB3830 (not issued)

SCHUMANN. Violin
    Concerto in d, op.
    posth
    Yehudi Menuhin (vln),   V 14913–6/M451
    PSONY   H DB3435–8/DB8448–51*
                              V m LCT6/*WCT28*

1939   *January 21*
    SCHUBERT. Symphony
        no. 4 in c, D417,
        'Tragic'
    PSONY   V 15426–9/M562
                          H DB3826–9/DB8700–3*
                  RCA m LP reissue during 1972

    February 21
    RESPIGHI. Fountains of Rome
    PSONY   V 15483–4/M576
                                  H DB3917–8

    SCHUBERT. Five German Dances
        and Seven Trios, D90
    PSONY   H DA1811–2/DA8411–2*
                                  V 2162–3

    Date unknown (authenticity unchecked)
    Brahms. Violin Concerto in D, op. 77
        Bronislav Hubermann (vln), PSONY   R m 2007

1940   *April 2*
    BRAHMS. Symphony no. 2 in D, op. 73
    PSONY   AC M412
                                  AC m RL3044

    April 30: live performance
    CHOPIN. Piano Concerto no. 1 in e, op. 11
        Josef Hoffman (pf), 'orch'
        (actually PSONY)   IPL m IPL502

June 24
SIBELIUS. Symphony no. 2 in D,
op. 43
PSONY   AC 11403–7D/M423
                                         AC m RL3045

August 2
SMETANA. Bartered Bride – Overture
PSONY   AC 19903D
                                         AC m HL7121
                                            F *CFE15029*

October 26: live performance
BEETHOVEN. Piano Concerto no. 4 in G, op. 58
   Josef Hoffman (pf), 'orch'
   (actually PSONY)   IPL m IPL503

November 3
MOZART. Symphony no. 25 in g,
   K185
PSONY   AC 11734–5/X217
MOZART. Piano
   Concerto no. 27 in
   B flat, K595
   Robert Casadesus (pf),   AC 11699–702D/M490
   PSONY   AC m ML2186
                                    AC m ML4791
                                   AC m 33C1028
November 16
BRAHMS. Academic Festival Overture,
   op. 80
PSONY   AC X200
                                         AC m ML2075
                                         AC m ML5126

RIMSKY-KORSAKOV. Capriccio
   Espagnol, op. 34
PSONY   AC 11477–8D/X185
                                         AC m RL3046
                                         AC m HL7075
BERLIOZ. Roman Carnival Overture,
   op. 9
PSONY   AC 11670D
                                          AC HL7121
                                            F *CFE15029*
                                          CBS m 72691

RAVEL. La Valse
    PSONY   AC 11640–1D/X207
                                         AC m RL3046
                                         AC m HL7075

December 16
BACH (arr. Barbirolli).
    Cantata no. 208, 'The
    Hunt,' BWV208 – Sheep
    may safely graze
    PSONY   AC 11575D/X200
DEBUSSY (orch. Büsser).
    Petite Suite – Ballet
    PSONY   AC 11641D/X207
DEBUSSY. First Rhapsody for Clarinet
    and Orchestra
    Benny Goodman (clar), PSONY   AC 11517D
MOZART. Clarinet Concerto in A,
    K622
    Benny Goodman (clar), PSONY   AC unissued
                                        (XCO29448–55)

1942   *April 11*
SIBELIUS. Symphony no. 1 in e,
    op. 39
    PSONY   AC 11923–7/M325
TCHAIKOVSKY. Suite no. 3 in
    G, op. 55 – Theme and
    Variations
    PSONY   AC 11826–7D/X226
                                        AC m ML4121

April 12
BRUCH. Violin Concerto
    no. 1 in g, op. 26
    Nathan Milstein (vln),   AC 11855–7D/M517
    PSONY   AC m ML2003
                                        AC m ML7083
                                        AC m RL6631

'An Elizabethan Suite' (arr.
    Barbirolli)
    PSONY (items recorded not   AC unissued
    specified)   (XCO32674–75)

1943   *December 31*
BAX. Symphony no. 3
HO   H C3380–5/C7593–8*

1944   *February 17*
VAUGHAN WILLIAMS.
    Symphony no. 5 in D
HO   H C3388–92/C7599–603*

September 18
WAGNER. The Mastersingers –
    Orchestral Suite from Act III
    (arr. Barbirolli): Prelude; Dance
    of the Apprentices; Procession of
    the Masters; Homage to Sachs;
    Finale
HO   H C3416–7

September 19
WAGNER. Rienzi – Overture
HO   H C3425–6
JOHANN STRAUSS II. Roses from the
    South, op. 338 – Waltz
HO   H C3408

1945   *February 16*
MENDELSSOHN. A Midsummer Night's
    Dream – incidental music, op. 61:
    scherzo
HO   H C3426
DELIUS (ed. and arr. Beecham). A
    Village Romeo and Juliet – Walk
    to the Paradise Garden
HO   H C3484

March 20
BEETHOVEN. Symphony no. 7 in A,
        op. 93
HO   H unissued
        (recording incomplete; only four sides recorded;
        matrix nos 2ER820/823/832/833)

MICHAEL HEMING. Threnody for a
    Soldier Killed in Action (arranged
    and developed by Anthony
    Collins from material found after
    Heming's death at the Battle of El
    Alamein in 1942)
    HO   H C3427

1946 *June 6*
    VAUGHAN WILLIAMS. Fantasia on a
    Theme by Thomas Tallis
    HO   H C3507–8
    RICHARD STRAUSS. Der
    Rosenkavalier –
    Orchestral Suite
    HO   H C3556–8/C7661–3*
                            H DB4240–2†
                    V m LBC1017/*WBC1017*

June 6–7
    WAGNER. Lohengrin – Prelude
    to Act III
    HO   H C3558/DB4242†

June 7
    CORELLI (arr. Barbirolli). Oboe
    Concerto
    Evelyn Rothwell (ob), HO   H C3540/DB4258†
    first movt only   H m CLP1840
    WAGNER. Lohengrin – Prelude
    to Act I
    HO   H C3545/DB4251†
    WEBER. Euryanthe – Overture
    HO   H C3560/DB4269†

1947 *January 2*
    BERLIOZ. Symphonie
    fantastique, op. 14
    HO   H C3563–9/C7664–70*

January 4
    ELGAR. Elegy for Strings, op. 58
    HO   H B9567

February 8
ROSSINI. The Thieving Magpie –
  Overture
  Augusteo SO   VdP S10535

February 10
CORELLI (arr. Barbirolli). 'Concerto
  Grosso' (arrangements for orch of
  movements from 12 Sonatas for
  violin and continuo, op. 5)
  Augusteo SO   VdP S10511–2

April 4
FAURÉ. Shylock – Suite, op. 37:
  Nocturne
  HO   H B9567

May 19
BEETHOVEN. Symphony
  no. 5 in c, op. 67
  HO   H C3716–9/C7718–21*
                              V m LBC1018/*WBC1018*

May 30
ELGAR. Bavarian Dance no. 2,
  op. 27
  HO   H C3695/C7705*
HUMPERDINCK. Hansel and Gretel –
  Overture
  HO   H C3623

September 25
ELGAR. Introduction and Allegro for
  Strings, op. 47
  HO   H C3669–70

October 23
ELGAR. Enigma Variations,
  op. 36
  HO   H C3692–5/C7702–5*

1948   *February 25*
PERGOLESI (arr. Barbirolli). Oboe
Concerto
Evelyn Rothwell (ob), HO   H C3731
MENDELSSOHN. Symphony
no. 4 in A, op. 90,
'Italian'
HO   H C3758–60/C7726–8
                                V m LBC*1021*/*WBC1021*

February 26
DELIBES. Sylvia – Suite
HO   H C3797–8
VAUGHAN WILLIAMS. Fantasia on
'Greensleeves'
HO   H C3819
                                            H *7ER5082*

March 10
STRAVINSKY. Concerto in D for String
Orchestra
HO   H C3733–4

April 26
GRAINGER. Irish Tune from County
Derry 'Londonderry Air'
HO   H C3819

April 29 and May 1
BRITTEN. Violin Concerto in d, op. 15
Theo Olof (vln), HO   H. unpublished
                                (2EA12949–56)

April 28 (side 3) and May 31, 1949 (sides 1 and 2)
SCHUBERT. Rosamunde –
Overture, D797, 'The
Magic Harp'
HO   H C3943–4/DB4294–5†
                                H m LBC*1047*/*WBC1047*

April 30
MENDELSSOHN. Hebrides Overture,
op. 26, 'Fingal's Cave'
HO   H C3770/*7R120*/*7P217*

May 1
IRELAND. These Things Shall Be
    Parry Jones (ten), Hallé Choir, HO   H C3826–7

December 4
GRIEG. Peer Gynt – Suite
    no. 1, op. 46
    HO   H C3921–2/DB4310–1†
                              V m LBC1017/*WBC1017*
MOZART (ed. Paumgartner).
    Oboe Concerto in C,
    K314
    Evelyn Rothwell (ob), HO   H C3954–5
    finale only   H m ALP2641 (SLS796)

1949 *March 3 and 5*
SIBELIUS. Symphony no. 7 in
    C, op. 105
    HO   H C3895–7/C7763–5*
               H m LHMV1011/*WHMV1011*

March 5
MOZART. Marriage of Figaro, K492 –
    Overture
    HO   H C3864

April 2
BEETHOVEN. Egmont – Incidental
    Music, op. 84 – Overture
    HO   H DB21139
                 H *7P233*

April 30
ELGAR. Serenade in e, op. 20
    HO   H B9778–9

May 1
DELIUS (arr. Fenby). Two Aquarelles
    HO   H C3864

May 3
IRELAND. Mai-Dun –
    Symphonic Rhapsody
    HO   H DB9651–2*/DB21232–3
                             (not used)

May 31

MENDELSSOHN. Octet in E flat, op. 20 –
    Scherzo (orch. composer)
    HO   H C3944
IRELAND. The Forgotten Rite – Prelude
    HO   H C3894

December 15 and 17
HAYDN. Symphony no. 83
    in g, 'The Hen'
    HO   H DB21076–8
                                                 H m ALP1038
                                                 H m LBC1060/
                                                   WBC1060

December 15 and February 2, 1950
ELGAR. Cockaigne
    Overture, op. 40
    HO   H DB9633–4*/
                                          DB21321–2 (not used)
                                                 H m BLP1065

1950   *February 2*
ELGAR. Dream Children no. 1,
    op. 43
    HO   H DB21594
                                                 H m HQM1122
DELIUS. Song of Summer
    HO   H DB9609–10*/
                                          DB21277–8 (not used)

MOZART. Cassation in G,
    K63 – Andante
    HO   H DB9609*/
                                          DB21278 (not used)

October 17
TCHAIKOVSKY. Swan Lake – Ballet,
    op. 20 (4. Waltz; 9. Act II:
    Introduction; 13. Second Dance
    of the Queen of the Swans; 14.
    Dance of the Little Swans; 24.
    Czardas)

HO (Laurance   H DB9549–50*/DB21185–6
Turner, vln)   (not used)
                    H m BLP1004
Nos. 4, 9, 13 and 14   H 7ER5106

October 19
BIZET. L'Arlésienne – Suite no. 1:
    Prelude; Adagietto; Suite no. 2:
    Farandole
HO   H DB21275–6 (not used)/DB9656–7*
                  H m BLP1004
           H m LBC1047/*WBC1047*

December 14–15
RUBBRA. Symphony no. 5
    in B flat, op. 63
HO   H DB9715–8*/DB21384–7
            V m LHMV1011/*WHMV1011*
                  H m BLP1021
                  H m HQM1016

December 18
FARNABY (orch. Rubbra).
    Improvisations on
    Virginal Pieces, op.
    50 – no. 4: Loth to
    depart
HO   H DB9715*/DB21387
                  H m HQM1122

1951   *May 4*
HAYDN. Symphony no. 96 in D
HO   H m ALP1038

December 20
DONIZETTI. Don Pasquale – Overture
HO   H DA2004
                  H 7ER5009
                  H m HQM1122

WEBER. Der Freischütz – Overture
HO   H DB21504
                  H m HQM1122

1952 *January 4*
TURINA. Danzás fantasticas, op. 22
HO   H DB9738–9*/DB21433–4 (not used)[1]

Orgia only   H ALP2641(SLS796)

April 5
MOZART. Divertimento no. 11
    in D, K251 – Minuet
HO   H m unissued
                          (tape nos 154–5)

April 9
LEHÁR. Gold and Silver Waltz, op. 75
HO   H DB21520
                               H *7ER5009*
                               V *ERAB13*
                               H *7P267*

May 21–22
BRAHMS. Symphony no. 3
    in F, op. 90
HO   H m BLP1015
            V m LBC1042/*WBC1042*

December 18–19
SIBELIUS. Symphony no. 2 in D, op. 43
HO   H m ALP1122
                               V m LBC1084

1953 *June 16 and September 29*
VAUGHAN WILLIAMS. Sinfonia
        Antartica (no. 7)
    Margaret Ritchie (sop), Hallé
    Choir, HO   H m ALP1102

July 27
VAUGHAN WILLIAMS. The Wasps –
        Overture
HO   H DB21623
                               H *7ER5082*
                               H *7P250*

[1] First commercial recording to be made in the rebuilt Free Trade Hall in Manchester.

August 31
HAYDN. Symphony no. 88 in G,
 'Letter V'
HO   H m unissued
GRIEG (orch. Barbirolli). Lyric Pieces
 Book VI no. 4 – Secret
HO   H DB21594

September 1
ELGAR. Introduction and Allegro for
 Strings, op. 47
HO   H m BLP1049

November 25
DEBUSSY. Prélude à l'après-
 midi d'un faune
HO   H m BLP1058
          H m ALP2641 (SLS796)
December 20
RIMSKY-KORSAKOV. Capriccio Espagnol,
 op. 34
HO   H m BLP1058

December 21
SCHUBERT. Symphony no. 9 in C,
 D944, 'Great'
HO   H m ALP1178
           V m LBC1085
December 23
LIADOV. The Enchanted Lake, op. 62
HO   H *7ER5026*

December 31
VAUGHAN WILLIAMS. Five
 Variants of Dives and
 Lazarus
HO (Jean Bell, harp)   H m BLP1049
           H m HQM1016

1954   *January 1*
IBERT. Divertissement for Chamber
 Orchestra
HO   H m ALP1244

January 2
VERDI. La Traviata – Prelude to
   Act I; Prelude to Act III
   HO   H *7ER5034*
                                                H m HQM1122

January 4
FAURÉ. Pelléas et Mélisande –
   Suite, op. 80
   HO   H m ALP1244
                                                H m HQM1122

January 5
'An Elizabethan Suite' (arr.
   Barbirolli)
      (Byrd: Earl of Salisbury's
      Pavan; Anon: The Irish Ho
      Hoane; Farnaby: A Toye;
      Giles Farnaby's Dreame;
      Bull: The King's Hunt)
   HO   H m BLP1065

February 10–11
SAINT-SAËNS. Carnival of the Animals
   Rawicz and Landauer (pfs), HO   H m ALP1224

February 11
JOHANN STRAUSS (arr. Landauer).
   Fantasy
   Rawicz and Landauer (pfs),   H m ALP1224
   HO   MFP m MFP2137
SUPPÉ. The Beautiful Galathea –
   Overture
   HO   H *7ER5034*
                                                H m HQM1122

June 8–9
ELGAR. Symphony no. 2 in E flat,
   op. 63
   HO   V m LBC1088
                                                H m ALP1242
June 9
JOHANN STRAUSS I (orch. Gordon
   Jacob). Radetzky March, op. 228
   HO   H *7ER5119*

June 14
VAUGHAN WILLIAMS. Tuba Concerto
    Philip Catelinet (tuba), LSO   H m BLP1078

November 11
CHABRIER. España
    HO   H DB21615
                                         V *ERAB13*
                                    H m BLP1058
                                    H *7ER5026*
                                    H *7P255*

1955   *January 12*
SIBELIUS. Four Legends, op. 22 –
    no. 2: Swan of Tuonela
    HO (Roger Winfield, cor anglais)   H m ALP1335
RICHARD STRAUSS (arr. Clemens
    Krauss). Die Liebe der Danae
    – symphonic fragment
    HO   H m ALP1335

January 12–13
VILLA-LOBOS. Bachianas
    Brasileiras no. 4
    HO   H m ALP1335

January 13
JOHANN STRAUSS II. Emperor
    Waltz, op. 437
    HO   H *7ER5119*
                                H m ALP2641(SLS796)

July 4–5
VAUGHAN WILLIAMS. Oboe
    Concerto
    Evelyn Rothwell (ob), LSO   H m BLP1078
                                    H m HQM1016

1956   *June 19*
VAUGHAN WILLIAMS. Symphony no. 8
    HO   P m NCT17000
                           Mer m MG50115/**SR90115**
                         P m GGC4061/**GSGC14061**
                         Van m SRV184/**SRV184SD**

June 20–21

BUTTERWORTH. A Shropshire Lad
BAX. Garden of Fand
    HO   P m CCT31000
                          Mer m MG50115/**SR90115**
                          P m GGC4061/**GSGC14061**

June 21

DELIUS. On Hearing the First Cuckoo
    in Spring(*a*); Fennimore and Gerda –
    Intermezzo; Irmelin prelude(*a*); A
    Village Romeo and Juliet – Walk
    to the Paradise Garden (ed. and
    arr. Beecham)(*b*)
    HO   P m CCL30108
                          P m GGC4075/**GSGC14075**
                          Van m SRV240/**SRV240SD**
(*a*) also on P *CEC32019*   (*b*) also on P **GSGL14137**

June 22

PURCELL (arr. Barbirolli). Suite for
    Strings, Four Horns, Flute and
    Cor Anglais
    HO   P m CCL30101
                          Mer m MG50125/**SR90125**

June 21 and 23

ELGAR. Enigma Variations, op. 36
    HO   P m CCL30101
                          Mer m MG50125/**SR90125**
                          Van m SRV184/**SRV184SD**
                          P m GGC4057/**GSGC14057**
    'Nimrod' only also on   P *CEC32023*
                          P **GSGC14137**

June 19, 20, 21 and 23

JOHANN STRAUSS II. Die Fledermaus, op 362 –
    Overture (a) (20/6); Annen Polka, op. 117 (b)
    (23/6); Perpetuum Mobile, op. 257 (c) (23/6);
    On the Beautiful Blue Danube, op. 314 – Waltz
    (d) (21/6); Gypsy Baron, op. 362 – Overture (e)
    (19/6); Tales from the Vienna Woods, op. 325 –
    Waltz (f) (20/6)

JOHANN STRAUSS II with JOSEF STRAUSS. Pizzicato
Polka (g) (20/6)
JOHANN STRAUSS I (orch. Gordon Jacob).
Radetzky March, op. 228 (h) (20/6)

HO	P m CCL30130
	Mer m MG50124/**SR90124**
	P m GGD0094/**GSGD10094**
	P m GGC4078/**GSGC14078**
	Van m SRV237/**SRV237SD**
(a) also on	P *CEC32003*
(a) also on	P **MST22**
(c) also on	P *CEC32003*
(d) also on	P **MST27**
(d) also on	P **GSGC14137**
(f) also on	P *CEC32004*
	P **SOS1**
(g) also on	P *CEC32003*
(h) also on	P *CEC32003*

December 11
DELIUS. Idyll
Sylvia Fisher, sop; Jess
Walters, bar, HO   P m CCL30108
P m GGC4075/**GSGC14075**
Van m SRV240/**SRV240SD**

ELGAR. Elegy for Strings, op. 58
HO   P m *CEC32023*
P **GSGC14137**

December 12
ELGAR. Introduction and Allegro
for Strings, op. 47
HO   P **GSGC14137**

December 12
ELGAR. Symphony no. 1 in
A flat, op. 55
HO   P m CCL30102–3
P m GGC4052/**GSGC14052**

December 13

MOZART. Symphony no.
    29 in A, K201
    Symphony no. 41 in C,
    K551, 'Jupiter'
    HO   P m CCL30106
                             P m GGC4060/**GSGC14060**
                           Van m SRV180/**SRV180SD**

1957   *May 3*

GERMAN. Nell Gwynn – Pastoral
    Dance; Country Dance;
    Torch Dance
    HO   P m CCL30129

HUMPERDINCK. Hansel and Gretel
    – Overture
    HO   P *CEC32004*

WALDTEUFEL. The Skater's Waltz,
    op. 183
    HO   P *CEC32005*

VAUGHAN WILLIAMS. Fantasia on
    'Greensleeves'
    HO   P unissued

LEHÁR. Gold and Silver Waltz,
    op. 75
    HO   P *CEC32005*

May 4

VIVES. Song (unspecified)
TURINA. Song (unspecified)
GRANADOS. Three Spanish Songs   P all unissued
FALLA (orch. Halffter).
    Seven Popular Spanish Songs
    Marina da Gabarain (mezzo-
    sop), HO   P *CEC32009*

May 21 – 22

BERLIOZ. Damnation of Faust, op. 24 –
    Hungarian March; Dance of the Sylphs;
    Will o' the Wisps
    HO   P m CCT31005
                             P m GGC4095/**GSGC14095**
    Hungarian March only   P **SOS1**

ELGAR. Cello Concerto
 in e, op. 85
  André Navarra (vlc), HO   P m CCL30103
           P m GGC4057/**GSGC14057**
RAVEL. Mother Goose – Suite
 HO   P m CCT31005

May 24
CORELLI (arr.
 Barbirolli).
 Oboe Concerto
 in F
  Evelyn Rothwell   P m CCL30127
  (ob), HO   P m GGC4065/**GSGC14065**

May 24–25
PERGOLESI (arr.
 Barbirolli). Oboe
 Concerto
  Evelyn Rothwell   P m CCL30127
  (ob), HO   P m GGC4065/**GSGC14065**

May 27
TCHAIKOVSKY.
 Symphony no.
 4 in f, op. 36
  HO   P m CCL30116
        P m GGL0300/**GSGL10300**
        P m GGC4028/**GSGC14028**
      Van P m SRV135/**SRV135SD**
May 28
SIBELIUS. Symphony
 no. 5 in E flat,
 op. 82
  HO   P m CCL30144
        P m GGC4022/**GSGC14022**
       Van m SRV137/**SRV137SD**
May 29
ROSSINI. William Tell – Overture
 HO   P m CCL30129

MENDELSSOHN. Hebrides Overture,
op. 26, 'Fingal's Cave'
HO   P m CCL30128
                                   P m GGL0301/**GSGL10301**
                                   P m GGC4095/**GSGC14095**
GRAINGER. Mock Morris; Irish
tune from County Derry
'Londonderry Air;' Molly on
the Shore; Shepherd's Hey
HO   P *CEC32022*

June 11–12
MAHLER. Symphony no. 1
HO   P m CCL30107
                                   P m GGC4074/**GSGC14074**
                                   Van m SRV223/**SRV223SD**

June 12
VERDI. Force of Destiny – Overture
HO   P m CCL30147/**CSCL70005**
                                   P m GGC4016/**GSGC14016**
                                   P m GGC4095/**GSGC14095**

June 13
TCHAIKOVSKY. Romeo and Juliet –
Fantasy Overture
HO   P m CCL30128
                                   P m GGL0301/**GSGL10301**

June 27–28
SUPPÉ. The Queen of Spades – Overture (a);
The Beautiful Galathea – Overture (b);
Light Cavalry – Overture (c);
The Jolly Robbers – Overture (d);
Morning, Noon and Night – Overture (e);
Poet and Peasant – Overture (f)
HO   Mer m MG50160/**SR90160**
                                   P m GGC4094/**GSGC14094**
                                              Mer **18094**
(a) and (c) also on   P *CEC32017*
(b) and (e) also on   P *CEC32018*
(c) also on   P **SOS1**
part of (c) also on   P **CSCL70007**

June 28–29
DvoŘák. Symphony no. 8 in G, op. 88;
    Scherzo capriccioso, op. 66
    HO   P m CCL30122/**CSCL70002**
                            Mer m MG50162
                            Van m SRV133/**SRV133SD**
                            P m GGC4069/**GSGC14069**
    Symphony – last movt only   P **CSCL70007**

June 29
Sibelius. Kuolema – incidental music,
    op. 44: Valse triste
    HO   Mer m MG50161/**SR90161**
                          P m GGC4076/**GSGC14076**

August 8
DvoŘák. Symphony no. 7
    in d, op. 70
    HO   P m CCL30145
                          Mer m MG50159
                    P m GGC4068/**GSGC14068**

August 9–10
Grieg. Peer Gynt – Suite no. 1, op. 46;
    Two Elegiac Melodies, op. 34;
    Symphonic Dances, op. 64   P m CCL30126
                    Mer m MG50164/**SR90164**
                    Van m SRV222/**SRV222SD**
                    P m GGC4077/**GSGC14077**
Tchaikovsky. 'Andante Cantabile'
    HO   Mer m MG50161/**SR90161**
                    P m GGC4076/**GSGC14076**
                              P **SOS1**

August 11–12
Haydn (attributed). Oboe Concerto in C
    Evelyn Rothwell (ob), HO   Mer m MG50041
                    P m CCL30127
                P m GGC4065/**GSGC14065**
Clarke. A Trumpet Voluntary
    William Lang (trpt), HO   P m CCL30129
                    Mer m MG50161/**SR90161**
                    P m GGC4076/**GSGC14076**

PONCHIELLI. La Gioconda.
    Dance of the Hours   P m CCL30129
    HO   Mer m MG50161/**SR90161**
                           P m GGC4076/**GSGC14076**

NICOLAI. The Merry Wives
    of Windsor – Overture   P m CCL30129
    HO   P *CEC32029*
                        Mer m MG50161/**SR90161**
                           P m GGC4076/**GSGC14076**

SOUSA. Stars and Stripes
    Forever   Mer m MG50161/**SR90161**
    HO   P m CCL30129
                             P *CEC32021*
                        P m GGC4076/**GSGC14076**

CHABRIER. Marche Joyeuse
    HO   P m CCT31005
                             P *CEC32021*
                      Mer m MG50161/**SR90161**
                        P m GGC4076/**GSGC14076**

MASSENET. Scènes alsaciennes – Sous les tilleuls
    (Under the Linden Tree)
    HO   Mer m MG50161/**SR90161**
                        P m GGC4076/**GSGC14076**
                                P **SOS1**

CHABRIER. Habañera
    HO   P unissued

August 13
DVOŘÁK. Serenade in d, op. 44
    HO (section)   Mer m MG50041
                             P m CCL30153
                      P m GGC4082/**GSGC14082**

December 28–29
VAUGHAN WILLIAMS. A London Symphony (no. 2)
    HO   P m CCL30134
                      P m GGC4012/**GSGC14012**
                      Van m SRV134/**SRV134SD**

December 30–31
SIBELIUS. Symphony no. 1 in e, op. 39
    HO   P m CCL30113
                      P m GGC4058/**GSGC14058**
                      Van m SRV132/**SRV132SD**

1958   *January 1*
BEETHOVEN. Symphony no. 1 in C, op. 21
   HO   P m CCL30132/**CSCL70001**
                            Van m SRV146/**SRV146SD**
                            P m GGC4081/**GSGC14081**

January 2
BEETHOVEN. Symphony no. 8 in F, op. 93
   HO   P m CCL30132/**CSCL70001**
                            Van m SRV146/**SRV146SD**
                            P m GGC4081/**GSGC14081**

August 20
TCHAIKOVSKY. Symphony no. 6 in b, op. 74,
    'Pathétique'
   HO   P m CCL30146
                    P m GGC4030/**GSGC14030**
                    Van m SRV148/**SRV148SD**

August 21–22
PUCCINI. La Bohème – Si sento meglio. . . Che
    gelida manina. . . Sì, mi chiamano Mimì. . .
    O soave fanciulla
PUCCINI. Madama Butterfly – Viene le sera. . .
    Voglietemi bene. . . Un a poco di vero. . .
    Quanti occhi fisi(*a*)
PUCCINI. Manon Lescaut – Dunque questa lettiga. . .
    Tu, tu, amore?. . . O tentatrice
PUCCINI. Tosca – E lucevan le stelle. . . Ah!
    Franchilgia. . . O dolci mano. . . Senti, l'ora e
    vicina. . . Amaro sol per te m'era
   Lenora Lafayette (sop), Richard Lewis (ten),
   HO   P m CCL30142
                    P m GGC4039/**GSGC14039**
        (*a*) also on P **GSGC14137**

August 23
SIBELIUS. Pohjola's Daughter, op. 49
   HO   P m CCL30144
                    P m GGC4022/**GSGC14022**
                    Van m SRV137/**SRV137SD**
HANDEL. Organ Concerto in B flat, op. 7/1
   Eric Chadwick (organ),   P m CCL30149
   HO, Valda   P m GGC4086/**GSGC14086**
    Aveling (continuo)

September 2

GOUNOD. Petite Symphonie in b for wind instruments
HO (section)   P m CCL30153
                              GGC4082/**GSGC14082**

HANDEL (ed. Rothwell and Mackerras). Oboe
   Concerto no. 1 in B flat
   Evelyn Rothwell (ob),   P m CCL30149
   Valda Aveling   P m GGC4086/**GSGC14086**
   (continuo), HO

September 2–3

HANDEL. Rodrigo – Suite
HO, Valda Aveling (continuo)   P m CCL30149
                          P m GGC4086/**GSGC14086**

September 3

HANDEL. Serse – Suite: Overture; Ombra mai fù;
   Sinfonia to Act III; Quelle che tutta; Gigue
   Richard Lewis (ten),   P m CCL30149
   Valda Aveling   P m GGC4086/**GSGC14086**
   (continuo), HO

DVOŘÁK. Legends, op. 59 – nos 4, 6 and 7
HO   P m CCL30145
                          P m GGC4068/**GSGC14068**

September 4

MASCAGNI. Cavalleria Rusticana – Intermezzo
HO   P m CCL30147
                          P m GGC4016/**GSGC14016**
                              Van **SRV250SD**

PUCCINI. Manon Lescaut – Intermezzo to Act III
HO   P m CCL30147
                          P m GGC4016/**GSGC14016**
                              Van **SRV250SD**
                                 P **GSGC14137**

ROSSINI (arr. Godfrey). William Tell – Ballet Music
HO   P m CCL30147
                          P m GGC4016/**GSGC14016**
                              Van **SRV250SD**
                                   P **SOS1**

Rossini. Semiramide – Overture
HO   P m CCL30147
                            P m GGC4016/**GSGC14016**
                                     Van **SRV250SD**

1959   *April*
Mozart. Die Zauberflöte, K620 – Overture
Weber. Oberon – Overture
Wagner. Tannhäuser – Overture
Beethoven. Leonora Overture no. 3, op. 72 (a)
HO   P m CCL30156
                                   P m GGL0302
                            P m GGC4089/**GSGC14089**
   (a) only   P **MST22**
Tchaikovsky. Marche Slav, op. 32
HO   P m CCL30154
                            P m GGC4029/**GSGC14029**
                      Van m SRV139/**SRV139SD**
Tchaikovsky. Symphony no. 5 in e, op. 64
HO   P m CCL30154
                            P m GGC4029/**GSGC14029**
                      Van m SRV139/**SRV139SD**
                                     P **MST27**
Dvořák. Symphony no. 9 in e, op. 95, 'From
   the New World'
HO   P m CCL30155
                      Van m SRV182/**SRV182SD**
                            P m GGC4070/**GSGC14070**
Beethoven. Piano Concerto no. 5 in E flat,
   op. 73, 'Emperor'
Mindru Katz   P m CCL30152/**CSCL70019**
   (piano), HO   Van m SRV138/**SRV138SD**
                            P m GGC4044/**GSGC14044**

June 5–6
Albinoni. Oboe Concertos: in B flat,
   op. 7/3; in D, op. 7/6
Cimarosa (arr. Benjamin). Oboe Concerto
A. Marcello (trans. Bonelli). Oboe
   Concerto in d
Evelyn Rothwell   Van m SRV191/**SRV191SD**
   (oboe), PAO   P m GGC4023/**GSGC14023**

September 1 and 2
NIELSEN. Symphony no. 4, op. 29,
    'Inextinguishable'
    HO   P m CCL30164/**CSCL70024**
                                P m GGC4026/**GSGC14026**
                                Van m SRV179/**SRV179SD**

September 2–3
BERLIOZ. Symphonie Fantastique, op. 14
    HO   P m GGC4005/**GSGC14005**
                                Van m SRV181/**SRV181SD**

September 4
DEBUSSY. La Mer
    HO   P m GGC4010/**GSGC14010**
                                Van m SRV177/**SRV177SD**

September 5
RAVEL. La Valse; Daphnis and Chloë –
    Suite no. 2*
    Hallé Choir*, HO   P m GGC4010/**GSGC14010**
                                Van m SRV177/**SRV177SD**

September 16–17
WAGNER. The Flying Dutchman –
    Overture (a); Lohengrin – Prelude to
    Act 1; The Mastersingers –
    Orchestral Suite from Act 3 (arr.
    Barbirolli): Prelude; Dances of the
    Apprentices; Procession of the Masters;
    Homage to Sachs; Finale; Tristan and
    Isolde – Prelude and Liebestod
    HO   P m GGDo094/**GSGD10094**
                                P m GGC4053/**GSGC14053**
                                Van m SRV149/**SRV149SD**
    (a) also on   P **MST22**

September 17–18
BRAHMS. Academic Festival Overture,
    op. 80; Double Concerto in a, op. 102
    Alfredo Campoli   P m GGC4009/**GSGC14009**
    (vln), André   Van m SRV136/**SRV136SD**
    Navarra (vlc), HO

September *18–19*
BRAHMS. Symphony no. 4 in e, op. 98
HO   P m GGC4037/**GSGC14037**
                             Van m SRV183/**SRV183SD**

1961 *April: Berne, Switzerland*
MENDELSSOHN. Symphony no. 4 in A,
        op. 90, 'Italian'
HO   CH m AM2248/**SMS2248**

Date unknown: London
RIMSKY-KORSAKOV. Capriccio Espagnol, op. 34
HO   CH m M961 (7-inch)

September 10: live performance in Budapest
SCHUBERT. Symphony no. 5 in B flat, D485
        Georges Enesco State SO   Elect m ECE0144

1962 *March 23–25*
FRANCK. Symphony in d
Czech PO   Sup m SUA10438/**SUAST50438**
                CR m 22160127/**22160128**

May 8–9
VAUGHAN WILLIAMS. Symphony no. 5 in D
        Philh   H m ALP1957/**ASD508**
                             A m 35952/**S35952**
                             H **ASD2698**

May 10
ELGAR. Serenade in e, op. 20
        SoL   H ALP1970/**ASD521**
                             A 36101/**S36101**
                             H 7ER5231/**RES4311**

May 11
ELGAR. Introduction and Allegro for
        Strings, op. 47
        SoL   H m ALP1970/**ASD521**
                             A m 36101/**S36101**
                             H **ASD2762**

N

VAUGHAN WILLIAMS. Fantasia on
   'Greensleeves'
    SoL   H m ALP1970/**ASD521**
                               A m 36101/**S36101**
                                     H *7P383*
                      H **ASD2642**(SLS796)

May 17
VAUGHAN WILLIAMS. Fantasia on a Theme
   by Thomas Tallis
    SoL   H m ALP1970/**ASD521**
                               A m 36101/**S36101**
                                   A **S3750**
                                   H **ASD2698**

August 27–28
ELGAR. Enigma Variations, op. 36
    Philh   H m ALP1998/**ASD548**
                               A m 36120/**S36120**

August 28
ELGAR. Cockaigne Overture, op. 40
    Philh   H m ALP1998/**ASD548**
                               A s 36120/**S36120**

August 28–29
ELGAR. Symphony no. 1 in A flat, op. 55
    Philh   H m ALP1989/**ASD540**
                                     S 60068
                      H **ASD2748**

August 29
ELGAR. Pomp and Circumstance Marches,
   op. 39 – no. 1 in D; no. 4 in G
    Philh   H *7ER5230*/**RES4310**
                      H m ALP2292/**ASD2292**
                               A m 36403/**S36403**
                                   A **S3750**

October 1
SIBELIUS. Symphony no. 2 in D, op. 43
    RPO   RD **4–15–9**
                    RD m RDM1028/**RDS5028**

December 17–18
TCHAIKOVSKY. Piano Concerto no. 1 in b flat,
    op. 23
FRANCK. Symphonic Variations for Piano
    and Orchestra
John Ogdon (pf), Philh   H ALP1991/**ASD542**
    A 36142/**S36142**

1964   *January 10, 11, 14 and 18*
MAHLER. Symphony no. 9
Berlin PO   H m ALP2047, ALPS2048/
    ASD596, ASDS597
    A m B3652/**SB3652**

April 20–21
ELGAR. Symphony no. 2 in E flat, op. 63
HO   H m ALP2061–2/**ASD610–1**
    Sera **SIB6033**
    H **ASD2748**

June 1
ELGAR. Falstaff, op. 68
HO   H m ALP2062/**ASD611**
    Sera **SIB6033**
    H **ASD2762**

June 2–3
SCHUBERT. Symphony no. 9 in C, D944
HO   H m ALP2085/**ASD632** (not used)
    H m ALP2251/**ASD2251**
    A m 36328/**S36328**

September 1–2
TCHAIKOVSKY. Serenade in C for Strings,
    op. 46
LSO   H m ALP2099 /**ASD646**
    A m 36269/**S36269**
    ASD2738
  Waltz only   A **S3750**
    H *7P383*
ARENSKY. Variations on a theme of
    Tchaikovsky, op. 35a
LSO   H m ALP2099/**ASD646**
    A m 36269/**S36269**
  Theme and variations 1, 2, 4, 6   H *7EG8958*

December 27–30
ELGAR. Dream of Gerontius, op. 38
Janet Baker   H m ALP2101–2/**ASD648–9**
(m-sop), Richard Lewis   A m B3660/**SB3660**
(ten), Kim Borg (bass), Ambrosian
Singers, Sheffield Philharmonic Chorus,
Hallé Chorus, HO
Angel's farewell only   H **ASD2642**(SLS796)

1965 *August 19*
ELGAR. Cello Concerto in e, op. 85
Jacqueline du Pré   H m ALP2106/**ASD655**
(vlc), LSO   A m 36438/**S36438**
                                        H **ASD2764**

August 20
DELIUS (arr. Beecham). A Village
Romeo and Juliet – Walk to the
Paradise Garden
LSO   H m ALP2305/**ASD2305**
                  A m 36415/**S36415**

August 30
ELGAR. Sea Pictures, op. 37
Janet Baker (m-sop),   H m ALP2106/**ASD655**
LSO   H **ASD2721**
                            A **S36796**
Where Corals Lie only   H **SEOM8**

August 25–27
PURCELL. Dido and Aeneas – complete
Dido   Victoria de los Angeles (sop)
Aeneas   Peter Glossop (bar)
Belinda   Heather Harper (sop)
Sorceress   Patricia Johnson (contr)
Second Woman   Elisabeth Robson (sop)
First Witch   Clare Walmesley (sop)
Second Witch ⎱
Spirit   ⎰ Sybil Michelow (m-sop)
Sailor   Robert Tear (ten)

Raymond Leppard   H m AN169/**SAN169**
(harpsichord continuo),   A m 36359/**S36359**
Ambrosian Singers, ECO

December 28
BAX. Tintagel
IRELAND. A London Overture
LSO   H m ALP2305/**ASD2305**
                                   A 36415/**S36415**

1966 January 23–24
SIBELIUS. Pohjola's Daughter, op. 49
HO   H m ALP2272/**ASD2272**
                                   Cap **SP8669**

SIBELIUS. Karelia – Suite, op. 11
HO   H m ALP2272/**ASD2272**
                                   Cap **SP8669**

    Intermezzo and Alla marcia only   *7P400*
    Intermezzo only   H **ASD2642**(SLS796)
SIBELIUS. Kuolema – Incidental Music,
    op. 44: Valse triste
HO   H m ALP2272/**ASD2272**
                                   Cap **SP8669**
                                     A **S3750**

SIBELIUS. Pelleas and Melisande, op. 46 –
    Incidental Music: no. 1
    At the castle gate; no. 2 A spring in
    the park
HO   H unpublished
SIBELIUS. Four Legends, op. 22 – no. 2:
    Swan of Tuonela
HO (Eric Fletcher, cor anglais)
                              H m ALP2308/**ASD2308**
                              A m 36425/**S36425**
                                    H **SLS799**
SIBELIUS. Four Legends, op. 22 – no. 4;
    Return of Lemminkaïnen
HO   H m ALP2272/**ASD2272**
                                   Cap **SP8669**
                                   Sera **6061**
SIBELIUS. Finlandia, op. 26
HO   H m ALP2272/**ASD2272**
                                   Cap **SP8669**
                                   A **S3750**

July 14
DELIUS. Song of Summer
    LSO   H ALP2305/**ASD2305**
                                    A 36415/**S36415**

DELIUS. Irmelin Prelude
    LSO   H m ALP2305/**ASD2305**
                               A m 36415/**S36415**
                                       A **S3750**
                             H **ASD2642**(SLS796)

ELGAR. Pomp and Circumstance Marches,
    op. 39 – no. 2 in a; no. 3 in c; no. 5 in C
    NPO   H m ALP2292/**ASD2292**
                               A m 36403/**S36403**

July 15–16
ELGAR. Froissart Overture, op. 19(a); Elegy
    for strings, op. 58; Sospiri, op. 70
    NPO   H m ALP2292/**ASD2292**
                               A m 36403/**S36403**
    (a) also on   H **ASD2762**

July 25–26
SIBELIUS. Symphony no. 2 in D, op. 43
    HO   H m ALP2308/**ASD2308**
                               A m 36425/**S36425**
                                   H **SLS799**

July 26–28
SIBELIUS. Symphony no. 7 in C, op. 105;
    Symphony no. 5 in E flat, op. 82
    HO   H **ASD2326**
                                   H **SLS799**

August 16–18, 20–27
PUCCINI. Madame Butterfly – complete

Cio-Cio-San	Renata Scotto (sop)
Suzuki	Anna di Stasio (m-sop)
Kate Pinkerton	Silvana Padoan (m-sop)
F. B. Pinkerton	Carlo Bergonzi (ten)
Sharpless	Rolando Panerai (bar)
Goro	Piero di Palma (ten)
Il Bonzo	Paolo Montarsolo (bass)
Prince Yamadori	Giuseppe Morresi (bass)
The Commissioner	Mario Rinaudo (bass)

Rome Opera House Chorus   H **SAN184–6**
and Orch   A m 3072/**S3072**
Excerpts from complete recording: H **ASD2326**;
7P401; **SEOM1**; **SEOM3**; **ASD2642**(SLS796);
A **S36567**

December 7–9
BRAHMS. Symphony no. 2 in D, op. 73
VPO   H **ASD2421**
     A **SDC3732**
BRAHMS. Academic Festival Overture, op. 80
VPO   H **ASD2433/ASD2589**
     A **SDC3732**

December 28–30
SIBELIUS. Symphony no. 1 in e, op. 39
HO   H **ASD2366**
     A 36489
     H **SLS799**

December 30–31
JOHANN STRAUSS I (orch. Gordon Jacob).
     Radetzky March, op. 228
JOHANN STRAUSS II. Perpetuum Mobile,
     op. 257; On the Beautiful Blue
     Danube – waltz, op. 314; Champagne
     Polka, op. 211 (a); Thunder and
     Lightning Polka, op. 324; Gypsy
     Baron – Overture, op. 362

RICHARD STRAUSS (arr. Barbirolli).
     'Waltzes from Der Rosenkavalier'
LEHÁR. Gold and Silver Waltz, op. 75
HO   Col **TWO180**
     Cap **SP8698**
     Sera **S60184**
(a) also on   A **S3750**
(b) excerpt also on   Col *DB8607*

December 31
BERLIOZ. Roman Carnival Overture
HO   H for release

1967   **May 4**

MAHLER. Lieder eines fahrenden Gesellen
 Janet Baker (m-sop), HO   H **ASD2338**
              A **S36465**
  Ging heut' morgen only   H **SEOM1**
MAHLER. Rückert Lieder – no. 4:
 Ich bin der Welt abhanden gekommen
MAHLER. Kindertotenlieder
 Janet Baker (m-sop), HO   H **ASD2338**
              A **S36465**

May 18–19

BEETHOVEN. Symphony no. 3 in E flat,
 op. 55, 'Eroica'
 BBCSO   H **ASD2348**
              A **S36461**
  third movt only   H **SEOM1**
              Sera **6061**

May 19

'An Elizabethan Suite' (arr. Barbirolli)
 (Byrd: Earl of Salisbury's Pavan;
 Anon: The Irish Ho Hoane; Farnaby:
 A Toye; Giles Farnaby's Dreame;
 Bull: The King's Hunt)
  BBCSO   H **ASD2496**

July 11 and 13

VAUGHAN WILLIAMS. A London Symphony (no. 2)
 HO   H **ASD2360**
              A **S36478**

July 13–14

SIBELIUS, Pelleas and Melisande, op. 46 –
 Incidental Music: no. 1 At the castle
 gate; no. 2 A spring in the park; no. 8
 The death of Melisande
  HO   H **ASD2366**
              H **SLS799**

July 14

VERDI. Force of Destiny – Overture
 HO   H for release

August 17–18
MAHLER. Symphony no. 6
    NPO   H **ASD2376–7**
                                  A **S3725**

August 19 and September 25
SCHOENBERG. Pelleas and Melisande, op. 5
    NPO   A **S36509**
                                H **ASD2459**

August 20–21
BRAHMS. Piano Concerto no. 1 in d, op. 15
    Daniel Barenboim (pf), NPO   H **ASD2353**
                                  A **S36463**

August 22
RICHARD STRAUSS. Metamorphosen
    NPO   H **ASD2377**

August 23
RAVEL. Shéhérazade
    Janet Baker (m-sop), NPO   A **S36505**
                                H **ASD2444**

December 4–8, 15, 18–19
BRAHMS. Symphony no. 1 in c, op. 68
    VPO   H **ASD2401**
                                A **SDC3732**
BRAHMS. Symphony no. 3 in F, op. 90
    VPO   H **ASD2432**
                                A **SDC3732**
BRAHMS. Symphony no. 4 in e, op. 98
    VPO   H **ASD2433**
                                A **SDC3732**
BRAHMS. Variations on a Theme of
    Haydn, op. 56a
    VPO   H **ASD2432/ASD2589**
                                A **SDC3732**

December 13
HAYDN. Cello Concerto in D
    Jacqueline du Pré (vlc), LSO   H **ASD2466**
                                  A **S36580**

December 21, 27–28
BRAHMS. Piano Concerto no. 2 in B flat,
    op. 83
    Daniel Barenboim (pf), NPO   H **ASD2413**
                                       A **S36526**

December 27–28
BERLIOZ. Les Nuits d'Été, op. 7
    Janet Baker (m-sop), NPO   A **S36505**
                                         H **ASD2444**
       Villanelle only   H **SEOM8**

1968   *January 28–29 and August 6*
    GRIEG. Peer Gynt – Incidental Music, op. 23
      Sheila Armstrong (sop), Patricia   Col **TWO269**
      Clark (sop); Ambrosian Singers;   A **S36531**
      HO
      3 excerpts also on   H **ASD2773**

August 6–8
DELIUS. In a Summer Garden; Koanga –
    La Calinda (ed. Fenby); Hassan –
    Entr'acte and Serenade (with Robert
    Tear, ten); Late Swallows (ed.
    Fenby); Summer Night on the River;
    A Song before Sunrise; On Hearing
    the First Cuckoo in Spring
    HO   H **ASD2477**
                                         A **S36588**

DELIUS. Fennimore and Gerda –
    Intermezzo   H unissued
    HO

August 12–21; October 8, 11 and 30
VERDI. Otello – complete
        Otello   James McCracken (ten)
        Iago   Dietrich Fischer-Dieskau (bar)
        Cassio   Piero di Palma (ten)
        Roderigo   Florindo Andreolli (ten)
        Ludovico   Alfredo Giacometti (bass)
        Montano   Leonardo Monreale (bass)
        A Herald   Gwynne Thomas (bass)
        Desdemona   Gwyneth Jones (sop)
        Emilia   Anna di Stasio (m-sop)

Ambrosian Opera Chorus,   H **SAN252-4**
   Children's Chorus, NPO   A **SCL3742**
   Cio m' accora only   H **SEOM2**
   Excerpts   H **ASD2690**

September 20
MARCELLO (ed. Rothwell). Oboe
   Concerto in c
   Evelyn Rothwell (ob), Valda   H **ASD2496**
   Aveling (continuo), HO
MONN. Cello Concerto in g (harpsichord
   continuo is based on Schoenberg's
   realisation and is edited by Valda
   Aveling)
   Jacqueline du Pré (vlc), LSO,   H **ASD2466**
   Valda Aveling (continuo)   A **S36580**

November 2
CORELLI (arr. Barbirolli). Oboe Concerto
   Evelyn Rothwell (ob), NPO   H **ASD2496**

December 12, 13, 18 and 20
DEBUSSY. La Mer; Trois Nocturnes
   OdP (Maîtrise de L'ORTF)   H **ASD2442**
                          A **S36583**

1969   *May 27*
BACH (arr. Barbirolli). Cantata no. 208,
   'The Hunt', BWV208 – Sheep may
   safely graze
   HO   H **ASD2496**
PURCELL (arr. Barbirolli). Suite for
   Strings, Four Horns, Flute and
   Cor Anglais
   HO   H **ASD2496**

May 27-28
SIBELIUS. Symphony no. 3 in C, op. 52
   HO   H **ASD2648**
                          H **SLS799**

May 29–30
SIBELIUS. Symphony no. 4 in a, op. 63
HO   H **ASD2494**
                                                H **SLS799**

July 16–18
MAHLER. Symphony no. 5
NPO   H **ASD2518-9**
                                                A **S3760**
        Adagietto only   H **ASD2642**(SLS796)
                                                Col *DB8778*
                                                Regal **SRS5103**

July 17–18
MAHLER. Rückert Lieder
Janet Baker (m-sop), NPO   H **ASD25189**
                                                A **S3760**
                                                ASD2721
                                                A **S36796**

July 19
TCHAIKOVSKY. Romeo and Juliet –
        Fantasy Overture
NPO   H incomplete

August 4–5
SIBELIUS. Scènes historiques, op. 25 –
        Festivo
HO   H for release
SIBELIUS. Rakastava, op. 14; Romance
        in C, op. 42
HO   H **ASD2494**
                                                H **SLS799**

August 6
GRIEG. Lyric Suite, op. 54
HO   H **ASD2773**
GRIEG. Sigurd Jorsalfar – Suite, op. 56:
        Homage March
HO   H **ASD2773**

August 18, 19, 21, 22, 25–27, 30
VERDI. Requiem Mass
        Montserrat Caballé (sop),   H **SAN267-8**
        Fiorenza Cossotto (m-sop),   A **SB3757**
        Jon Vickers (ten),
        Ruggero Raimondi (bass),
        NP Chorus and Orch
        Sanctus only   H **ASD2642**(SLS796)

September 26–27
RICHARD STRAUSS. Ein Heldenleben,
    op. 40
    LSO   H ASD2613
                             A S36764

September 27
WAGNER. The Mastersingers –
    Prelude to Act 1
    LSO   H ASD2642(SLS796)

October 1
TCHAIKOVSKY. Francesca da Rimini
    Overture, op. 32
    NPO   H ASD2738

1970   *May 21–22*
SIBELIUS. Symphony no. 6 in d, op. 104
    HO   H ASD2648
                             H SLS799

May 22
GRIEG. Norwegian Dances, op. 35
    HO   H ASD2773

July 15–17
DELIUS. Appalachia (with Alun
    Jenkins, bar; Ambrosian Singers);
    Brigg Fair
    HO   H ASD2637
                             A S36756
    Rehearsal sequence from   m ALP2641(SLS796)
    Appalachia

PART TWO
The voice of Barbirolli

Commercial recordings

1951   'Festival Towns of Britain' – Cheltenham
Sir John Barbirolli recalls his memories
of the town   RSL 448–51*
(coupled with 'Brighton': not by Barbirolli)

1962   *December*
Sir John Barbirolli introduces
recordings by Yvonne Arnaud

HSP m RLP10

1964   *April 21: Kingsway Hall*
Sir John Barbirolli in conversation
with Ronald Kinloch Anderson

H m ALP2641 (SLS796)

1966   *May 8: ITV*
Sir John Barbirolli in conversation
with Eamonn Andrews

H m ALP2641 (SLS796)

1970   *July 16: Kingsway Hall*
Sir John Barbirolli rehearsing
Delius's Appalachia

H m ALP2641 (SLS796)

Private recording

1969   *December 18*
Talk on Radio 4 at 21.40 hours   BIRS m tape

PART THREE
Private and 'off-the-air' mono recordings

In the possession of Lady Barbirolli

1937 *January 10*
WAGNER. Orchestral excerpts (unidentified)
    PSONY

November 7
SCHUMANN. Symphony no. 4 in d, op. 120
    PSONY

1938 *April 3*
LISZT. Piano Concerto no. 1 in E flat – first
    movement only
    Levitzki (pf), PSONY

April 17
PURCELL (arr. Wood). Trumpet Voluntary
DELIUS. Appalachia (incomplete)
    PSONY

April 18
BEETHOVEN. Symphony no. 5 in c, op. 67
    PSONY

April 23
STRAVINSKY. The Firebird – Suite (1919 version)
    PSONY

October 20
BERLIOZ. Benvenuto Cellini – Overture
  PSONY

October 30
GRIFFES. The White Peacock
  PSONY
WEBER. Oberon – Overture
  PSONY

1939 *January*
HAYDN. Symphony no. 104 in D, 'London'
  PSONY

April
ROSSINI. Petite Messe Solennelle
  Soloists, Westminster Choir, PSONY

October 15
FRANCK. Symphony in d
  PSONY

December 17
MAHLER. Symphony no. 5 – Adagietto
RAVEL. Daphnis and Chloë – Suites 1 and 2
  PSONY

December 24
WEINBERGER. Christmas.
  PSONY

1940 *April 11*
HERMANN. Moby Dick
  CBS Broadcasting Orch.

September 18
PERGOLESI (arr. Barbirolli). Oboe Concerto
  Evelyn Rothwell (ob), PSONY

1941 *April 20*
BENJAMIN. Overture to an Italian Comedy
  PSONY

1942 *March 22*
ANTHONY COLLINS. Overture: Sir Toby and
    Sir Andrew
    PSONY

1943 *February 23*
CORELLI (arr. Barbirolli). 'Concerto Grosso'
    PSONY

1944 *December 26: live concert in Philips Canteen,*
    Eindhoven, Holland
GRAINGER. Tune from County Derry,
    'Londonderry Air'
JOHANN STRAUSS II. Tales from the Vienna
    Woods – waltz
Interviews
'Auld Lang Syne'
    HO

1950 *October 6*
CASTELNUOVO-TEDESCO. Oboe Concerto
    Evelyn Rothwell (ob), HO

1951 *March 9*
CHAUSSON. Poème de l'amour et de la mer
    Kathleen Ferrier (contr), HO

date unknown
STRAVINSKY. The Firebird – Suite (1919 version)

date unknown
POPPER. Cello duet
    John Barbirolli (vlc), Lauri Kennedy (vlc)

date unknown
RICHARD STRAUSS. Oboe Concerto
    Evelyn Rothwell (ob), HO

date unknown
LOEILLET. Trio in b
    Evelyn Rothwell (ob), Daisy Kennedy (vln),
    John Barbirolli (vlc)

date unknown
FULEIHAN. Piano Concerto no. 2
    Eugene List (pf), PSONY

Other private recordings

1939   *April 16*
WAGNER. Tristan und Isolde – Act II

Tristan	Eyvind Laholm (ten)
Isolde	Kirsten Flagstad (sop)
Brangaene	Enid Szantho (m-sop)
Koenig Marke	John Gurney (bass)
Melot ⎫ Kurvenal ⎭	Daniel Harris (bar)

'orch' (actually PSONY)

Because of an omission in the original transcriptions, it was necessary to insert 37 bars, beginning at 'Lass' mein Liebsten ein'. This section was taken from a performance of 21 December 1939.

1953   *June 4: Live performance at the Royal Opera House, Covent Garden*
VERDI. Aïda – Act III

Aïda	Maria Callas (sop)
Amneris	Giulietta Simonato (m-sop)
Radames	Kurt Baum (ten)
Amonasro	Jess Walters (bar)
Ramphis	Giulio Neri (bass)
King	Michael Langdon (bass)

ROH CG Chorus and Orch

1969   *December 18: Sir John Barbirolli's 70th birthday concert, given at the Free Trade Hall, Manchester, 19.30 hours (private recording held at the British Institute of Recorded Sound)*
ELGAR. Introduction and Allegro for Strings, op. 47
VAUGHAN WILLIAMS. Symphony no. 6 in e
BEETHOVEN. Symphony no. 7 in A, op. 92
Speech at the conclusion of the concert
HO

Other private recordings of many major Barbirolli interpretations are known to exist.

Index